The Films
of Johnny Depp

ALSO BY WILLIAM B. PARRILL

European Silent Films on Video:
A Critical Guide (McFarland, 2006)

The Films
of Johnny Depp

WILLIAM B. PARRILL

McFarland & Company, Inc., Publishers
Jefferson, North Carolina, and London

I would like to express my appreciation
to Jeff Bell for his assistance,
to Ken Mitchell for directing me to "Into the Great Wide Open,"
and to all my friends at Southeastern
who have discussed films with me.
Without the help of my wife Sue,
this book would never have been finished.

LIBRARY OF CONGRESS CATALOGUING-IN-PUBLICATION DATA

Parrill, William.
The films of Johnny Depp / William B. Parrill.
p.   cm.
Includes bibliographical references and index.

ISBN 978-0-7864-4022-1
illustrated case binding : 50# alkaline paper

1. Depp, Johnny — Criticism and interpretation.   I. Title.
PN2287.D39P37   2009   791.4302'8092 — dc22 [B]   2009019987

British Library cataloguing data are available

On the cover: Johnny Depp as Jack Sparrow in *Pirates of the
Caribbean: The Curse of the Black Pearl*, 2003 (Photofest);
background Auguste Mayer, 1836, title unknown, oil on canvas,
41" × 63"; border and banner ©2009 Shutterstock

Manufactured in the United States of America

McFarland & Company, Inc., Publishers
Box 611, Jefferson, North Carolina 28640
www.mcfarlandpub.com

To the women in my life:
Sue, Gretchen, Haley, Emily and Del

Table of Contents

Preface 1

Introduction 3

THE FILMS

Preface

I can remember precisely the exact moment I realized that Johnny Depp was an actor of extraordinary power. Some four years ago my wife Sue had a knee replacement operation. As she roused herself to consciousness from the depths of pain killers, she mumbled something that sounded like "Johnny Depp." When I leaned toward her to hear her better, she spoke clearly: "Do you know Johnny Depp's telephone number?" I realized at that moment that a name of such talismanic power, that could penetrate so deeply into the subconscious, must belong to an extraordinary actor, or to an extraordinary sex object, or at least to someone extraordinary.

I do not mean merely that he was unusual, but that he possessed a hidden quality which distinguished him, so far as I could tell, from all other film actors. In an attempt to identify that quality, I asked many people what they thought it might be. The majority of the people I spoke to thought that Depp was an outstanding actor, but were essentially clueless in attempting to isolate his uniqueness.

I am convinced that the best way to appreciate Depp's uniqueness is to examine each of the films in which he appears in chronological order as entities unto themselves. In many of them, Depp is not a major actor, but even in his smallest role he leaves an indelible impression. Why have his cameos been so successful? Why did he choose a particular film? What did he contribute to it? What is his relationship to earlier film actors, especially to Marlon Brando and the silent comics? How has his admiration for the Beats influenced his choice of roles and his acting? How has his projection of an androgynous sexuality influenced both his choice of roles and his acting of them? What view of America has he projected in his films? How has Depp's relationship with his directors, particularly Terry Gilliam and Tim Burton, shaped his — and their — films? What is the vision of America projected in his films, both by native and foreign directors? What are the religious implications of his films, particularly the idea of sacrifice lurking in the background — and occasionally in the foreground — of so many?

An internet site announces — on what authority I neither know nor care — that Johnny Depp's IQ is 120 — or 119 — and asks the viewer to see if he is "smarter" than Johnny Depp. Trust me, you are not, nor am I. How Depp achieved his current status cannot be measured by a test but by a question: How is it that a basically self-educated young man from Kentucky, with no particular cultural or monetary advantages, somehow managed to become the representative actor of his time?

While I do not pretend to have answered the question, I have attempted to analyze the process by which it came about, film by film.

Introduction

How Pleasant to Know, Mr. Depp

Johnny Depp was born at the wrong time. He should have been born forty or so years earlier so that he could have walked the streets of morning with James Dean before Dean's untimely death on that California highway. He should have met Hunter S. Thompson at the peak of his career when he was writing *Fear and Loathing in Las Vegas*, before his talent was devastated by alcoholism and drug addiction. He should have hung out with Jack Kerouac, ridden with Ken Kesey and the Merry Pranksters, and gone to the Actor's Studio when that name meant something and the people who had gone there were the wonders of the world. He should have been in a film with Marlon Brando when that Prince of Players still took acting seriously and before he had turned himself into a bloated hulk who parodied his art and ridiculed his former self onscreen. He should have worked with Elia Kazan and Nick Ray, two great directors who privileged the art of screen acting and inspired James Dean to greatness. These and other exemplars of the sixties were dead or exiled, and Depp was, for the most part, left with only their examples to guide him.

Time passed and popular culture darkened. Viet Nam was followed by despair and violence in the cities. Pot gave way to cocaine and then to crack. As the 1960s and its cultural icons receded into the historical past, they were never replaced. They left a hole in the popular culture which no one filled. In film and literature, pretenders abode their destined hours and went their way. The Beat generation gave way to the "new" journalism, and the "nonfiction" novel — Capote's *In Cold Blood*, Tom Wolfe's *The Electric Kool-Aid Acid Test*, Hunter S. Thompson's *Fear and Loathing in Las Vegas* — came and went. The heirs of Brando and Dean — Al Pacino and Robert De Niro, perhaps? — have hardly matched the great originals. And what film director now has the white heat of Elia Kazan or Nick Ray when they were working at their best, or even their second-best?

Which leaves us with Johnny Depp. All great artists revere their predecessors and transcend them, at the same time honoring and rejecting. The argument here is that Johnny Depp, alone among film actors of the present day, or indeed of days past, has deliberately created a body of work honoring both the silent clowns of the early years of the century and the beat generation of the 1960s. The ghosts of Charlie Chaplin, Buster Keaton, Hunter S. Thompson, Marlon Brando, James Dean and other cultural icons haunt his films. It would, of course, be presumptuous to argue that Johnny Depp has changed the age in any way, but he has certainly opened an argument for the actor as auteur, as a prime mover of the artistic process.

Until recently, Johnny Depp has, for some twenty years, received constant, harping criticism for his choice of roles. Reviewers say that if he had taken this role or that role, if he had taken *Speed*, say, he would have been a big star long ago. Perhaps, but he would not have been Johnny Depp, would not have created a persona that would justify either *The Libertine* or *Pirates of the Caribbean*. The only real choice an actor has consists of the roles he turns down. In the roles he has taken, Depp has, with minor exceptions, left his mark upon the film, turned it this way and that into a Depp film. True, it may also be a Tim Burton film or a Terry Gilliam film, but it is a Johnny Depp film and precious for that reason.

Some time back, the New Critics saw art as completely pure, as existing beyond space, time and historical context. While this approach worked well with poetry, the purest of the arts, it came a cropper with Shakespeare and performance art. Proteus-like, the performers changed and shaded the characters of Prince Hal, Hamlet and Prospero so that sometimes it was almost impossible to tell whether they were noble heroes or something much less noble, perhaps even vile. And what of film, the newest and least respected of the arts, who made actors rich household words but diminished their power at the hands of the studios and the directors? Some film directors (and among them some of the greatest) — most notably, perhaps, Fritz Lang, Alfred Hitchcock, and Stanley Kubrick — hardly seemed to be interested in actors at all, except for how they photographed against the décor.

The role of the actor in big-budget dramatic films today is sadly diminished. The screenplay is sold on the basis of what has been successful (that is, profitable) in the past, the director is chosen on the basis of his (it is almost always a man) track record, the main actors are picked for their popularity and their affordability (that is, for their Q rating), and the film is shot. And the resulting product itself is generally at the mercy of the ubiquitous computer-generated imagery, which often leads the way, with the poor player trailing a long way behind. While the sequence listed here does not always occur in this order, it is clear that the actor is only one part of the equation, and usually not even the most important part.

This book is concerned not with Johnny Depp's personal life, but with his films. Since his meteoric rise to fame in the television series *21 Jump Street* in 1987, he has been a creature of the media, and his every step has been endlessly recounted and evaluated in the tabloids, on television and latterly on the internet. Depp was, however, almost from the first, recognized as unusual in some way, as "a person of interest" from whom much might be expected, at least if he did not crash and burn. Before *Pirates of the Caribbean*, his choice of films has been regarded as wildly eccentric; but with only one or two exceptions, each of these choices represented what he believed to be genuine creative opportunities. When these films are taken in sequence, they represent not only trial and error, but a steady if sometimes uncertain growth both in his development as an actor and as a kind of philosopher of the screen who presented in non-judgmental fashion a darker and, at the same time, more sympathetic image than any great film star of the sound period. The real question then becomes: How did the personalities which Depp projects in his films become, in the jargon of the criticism of the day, such potent signifiers? The answer is found in his films.

That answer, although subject to endless debate and qualification, includes his appearances in films done by foreign directors examining America's image, his non-judgmental analysis of the characters he plays, including their understanding — or lack of it — of their motives and sexuality, his willingness to subordinate his own character to the demands of the film, his ambiguous mixing of humor and drama, and his intuitive understanding of—and homage to—the great players of cinematic history.

The Haunted Palace: The Mind of Johnny Depp

> "Yet it [the mind] creates transcending these,
> Far other Worlds and other Seas,
> Annihilating all that's made
> To a green thought in a green shade."
> (Andrew Marvell, "The Garden")

Artists have always been fascinated by the mind's ability to contain contrary ideas, emotions, attitudes and, yes, personalities, and have attempted to explain those contradictions. Emerson said, "A petty consistency is the hobgoblin of little minds." Walt Whitman, his disciple, said that he—speaking as the voice of the American people—contained "multitudes." Whitman meant, of course, the poet and not the man. Shakespeare alone seemed to contain the world, but the world he claimed was the world he created with the poet's eye "in a fine frenzy rolling." While he always spoke of players sympathetically, there is nothing to show that he claimed a special creative place for them. The question, however, is an open one, and the principal actors have an honored place in his monument, the First Folio of his plays (1623).

Only the actors, even the greatest of them, were exempt. No one ever claimed that Brando or Olivier, by common consent two giants who shared the world between them, were auteurs. Certainly, neither ever claimed that exalted status. Olivier gave Shakespeare—the writer—full credit. Brando disdained actors as a group, and all he ever wanted was a full salary and a share in the creative process.

Of course, film buffs are always ready to argue the prospective merits of actors, but the standards are vague and the arguments are always inconclusive. Film directors, when they have the power of choice, are quick to choose actors who represent a version of themselves: John Ford/John Wayne, David Lynch/Kyle MacLachlan, D. W. Griffith/Lillian Gish, Clarence Brown/Greta Garbo, and a few other dynamic duos. A few writers also see individual actors as versions of their own complicated egos. Charlie Kaufman's brilliant screenplay for *Being John Malkovich* is an argument for the actor as auteur. Reviewers were quick to point out that no one would ever do a serious fiction film called *Being John Wayne* or *Being Sylvester Stallone*. They would, of course, be suitable subjects for burlesque, but hardly for a sober treatment. The reason for this, of course, is that they have, at least on the screen, no inner life. Everything is projected on the screen, and they are what you see. The standard Hollywood version for projecting thought on screen is to show an actor at a typewriter looking out the window, or, like Dr. Zhivago, riding through a beautiful snow-covered landscape with his sweetie while worrying about the revolution disrupting his poetry writing.

The complexity and depth of the roles that Johnny Depp has played may profitably be compared to rooms in "The Haunted Palace," a poem by Edgar Allan Poe contained in his famous story "The Fall of the House of Usher" (1839). According to Richard Wilbur, "The House of Usher is, in allegorical fact, the physical body of Roderick Usher, and its dim interior is, in fact, Roderick Usher's visionary mind" (Poe 393). Poe pretends that what he is depicting is the mind of Roderick Usher, but we know that it is, in reality, his own. Thus, Poe's haunted palace represents in surrealistic fashion Roderick Usher's mind and, for the present purpose, the creative mind of Johnny Depp. Each room in our haunted palace contains characters from Depp's mind, and the guide, Mr. Poe, who is soft-spoken and neatly but shabbily dressed, has a remarkable resemblance to him. Each room is individually furnished in an appropriate style, and Cry-Baby Walker, J. M. Barrie, Lord Rochester, Ichabod Crane, Sweeney Todd and the rest have been allowed to choose their own decorations. Captain Jack stalks a widow's walk on the crenelated battlement. Mr. Poe has graciously allowed Bon-Bon and Lt. Victor to share a room together.

Of course, this palace is not what most people would call Johnny Depp's real mind, which we may assume is what gets him through the day in more or less the same way all our minds get us through the day. It is his artistic mind.

Faces and Sacrifice

We have characteristic images of iconic film actors, often beyond any ability they may have. For example, there is forgiveness in physical grace, instances that remain with us a lifetime. Some twenty minutes into *The Four Horsemen of the Apocalypse*, Valentino steps onto the dance floor and performs the tango while glued to a woman who, at least as far as the audience is concerned, might as well not be there. James Dean moves instantly from sullen outrage to open rebellion and pushes cakes of ice down a chute in *East of Eden*. Five minutes into *Shane* there is an unexpected sound, Alan Ladd turns, twisting like a cobra, and a gun magically appears in his hand. And the fluid athletic grace of Douglas Fairbanks, Burt Lancaster and John Travolta made them stars before they learned to act, and sometimes kept them stars after that ability had faded.

But moviemaking is also an art of faces, and there is a grace in stillness too. The stillness of Garbo's face at the end of *Queen Christina*, the resignation on Burt Lancaster's face when he learns that the killers have arrived, the alert watchfulness registering something between stoic resignation and grim determination which we have so often seen on the face of Buster Keaton, an actor whom Depp much admires and with whom he is explicitly compared in the opening of *Benny & Joon*.

Johnny Depp has many faces. It was, especially when he was younger, a face of extraordinary beauty, and it was guilt-free and non-threatening. It promised an afternoon of pleasure without being a threat to the husband and children. It promised an evening of pleasure with Don Juan at an expensive restaurant, an elevator ride to pleasure, a dream fulfilled.

Depp's face, like that of Garbo, is best seen in repose. The famous shot of Garbo at the end of *Queen Christina* (1933) is essentially a blank, a mirror in which every viewer can see what he or she wants. At the end of *Dead Man*, William Blake sets out upon the endless ocean of life — or whatever ocean it is — and his "sea canoe" disappears into the vastness. He has been dying for a long time — throughout most of the movie, in fact — and his face shows that he has accepted the inevitable. At the end of *From Hell*, Inspector Abberline, an opium addict, has prepared himself for death by leaving coins for the ferryman Charon to take him across the river into the land of the dead. (In an alternate, rejected version included on the DVD, the ending is the same, but the locale has been changed to a romantic Oriental opium den.) Although different interpretations of the ending of the film are certainly possible, the consensus is that Abberline has sacrificed himself to protect the woman he loved. But the discussion does not end there, and the scapegoat/sacrifice lurks beneath the surface of many of Johnny Depp's films, including, at least indirectly, all of those done with Tim Burton.

Although films made outside the Hollywood mainstream have furnished enduring images of faces — Falconetti's in Dreyer's *Passion* and Jim Caviezel's in Gibson's *Passion* — Hollywood films generally allow two forms of "sacrifice" — for love and for country. The two are sometimes even allowed to conflict with each other, as in *Queen Christina*, but the idea of religious sacrifice is beyond the pale, unless it is set within a carefully agreed majority context purged of any religious sect or doctrine. The problem, of course, is that the idea of sacrifice, which is always exemplified in the face, is so deeply embedded in all cultures that it cannot be purged.

Largely under the influence of René Girard, who opened the discussion, the idea of the relationship between the scapegoat and sacrifice has taken center stage in recent literary discussions, and as the debate widens, the films of Marlon Brando and Johnny Depp will merit particular attention. Derek Hughes' *Culture and Sacrifice: Ritual Death in Literature and Opera* should prove valuable in stimulating the discussion.

Johnny Depp and Silent Films

Kevin Brownlow called his famous book about Hollywood filmmaking in the 1920s *The Parade's Gone By* to indicate the rapidity and completeness of the change from silents to sound. The revolution, coinciding as it did with the coming of the Great Depression, followed by World War II, seemed to foster a sort of instant amnesia in which silent films were instantly forgotten. The question then becomes: What could a youngster named John Christopher Depp growing up in the wilds of Owensboro, Kentucky, and in Miramar, Florida, in the sixties and seventies have seen on television and in the movie houses?

The quick answer, of course, would be, "not much," but the answer is not quite as clear as we might suppose. Johnny Depp grew up in a period when silent movies were once again being seen after a hiatus of some three decades. Critically, the renaissance had begun with the film reviews of James Agee, and flowered with his essay in *Life*, "Comedy's Greatest Era," which was the cover story for September 3, 1949, and which received an enormous response. Of the three great clowns of the silent period discussed by Agee — Chaplin, Lloyd and Keaton — Charlie Chaplin was rich, living in exile in Switzerland and preserving his films in an hermetically sealed vault; Harold Lloyd, no less rich, was living in mildly eccentric seclusion; but Buster Keaton was poor and ready to work. And work he did.

The arrival of television in the late 1940s aided in the revival of silent films. Although the television stations had close to no interest in silent movies, the demand for product, as it was called, was insatiable, eventually encompassing twenty-four hours a day, day in and day out, year in and year out. Denis Meikle gives it as fact that Depp watched *Silents Please*, a half-hour show which survived for only one season, 1961–1962, but which ran seemingly forever in syndication (24). *Silents* showed classic silent movies from the collection of Charles Killiam, with commentary by Ernie Kovacs. By today's standards, the prints were miserable and the projection speed too fast, but the commentary was generally astute. The feature films listed in the Killiam catalogue include Barrymore's *Dr. Jekyll and Mr. Hyde* (1920, Keaton's *The General* (1927) and Chaney's *The Hunchback of Notre Dame* (1923) and *The Phantom of the Opera* (1925). By the 1970s, interest in silent films, although still a minority taste, was growing. In 1971, Orson Welles hosted a series called *The Silent Years*. While the prints were still poor by today's standards, Welles' excellent commentary is occasionally included as a DVD extra. By 1975, Lillian Gish — Mother Hollywood — supplied PBS TV commentary for films from the Blackhawk collection, the original source for David Shepard's Film Preservation Associates collection. Silent movies were clearly on the move.

The evidence shows that toward the end of Depp's four years on *21 Jump Street*, Depp, with the assistance of his co-star Peter DeLuise, began to improvise both dialogue and bits of business. DeLuise was, of course, the son of Dom DeLuise, a comic probably best known for his appearance in Burt Reynolds movies, and the youngster's comic timing and his knowledge of earlier clowns had doubtlessly been learned at his father's knee.

As Depp's confidence grew, and as his influence on the series increased, references to early films began to appear on *21 Jump Street*. In "La Bizca" (the cross-eyed woman), broadcast on February 26, 1990, Hanson (Depp) and Penhall (DeLuise), far away from Jump Street in the doo-doo of some unnamed police state south of the border, teach a woman who understands little or no English how to properly enunciate Laurel and Hardy's famous phrase "another fine mess." The phrase had been popularized by Johnny Carson, a great admirer of Laurel and Hardy, on *The Tonight Show*. A later episode, "How I Saved the Senator," broadcast May 7, 1990, clearly shows Depp's admiration for silent film comedy. When the Jump Street Squad saves the life of a senator, a beautiful wannabe filmmaker, played by Elena Wohl, inspires the Jump Street crew to tell their stories. Hanson's, by far the most interesting, is a one-reel, silent (with music), pixilated, black and white film, with Depp doing an excellent Chaplin imitation. Depp plays a waiter in a swanky restaurant who foils an anarchist. The film probably most closely resembles the restaurant sequence in Chaplin's Mutual two-reeler *The Rink* (1916). The anarchist was, of course, a standard villain of the period, and can, for example, be seen in Chaplin's *East Street* (1917). Although a look at the Chaplin Mutuals will quickly prevent any adventurous critics from overvaluing the *Jump Street* homage, the faux film is one of the high points of the entire series. Clearly, when Depp left what he called his period of "indentured servitude" on *Jump Street*, he was familiar with the late silent-early sound films of Laurel and Hardy, as well as with Chaplin's Mutual series, which many critics believe to be Chaplin's best work.

Buster Keaton probably did more than anyone else to help the renaissance. He appeared in movies, both lowbrow (DeMille's *The Greatest Show on Earth*) and high (Samuel Beckett's *Film*); on television in a series of popular commercials (Alka-Seltzer, Simon Pure Beer, and others); and in series, including a famous episode of the *Twilight Zone* ("Once Upon a Time"). Although few of the silent clowns continued into the television era, their legacy certainly did.

Red Skelton, for example, an enormously popular comedian whose show (*The Red Skelton Show*) ran from 1955 to 1970, was a master of pantomime who admired and imitated Keaton. When stuck with the problem of extricating himself from a closet guarded by a lion in the 1948 film *A Southern Yankee*, Skelton reportedly called on Keaton to solve the problem. The idea probably originated in the fertile mind of director Eddie Sedgwick, who had worked with Keaton on many of his best silent films.

In some Depp movies, including *Benny & Joon*, *Don Juan DeMarco*, and the three *Pirates of the Caribbean* entries, the influence of silent films is open and apparent. *Benny & Joon* is clearly an homage to silent comedy. The picture opens with a montage sequence that includes a train traveling toward a northwestern town across a rural landscape. The camera moves in close to a window showing a book, *The Look of Buster Keaton*, by Robert Benayoun, a French film critic and director, and a great admirer of Jerry Lewis, with whom Depp had just worked on *Arizona Dream*. The book lowers to reveal the face of Johnny Depp; he's wearing Keaton's porkpie hat and looking startlingly like the great silent clown before booze and cigarettes ruined that magnificent face. The shot is visually striking and totally out of context. Whether the shot originated with Depp or director Jeremiah Chechik, it confidently, even stridently, introduces the subtext of the film's physical comedy. The screenplay for *Benny & Joon* was written by Barry Berman, formerly a clown for Ringling Brothers, Barnum and Bailey Circus. In the credits, he received an additional listing as adviser for the "physical comedy," with which the film abounds.

Both Tim Burton and Johnny Depp have often spoken of their admiration for early films, by which they mean films of the entire silent period and of the expressionistic American horror pictures of the 1930s. Of course, Burton has always been an acute student of early cinema. He began his career with Disney, knew many of the old-timers who had been with Disney since the beginning (or near it), and his whole career, it could be argued, in a continuation of the silent film tradition.

What is clear is that Johnny Depp is essentially an actor acutely aware of the history of film, and who has been strongly influenced by silent film acting — not in any consciously theoretical way, but as a living embodiment of a nearly extinct tradition.

The Divided Self

The great gift which silent comedy gave to Johnny Depp is that "nothing sticks to him." Silent comedians and their low fellows of the sound period, such as the Three Stooges, wreaked indiscriminate and sometimes complete destruction wherever they went. No matter — they were forgiven and sent out to destroy again. Keaton's face, like Depp's, is alive to every nuance and sensibility, and he can look at earthquakes and train wrecks without blinking. His feelings are hardly shown at all, and must be read from his actions. Keaton played one character, but Depp plays many. What Depp learned from Keaton was that characters can have an inner life separate from the one actors spend their lives learning to express. Almost all actors want to show the viewer the depths of the character they are playing. Depp has an arsenal of ways to make behavior plausible without allowing it to be put on display before the multitudes.

Depp's characters always have — or seem to have, which is, in art, the same thing — a hidden self, a divided personality, a "secret window" that may or may not be revealed in an individual film. Unrevealed and happy, the self is a comedian, but like the characters in a story by Edgar Allan Poe, the comedian comes apart under stress. He may take opium for solace or even a cornucopia of drugs. He may decide to become a famous poet and seek out a wise Native American, and take a canoe ride on the ocean of life. He may decide to go to work on his enemies with a straight razor. He may even decide to become an omni-sexual pirate king to whom nothing is forbidden.

Depp's personality can turn on a dime. Recent critics of Shakespeare's Iago, in *Othello*, have declared him a sociopath — that is, a person who has to construct his own personality. Of course, without feelings or emotions he is unable to do so and wanders in a wilderness of evils. It is unclear whether any actor could successfully portray Iago as a sociopath. It would require an actor to imitate a man with no feelings pretending to have feelings. The argument here is not that the hidden self is a sociopath, but simply that he could be. At any rate, he can turn in an instant from bonhomie to slashing away with a razor or killing people and burying them in a secret garden. Or he might just be a handsome, well-dressed man who likes to have guiltless sex with women in an endless elevator ride. Or even better, perhaps a "porterette" of astonishing skill and style who performs in a prison yard and smuggles packages in and out of a Havana prison. And he might even look like John Dillinger or Johnny Depp.

The Auteur

What are the sources of Johnny Depp's appeal? What is unique about him? How is he different from other important actors? Why does he so often seem superior to the movie that he is in? Why is he better than George Clooney, Sean Penn, Brad Pitt or other contemporaries? Although famous actors make enormous amounts of money, they are seldom considered seriously in film criticism. What does the term "author" or "auteur" mean anyway? And is the director the only candidate for that revered name? Could an actor with special abilities — say, Johnny Depp — possibly qualify?

The romantic critics regarded originality and its partner, imagination, as the greatest of literary virtues, and elevated Shakespeare to the top of the heap. Early film critics wrote about the "producer" of the photoplay, but ran into trouble deciding who he was. During the postwar period, the French, always more alert to critical trends than the Americans, decided the film's director was the auteur, or author; but the term was elastic and shifting, since all the accepted directors had a generous share of poor movies which had to be explained in one way or another. And then there were creative people who made admired movies but who never directed. Popular writers on film elevated Buster Keaton and Harold Lloyd to auteur status without the high-brow critics even noticing. Producer Val Lewton, another revered figure, made wonderful low-budget horror movies and never directed a single film.

Since the concept of the director or writer was unknown, or alien, to the new art of film, the first author was the "producer," a term which usually meant the person, almost always a man, responsible (or who could claim responsibility) for the film. He could be a producer — that is, the man who put up the money, or the man who directed the film, or both. The most notable of the first generation of producers, the men who made the movies, were the Lumière brothers and Georges Méliès. Today the Lumière brothers would be considered the producers of their films, but Méliès was an auteur in the modern sense because he produced his films, wrote the scripts, designed the sets, often acted in them and directed them. These early filmmakers quickly developed the concept of the company which produced the film as an emblem of quality, but were soon forced to drop it with the burgeoning popularity of the developing stars of the early screen. During the silent period a few directors established themselves as images of quality — D. W. Griffith, Cecil B. DeMille, Erich Von Stroheim, and F. W. Murnau among them — but never made much of a dent in the public consciousness. Charlie Chaplin, Buster Keaton, Douglas Fairbanks and Mary Pickford established and maintained a tradition of loyalty matched by few later stars. To a greater or lesser extent, they controlled the making of their films. Film reviewing quickly became part of the business of publicizing motion pictures, but was, for the most part, controlled by the film companies (as, to a surprising extent, it remains). Early film books in America, such as Vachel Lindsey's *The Art of the Moving Picture* (1915), were little more than subjective introductions to a complex subject.

Elsewhere, however, especially in the USSR, making films and writing about them became a blood sport which began to influence writers outside Russia, both in translation and in indigenous writings. Huntley Carter's *The Theatre and Cinema of Soviet Russia* (1924), Paul Rotha's *The Film Till Now* (1930), and V. I. Pudovkin's *Film Technique* (tr. 1929) were substantial works which attempted a serious examination of the relationship between film and society. After World War II there was a new interest in film studies in all areas — practical, historical, and theoretical — with the French leading the way. Repression in the USSR and in Germany had largely killed off, often literally, film criticism. In France, Robert Brasillach, one of the most famous movie critics of the World War II period, was executed as a traitor, but that apparently had more to do with his fascism than with his film writing.

During the war, French filmmaking had continued to enjoy a remarkable degree of freedom, considering the circumstances, and budding French filmmaker/critics soon developed a vigorous debate attempting to justify their preference for American movies. The concept of originality, which had bedeviled literary criticism since the Romantic period, became a focal point as a standard of value. The problem was that popular films were mass produced and required a number of people with individual expertise in various disciplines, including, among others, writers, set decorators, photographers, and directors. How could we distinguish what had value from drivel? The answer was the so-called "auteur theory."

Many writers have claimed that the auteur theory is not really a theory at all, but a standard of discrimination. The maze of claims and counter-claims has been sorted through by Jeff Bell, and the interested reader may safely be guided by his clear analysis in his essay "The Director Function: Auteur Theory and Poststructuralism." François Truffaut started the debate with a 1954 essay, "A Certain Tendency of the French Cinema," whose fame may outlive his films. Truffaut thought that the old guard was a stuffy bunch, and he was interested in justifying the director as an original contributor to the so-called "tradition of quality" which he claimed saw the director strictly as a *metteur-en-scène*, a man who moved the characters around to tell the great stories literature had supplied. Truffaut argued that this was wrong, and that the person who establishes "a unified subject that serves as the sole source of creative output" is, of course, the director (Bell 188). This applied even, or especially, to American directors who, working within the studio system, nevertheless managed to impose their own personalities upon often recalcitrant material. In America, Andrew Sarris contentiously supported the auteur theory against all comers and helpfully ranked the directors for the uninitiated in books and essays.

Jeff Bell's argument mediates between the extremes of those who see the director as the be-all and end-all of filmmaking, and those who privilege "the linguistic signs of the traditional written narrative" (150). Truffaut's argument was hardly disinterested; he was attempting to supply a theoretical justification for the films he and other members of the so-called *nouvelle vague*, or new wave, were making. This argument has, however, the advantage of including the great French films of the "tradition of quality"—for example, *Children of Paradise* and the films of Jean Renoir and Raymond Bernard—but it also allows room for other claims of authorship.

Auteur hunters paid close attention to minutiae, examining who was and who was not allowed to light each others' cigarettes in the films of Howard Hawks, and other recurring events and symbols. Obviously, the director was responsible. Other claimants, however, have found few supporters. Gore Vidal and William Goldman, both novelists and writers of screenplays, individually floated the idea of the writer as auteur without much success. Nonetheless, their argument that the nearly sacred word "auteur" should often be considered as plural certainly makes sense. Can there be any doubt that Robert Towne's screenplay for Roman Polanski's *Chinatown* (1974) was absolutely essential for that film's greatness?

The concept of the director (or filmmaker, as he/she is generally called) as auteur is accepted by most young film students as a matter of fact. In some cases, however, the idea of the actor as auteur has been accepted as well, almost without comment. Buster Keaton, who never claimed a single directorial credit during his entire career, is now universally regarded as an auteur, the equal—perhaps even the superior—of Chaplin, who set the gold standard for comedy. The whole idea of the actor as auteur would have struck Keaton, a meat and potatoes man if ever there was one, as absurd.

It is certainly worthy of note that none of the early auteur critics believed control of all aspects of filmmaking was necessary to qualify a subject as an auteur. Their criticism began as an attempt to justify the Hollywood films they liked, despite their standard, cookie-cutter production. The grace notes, or bits of business, they found in the work of even a bottom-feeder like Edgar G. Ulmer might qualify him for the title. If we accept these grace notes, or business, as a qualification, then we must admit that an actor could qualify.

The question then becomes: What sort of actor would it take, and how could he qualify? Would Marlon Brando, Depp's mentor and the man who is generally credited with revolutionizing film acting, qualify? The answer is clearly yes, but only in a small number of roles, which would include *A Streetcar Named Desire*, *On the Waterfront*, *Last Tango in Paris* and *The Godfather*, and perhaps one or two others. Certainly, Brando is not unique in making movies in which he did not believe — after all, actors have to eat, too — but he is unusual, if not unique, in allowing his dislike to show so visibly. For example, his detestation for Chaplin's *A Countess from Hong Kong* is visible in every frame of that film in which he appears.

In ways which are unique, but not beyond all conjecture, Johnny Depp embodies silent film techniques in his performances. He is androgynous, an equal opportunity sexual object, an effeminate leading man with a haze of hippieness surrounding him. While Anthony Lane believes that Chaplin originated the breed, it is probable, perhaps certain, that there are effeminates lurking somewhere in Shakespeare's *Twelfth Night* and *The Tempest* (Lane, *Dead Man's Chest*). All of Depp's performances embody not only the external aspects of personality — which is what all good actors do — but also an inner self which defies analysis. Additionally, his admiration for and homage to the Beat culture of the 1960s enriches his performances and places them in an historical context. There is no evidence that Depp has ever worked against the grain of a movie in which he appeared. He is a shape-shifter who has always subordinated himself to the demands of the film as a whole, and he has always loyally supported his films, sometime doing publicity for them years after they were made. Depp has made poor movies — he has even directed one of them — but he has never betrayed the shape of them. He has never betrayed the film by being better than the film itself, as alpha male actors often have. This, more than any other factor, has hindered him from being recognized as the greatest player of his time and as one of the few actors of today qualified to be given the honorific of auteur.

Depp believes that acting is, or should be, an expression of the artist's personal feelings, although not necessarily his political beliefs. He admires the free-wheeling counter-culture of the sixties and believes that art should in some way express its values, but he is the least dogmatic of prophets. Beyond a belief in absolute freedom of expression, he makes no attempt to convince the audience of the validity of his beliefs. Depp is not an intellectual. He does not, like Oliver Stone or George Clooney, make political films. Like Buster Keaton, he is largely self-educated and operates primarily on instinct and imitation. His best audience is children. He is an overlord surveying in a non-judgmental fashion the weirdness of the characters he inhabits. That is his gift to the audience.

And he is the most generous of actors. He always subordinates himself to the film, and he has often disappeared into a role and left others to take the laurels. In *What's Eating Gilbert Grape*, for example, he allowed the young Leonardo DiCaprio to do the Rain-Man shtick — all grimaces and jerky movements — without hindrance, and to be nominated for an Academy Award. But watch the movie two or three times today and see who is doing the real acting.

Johnny Depp is unusual, perhaps unique — in his ability to bring minor roles — what are usually called cameos — to life. His impersonation of the flamboyant Bon-Bon in *Before Night Falls* is probably the most famous. Although onscreen for only seconds, Depp was so impressive that one writer suggested that he should have won an Academy Award for his performance. His other cameos are nearly as effective, and usually tell a story which is complete in itself. The story is never in conflict with the content of the film itself, but is always an augmentation of it. In other words, he is always acting in the same film, not in another one with no relationship to the one in which he appears. In this he is unlike his famous mentor Marlon Brando, who never bothered to conceal his contempt for the many films he appeared in which he, for one reason or another, detested.

The essential Johnny Depp is apparent everywhere in his films, but he is not easy to define. For some, he is a philosopher of the self, a dark prophet who holds a mirror up to nature. For others, he is a non-judgmental child who invites everyone to join with him in his guilt-free games. No matter how young or old we are, he promises to absorb our guilt and keep us free. My attempt has been to turn and follow him.

THE FILMS

1984 *A Nightmare on Elm Street*

Baby Face

"What, will the line stretch out to the crack of doom?"
(Shakespeare, *Macbeth*)
"Them that dies will be the lucky ones."
(Long John Silver, *Treasure Island*)

Johnny Depp and Freddy Krueger arrived onscreen together. Depp's first screen appearance was as one of Freddy Krueger's victims in the first of a series of *Nightmare on Elm Street* movies, which, in one form or another, bids fair to stretch out to Shakespeare's "crack of doom." Up-and-coming director Wes Craven wrote and directed this thriller about child molester Freddy Krueger's return from the dead as a so-called "dream demon" who attacks and kills potential victims when they fall asleep. The film solidified Craven's career as a master of the horror film aimed directly at the teenaged audience. Although more limited in content and imagination than the great horror films of the past, today's low-budget slasher films remain the most surefire moneymakers around.

Wes Craven (b. 1939) entered filmmaking in 1972 with *The Last House on the Left*, a low-budget horror movie. Craven had both talent and a sure eye for popular taste. In the following years he turned out a series of films whose popularity ensured both work for the director and appreciation from his fans. Although lacking major stars, his films combined talented — and sometimes not so talented — newcomers, such as Johnny Depp, aging stars and attractive television performers. *Swamp Thing* (1982), based upon a comic book, starred the still-elegant French star Louis Jourdan and television temptress Adrienne Barbeau. Craven's professionalism and the success of his so-called "franchise" films (*The Last House on the Left, A Nightmare on Elm Street, The Hills Have Eyes*) eventually moved him into the Hollywood mainstream with *Music of the Heart* (1999). Starring Meryl Streep and, as they say, "based on a true story," *Music* was a biopic about the problems of a Harlem violin teacher. Although predictable, the film won an Academy Award nomination for Streep and was widely admired. Still, Craven somehow felt uncomfortable in the mainstream and quickly moved back into the environs of the horror genre.

The *Nightmare on Elm Street* series was produced by New Line Cinema and was largely responsible for the growth of the company which eventually went public and produced the enormously popular (but much more expensive and prestigious) *Lord of the Rings* trilogy. The *Nightmare* series includes *A Nightmare on Elm Street* (1984), *Freddy's Revenge* (1985), *Dream Warriors (1987), The Dream Master* (1988), *The Dream Child* (1989), *Freddy's Dead: The Final Nightmare* (1991), *Wes Craven's New Nightmare* (1994), and *Freddy vs. Jason* (2003), with more on the way. According to the commentary on the DVD, the studio was not completely happy with the second film of the series, *Freddy's Revenge,* which took the claw-handed avenger out of the dream world and put him into the real world. The third film quickly returned him to the dream world, where he is, of course, invulnerable and eternal.

Billed on the two-disc DVD as "the chilling masterpiece that spawned the greatest horror franchise in film history"—clearly a considerable statement—A *Nightmare on Elm Street* revived the moribund horror genre and started Johnny Depp on his film career. It also made Robert Englund, who played Freddy, a genre favorite who became instantly recognizable to teenagers, even without his makeup. John Saxon, an honorable actor who has had an up and down career (which included co-starring with Marlon Brando in *The Appaloosa* [1966]), is the only actor in *Nightmare* with any considerable reputation at the time the film was made. Saxon plays the police-chief father of Heather Langenkamp, who plays Nancy Thompson (and who was to reprise, so to speak, the character in the third Freddy movie). Ronee Blakley, who had been nominated for an Academy Award as Best Supporting Actress for Robert Altman's masterpiece *Nashville* (1976), unfortunately seems adrift here. Fragile and heartbreaking in Altman's film, she seems never to have found another director who could utilize her talent.

Unlike his contemporary, Canadian-born David Cronenberg, Craven has not received good press. David Thomson fairly represents the negative case. Although Thomson noted that Craven began with a "modernization" of Bergman's *The Virgin Spring,* he concluded: "His concern has been to shock, and to profit from it" (*New Biographical Dictionary*). Neither Thomson nor the present writer doubts that Craven's "postmodern self-reflection ... amounts to a frenzied, disdainful redoubling of nastiness because no one really believes in it," no matter how many young graduate students see "tenure beckoning" with learned treatises on Craven's violence. Cronenberg, by comparison, is perhaps even more violent; but horror, for him, is, to quote Thomson again, "not a game or a meal ticket; it is rather the natural expression for one of the best directors working today." Often brilliant, but, until recently, wildly uneven, Cronenberg in his full maturity has produced a series of brilliant films which—for want of a better word—may be called gothic, showing both the depth of man's predatory violence and his infinite capacity for self-deception: *Spider* (2002), *A History of Violence* (2005) and *Eastern Promises* (2007). It is to be hoped that Cronenberg and Johnny Depp will make a film together in the near future. Craven, however, may be comforted by his box-office returns.

Despite the popularity of *A Nightmare on Elm Street,* no one at the time seems to have paid any particular attention to Depp. He appears early in the film, a teenager telling lies to his mother on the telephone. He is aided in the process by some not-very-convincing sound effects from a boom box. He is a slender, extraordinarily good-looking, rosy-cheeked teenager; and as soon as the viewers see Freddy Krueger sharpening his artificial fingernails, they are immediately fearful that he will not make it to the end of the film. Indeed, he does not, but this is a "dream film" with a "dream killer," and he is resurrected at the end only to be threatened again.

The enormous box-office generated by the film guaranteed another Elm Street film, and another, and so on, but no one at the time seems to have suspected either that the young actor might have had something to do with the film's box-office success or that he might become one of the leading actors of his time.

1985 *Private Resort*
Horny Crunchies Winner

In *Private Resort*, Johnny Depp is top-billed, after Rob Morrow, in an R-rated teenaged comedy of adolescent lust at a "private resort." As might be expected of an R-rated adolescent film with what turned out to be, at least eventually, an enormously popular young star, there are, apparently, several versions of the movie. The DVD version currently available clocks in at 82 minutes, the length given by *Variety* for the theatrical release. A writer on the IMDB site states that he saw a television version which began with Morrow and Depp winning a trip to the private resort off the box-top of a cereal called "Horny Crunchies or something like that." This is probable. The DVD version takes place entirely at the resort, with only a passing reference to explain how our two lust-ridden protagonists got there; and preparing the film for a network television audience would certainly have required drastic reediting for a movie already too short to fit into a two-hour time slot. Outtakes were often used to fill up the necessary time period. Presumably, the makers of the film wanted to waste no time before cutting to the nearly naked women on the beach.

The film begins in near chaos, proceeds quickly to chaos, and winds down to near chaos. The formula is well described by the *Variety* reviewer as "nubile women on display, teen antics and rock music." While *Private Resort* has the necessary ingredients, only the women are up to the mark. The cast lacks the split-second timing needed for slapstick comedy, and the music is forgettable. The reviewer may think that slapstick is "old hat," but it has been old hat for a long time and still works, at least in the right hands.

Unlike Bob Clark's enormously popular adolescent comedy *Porky's* (1982), which was set in the 1950s, *Private Resort* has no cultural context. The resort is clearly expensive, but seems to be caught in an alien time warp. It is populated almost entirely by beautiful, nearly naked young women, with only an occasional older person brought in to move the story along and give the viewer someone to root against.

George Bowers' short career as a director of low-budget films ended with *Private Resort*, but he has continued to work in the industry as an editor. Notable recent work includes *Walking Tall* (the 2004 remake of the 1973 Joe Don Baker classic) and *From Hell*, which reunited him with Johnny Depp (2001), although in a different capacity.

Rob Morrow, originally top-billed ahead of Johnny Depp, has not managed to equal Depp's success, but has continued to work steadily on television with an occasional film role tossed in. He recently played a doctor in the popular film *The Bucket List* (2008).

By contrast, Hector Elizondo (b. 1936), "the Maestro" in *Private Resort*, has had a distinguished fifty-year career as a second banana on stage, screen and television, both with and without his toupee (or, in at least one famous appearance, both with *and* without). Much of his best work has been done with director Garry Marshall, notably in *The Flamingo Kid* (1984), *Pretty Woman* (1990) and *Runaway Bride* (1999), among others. He also appeared as a regular in the short-lived television series *Cane* (2007), and in Mike Newell's big-screen version of Garcia Marquez's *Love in the Time of Cholera*. In *Private Resort*, Elizondo—or, rather, his rug—receives a really bad haircut, and in his quest for vengeance he is further humiliated. Marshall must surely have seen *Private Resort* and have realized that Elizondo and his toupee presented a rich source of material for comedy. The result was Elizondo's performance in *Pretty Woman*.

Andrew Clay, the stand-up comedian later known as Andrew "Dice" Clay (and star of *Ford Fairlane*), appears in a series of slapstick gags toward the end of the film. Clay was later attacked for his alleged sexism and substantially exiled from network television for a time on the grounds of political incorrectness. Although he continues to perform, he has never managed to regain his earlier popularity.

Several of the women manage to make an impression. Dody Goodman, a comedienne who often appeared on *The Tonight Show with Johnny Carson*, is miscast as a lecherous, rich older woman. Hilary Shapiro and Leslie Easterbrook do effective work, at least as long as they can manage to keep their clothes on.

Depp is so young that what seems to be baby fat still clings to his round face, and his body seems almost frail. He is, or wants to be, a sex machine. The *Variety* reviewer, who seemed to assume that Depp was the sole star, wrote: "Depp is doing his thinking with another part of his body than his brain, trying to hop in the sack with every girl in sight, including the genre's inevitable older woman, statuesque Leslie Easterbrook."

The film received few reviews. *Variety* reviewed it in December, but noted that it had received only a very limited release earlier in the year and then had gone straight to video. The film seems to have done little or nothing to further Depp's career, and has been, according to Denis Meikle, "[e]ffectively stricken from the biographical record by its embarrassed star" (49). Later writers have duly noted Depp's nude scene some fifteen minutes into the film without believing that it did anything to improve a bad movie. A recent biography of Depp notes, however, that the nude scenes (mostly shots posterior, and not particularly revealing by current standards) "have made *Private Resort* a kind of Collector's item for Depp Fans" (Blitz 18).

The split-second timing necessary for physical comedy is almost totally lacking in *Private Resort*, and the youngster with the chubby cheeks is nearly lost in a sea of near-nudity—almost, but not quite. Still, as far as this film is concerned, it is only hindsight, so to speak, that would allow anyone to forecast him a future as a great actor.

1985 *Lady Blue*
"Birds of Prey," TV Episode

Johnny Depp appeared in an episode entitled "Birds of Prey" (Episode 4), broadcast on October 10, 1985, of the short-lived television series *Lady Blue*. The series, which starred Danny Aiello, Ron Dean and Jamie Rose (as the lady policeman of the title), began as a television movie pilot broadcast on April 15, 1985. According to the IMDB, Lorenzo Clemens, Terry Ferman and David Oliver appeared in the episode. Presumably the stars did also. According to one report, the series was considered too violent for the times. A montage of Johnny Depp scenes, dubbed in Spanish, may be seen at: *http://www.youtube.com/watch?v=amklJRdZzWA&feature=related* (Accessed May 20, 2008).

1986 *Platoon*

Learning the Craft

"Sarge, you wanna tell me which way to go. I wanna
figure this out." (Pvt. Gator Lerner)
"Only the dead have seen the end of war." (Plato)

After serving in the infantry in Viet Nam, and taking film classes at New York University (where Martin Scorsese is said to have been one of his teachers), Oliver Stone achieved notable success as a script writer before becoming a director. His early screenplays include *Midnight Express* (Alan Parker, 1978), for which he won an Oscar, and stints on *Conan the Barbarian* (John Milius, 1982), *Scarface* (Brian De Palma, 1983), *Year of the Dragon* (Michael Cimino, 1985) and *8 Million Ways to Die* (Hal Ashby, 1986). After directing two genre entries, *Seizure* (1981) and *The Hand* (1986), Stone came into his own with *Salvador* (1986) and *Platoon* (1986). Stone combines a pulp journalist's flair for the sensational with a take-no-prisoners narrative thrust reminiscent of Sam Fuller, both in treatment and subject matter. His subjects have included JFK, the Doors, Nixon, Wall Street, Alexander the Great, the National Football League, the World Trade Center destruction and George W. Bush. The good will generated by *Platoon* has long since evaporated, and Pauline Kael's famous retirement jibe that "the prospect of having to sit through another Oliver Stone movie is too much" appears to have carried the day. Despite his early critical success, Stone's reputation seems to be in permanent free-fall.

And yet, when so many movies are composed of seemingly endless explosions, who else has given so much attention to the forces of American society? Tom Wolfe, one of the founding fathers of the so-called new journalism, has praised *Any Given Sunday* (1999), a study of the workings of the National Football League, for doing what American novelists should be doing and are not—that is, showing how a great American institution works. Wolfe began his career as a non-fiction chronicler of American society and knows whereof he speaks. Coarse, crass and crude Stone's movies may be, but they are alive, and no other American filmmaker, liberal or conservative, has combined Stone's narrative flair with big-budget expertise in dealing with quintessentially American subjects.

Platoon was widely and favorably reviewed, was popular in theaters around the world, and won a ton of prizes, including four Academy Awards: Best Picture, Best Direction, Best Film Editing and Best Sound. The film appeared toward the end of a cycle of movies which dealt more or less directly with the Viet Nam incursion. The series included Sidney J. Furie's *The Boys in Company C* (1978), Ted Post's *Go Tell the Spartans* (1978) and *The Deer Hunter* (1978). Stanley Kubrick was, as usual, behind the curve, and *Full Metal Jacket* did not appear until 1987, nearly ten years later. All of these films have much to recommend them. The account of basic training in *The Boys in Company C* clearly influenced the magnificent first half of *Full Metal Jacket*. *Go Tell the Spartans* echoes the message allegedly sent back from Thermopylae by the 300 Spartans: "Here we died as they commanded. Go tell the Spartans"; and the scene of the soldiers, who have no memory of history, moving across the graveyard of the French who died in Indo-China is unforgettable. Unquestionably, the disaster of *Heaven's Gate*, which effectively put an end to Michael Cimino's career, has unfavorably influenced our perception of *The Deer Hunter*. Even so, many parts of the film, but especially the opening forty-five minutes, are permanently etched in film history. Although Stanley

Kubrick, as usual, went to fanatical lengths to ensure the accuracy of *Full Metal Jacket*, he had no interest in allocating blame to any particular group. He presented war as permanent and eternal because it is rooted in the black heart of man himself.

Platoon opens with a short scene of recruits arriving by cargo plane at a Viet Nam air base. As they leave the base, they watch body bags being loaded onto the same plane for its return to America. The film then moves immediately into the jungle, where every bush can hold a booby trap or a sniper. The men of the platoon, many of whom are based on, or are composites of, soldiers that Stone knew in combat, are generally more individual and believable than the characters in World War II films, who were usually characterized by a regional tic or speech characteristic. They are foul-mouthed, dope smoking, cynical and fatalistic to the core. They are from the lowest rung of the economic and social scale, and they know that innocent people are often killed in the heat of combat. The movie is about the limits of what is acceptable.

The moral poles of the film are represented by scar-faced Sgt. Barnes (Tom Berenger) and Sgt. Elias Grodin (Willem Dafoe). As the film moves toward its conclusion, which defends the murder of Barnes in the name of morality, the war goes on. The new soldiers become old soldiers, or dead soldiers, and the film ends where it began.

While some critics praised *Platoon* for its lack of "big symbols"—*The Deer Hunter* seems to have been the culprit here — others saw it as expressing the moral malaise of America. Yet others saw it as simply muddled. Sydelle Kramer wrote: "Stone never considers that we might have brought our corruption with us. A country sunk into self-indulgent lassitude, a people nurtured by delusions and shadowy propaganda dreams, a culture soured on its own ideals." This seems wide of the mark, since it is difficult to see how this could apply to any of the men in the film, even to Pvt. Taylor (Charlie Sheen), who delivers the voice-over commentary.

Platoon has not aged well. Like all of Stone's films, it is overheated and full of symbolism and commentary that seems, at least with the hindsight of more than two decades, unnecessary and redundant. The crucifixion imagery of Elias has often been criticized, but it was certainly thought appropriate at the time, as was the voice-over of Pvt. Taylor, which was taken to represent a voice of reason in a world of insanity. We are told that Taylor had been to college and, we presume, was therefore qualified as a narrator. Unfortunately, the voice-over only states more explicitly what is already explicit in the film itself.

The strength of the film is in its location footage, with the Philippines standing in for Viet Nam; in its first-hand knowledge of military terminology and usage; and, perhaps most of all, in its realistic differentiation of a variety of individuals. Depp's Pvt. Lerner, unfortunately, is not one of those individuals. We are simply not told enough about him to see him as an individual, and the contemporary reviews of the film, naturally enough, seldom, if ever, mention Depp. In his DVD commentary, Stone says that Depp was still learning his craft, but that he would like to work with him again. There is nothing to indicate that the director thought particularly highly of him at the time.

In *Platoon*, Depp plays Pvt. Gator Lerner, who serves as translator for the platoon. Although an uneducated Cajun, if that is what his name indicates, would seem an unlikely candidate for such a job, Depp, according to Stone's commentary on the DVD, learned some phrases of Vietnamese for the role. He is shown translating and is present during the massacre, apparently filmed as a small version of the My Lai massacre, and is shown carrying a young girl out of the burning village. Later, during an ambush, Big Harold (Forest Whitaker) asks about him. The reply is: "He's over there, by the log." Gator is carried off on a stretcher and is last seen being loaded onto a copter. Whether he is dead, dying or recovering, the film does not say.

According to legend, Depp's progress in the movies was slowed when important scenes in *Platoon* ended up on the cutting room floor. Brian J. Robb, for example, states that it "was in the editing that Johnny Depp's performance as the translator Lerner suffered the most," but offers no evidence to support his assertion (23). Legend was wrong, and the legion of fans who hoped that the 20th Anniversary Edition of *Platoon* (2006) would contain significant unpublished footage of Johnny Depp were disappointed. Only two new scenes included as extras contained footage of Depp. In the first, he says that everybody is interested only in "making money and looking out for themselves." In the second, he tells the Sergeant that he "has to figure something out."

1986 *Slow Burn*
Film Noir Lite

"$200 a day plus expenses" (Eric Roberts in *Slow Burn*)

Although Johnny Depp always speaks of *Private Resort* and *Slow Burn* as bad movies, almost all beginning film actors have appeared in films as bad or worse, and few of them have gone on to forge careers as successful artistically as Johnny Depp. *Slow Burn*, made for "pay television," as it was then called, is a violent movie, incorrectly described by Brian Robb as a "sub–Hitchcockian thriller" which attempts "to evoke the spirit and atmosphere of 1940s film noir" (20). Certainly the specific model for plotting and dialogue is Howard Hawks' *The Big Sleep* (1946), and anyone familiar with that famous film is unlikely to discover anything new in either the plotting or the dialogue of *Slow Burn*. In acting, dialogue and plotting, *Slow Burn* is clearly film noir lite — and very well lighted; the location shooting in the bright California sunlight and in realistic interiors would seem to disqualify the film as noir of any type.

A gumshoe, young by noir standards, is hired to track down a wife and child whom the husband abandoned some years before. The son turns out to be dead, but another teenager, played by Johnny Depp in a brief appearance, is mistaken for him and eventually murdered. The blond and sexually insatiable femme fatale, a standard prop in such films, turns out to be no better than she should be. The script is serviceable, but the patter seems to belong to some other, better movie.

Considering the budget and rehearsal time, the performers are generally effective. Beverly D'Angelo is an attractive actress best known for her appearance in the National Lampoon Vacation movies with Chevy Chase — *Vacation* (1983), *European Vacation* (1985), *Christmas Vacation* (1989) and *Vegas Vacation* (1997) — but she can also be effective in more serious roles, as in *American History X* (1998).

Eric Roberts, the older brother of star Julia Roberts, was effective early in his career in tough-guy roles, but quickly settled into supporting roles in films and television. He is probably best seen in Frank Pierson's *King of the Gypsies* (1979) and in Andrei Konchalovsky's *Runaway Train* (1985). Adapted by the director from a screenplay by Akira Kurosawa, *Runaway Train* is sort of a *Moby Dick* on the rails, and reads as if Abel Gance had come back from the dead to redo *La Roue* (1923) or Robert Aldrich's *Emperor of the North* (1973). At the beginning of *Slow Burn*, Roberts seems uncertain, but he gets better as the film goes along. Henry

Gibson, then famous for his spots on *Rowan and Martin's Laugh In*, appears briefly, and Dan Hedaya is excellent as a blackmailed father attempting unsuccessfully to save his son.

The problem with *Slow Burn* is not the script, the cast, or the location shooting, but the stolid direction. (Blitz and Krasniewicz wrote incorrectly that the film is set in south Florida [18]). A few continuity problems may be forgiven, considering the movie's low budget. For example, when Eric Roberts takes off after another car that is speeding away, the other car is shown to be stopped, when a second ago it had clearly been moving. Perhaps because of budgetary restraints, many details of the film seem generally wrong, from Eric Roberts' dress to the photographs and gallery installations, which are low-rent and unconvincing. Occasionally, however, especially towards the end, the pacing picks up and the movie gains some energy. It is probable that the English-born director's lack of first-hand knowledge of the flora and fauna of upscale life in the California desert injured the film.

In addition to *Slow Burn*, Chapman directed three other independent films during the 1980s: *Hussy* (1980), with a young Helen Mirren; *Strangers Kiss* (1983), with Peter Coyote and Chapman's then-wife, Victoria Tennant; and *Heart of Midnight* (1988), with Jennifer Jason Leigh. Considering the actors involved, all of these films would merit a second look. Apparently, Chapman's career as a director was not notably successful and was, for whatever reason, abandoned.

According to the biographical entry on the Internet Movie Data Base written by Chapman himself, he now writes non-fiction and screenplays. Notable recent screen work includes (with others) *Runaway Jury* (2003) and *Black Water Transit* (2008). He is the great-great-grandson of Charles Darwin, and has written extensively on the creationism controversy.

Slow Burn attracted little attention, and, apparently, Depp attracted none at all. (Although the film was released on VHS, it has not, as of 2009, been released on DVD.) Those who have watched the movie since Depp became famous have not been any kinder. A recent critic wrote, quite accurately, "Johnny Depp is very young in this one and has an awful 80's haircut. He chews gum and tosses a soccer ball around for about 5 minutes and that is all we get to see of him" (Blitz 18). That is, of course, except for a shot of his beautiful corpse.

At the time *Slow Burn* was made, Roberts was, of course, much better known than Johnny Depp. Twenty years on, Eric Roberts is best known as the older brother of his famous sister and has essentially been reduced to bit parts. By comparison, Johnny Depp is one of the most recognized faces in the world. It is unlikely that anyone could have predicted this outcome, at least on the basis of *Slow Burn*.

1987–1990 *21 Jump Street*
Teenage Heartthrob

Episodes that contain notable performances
or bits of business by Johnny Depp are marked •.

The IMDB gives complete cast listings but does not, at least at the time of this writing, include writing and directing credits, which are listed below. Although the five DVD sets published by Anchor Bay contain all 103 episodes, some episodes do not have Depp in them at all, and in others he appears only briefly. What is needed is a single inexpensive set containing selected episodes of Depp's performances.

Although Johnny Depp's career was in turnaround when the producers of *21 Jump Street* called, Depp initially refused the role of Tom Hanson, hoping that his role in *Platoon*, which was, in reality, little more than a cameo, would lead to better offers from Hollywood. These offers were not forthcoming, and when Jeff Yagher was replaced during the shooting of the two-part pilot and the offer was repeated, Depp accepted.

21 Jump Street is a television series concerning the adventures of a group of young undercover policemen assigned to investigate high school crime. The series began in 1987 and ran for five seasons on the Fox Television Network. Because the Jump Street Squad was stationed in a deconsecrated or abandoned church, the series was originally entitled *Jump Street Chapel*. The name was changed because of its religious connotations, although the church's stained glass windows are clearly visible.

The series was originally produced by Stephen J. Cannell and Patrick Hasburgh, but Hasburgh soon dropped out. According to Cannell, he was approached by Barry Diller to produce a television series for the fledgling Fox Television Network. In an attempt to compete with the established networks, Fox offered a guaranteed thirteen-week shoot without the production of a pilot episode. Beyond approval of the program concept and the cast, Fox offered a free hand. The series, which was shot in Vancouver, British Columbia, reached its target goal of teenagers and on August 23, 1987, enjoyed the distinction of being the first Fox show ever to beat one of the "big three"— ABC, NBC and CBS — in its time slot. According to Alex McNeil, the series moved into syndication after three and a half seasons (870).

Jump Street was designed as an ensemble series, and an episode typically involved at least two stories linked together only by the squad members. Romantic alignments shifted and blurred. As the characters— and the series— aged, the high school format was not dropped so much as ignored, and any pretense at dealing with the problems of teenagers was largely abandoned, especially in the later episodes. As might be expected in a series filmed so rapidly, the episodes contain occasional continuity errors, and proper names do not always agree either within an episode or with those given in the credits.

The Jump Street group included Tom Hanson (Johnny Depp), Judy Hoffs (Holly Robinson Peete), Doug Penhall (Peter DeLuise), Captain Jenko (Frederic Forrest in the two-part pilot and the first four episodes), Captain Fuller (Steven Williams, who replaced Frederic Forrest), Harry Truman Ioki (Dustin Nguyen), Sal "Blowfish" Banducci (Sal Jenco), and Dennis Booker (Richard Grieco, who became a regular in Season Three). In a spin-off, Grieco reprised his role as Detective Booker in a series of his own, *Booker*, which lasted one season.

According to Hal Erickson, the gifted Frederic Forrest was replaced when young viewers complained on a Fox complaint "hot-line" that they could not "relate" to the idea of a sixties flower child growing into a mellow police officer in charge of an undercover group of young cops (1989: 288). It is, however, more likely that the film's producers simply decided that more contrast, bringing potential opportunities for conflict, was needed between the authority figure and the young Jump Street Squad.

The popularity of Johnny Depp quickly became apparent, and he became the focus of an enormous amount of media attention. By all accounts, Depp began by doing what the producers wanted him to do: he spoke positively of the show before the media and praised its "socially healthy themes." He even answered fan letters himself, and he said that he "started off by phoning up the girls who wrote me, but that was expensive" (Blitz 25). And unlikely.

But Depp, whose baby face concealed a "vaulting ambition," soon came into conflict with the producers, who naturally enough wanted to show off his baby face. Depp wanted to appear

21 Jump Street's original Jump Street Squad. Clockwise from top left: Peter DeLuise, Johnny Depp, Dustin Nguyen, Frederic Forrest, and Holly Robinson Peete.

in disguise — after all, wasn't that what the Jump Street unit was supposed to do — and to improvise dialog appropriate for the character.

Just as doctors' series regularly feature a disease of the week, *21 Jump Street* featured a high school crime of the week. Problems, usually of a criminal nature, included racial discrimination and racial tension, teen prostitution, drugs (including designer drugs; baby-selling to buy drugs; juvenile abuse at expensive detox centers for rich kids,; sales of crack cocaine, steroids, ecstasy and heroin; drug testing, and addiction), computer hacking, attacks on disabled people, sexual molestation (including incest), high school loan sharking and extortion, child care, rape, pornography, the witness protection problem, gang violence, massage parlors, AIDS and venereal disease, mercy killings, gun possession, date rape, high school rape and cover-up, high school pregnancy, gay bashing in a military school, problems of Vietnamese refugees, mental retardation, religious cults, boot camps for troubled youths, dangers of police work, toxic waste, automobile chop shops, brutality in the military during basic training, corruption in college athletics, loan sharks and gambling, and abuse of freedom of speech by the media. Most of the early shows dealt with specific abuses in high school, but as time passed, many of the locales, such as the chemistry lab in "Research and Destroy," seem perched somewhere between high school, college and no-man's land. The numerous popular culture references of the first season grew fewer and fewer, the acting broader, and the episodes more violent.

Depp's problem was that he identified himself so completely with the counterculture the Jump Street Squad was investigating that he thought he was on the wrong side. When it became apparent to the producer and the network that Depp was enormously popular and increasingly unhappy, they quickly prepared for his replacement and brought in two young men who closely resembled him — Richard Grieco and, later, Michael Bendetti. When Grieco spun off into his own series, he was replaced by Bendetti. Both Grieco and Bendetti, although larger men, closely resembled the young star, but completely lacked his charisma. The result: Instead of replacing Johnny Depp, as the producers devoutly wished, they made viewers more acutely aware of his absence.

Co-star Peter DeLuise gained weight rapidly, and his liking for junk food became a staple, so to speak, of later episodes. Peter DeLuise's younger brother Michael appeared in eleven episodes, not to mention a third brother, David, who appeared in one episode.

21 Jump Street was Acting 101 for Depp's career. Beginning actors tend to overplay when someone overplays opposite them, and, at least in the beginning, Depp customarily followed suit. The early episodes in which Depp appeared opposite the skilled Frederic Forrest, who usually low-balled his scenes, are notable exceptions. Peter DeLuise's skilled timing and particular emphasis, doubtlessly honed in youthful repartee with his gifted comedic father Dom DeLuise, played off neatly against Depp's understatement — or at least they did after Depp had figured out what was going on. As might have been expected from someone with his background, DeLuise was comfortable with improvisation, even when the lines did not necessarily further the script, as in the following exchange in which DeLuise does not even appear to hide the fact that he is supposed to be checking IDs:

Penhall: What's your sign?

Hanson: Why, do you want to buy me a drink? ("Say It Ain't So, Pete")

One of the pleasures of sloughing though the 103 episodes of *21 Jump Street* is looking for familiar faces. The most famous of these are rosy-cheeked Brad Pitt, the only actor who may be considered Depp's equal in star power; Vince Vaughn (*Wedding Crashers, Fred Claus*); and Josh Brolin (*Wicker Park, No Country for Old Men*), who was originally considered for Depp's role. Others less well-known include Bridget Fonda, Pauly Shore, Rosie Perez, Kareem Abdul-Jabbar, Sherilyn Fenn, Jason Priestley, Christina Applegate, and, of course, John Waters, who was to direct Depp's next movie. Still others, who are hardly known at all, distinguished themselves, and now, with the help of the IMDB, the viewer can discover their work. To cite only one example, the beautiful Jensen Daggett goes one-on-one with Johnny Depp in Season 4's "Awomp-Bomp" and comes out a winner.

Depp's growing unhappiness with the show, well documented by Denis Meikle, became more apparent when Richard Grieco joined the cast as a Depp substitute. Grieco resembled Depp, and their appearance together gave the series a schizophrenic air. When the pair was together in the same scene, the tension was visceral. As the series aged, Depp's attention to the nuances of meaning in his dialogue, usually careful and exact during the first season, became less exact, often with damage to the continuity. Unfortunately, DeLuise's acting, hardly notable for its restraint in the best of times, became broader, even manic, and Depp sometimes followed his lead. The improvisation often left other cast members adrift, and some of the dialogue in the fourth season is nearly incoherent.

Depp, of course, did not care. What Meikle calls "a 15-hours-a-day, 9-months-a-year apprenticeship in television" was over (88). Depp later described the series as "assembly line stuff ... borderline fascist" (*Burton on Burton* ix). His period of "indentured servitude" was over; the phrase, however, seems a bit harsh for a largely inexperienced young actor making $45,000 an episode. In his DVD commentary, Stephen Cannell notes that Depp has a poor opinion of the series, but praises his work ethic. This does not mean, of course, that as time passed there was no tension on the set. Steven Williams says that Depp wanted to don disguises in order to play different roles. After all, the Jump Street Squad members were undercover, were they not? Of course, the producers and the public wanted Johnny Depp, the charismatic young man with the striking good looks and the quicksilver personality, and not some actor doing a shtick. But with at least three male actors who looked alike, and Depp attempting to disguise himself during his increasingly rare appearances, the audience was understandably confused at times.

Whatever criticism Depp may have made then or later is largely unjustified. *21 Jump Street* gave the young actor what he desired, an entrée into feature filmmaking.

SEASON ONE

Episodes 1–2: Untitled Pilot (April 12, 1987) •
Writ: Patrick Hasburgh; *Dir:* Kim Manners

Although Tommy Hanson has graduated at the top of his class at police academy, his lack of experience and sometimes impulsive behavior are considered a liability in police work. His extremely youthful appearance, however, make him a natural for an undercover unit, headed by Captain Jenko, investigating crime in urban high schools.

The pilot concerns a middle-class high-school junkie who is being terrorized and extorted with increasing violence by a vicious black youth named Tyrell. The characters are pasteboard, the stunts, including automobile chases and fist fights, are well-staged by veteran stunt coordinator Gary Combs, and the references to pop culture are numerous. Pop references include Sid Vicious, Steve Garvey, *Pretty in Pink*, Jim Morrison and *Fast Times at Ridgemont High*.

From the beginning, the producers knew who the star was and what they were selling, but they were not always sure how to package it, and it feels strange to hear Depp defending the establishment and giving the young junkie an anti-drug lecture: "A guy messes up once. It doesn't mean his whole life is over." At one point Depp even confesses to being a Republican.

Episode 3: "America, What a Town" (April 19, 1987) •
Writ: Bill Nuss; *Dir:* Larry Shaw

This episode skillfully combines two stories, the adventures of a Polish exchange student (well played by Tracy Lin) and the Jump Street Squad's breaking up of an automobile racket operating from a high school shop. While it is extremely unlikely that such a complicated scam would have been able to operate out of a high school shop class, it is clearly explained.

The Polish student's amazement at the decadent abundance of an American mall, and her growing admiration for capitalism, is strictly old-hat, dating back to Greta Garbo in Ernst Lubitsch's *Ninotchka* (1939) and forward to Robin Williams in *Moscow on the Hudson* (1984), which may have been the model here. Tracy Lin's portrayal is broad, and her accent keeps slipping in and out, but she's effective nonetheless. The episode's best bit of business involves Depp giving DeLuise an enormously long automobile title number to remember, and shows that Depp was already mastering the killer timing he was later to perfect.

Episode 4: "Don't Pet the Teacher" (April 26, 1987)
Writ: Clifton Campbell; *Dir:* Les Shelton

This effective episode shows how quickly the producers of the series realized their young star's romantic appeal. Sent undercover (as usual) to investigate mysterious doings at a high school, Hanson is immediately smitten by the charms of a beautiful young teacher, and she is, of course, smitten in return, although she desperately attempts to control her illicit urges. Had the situation been real, under the more enlightened legal systems of most states today, Miss Chadwick, well played by Leah Ayers, would probably not have been treated with such freedom and would have been charged with carnal knowledge of a juvenile.

The mystery is of only moderate interest, and the experienced viewer is likely to spot the culprit long before the Jump Street police have collared him.

Episode 5: "My Future's So Bright I Gotta Wear Shades" (May 3, 1987)
Writ: Bill Nuss; *Dir:* Gary Winter

While investigating a drug-induced death at an expensive prep school, the Jump Street Squad eventually put pressure on one of the boys, played by Josh Brolin, to cop a plea.

The title of the episode comes from the interrogation when the young dope smuggler tells the Jump Squad: "My future's so bright..." and then puts on his dark sunglasses without finishing the sentence.

Josh Brolin, the son of James Brolin, is one of the few young actors from *21 Jump Street* who later managed a successful career in film. His performance is memorable for the expressiveness of his close-up when he tells the police that he is going to turn state's evidence and testify against his associates.

In a coda, the Jump Street Squad speaks about the evils of cocaine and exhorts the audience to call 1-800-COCAINE.

Episode 6: "The Worst Night of Your Life" (May 10, 1987)
Writ: Patrick Hasburgh; *Dir:* Rob Bowman

In a poorly written and poorly motivated episode, the Jump Street Squad is sent to investigate a series of arsons at an exclusive all-girl Catholic school. The events seem unmotivated, but Holly Robinson gives an attractive performance, and Depp looks great in his prom togs—but here, as in real life, he refuses to dance.

Episode 7: "Gotta Finish the Riff" (May 17, 1987)
Writ: Patrick Hasburgh and Bill Nuss; *Dir:* Kim Manners

After the two-part pilot and four episodes, Frederic Forrest, who played Captain Jenco, the head of the Jump Street Squad, was replaced by Steven Williams, as Captain Adam Fuller, the squad's new leader. Forrest, a gifted actor who never quite became a leading man, achieved early fame in *When the Legends Die* (1972); in the opinion of some critics, including F. Scott Momaday, he offered perhaps the best portrayal of a Native American on film. Forrest's memorable closing line — "I want to be with the horses" — ranks in context as one of the most effective on film. A favorite actor of Francis Ford Coppola, Forrest was doubtlessly replaced because his laid-back style was too similar to that of the young Jump Street Squad, and it was felt that a harder-edged, more by-the-book character was needed.

The episode opens with the funeral of Captain Jenco, killed by a drunken driver. A month later, the Jump Street Squad is reconvened under the direction of the no-nonsense Captain Adam Fuller. When the authoritarian principal of Grant High School is threatened, Hoffs and Hanson are sent in, armed, to pose as high school students. The action scenes are well filmed, and there is some effectively tough dialogue. For instance, when she is frisked, Hoffs says, "Let me know if you find something you like."

Episode 8: Bad Influence (May 24, 1987)
Writ: Paul Bernbaum; *Dir:* Kim Manners

"Bad Influence" is a good example of the *Jump Street* formula. While it deals with serious problems— drug addiction, teenage prostitution, and amoral youngsters— it also has a sense of humor designed to appeal to a young audience. In a PG-13 version of a line that might have come from *Knocked Up* (2007), one of the horny young men with a large amount of money in his pockets tells his companion: "Jordy, there are full-figured women inside of those doors waiting to cater to our every need."

The bad news is that Johnny Depp plays only a minor role in the proceedings, although he does get to use his doofus expression a time or two.

Episode 9: "Blindsided" (May 31, 1987)
Writ: Jonathan Lemkin; *Dir:* David Jackson

While working undercover at a local high school, Hanson discovers that a troubled young woman, brilliantly played by Sherilyn Fenn, has been molested by her father. By current standards, the solution is simplistic. Hanson opines to the girl, "What he's got is a disease. It's not like it can't be dealt with."

Blindsided is replete with wonderful dialogue and bits of business, both humorous and emotional, and supported by strong acting by Depp and Fenn. The best bit concerns a young man whose bathroom visits are inhibited by the drug business being conducted there.

Episode 10: "Next Generation" (June 7, 1987)
Writ: Paul Bernbaum; *Dir:* David Nutter

Penhall becomes a babysitter for the child of an airline stewardess, and Hanson joins the Scholastic Bowl and is nominated for class president against his will. The episode's best line comes when Captain Fuller tells Penhall, "Pee Wee Herman [then still unsullied by a late obscenity charge] is more qualified than you [as a babysitter]."

Episode 11: "Low and Away" (June 14, 1987) •
Writ: Bill Nuss, Paul Bernbaum; *Dir:* Bill Corcoran

The Feds ask the Jump Street Squad to protect the son of a famous gangster in the witness protection program, as the lad is about to testify in a trial. This well-acted story has a gifted young baseball pitcher, divided loyalties, a touch of inter-racial romance (still unusual in 1987), a combined chase/shootout with a spectacular car stunt (courtesy of Gary Combs), and Johnny Depp with a shotgun. It is unfortunate that Depp has never made a moonshine movie.

Episode 12: "16 Blown to 35" (June 21, 1987

Writ: Clifton Campbell; *Dir:* James Whitmore, Jr.

The Jump Street Squad is out to bust a pornographer recruiting high school kids for "modeling careers," which are, of course, actually entrees into pornographic movies.

The episode's title refers, of course, to 16mm film being blown up to 35 mm, the theater standard in 1987. Only a few pornographic films were shown in legitimate movie theaters, and by 1987 video tapes for purchase and rental had transformed and enormously enlarged the industry. The downtown grind houses had disappeared, and pornographic films had entered the television sets of middle–American homes.

While "16 Blown to 35" deftly mixes the comic (Captain Fuller's problems with his son) and the serious (high school girls and pornography), it is less successful in its treatment of the latter. While the episode leaves open the question of why a high school would allow an ersatz modeling contest on campus, it does attempt to deal honestly with the glamour of "modeling" and why a young girl would allow herself to be enticed by such a shabby enterprise. When Judy Hoffs, in another excellent performance by Holly Robinson, deliberately exposes the day's shooting, we are convinced of her real concern for a young girl about to take the wrong path.

Johnny Depp makes little more than a token appearance, although we do learn that Hanson collected baseball cards when he was young.

Episode 13: "Mean Streets and Pastel Houses" (June 28, 1987)

Writ: Jonathan Lemkin; *Dir:* James Whitmore, Jr.

When an increasingly violent teenage gang masquerading as members of the KKK sends a young man to the hospital, the Jump Street Squad goes undercover to investigate. Hanson describes the gang as a "weird deviant aboriginal off-shoot ... just another sub-culture — breaking rules, pecking order, that kind of thing." The kicker, of course, is that Hanson fits the description better than any of the gang members.

SEASON TWO

Episode 1: "In the Custody of a Clown" (September 20, 1987) •

Writ: Clifton Campbell; *Dir:* Kim Manners

The producers, recognizing "In the Custody of a Clown" as a particularly strong episode, chose to begin the second season with it, rather than the two-part "Besieged," which originally had been intended to open the season. The episode has a double plot, with the two intertwined stories echoing each other. A young boy, the center of a bitter custody dispute, arranges his own "kidnapping," with the assistance of his grandfather.

Old pro Ray Walston, veteran of stage (*Damn Yankees*), screen (Billy Wilder's *Kiss Me, Stupid*) and television (*My Favorite Martian*) is broadly amusing as the crotchety judge who oversees the kidnapping hearing.

Hanson, dressed in drag, assists in capturing the perpetrator. Depp is a wonder to behold, wearing a blond wig and pearl earrings; when he doffs the wig, he becomes an androgynous object of desire unequaled since the heyday of Greta Garbo. "They don't pay me enough for this," he opines sadly.

Episodes 2–3: "Besieged" (September 27, 1987)
Writ: Jonathan Lemkin; *Dir:* Bill Corcoran

In a two-part episode, the Jump Street Squad attack the then new menace of crack cocaine, including the increased violence, prostitution and police corruption it brings with it.

Episode 4: "Two for the Road" (October 11, 1987)
Writ: Paul Bernbaum; *Dir:* Steve Beer

"Two for the Road" deals with three related hot-button issues: mercy killing, false IDs and drunk drivers. Captain Fuller is charged with drunken driving when he fails a breathalyzer test at a random police stop; the Jump Street Squad busts a counterfeit ID racket; and a young man involved in a fatal accident which left his friend a quadriplegic shoves him into the drink and drowns him to ease his suffering.

A young Pauly Shore scores as the ID forger Kenny Ryan. When he is arrested, he assumes that the Jump Street Squad's badges are counterfeit and expresses his admiration.

Episode 5: "After School Special" (October 18, 1987) •
Writ/Dir: David Jackson

"High School Hell" would have been a better title. After a young thug pulls a gun and shoots a teacher in class, Captain Fuller goes undercover as his replacement. The students in *The Blackboard Jungle* are pacifists compared to this group. Ideologically, the episode is a mess, and the delinquency seems to be shared equally between the students and the teachers. The result is repugnant.

As compensation, an amusing subplot deals with the decision by Tom Hanson's mother to move in with her boyfriend and maybe marry him. Depp's scenes are amusing and well acted, particularly a bowling competition between Hanson and the boyfriend.

Episode 6: "Higher Education" (October 25, 1987)
Writ: E. Paul Edwards; *Dir:* Larry Shaw

After Ioki is accused of impregnating a student while working undercover at a local high school, the Jump Street Squad chases down the culprit. At one point, Hoffs (who has been given an egg to take care of as if it were a child) asks drolly "Do you have a brown egg?"

Episode 7: "Don't Stretch the Rainbow" (November 1, 1987)
Writ: Patrick Hasburgh; *Dir:* Kim Manners

"Rainbow" is a melodramatic but effective Romeo and Juliet story about trouble at a racially mixed inner city school. The daughter of the black principal of Lincoln High (so-called in the film, but named Bugard High on the DVD cover) and a star white athlete fall in love, and the girl becomes pregnant. Hoffs and Hanson work to quell the ensuing riot. Martin Luther King's "I Have a Dream" speech plays over the closing credits. Depp does effective work in the action scenes. In the comic underplot, Penhall and Blowfish compete as standup comedians.

Episode 8: "Honor Bound" (November 8, 1987)

Writ: E. Paul Edwards; *Story:* Stephen J. Albert & Scott Smith and E. Paul Edwards; *Dir:* Bill Corcoran

After an epidemic of gay bashing breaks out near a military school, Penhall and Hanson are sent undercover to investigate. When one of the victims dies, an accused cadet cites the honor code and refuses to testify. In the end, the episode attempts (unsuccessfully) to justify the honor code.

In an episode rich in one-liners, Penhall has the best one. After being told he will have to leave the academy, and that his "accusations" will not get him reinstated, Penhall flashes his badge and says with perfect timing, "That's OK, I already have a day job."

Episode 9: "You Oughta Be in Prison" (November 15, 1987)

Writ: Bill Nuss; *Dir:* Kim Manners

Penhall and Hanson are sent to guard an egotistical movie star, but when Hanson takes a bit part, he is recognized by a prisoner (well-played by Reginald T. Dorsey, reprising his role from the pilot), who vows revenge. At the climax, Hanson subdues the victim of his "environment," but the film star gets the credit. The television audience, however, was not deceived and knew who the real star was.

Guest stars include Shannon Tweed, famous at the time as a Playboy Playmate, and Tony Todd, who later starred in *Candyman*.

On the DVD commentary, recorded in April 2004, Peter DeLuise notes that Depp put "an extra gym sock in a place I don't like to talk about." Although there is no definitive proof, visual evidence would seem to support the base allegation. According to Ernest Hemingway, Spanish bullfighters use a similar subterfuge. Sacha Baron Cohen, who plays a robust fraud who calls himself Signor Adolfo Pirelli, and is done in by Sweeney Todd in Tim Burton's film of the same name, has also been, perhaps unjustly, accused of the same deception. Cohen's history as the fraudulent *Borat* in the hit 2007 film does not, however, inspire confidence in his veracity.

Episode 10: "How Much Is That Body in the Window?" (Nov. 22, 1987)

Writ: Clifton Campbell; *Dir:* Neill Fearnley

The title is clever, combining as it does the idea of death, a beautiful body on display, and a popular song. When a young female gymnast dies of steroid abuse during a competition, Penhall and Hoffs are sent to investigate. Unfortunately, the laws dealing with the use of steroids are inadequate, and both the script and the squad have only limited success in dealing with a particularly complex subject. The script mentions DMSO (at that time being touted by *60 Minutes* as a kind of wonder drug), collagen, testosterone, blood doping, cortisone self-injection, and "roid rage." The episode shows, if indeed it needed to be shown, that as early as 1987, gym rats and high school athletes were already universally aware of the dangers of steroids. The episode, of course, is largely silent on the use of steroids in professional athletics.

Meanwhile, Hanson, who has decided to become a Big Brother to a troubled youth, enjoys an onscreen kiss (inaugurated by actress Dorothy Parke, who plays the woman running the program), but ultimately decides the program is not for him. The program may not be, but at episode's end the woman is clearly available to fill the "void" in his life. She is clearly a stand-in for the multitude of teenaged fans who would liked to have changed places with her.

Episode 11: "Christmas in Saigon" (Dec. 20, 1987)
Writ: Bill Nuss; *Dir:* Kim Manners

The Christmas episode for 1987 deals with the plight of Vietnamese refugees. Ioki turns out to be a Vietnamese youth who concealed his identity. The flashbacks skillfully mix authentic film of the fall of Saigon with new footage of Ioki's story. The episode is unusual for having no subplot. Depp has little to do, but Dorothy Parke returns as his romantic interest.

Episode 12: "Fear and Loathing with Russell Buckins" (Dec. 20, 1987) •
Writ: Gary Skeen Hall; *Dir:* Kevin Hooks

In an entertaining episode, Tommy Hanson meets Russell Buckins, an old high school friend, leaves his job, disregards a subpoena, wrestles a bear, runs over a steer (wrongly described in the film as a cow), and reconnects with a high school sweetheart three hours before her wedding. In the underplot, Penhall is sent back to police school to hone his procedural skills.

In its demonstration of Depp's increasing reactive skills, the episode is prophetic of the actor's future career in the title, and in Russell Buckins' iteration of Hanson as a "dead man."

Episode 13: "A Big Disease with a Little Name" (Feb. 7, 1988) •
Writ: Patrick Hasburgh; *Dir:* Neill Fearnley

In an episode in which viewers can almost see Johnny Depp's talent burgeoning before their eyes, *21 Jump Street* confronts AIDS. Hanson is sent into a high school to protect a young man who has AIDS, and the growing understanding between the two youths is movingly depicted. Largely ostracized by his family, and ignored or persecuted by his high school classmates, Harley (well played by Philip Tanzini) is searching for whatever consolation he can find. Since this is television for the masses, religious consolation is not possible, although clearly political correctness is. "God Bless America" is misread as a statement, when it is, as the grammar clearly shows, a prayer: "America, America, [may] God shed his light [substituting for grace] on thee, and [may he] crown thy good with brotherhood from sea to shining sea." The grammar shows the parallel use of the subjunctive; if it were a statement, the second verb would have been "crowned."

The episode stands as a kind of time capsule of the late 1980s, depicting the paranoia surrounding the nearly universal fear of contracting AIDS through casual contact. The scenes between Tanzini and Depp are electric. Tanzini has the more emotional role, but the understated sensitivity of Depp's performance approaches the miraculous.

A comic subplot deals with Penhall's romantic difficulties.

Episode 14: "Chapel of Love" (February 14, 1988)
Writ: Bill Nuss & Jonathan Lemkin; *Dir:* Michael Robison

Left dateless on Valentine's Day, the Jump Street group, minus Hoffs, who arrives late, decide to play poker. Each has a more-or-less humorous story to tell about a failed romantic encounter, except for Hanson, who speaks last and tells how his policeman father was killed on duty after driving Tommy and his date to a party. The story is short and underwritten, but Depp's reactions are realistic and believable.

Episode 15: "I'm OK, You Need Work" (February 21, 1988)
Writ: Clifton Campbell; *Dir:* Neill Fearnley

"I'm OK" campaigns for constitutional protection of young people who are committed by rich parents to expensive but ineffective and sadistic rehabilitation centers. Hanson goes undercover to investigate, immediately gets into trouble and is scheduled for "behavior mod." Doped up and shipped out, Hanson is eventually rescued by the Jump Street Squad.

The episode combines some deft acting by guest stars Christina Applegate and James Stephens (*The Paper Chase* series). Like his idol Marlon Brando, Depp takes abuse effectively and delivers some neat lines.

Episode 16: "Orpheus 3.3" (February 28, 1988) •
Writ: Bill Nuss; *Dir:* James Contner

When Hanson and his girlfriend Amy stop at a convenience store, a robber, frightened when Amy drops some items, fatally shoots her. According to the store's surveillance tape, the shooting took 3.3 seconds. Hanson goes into a deep funk, plays the tape obsessively and imagines killing the culprit and saving the girl. Eventually, he succeeds in tracking the killer down and comes to terms with his grief.

"Orpheus 3.3" is a mod variation of Michelangelo Antonioni's *Blow-Up* (1966), a critical favorite by an auteur more respected in 1988 than now. The episode is perhaps also indebted to Francis Ford Coppola's *The Conversation* (1977). The obsessive, repetitive watching of the tape in hopes of discovering a clue, and the resulting nearly paranoid wish fulfillment, has a surprisingly melodramatic effectiveness and complexity rare in the *Jump Street* series. The seedy television ambience, standing in for Antonioni's fashionable elegance, is closer in tone to Sam Fuller's *Pickup on South Street* (1953) and is augmented by a touch of standup comedy.

Episode 17: Champagne High (March 6, 1988)
Writ: Paul Bernbaum; *Dir:* Larry Shaw

After crime breaks out at a high school which has recently begun busing poor kids into a rich neighborhood, Penhall and Hanson, posing as the rowdy McQuade brothers, are sent to the school to investigate. Unfortunately, the situation, which would seem to indicate a serious discussion of class and racial conflict, quickly disintegrates into melodrama. It is unclear why the rich kids would be sent to a public school, or why the public school would be so racially pure, with not a minority student in sight.

At some point, Depp, aided and abetted by DeLuise, began to improvise bits of business in good method-acting style, but not always to the benefit of the story. DeLuise stuffs himself with food in a fair imitation of John Belushi in *National Lampoon's Animal House*, which was currently in theaters when the episode aired. Depp dresses in a variety of scarecrow outfits and attempts to out-ham DeLuise. He had not yet mastered the secret of underplaying against over-the-top actors.

Episode 18: "Brother Hanson & the Miracle of Renner's Pond" (March 13, 1988)
Writ: Eric Paul Jones; *Dir:* Bill Corcoran

When a large number of biology textbooks are burned in a conservative school, Hanson discovers that most of the community supports the teaching of a literal interpretation of the Bible. A teacher believes that his son has been brought back from the dead to serve as witness, and he pressures the boy into evangelizing. In the melodramatic conclusion, the young man threatens to throw himself from a high place to prove his miraculous power, as Simon the Magician had done in *The Silver Chalice* (1955). Of course, Simon — wonderfully played by a young Paul Newman — killed himself. Fortunately the young man's penitent father talks him out of the exploit. Newman also apparently repented and apologized in the trade papers.

Episode 19: "Raising Marijuana" (April 17, 1988)
Writ: Jonathan Lemkin; *Dir:* Bill Corcoran

In an episode in which Hanson does not appear, Hoffs goes undercover to capture a marijuana kingpin who is using teenagers to smuggle dope by the ton.

Episode 20: "Best Years of Your Life" (May 1, 1988)
Writ: Jonathan Lemkin; *Dir:* Bill Corcoran

In a talky but unconvincing episode, Hanson and Penhall develop feelings of guilt because of their inability to come to terms with the suicide of a teenage boy at a school where they are working undercover. The chief interest of the episode today is not the psycho-babble, but the appearance of a pudgy-cheeked Brad Pitt in a supporting role. Here, for the first (and perhaps the last) time, the two leading heartthrobs of their generation go toe-to-toe dramatically. The result is hardly as interesting as one might expect, but Depp (as one might expect) is better dressed.

Episode 21: "Corey and Dean Got Married" (May 8, 1988)
Writ: Clifton Campbell; *Dir:* Kim Manners

Johnny Depp makes only a token appearance at the beginning of this episode, which deals with a teenage romance gone terribly wrong.

Episode 22: "School's Out" (May 22, 1988)
Writ: Eric Blakeney; *Dir:* Kim Manners

With the Jump Street Squad waiting to hear if their budget will be renewed for the following year, Hanson goes to a high school to ferret out a "mad bomber" who has been detonating toilet bowls. What he discovers instead is a young man with a shady past who makes straight A's and lives in the school's boiler room.

SEASON THREE

Episode 1: "Fun with Animals" (November 6, 1988)
Writ: Eric Blakeney; *Dir:* James Whitmore, Jr.

When Hanson becomes convinced that Officer Dennis Booker, working with Hanson on a racism investigation at a high school, raped a young woman, he accuses him before Fuller.

Episode 2: "Slippin' into Darkness" (November 11, 1988)
Writ: Clifton Campbell; *Dir:* James Contner

After a group of teenage vigilantes, who call themselves the Street Rangers, disrupt the work of the police, the Jump Street Squad goes undercover to investigate. Of course, the Rangers turn out to be more hindrance than help.

When a gang member asks Hanson if he wants to make some "quick cash," Hanson asks if it is a "trick question."

Episode 3: "The Currency We Trade In" (November 20, 1988) •
Writ: Eric Blakeney; *Dir:* Eric Blakeney

Penhall becomes a media star by taking out a killer in a seafood restaurant, and hits the skids when he wrongly accuses a man of molesting his young daughter. In an amusing understory—which is so good that it seems to belong to some better series—Hanson's blind date with an assistant district attorney is a disaster, one he later salvages by pretending to be her husband. Peri Gilpin is sensational as the girl. The film shows conclusively that Depp would be wonderful in the romantic comedies which he has hitherto disdained.

Episode 4: "Coach of the Year" (November 27, 1988)
Writ: Bill Nuss; *Dir:* James Whitmore, Jr.

Penhall goes undercover to investigate a famous high school football coach after a player is paralyzed. In an episode as relevant today as it was twenty years ago, the coach, well played by Robert Conrad in macho mode, is given a pass by a venal politician and by his adoring public. Depp is in fine form in a brief appearance in which he is interrupted as he is about to ravish the assistant district attorney on her desk. Although apparently the same character romanced in the previous episode, she is now played by a different actress, this time by Yvette Nipar in a recurring role.

Episode 5: "Whose Choice Is It Anyway?" (December 11, 1988)
Writ: Michelle Ashford; *Story:* David Abramowitz; *Dir:* Bill Corcoran

"Choice" is an anti-abortion story in which Depp does not appear. The title is incorrectly given on the IMDB as "Whose Choice Is It Anyways?"

Episode 6: "Hell Week" (December 18, 1988)
Writ: Bill Nuss; *Dir:* Jonathan Wacks

The Jump Street Squad is sent to investigate violence on a college campus during Hell Week. Depp's stoic endurance of his suffering during his initiation ceremony foreshadows his sufferings in later films.

Episode 7: "The Dragon and the Angel" (January 15, 1989) •
Writ: E. Paul Edwards; *Dir:* Jefferson Kibbee

In a timely episode, Harry infiltrates a Vietnamese high school gang and discovers that the editor of a communist newspaper sends money to his grandmother, still in Viet Nam. The editor's argument of more than twenty years ago echoes events today. He says that America's government "creates wars that keep a stream of refugees coming here to provide domestic help for its rich." In a hilarious subplot, Penhall shoots Hanson in the rump during a shootout. Overcome by guilt, he becomes overly solicitous and buys Hanson a so-called "doughnut," which Hanson indignantly rejects as a "whoopee cushion." A fake psychiatrist only augments Penhall's guilt. Although Hanson is shown with his butt trussed up in the air, the viewer is, perhaps fortunately, spared a shot of the wound. The hero (invariably a youngster) being shot in the ass has long been a standard source of cinematic humor. One notable example can be found in Sam Peckinpah's *Major Dundee* (1965).

"The Dragon and the Angel" shows *Jump Street* at its best—a mixture of action, social commentary and humor designed to appeal to a young audience.

Episode 8: "Blue Flu" (January 29, 1989)
Writ: Clifton Campbell; *Dir:* Bill Corcoran

Tensions erupt when the police officers go on strike. Hanson makes only a brief appearance.

Episode 9: "Swallowed Alive" (February 5, 1989) •
Writ: Eric Blakeney; *Dir:* James Contner

Although "Swallowed Alive" is much too ambitious for an hour time-slot, Depp powerfully takes center stage in the investigation of a juvenile prison facility. In a scene in which Hanson meets a girl brought in for a sexual tryst, Depp, zonked out, tears rolling down his cheeks, crazed from the injustices of the prison and whatever he has been drinking from an old motor oil container, seems to represent all suffering humanity. The girl, clueless, says, "What a waste." The episode is perhaps as pure an example of star power as the small screen has produced.

Episode 10: "What About Love?" (February 12, 1989)
Writ: Michelle Ashford; *Dir:* David Jackson

The episode deals with the romantic entanglements of the Jump Street Squad, particularly Hoffs, who becomes involved with a married man, well played by Michael Laskin, and is forced to consider filing a charge of sexual harassment. Hanson makes only a brief appearance.

Episode 11: "Wooly Bullies" (February 19, 1989)
Writ: Bruce Kirschbaum and Eric Blakeney & Bill Nuss; *Dir:* Bill Corcoran

In a generally amusing episode, told largely in flashback, the Jump Street Squad swap stories about bullying. Hanson's story tells of his problem with a young Amazon who persecutes him relentlessly until he invites her to a grade school dance. The cast includes not only Peter DeLuise, but also his younger brother Michael and their father, comedian Dom DeLuise. A young Laurenz Tate scores as the adolescent Captain Fuller.

Episode 12: "The Dreaded Return of Russell Buckins" (February 26, 1989)
Writ: Marc Abraham and Paul Bernbaum; *Dir:* Rob Iscove.

When Russell Buckins gives the undercover Jump Street Squad unwanted publicity, Hanson is suspended and seeks out his old companion. Angelo Tiff returns as Buckins, but the magic of the first episode is largely missing; however, the scene in which Hanson jumps on Russell's back is particularly amusing.

Episode 13: "A.W.O.L." (March 19, 1989)
Writ: Glen Morgan and James Wong; *Story:* Peter L. Dixon, Glen Morgan and James Wong

When a recruit attacks a brutalizing sergeant, goes AWOL and returns to high school, Penhall and Hanson are sent to bring him back. The number of writers involved clearly shows that the resulting melodrama involving a mountain rescue was as unconvincing then as it is now.

Episode 14: "Nemesis" (March 26, 1989)
Writ: Jim Truby; *Dir:* Ken Wiederhorn

In a role which Depp refused, Richard Grieco, as Dennis Booker, goes undercover to expose a drug ring and suffers a psychological crisis. The script is particularly weak.

Episode 15: "Fathers and Sons" (April 9, 1989)
Writ: John Truby; *Dir:* Jefferson Kibbee

The Jump Street Squad's investigation of the mayor's son is compromised when Hanson's girlfriend, well played by Yvette Nipar, informs her superiors, who suspend the operation. Hanson's rejection of her attempt at reconciliation at the end of the episode seems to belong to some new and better film.

Episode 16: "High High" (April 23, 1989)
Writ: Eric Blakeney and Bill Nuss; *Dir:* Mario Van Peebles

The Jump Street Squad infiltrates a creative arts high school to expose a dope dealer. Penhall auditions for a class by playing Ralph Kramden (Jackie Gleason) of *The Honeymooners*. Unfortunately, Hanson, who should have played Ed Norton, is merely an onlooker. "High High" is an early directing credit for Mario Van Peebles, whose varied directing career includes *New Jack City*. He is the son of Melvin Van Peebles, who directed the legendary exploitation film *Sweet Sweetback's Baadasssss Song* (1971).

Episode 17: "Blinded by the Thousand Points of Light" (April 30, 1989)
Writ: Glen Morgan & James Wong; *Dir:* Jorge Montesi; *Cast* Bridgit Fonda

The Jump Street Squad, minus Hanson, search for a missing young male hustler.

Episode 18: "Next Victim" (May 7, 1989)
Writ: Bruce Kirschbaum; *Dir:* James A. Contner

In a didactic script illustrating the dangers and responsibilities of free speech, Richard Grieco, replacing Johnny Depp, who refused the role, impersonates a radio hate-jockey.

Episodes 19–20: "Loc'd Out (Partners)" •
Part 1 (May 14, 1989) — *Writ:* Michelle Ashford and Eric Blakeney / Part 2 (May 21, 1989) — *Teleplay:* Eric Blakeney and Bill Nuss; *Story:* John Truby and Glen Morgan and James Wong

"Loc'd Out," or "Partners," is perhaps the most elaborate of the Jump Street stories, combining well-shot action and effective location sequences. Nonetheless, despite — or because of — the elaborate writing credits, the story, particularly the second part, lacks credibility.

In an hilarious scene, Hanson, picked to infiltrate a teenage gang, takes lessons to learn to impersonate a gangster named Mad Dog 2 (Mad Dog 1 is deceased); but, unable to master the argot, he is given another name and taught the mastery of the stare-down. Eventually, Hanson infiltrates not one but two gangs, is accused of killing a cop, and, as the third season ends, is tried and convicted.

Season Four

Episode 1: "Draw the Line" (Sept 18, 1989)
Writ: Glen Morgan & James Wong; *Dir:* Kim Manners

In an extremely unlikely series of events, Booker has Hanson paroled for twenty-four hours to attend Ioki's (non-existent) funeral, and the Jump Street gang eventually prove that Hanson is innocent. There is a lot of unfunny business about Penhall's battle with his VCR in his attempts to tape sporting events.

Episode 2: "Say It Ain't So, Pete" (September 25, 1989)
Writ: Bill Nuss; *Dir:* Jefferson Kibbee

In an episode which seems to have been locked away somewhere in a time capsule, Ioki returns to work, and Penhall and Hanson go undercover to expose illegal gambling. A quarter of a century later, when legal gambling is ubiquitous, the penny-ante gambling of the Jump Street Squad, presented as a counterpoint to show that gambling is everywhere, seems gratuitous.

Episode 3: "Eternal Flame" (October 2, 1989) •
Writ: David Stenn; *Dir:* Mario Van Peebles

While working undercover at what seems to be a teenage strip club, Hanson is recognized by a former flame (the ravishing Kim Valentine), who is married to the club owner (Michael Des Barres). The ridiculous script is given considerable dramatic bite, especially in the nightclub scenes, by Van Peebles' imaginative direction and by the chemistry between the two leads.

Episode 4: "Come from the Shadows" (October 9, 1989)
Writ: Larry Barber and Paul Barber; *Story:* Larry Barber & Paul Barber and Sharon Elizabeth Doyle

"Shadows" is a story about a priest selling babies from El Salvador in which Depp does not appear.

Episode 5: "God Is a Bullet" (October 16, 1989)
Writ: John Truby; *Dir:* Jefferson Kibbee

This is an unconvincing story of a high school principal who uses boot-camp methods to reform a high school. Depp was right to turn this turkey down.

Episode 6: "Old Haunts in the New Age" (October 30, 1989) •
(Note: The IMDB has incorrect title.)
Writ: Glen Morgan and James Wong; *Dir:* Jefferson Kibbee

In a farcical Halloween story involving apparently supernatural happenings, the Jump Street Squad investigates arson at a high school. The humor is broad and generally misses the mark, but Depp in a Mohawk haircut imitating Robert De Niro from *Taxi Driver* is a hoot.

The sportive Gothic story, perfected by Washington Irving in "The Legend of Sleepy Hollow" and "Rip Van Winkle," goes back to the earliest days of cinema. Paul Leni's *The Cat and the Canary* (1927) is a notable example.

Episode 7: "Out of Control" (November 6, 1989) •
Writ: Thania St. John; *Dir:* Mario Van Peebles

Although *21 Jump Street* is not a series renowned for its stunts, "Out of Control" is a notable exception, containing two breathtaking sequences by stunt coordinator Gary Combs.

The first is an automobile sequence showing a woman astride two racing automobiles, a foot on each one; and the second is a roller-coaster sequence in the dark, with Hanson chained to a track as the roller-coaster bears down on him. The sequences seem to have caught Depp's interest, since he is notably more intense and serious than usual. Christine Elise is outstanding as a young woman whose emotions become intense only during near-death experiences.

Episode 8: "Stand By Your Man" (November 13, 1989)
Writ: Michelle Ashford; *Dir:* Daniel Attias

When Hoffs is raped by a medical student, she quickly learns that convicting the culprit will be nearly impossible. In an amusing scene, Penhall enlightens Hanson about the mysteries of women.

Episode 9: "Mike's P.O.V." (November 20, 1989)
Script: Glen Morgan & James Wong; *Story:* John Truby; *Dir:* Jorge Montesi

When a high school teacher is killed by a drive-by shooter on a bicycle, Hanson and Penhall are sent undercover to investigate. The story is unusual, at least in the *Jump Street* series, for being told visually largely from the point of view of the murderer. While hardly *Crime and Punishment*, the story is reasonably effective, although the motive — "It seemed a reasonable way to get these guys to like me" — is not. Hanson has some brief improvisation. Vince Vaughn has a bit part.

Episode 10: "Wheels and Deals: Part 2" (November 27, 1989)
Writ: Thania St. John; *Dir:* Jefferson Kibbee

Part 1 aired on *Booker*, as "Deals and Wheels," but is included in the complete fourth season DVD collection of *21 Jump Street* as a prequel to "Wheels and Deals." The episode aired on November 26, 1989, a day before its continuation on *21 Jump Street*. Richard Grieco's character, Booker, began life on *21 Jump Street*, presumably as a replacement for Johnny Depp, but switched to his own series, which lasted only one season. Part 1 deals with Booker's attempt to bring a crime lord, Raymond Crane, to justice. In Part 2, the Jump Street Squad infiltrates a motorcycle gang to expose Crane. The episode is notable for Gary Combs' excellent stunt work, but Depp, in his brief appearances, scarcely bothers to conceal his disdain.

Episode 11: "Parental Guidance Suggested" (December 4, 1989)
Writ: Sam Bushwick and Glen Morgan & James Wong; *Dir:* Jeffrey Auerbach

In an episode in which Depp does not appear — or is that Hanson struggling with a fake skeleton in a high school science class? — the Jump Street Squad fights parental abuse of teenagers and neighborhood robbery.

Episode 12: "Things We Said Today" (December 18, 1989)
Writ: Glen Morgan & James Wong; *Dir:* Tucker Gates

In an episode in which Depp is a no-show, Ioki confronts a face from the past. Dirk Blocker, son of Dan Blocker (*Bonanza*), appears in a supporting role.

Episode 13: "Research and Destroy" (January 8, 1990)
Writ: Gary Rosen; *Dir:* Jefferson Kibbee

In an episode which veers wildly from farce to tragedy, the Jump Street Squad infiltrates a chemistry laboratory to investigate designer heroin. By this point in the series, Depp's performances had become increasingly eccentric, as if he were trying in some way to sabotage his popularity.

Episode 14: "A Change of Heart" (January 15, 1990)
Writ: Michelle Ashford; *Dir:* Jan Eliasberg

In a story involving a husband who murders his wife's lesbian lover, and in which Captain Fuller finds romance, Depp has only a cameo. Whatever else the episode may be, it is a time capsule of the sexual attitudes of twenty years ago.

Episode 15: "Back from the Future" (January 29, 1990) •
Writ: David Stenn; *Dir:* Peter DeLuise

By some mysterious means, the Jump Street Squad, fifty years into the future, are contacted to tell tales of their adventures. Since most of the episode is composed of clips from the entire series, going back to Captain Jenco and the earliest days of the show, "Back from the Future" is the essential *21 Jump Street* episode. The ridiculous old-age makeup among the group is a particular attraction. Twenty years on, old Hanson's statement that a cure for AIDS has been discovered appears to be wishful thinking.

Episode 16: "2245" (February 5, 1990) •
Writ: Michelle Ashford & Glen Morgan & James Wong; *Dir:* Kim Manners

"2245" is a somber story, told largely in flashbacks, of the last days of a young thug condemned to death by lethal injection. Josh Richman is excellent as the condemned man who wants Sean Penn to play him in the movie, and a young Rosie Perez offers strong support as his girlfriend. Johnny Depp, recognizing a strong script, is suitably restrained.

Episode 17: "Hi Mom" (February 12, 1990)
Writ: Bill Nuss; *Dir:* James Whitmore, Jr.

In an episode dealing with various types of corruption in college athletics, as pertinent today as it was when it was first broadcast, the Jump Street Squad infiltrates a large university. Kareem Abdul-Jabbar has only a brief supporting role, but gets a picture on the DVD jacket.

Episode 18: "Awomp-Bomp-Alobomb, Aloop" (February 19, 1990)
Writ: Glen Morgan & James Wong; *Dir:* Jorge Montesi

When the Jump Street group tire of freezing in the middle of winter, Penhall and Hanson head south for a spring break. Along the way, Hanson meets his future in the person of Baltimore film director John Waters as a kind of psychedelic bus driver (courtesy of the Merry Pranksters?). In an improbable plot development, Hanson is cheated out of sharing a blanket with the beautiful Jensen Daggett. Perhaps awed by Daggett's beauty, Depp gives an unusually restrained performance.

Episode 19: "La Bizca" (February 26, 1990) •
Writ: Larry Barber & Paul Barber; *Dir:* David Nutter

Richard Roundtree, the original *Shaft*, guest-stars in a brutal and violent episode which cannot have held much interest for the teenaged audience. Penhall and Hanson go to strife-ridden El Salvador to find Penhall's wife. There they discover that she has been murdered, and eventually bring back her sister's young son to America. In an interesting interlude, which surely must not have been in the original script, Hanson and Penhall teach the boy's mother to appreciate Laurel and Hardy's "another fine mess" routine. While the interlude is unsuccessful in context, it implies a score of possibilities. The revolutionary Rosina is called "La Bizca," the cross-eyed woman, because of the way she sights a weapon.

Episode 20: "Last Chance High" (March 19, 1990)
Writ: Michelle Ashford; *Dir:* Kim Manners

In an episode which moves from coarse comedy to serious social problems within seconds, Penhall and Hanson infiltrate a high school for socially maladjusted students. The interchanges between Depp and DeLuise are broad and apparently totally improvised, often at the expense of continuity.

Episode 21: "Unfinished Business" (April 9, 1990)
Writ: Julie Friedgen; *Story:* Julie Friedgen and Geri Jewell & Marc Powell; *Dir:* Daniel Attias

In an episode in which Depp does not appear, Hoffs poses as a disabled person to catch an attacker.

Episode 22: "Shirts and Skins" (April 30, 1990)
Writ: Larry Barber and Paul Barber; *Dir:* Jorge Montesi

Depp, unfortunately, is a no-show in an episode in which the Jump Street Squad infiltrates a neo–Nazi group to see who killed one of its leaders. Depp would have been interesting as a Gestapo type.

Episode 23: "How I Saved the Senator" (May 7, 1990) •
Writ: Gary Rosen; *Dir:* James Whitmore, Jr.

When the Jump Street Squad saves the life of a senator, a wannabe moviemaker inspires the Jump Street Squad to tell their stories. Hanson's story, by far the most interesting, is a one-reel pixilated silent movie in which Depp, doing his best Chaplin-waiter imitation, foils an anarchist. During the chase ending of the movie, the Jump Street Squad imitates the Keystone Kops. The movie, one of the high points of the entire *Jump Street* series, is essential viewing for anyone interested in Depp's development as an artist. Elena Wohl (as Elena Stiteler) scores as the would-be moviemaker.

Episode 24: "Rounding Third" (May 14, 1990)
Writ: Gary Rosen; *Dir:* Jefferson Kibbee

Depp does not appear in a story about Penhall, his ward, and little-league baseball.

Episode 25: "Everyday Is Christmas" (May 21, 1990)
Writ: Glen Morgan & James Wong; *Story:* David Gascon, Glen Morgan and James Wong

21 Jump Street winds down when Penhall, as a disciplinary measure, is transferred to the regular police force. Depp is a no-show.

Episode 26: "Blackout" (July 16, 1990)
Writ: Larry Barber and Paul Barber; *Story:* Adam McElroy; *Dir:* Tucker Gates.

According to the IMDB, "Blackout" was originally broadcast on July 16, 1990, as the concluding episode of Season 4. It is, however, included as the first episode of Season 5 of the DVD collection. Since Depp does not appear in any of the episodes of Season 5, his marquee name was presumably included to mislead potential buyers into thinking that Depp appeared in all, or at least some, of the season's episodes.

The episode combines teen terror, going back as far as *The Blackboard Jungle* (1955), and elements of various horror movies in an improbable tale of high school students forced to remain at school after dark because of flooding. The ensuing blackout and reign of terror, eventually quelled by the Jump Street Squad, is less interesting than the struggle between a young man's wish to conform and the demands of his conscience, exemplified by the girl he has been dating. "Blackout" is effective, and its blunt language, although muted by today's standards, must have been startling a quarter of a century ago. Holly Robinson does well in her role, but Johnny Depp is hardly more than a figure fleeing down the high school corridor.

"Blackout" was Depp's farewell to *21 Jump Street*. His replacement, Michael Bendetti, apparently chosen for his resemblance to Grieco (who had been chosen because he resembled Depp), had none of Depp's charisma, and the series became increasingly unfocused. Depp's final word on the series: "I'd rather pump gas.... I'd never do it again, ever — there's not enough money in Los Angeles" (Meikle 90). In his 2002 Actors Studio interview, he said that working on the series was a terrific three-and-a-half-year learning experience: "I'd been turned into this product. Someone else's product."

1989 *Cry-Baby*

The Rebel

"His kind of music isn't even on the Hit Parade."(Mrs. Vernon-Williams)

Johnny Depp moved from what he has spoken off as a kind of indentured servitude to the freedom of John Waters' *Cry-Baby*. Tom Hanson was the character that Johnny Depp had been playing on *21 Jump Street*, but Cry-Baby Walker was the character that he wanted to play — a rebel against the dominant culture — and the flamboyantly gay, pencil-mustachioed master of bad taste, John Waters, was just the man to take him where he wanted to go. Depp had bonded with Waters when he appeared on an episode of *21 Jump Street*. Now, for the first time in his career, Depp had been given an opportunity he approved of.

The film was a win-win situation for both actor and director. It represented an enormous step up financially for Depp, who reportedly received $1,000,000 for his work on the film; but it was also, courtesy of Johnny Depp, a step up for the Baltimore filmmaker, who was promoted from the miniscule budgets of his earlier films to studio backing and a $12,000,000 budget.

John Waters (born 1946), who justly contends with writer and grouch H. L. Mencken, filmmaker Barry Levinson (*Good Morning, Vietnam*), and producer David Simon (*The Wire*)

Ricki Lake (as Pepper Walker), Johnny Depp (as Cry-Baby Walker) and former porn star Traci Lords (as Wanda Woodward) in *Cry-Baby*.

for the honorific of the "Sage of Baltimore," began his career with "gleeful vulgarity and tastelessness represented through sorrowful production values" (Allon 58). His early films, especially *Pink Flamingos* (1972), *Hairspray* (1988), and *Polyester* (1981), are considered masterpieces of trash cinema by aficionados of such movies. Reaction to these films—and to his humor—is intensely personal, and they will always appeal only to a minority of viewers.

Ariel Levy defines Waters' interests as "art, sex, drugs, and transgressions," orchestrated by the man William Burroughs called "the Pope of trash." To cite only one example, in *Female Trouble*, Divine, in the female role, performs fellatio on her own son. "Oh, Mama, you're the best," the son enthuses (21). Waters continues to peddle his art in its pure—or, more accurately, its impure—form while allowing Hollywood and John Travolta in a fat suit, among others, to tone it down for the multitudes. With *Cry-Baby*, he moved briefly into mainstream Hollywood filmmaking, but he has never been comfortable there, and his work is more appealing to the mass public when toned down by others.

Plays based on the films of John Waters have had mixed receptions. *Hairspray* was turned into a Broadway musical which won eight Tonys, was exported to London, and was made into a hit film. The movie, however, is the original and the others, no matter how expensive, are only cheap imitations. *Cry-Baby* was not so fortunate. The musical, starring James Snyder, opened on Broadway on April 24, 2008, and closed on June 26 after 113 performances. Although it received four Tony nominations, it did not win any awards and is estimated to have lost more than $10,000,000 plus capitalization.

The eccentric but effective casting of *Cry-Baby* involved old-line Hollywood, the good, the bad and the ugly. Old line, or second-line, Hollywood was represented by Troy Donahue and David Nelson. The romantic lead, young and charismatic Amy Locane, who seems to have been picked for her talent, represented the good. The bad came in the forms of Susan Tyrrell, who, according to Waters, customarily introduced herself by saying, "Hello, I'm Susan Tyrell, and I have the pussy of a twelve-year-old"; Traci Lords, fresh from a career as an under-aged porn star; Joe Dallesandro, famous for his association with Andy Warhol; and Patricia Hurst, then famous for her association with the Symbionese Liberation Army. And the ugly was clearly represented by Iggy Popp, a particular favorite of Johnny Depp, and Kim McGuire as "Hatchet Face." Pretending to be bad, Johnny Depp seems to have wandered between the groups indiscriminately.

To say that *Cry-Baby* has a plot would probably dignify the sequence of events in the film beyond its merit. In a city divided between up-tight and hang-loose elements, Cry-Baby Walker is unjustly persecuted, prosecuted and sent to prison, where he organizes a dance team. Of course, he is ultimately released and reunited with his no-longer up-tight sweetie. Generically, *Cry-Baby* is a Romeo and Juliet story; unlike *West Side Story*, however, it has plenty of laughs along the way and a happy ending. It is also a cultural time machine, with director Waters happily pointing out the pleasure and incongruities of life in the 1950s between the so-called "squares" and "drapes" of Baltimore. Strangely, although "square" morphed from a word taken from carpentry to represent an honest man to a word to represent a person out of touch with the cutting edge of popular culture, "drape" did not enter the mainstream and, through no fault of Waters, seems to have been confined largely to Baltimore and its environs.

Waters is too genial a host, and his brush too broad, for satire, and *Cry-Baby* may more accurately be described as burlesque. This should not, however, be taken as a term of disparagement; indeed, neither Waters nor Depp is interested in satire. They are too affectionate and in love with their characters for that. Depp seems to have been doing a tryout as a young Don Quixote, and may yet star in a movie about Cervantes' immortal tilter at windmills.

The reviews of *Cry-Baby* were overwhelmingly favorable, but generally regarded John Waters as having sold out to the commercial mainstream. In his review, Edmond Grant moaned that Waters had shed his nasty side this time around and had contradicted the "attitude exhibited in his earlier films ... that anything society considers gross, degraded, and abnormal is actually beautiful and worth reveling in." Grant called the result "a thoroughly enjoyable broad comedy that is by no means indicative of its director's work." Peter Rainer believed that what the film lacked was "not so much the subversiveness of his [Waters'] earlier movies as the weirded out invention. Too much of *Cry-Baby* is indistinguishable from what it is supposed to be lampooning."

Anne Billson wrote that the film zips through its "plot premise" in the first half- hour and then devotes the remainder of the movie "to musical numbers and set-piece clichés" about prison films, chicken runs and Rita Hayworth's strapless gown in *Gilda*. She added that if Waters has moved toward the mainstream, it is because society has become more acceptable of outrageousness. Terry Kelleher made the point more succinctly: "If trashy nostalgia ain't what it used to be, John Waters has only himself to blame."

A few critics seemed unable to appreciate *Cry-Baby* at any level. David Edelstein strangely criticized the film for not having "a vein of sincerity." How could that have improved the movie? Could he have seen any of John Waters' other films? Suzanne Moore called *Cry-Baby* "good, clean fun, but too self-consciously cute to be really successful."

In retrospect, it can clearly be seen that the financial success of the film was due almost entirely to the popularity of its youthful star. Some writers, attempting to fit *Cry-Baby* into Waters' oeuvre, scarcely mentioned Depp. Others, however, sought to identify his appeal and to place it within an historical context they could understand. Anne Billson called Depp "a *bona fide* teen idol" (Billson). Jack Kroll made the customary comparisons to James Dean and Elvis Presley. Richard Corliss wrote that Depp brought "big-screen grace and swagger" to the film, "no mean achievement" since he was "guying his own image." This provides a clear insight into both the film and the emerging genius of Johnny Depp.

David Denby was enthusiastic and called Depp "a shining modern descendent of Elvis, with a soft, hoarse voice, slick black hair and the cruel cheekbones of the original." Depp had, however, a "level of consciousness" that Presley never had, which makes him vulnerable so that tears can drip down his cheek. Denby, in a memorable phrase, called Depp "Emblematically Moist," and concluded that he was "a very shrewd, sensual performer" who "could become a big movie star."

Certainly, Depp dressed in an Elvis outfit and twanging on a guitar is a joy to watch. He has padded shoulders, a spit curl, and a coat with white tails. Later he tears open his shirt to show a tattooed electric chair on his chest, worn in homage to his parents. "Electricity killed my parents," he explains helpfully. Elvis never matched that.

Although comparisons of Johnny Depp to Elvis Presley and James Dean seemed relevant at the time *Cry-Baby* was released, they seem today to have been somewhat off the mark. Depp's lip-synching (to the singing of James Intveld) was perfect in *Cry-Baby*, but he was not a natural singer or dancer, nor did he pretend to be. Later, in *Sweeney Todd*, he did his own singing, but that was done in the pursuit of the character and of the film, not to fulfill any career design. Elvis, by comparison, was never much of an actor and, because of the influence of Colonel Parker on his career (or perhaps because of his lack of ambition in that direction), never aspired to be.

The comparison to James Dean was, and is, closer. Dean appeared in only three major films, all of them by directors skilled in all aspects of filmmaking, including the manipulation of temperamental actors. Both Elia Kazan (*East of Eden*) and Nicholas Ray (*Rebel Without a Cause*) managed through sometimes complicated manipulations to get classic performances from Dean as a young rebel suffering, for whatever Freudian reason, from the misunderstanding of his family and the injustice of the system. Psychologically, the two characters are exactly the same. George Stevens, however, was old school, and integrated Dean's character into an epic film in which he plays what is essentially a supporting role. Dean's characterization in *Giant* is less assured, perhaps because Stevens was less successful in communicating with his moody young actor. It is, however, at least an open question whether Dean, at that point in his career, would have been successful in developing a persona broad enough to encompass characters other than young rebels.

Although John Waters designed *Cry-Baby* as an ensemble piece and peopled it with situations and characters based upon his own slanted — or, some would say, warped — view of reality, Depp was the glue that made it a hit, "the observed of all observers," then as now.

1990 *Edward Scissorhands*

Cutting Edge Drama

"The villagers never liked you." (Sylvia Plath, "Daddy")
"We actually have known each other before the invention of cinema."
(Tim Burton on his relationship with Johnny Depp)
"Let's cut the comedy for a while." (Bill)

In a perfect world, all actors would discover, or be discovered by, the person who would define their essential character, the person who would define the parameters of the character they were — by talent, temperament, experience and appearance — most suited to play. For one reason or another (lack of talent, misalignment of the stars, perverseness, or whatever), most actors are doomed to wander between the worlds without ever discovering their professional soul mates. Sometimes it seems that only one director will be able to utilize to the fullest those quicksilver characteristics. Apparently, only David Lynch knows how to use Kyle MacLachlan to his full potential, as he's so perfect for Lynch but so stolid in nearly everything else. John Wayne was wandering between the worlds until John Ford made him a star in *Stagecoach*, and even when other directors used his character successfully, as Hawks did in *Red River*, they did not, as Hawks claimed, reinvent the character, but merely aged him.

According to Johnny Depp in his preface to *Burton on Burton,* he was going through a self-destructive period which a former agent had described as "good medicine for unemployment" when he was sent a script which caused him "to weep like a baby" (ix). Although Depp felt that no director in his right mind would hire him for such a role, his agent convinced him to fly to Los Angeles to meet Tim Burton. After weeks of "researching the part," whatever that may mean, he was in despair until the telephone rang and he was told he had gotten the role.

Although only some three years older than Johnny Depp, Tim Burton had already established himself as a creative artist capable of turning out successful and distinctive commercial films. After winning a scholarship from the Disney studios, he was put to work on Disney's animated film *The Fox and the Hound*. Although he later complained that he could neither draw nor imitate the in-house Disney style, he was allowed to create his own short films. In retrospect, the time spent at Disney seems to have been an extremely creative period which allowed a talented artist to find his own way.

Burton's apprentice films, before moving into features, included *Vincent* and *Hansel and Gretel* (both 1982); *Frankenweenie*, a film about Victor Frankenstein's dog (1984); "Aladdin and his Wonderful Lamp," for *Shelley Duvall's Faerie Tale Theatre* on *Showtime* (1984); and "The Jar" for *Alfred Hitchcock Presents* (1985). Burton's first feature, *Pee-Wee's Big Adventure* (1985), was enormously popular, especially with children. Pee-Wee Herman, the eponymous lead, was a mad child/adolescent who resembled Jerry Lewis at his most manic. Paul Reubens, the star of an enormously popular children's television show, played the lead in Burton's equally popular film. Burton, who has always had an instinctive understanding of children, caught the sprightly, slightly anarchic quality of the character perfectly. Unfortunately, Reubens was brought up on an obscenity charge, his television career was ruined and his impersonation of Pee-Wee as a wild child was permanently scuttled, although he did surface later as a subdued character actor.

Burton moved from strength to strength. *Beetlejuice* (1987), a good-natured parade of ghoulishness, starred little-known Michael Keaton as a sprightly apparition, with a young Winona Ryder in support. Burton's clout was now so great that he was chosen to direct *Batman* (1989), starring Keaton, cast against type as the caped crusader, and Jack Nicholson as the Joker. Although not all of the critics were enamored of Keaton, Nicholson's Joker was widely praised and, in some aspects at least, definitive. The Joker's clattering teeth at the end of the film, presumably all that remained of him, was typical of Burton's ability to scare a mainstream audience without antagonizing them. Heath Ledger darkened the Joker into a depressive, but his portrayal is quite without the manic expressiveness Nicholson gave to the role.

Tim Burton has said that the idea of Edward originated from a reading of Caroline

Thompson's novel *First Born*, which was about "an abortion which came back to life." When he met Thompson, he said they bonded because she did not overanalyze everything, "so there wouldn't have to be a lot of grade school psychology going on in terms of discussing the project." He imagined a creature "who wants to touch but can't ... the feeling that your image and how people perceive you are at odds with what is inside you" (Salisbury 87). Burton and Thompson wrote the script together and presented it to the studio as a fait accompli.

A kindly old lady is telling her young grandson a bedtime story. In an under-populated pastel town, a clueless Avon lady named Peg Boggs, played by Diane Wiest, is attempting unsuccessfully to sell her wares. She is turned away abruptly by, among others, a teenager and a lustful housewife attempting to seduce a plumber ("Housewives get lonely, too"). Finally, she drives up a mountain to a mansion situated high above the town. The mansion, a gothic monstrosity, has elaborate lawns decorated by complex figures of animals carved from hedges.

Here Peg finds an incomplete young man with frizzy hair, a scarred pale face, leather clothing, and shears for hands. As it turns out, his creator, the "Inventor," has died before he could finish the job, and his creature must make do with his mastery of the shears instead of the more adaptable hands. While they are great for topiary work and hairdressing, they are distinctly wrong for performing everyday tasks. (How Edward manages the functions of everyday life is one of the mysteries of the film.) Peg is kind-hearted, takes Edward home with her, and makes him a part of her family. At first, Edward is an interesting object of curiosity, but he knows nothing of the intricacies of suburbia and is unable to fit in. Peg's nubile young daughter, a cheerleader, becomes interested in Edward, but her jealous and evil boyfriend frames Edward, and the film ends tragically. However, here, as in the later *Charlie and the Chocolate Factory*, Burton takes the curse off his dark materials by returning to the old lady and her grandson, and pretending that it is only a story.

The cast is strong throughout. Dianne Wiest is perfect as Peg, the Avon lady, and received an Academy Award nomination as a reward. Her whole dim, bland lack of understanding of the matter at hand, no matter what that is, is perfectly expressed in her dress and mannerisms. Winona Ryder (b. 1971) is a gifted actress who, as the world knows, had a long, apparently turbulent romance with Johnny Depp. She became a star in Burton's *Beetlejuice* and appeared in leading roles in a number of outstanding films, including *Dracula* (1992), Martin Scorsese's *The Age of Innocence* (1993), *Little Women* (1994), and *Girl Interrupted* (1999). Unfortunately, her career declined rapidly after she was accused of shoplifting, and, although she has continued to act, she seems, for whatever reason, to have lost her way.

Alan Arkin, although never a major star, has had a long and successful career, usually in comic roles. His first important credit, in *The Russians Are Coming* (1966), defined his persona, and he has continued to hone it. Among his notable appearances are *The In-Laws* (1979) — "serpentine, serpentine" — and *Little Miss Sunshine*, for which he received an Academy Award for Best Supporting Actor in 2007. Conchata Farrell was superb as a mail-order bride opposite Rip Torn in *Heartland* (1979). Kathy Baker was memorable in the underrated *Jacknife*. Anthony Michael Hall, superbly villainous as the teenaged thug Jim, went on to play the lead in a television series based (like an earlier film version) on Stephen King's *The Dead Zone* for six seasons. All in all, *Edward Scissorhands* sports a great cast.

With the exception of Jim, none of the characters are bad, only misguided. They seem to be caught in a 1960s time warp. After all, they live in a pastel suburbia and apparently have little experience with the outside world. They act according to their understanding. Peg uses her Avon products to conceal Edward's scars, and the others treat him as they would anyone else. They simply do not understand how different Edward is, and, assuming that his abilities are the same as their own, they condemn him almost out of hand.

Snip-Snip: *Edward Scissorhands.*

Reviewers were enthusiastic. The anonymous reviewer in *Variety* wrote, "The film takes a boy whose arms end in pruning shears, and makes him the center of a delightful and delicate comic fable." The writer saw "a sizable b.o. reward" if Fox could figure out a way to convince the public that the film "isn't too strange." Although the reviewer's belief that the film "sags" toward the end, a recurrent criticism of Burton's films, he/she adds that the story-within-a-story allows for a recovery. According to the reviewer, the film is stuck stylistically "in the early '60s where women subsist on voracious gossip and men return home en masse, sweeping nightly into the cul-de-sac in a parade of headlights." He/she was enthusiastic about the "former TV teen idol," and wrote that Depp gives "a sensational reading of Edward as a sad funny clown with a Chaplinesque shuffle" forced "to express himself with his eyes and bizarre movements." David Sterritt called Burton a "profoundly offbeat filmmaker," but noted that people were not "weirded out," but were responding warmly to the film at the box office. Sterritt even compared it to *Twin Peaks*, then at the height of its popularity on television. Sterritt described Edward as "a wistful teen who doesn't fit in with the other kids," and emphasized the film's lesson of tolerance for people who are different. He thought, however, that the film's "cloying tone" and "stale narrative devices" worked against its "engaging — if not brilliant — fantasy."

Richard Corliss called *Edward* "a witty comedy of manners that arcs into a poignance," and "a Christmas movie only a Grinch could hate." David Ansen wrote that *Edward* is a "film of splendidly original, brightly lit surfaces— Burton inverts middle-class tackiness with surreal lyricism." John Leland, however, was unimpressed, writing that the film was "bankable Hollywood formula," and that Burton "just seems to think kids' stuff is really neat."

In many ways, the film is, as Tim Burton has acknowledged, an homage to Vincent Price. It was Price's last movie and formed a suitable climax to his career as the last of the great stars of horror films, a distinguished group which stretched back to Lon Chaney and included Boris Karloff and Bela Lugosi. By the time Depp and Burton made *Ed Wood* some years later, the classic Hollywood horror film had already receded into the past and had become, at least in the minds of its makers, an historical object.

Price was, by all accounts, an erudite man with a wide range of interests. A collector himself, he spent a short time selling quality, but comparatively inexpensive, art to the masses through Sears-Roebuck. He came to the horror film comparatively late in his career after a successful, but hardly spectacular, stint as a character actor and sometime villain. He was magnificent in Sam Fuller's *The Baron of Arizona* (1950). His roles in *House of Wax* (1953) and *The Fly* (1958) transformed him into a horror icon, and his films with Roger Corman, loosely — sometimes much too loosely — based on the stories of Edgar Allan Poe, were sure moneymakers.

Burton says that he had originally thought of his poem "Vincent" as a children's book, but then was given the opportunity to film it in stop-motion. As a youth, Burton had admired the old Vincent Price movies, and the seven-year-old boy in the film goes in and out of his own reality. He believes, at least intermittently, that he is Vincent Price. The poem ends with a quote from "The Raven." According to Burton, the people at Disney thought that Vincent dies at the end of the film; the director himself, however, believes that the evidence is not conclusive. Of course, the suits at Disney wanted to have "the light click on and have his dad come in" and show that the whole film had been a dream. Burton says that was his "first encounter with the happy ending syndrome" (Salisbury 16). It was, however, not the last.

With the bravado of youth, Burton approached Price and asked him to read the poem in a voice-over. The actor, then living in comfortable retirement, readily agreed. With Price on hand, and with the able assistance of animator Rick Heinrichs, stop-motion animator

Steven Chiodo and cameraman Victor Abadov, the black and white film was completed in two months (Salisbury). The result was delightful. (*Vincent* is included as an extra on the DVD versions of Burton's *The Nightmare Before Christmas*.)

Although *Vincent* was done in the German expressionistic style of the 1920s, Burton has said that the film was specifically influenced by Dr. Suess. Flattered by the poem and the homage it represented, Price somehow managed to make a major work out of a jeu d'esprit. Price felt that the poem captured perfectly what he called the preposterous aspect of many of the Roger Corman horror films which had made him famous. The Corman/Poe movies included *The House of Usher* (1960), *The Pit and the Pendulum* (1961), and *The Raven* (1963), among others. Later films, such as *The Abominable Dr. Phibes* (1971), yet another clone of the Lon Chaney 1925 silent *The Phantom of the Opera*, its sequel *Dr. Phibes Rises Again* (1972) and *Theatre of Blood*, (1973), about an old Shakespearean actor who takes revenge on his critics by killing them off in Shakespearean fashion, mined the same vein. (A notable exception is *Witchfinder General*, in which he played so-called "Witchfinder General" Matthew Hopkins as pure evil.)

J. Hoberman's description of *Edward Scissorhands*' merits was all over the lot. He called Burton "the reigning master of the Looney Tune gothic," and an "American *Kinderkultur* in heroic, horrific form, each of whose films might be entitled *The TV Cabinet of Dr. Caligari*." In rare, metaphoric form, Hoberman described Burton as a child of the autistic generation whose Edward projects the fear of being touched on everyone he meets. The film was "a child's bedtime story, set inside a virtual snow-shake paperweight," which had, nonetheless, "a steely masochistic edge" with razor blades concealed inside. Edward himself was, in Hoberman's memorable phrasing, "a creature of the weirdest Weimar," with his wild hair, scarred face, and "a nervous pattern of snipping his shears." Hoberman praised Depp for "a brilliantly behavioral performance," and believed that his eyes were a mirror of his "evident physical discomfort."

The basic purpose of any film review is to tell the viewer whether to shell out his hard cash to see the movie. The greatest reviews fall into one of two types: the first explains a movie which the audience is predisposed not to like, but should. Pauline Kael's reviews of Peckinpah's *The Wild Bunch* and Altman's *Nashville* are examples of this type. The second type, of which Hoberman's review is an example, explains a movie which is art masquerading as popular entertainment. All sorts of works pretend to be art but are actually trash. By locating *Edward Scissorhands* firmly in film history, Hoberman put the argument for the movie's greatness fairly and squarely.

Hoberman compared Burton to David Cronenberg and David Lynch as examples of errant sensibility. A critic nearly two decades later would also mention the Coen brothers. All of these filmmakers operate at the fringes of the Hollywood establishment. Burton, however, is at the center. He began with Disney, the Goliath of mass entertainment. and although he has often been critical of Disney, he has always spoken appreciatively of the opportunities the company gave him.

1991 *Freddy's Dead: The Final Nightmare*

Opra Noodlemantra

Johnny Depp made a cameo appearance in *Freddy's Dead: The Final Nightmare*, the sixth entry in the Wes Craven slasher series. Despite the title, it is unlikely that many fans were deceived into thinking it was the last of its line. In addition to Depp, the film's "guest stars" included Tom Arnold, Roseanne Barr, and Alice Cooper, each of whom was noisily dispatched in turn to the none-too-silent "silent halls of death."

In the film, a haunted teenager wakes from a troubled sleep. He has been smoking pot and is perhaps hallucinating. The television set is on. Clutching hands reach out from the set, and his friend Carlos, or his ghost, tells him to "get out." Groggily, he ignores this excellent piece of advice. He wakens. The television set is showing test patterns—remember them? Johnny Depp appears, making a public service announcement. He holds up an egg and announces, "This is your brain." He cracks the egg and into a hot skillet, where it sizzles. "Question?" Freddy Krueger appears suddenly and zaps Johnny with the skillet. "It looks like a frying pan and some eggs to me," he opines sagely.

In the film's credits, the "Teen on TV" is billed as "Opra Noodlemantra." Could this be Depp's revenge for the anti-drug announcement Depp was required to make for *21 Jump Street*? All in all, it made for a memorable departure from the series.

1991 *Into the Great Wide Open*
A Music Video

While Johnny Depp and Faye Dunaway were waiting for director Emir Kusturica to recover from his depression so that shooting on *Arizona Dream* could resume, they made a music video with Tom Petty. The video, *Into the Great Wide Open*, which runs for more than six minutes, furnished the lead track and title for Petty's 1991 album, and was, of course, released before *Arizona Dream*. Petty supplied the music, and Depp played the lead in a somber story of disillusionment set to engaging music and lyrics. Country boy Eddie Rebel comes to the Big City, gets a tattoo and a girlfriend, moves into an apartment with her, gets a job at a nightclub, becomes successful in the music business, rises to the top of the charts, watches his life fall apart under stress, is "axed" and leaves town. Despite its extreme length for a music video, *Wide Open* was enormously popular on MTV.

Although outside the scope of this book, Depp's music videos, both those in which he appears and those which make unauthorized use of his image, deserve close study. They furnish the raw material for the study of fame, its glamour and its pitfalls in our time.

1992 *Arizona Dream*
A Foreigner's Dream

American muse, whose strong and diverse heart,
  So many men have tried to understand,
But only made it smaller with their art
  Because you are as various as your land.
(Stephen Vincent Benét, *John Brown's Body*)

Faced with a variety of choices after the success of *Edward Scissorhands*, Johnny Depp, as usual, took the path "less traveled by," and starred in what is, in effect, a European art film about America. The film, originally entitled *The Arrowtooth Waltz*, was released under the title *Arizona Dream*— at least to the few people who managed to see it. Bosnian émigré director Emir Kusturica had recently received rave reviews and international acclaim for *Time of the Gypsies* (*Dom za vesanje*, 1988). (Kusturica's film is not to be confused with Frank Pierson's popular *King of the Gypsies* from a decade earlier.) The film was an international project which had started as a screenplay by David Atkins, who had been in Kusturica's film class at Columbia University and who received screen credit. Atkins' only other significant credit to date is *Novocaine* (2001), with Steve Martin, which he also directed. The original title, *The Arrowtooth Waltz*, refers to the protagonist's dream of himself as an Eskimo capturing a rare fish called an arrowtooth halibut and bringing it back to his igloo. The title was, of course, discarded as unintelligible to a mass audience — or, for that matter, even to a select one.

Co-stars Jerry Lewis and Faye Dunaway were both on the downside of careers which had yielded them fame, money and considerable acclaim. The team of Dean Martin and Jerry Lewis had made some of the most popular films of the 1950s, and Lewis had become a particular favorite of the French critics. (This idea was, in the view of many American critics, a sure sign of the decadence of French film criticism.) Both Martin and Lewis were ambitious, and success drew them apart. Martin went on to a notable career as an actor, singer and full-fledged member of the famous Rat Pack, but Lewis, who had developed a huge cult following in France, had ambitions as a serious actor and auteur, but was never able to equal his earlier success. Without Martin's sophistication, his character hardened, and even a stint on television and a leading role opposite Robert De Niro in Martin Scorsese's *The King of Comedy* (1982) did nothing to revive it. Faye Dunaway, who was for a decade or so a major star, became famous in Arthur Penn's *Bonnie and Clyde* (1967), won an Oscar for *Network* a decade later, and gradually slipped into what were basically supporting roles. Like Dunaway, supporting actor Michael J. Pollard came to prominence with *Bonnie and Clyde*, and even had leading roles in *Dirty Little Billy* (as Billy the Kid) and *Little Fauss and Big Halsey* (1973) before slipping back into supporting roles in less prestigious films.

Released only belatedly in America on June 7, 1995, by Kit Parker Films, *Arizona Dream* grossed a miserable $112,547. According to *Box Office Mojo*, its widest release in the USA included only three theaters. Ten years after shooting, the film was released on a region 2 PAL DVD. It has not, as of 2009, been released in any form in the USA. In the old days (that is, before video), the film might have opened in a few art theaters, established itself as a cult movie, and have gotten at least a somewhat larger gross; but it would, in any case, have remained caviar for the multitudes. According to producer Claudie Ossard, *Arizona Dream* was financially successful in France and became a cult film there.

For the DVD, Johnny Depp gave an interview on February 12, 2002, to producer Ossard. She asked the questions in French, and Depp responded in English. The interview gives considerable insight into both the problems of the movie and Depp's commitment to the project. The filming took about a year, with a three-month break when director Kusturica went into a deep depression. Although Depp was free to take other jobs, he bided his time, making a music video with Dunaway. After waiting some hours to begin filming one morning, Lewis approached him and said, "Well, kid, the director is sitting over there alone under a tree." Apparently, chaos in Yugoslavia and in the director's head had caused him to shut down. He said he felt like a drowning man who rises to the surface only to sink again. It approaches the miraculous that the film was ever finished at all. Depp, as always, remained committed to the project and has done everything he could to publicize the film.

Arizona Dream is a foreigner's fantasy of America in a period of decline. Influenced by the South American novels of magical realism, especially those of Gabriel García Márquez, Emir Kusturica's film is a magical realist dream based upon a tourist's view of the American west peopled by old movie stars and fueled by dreams of vast spaces, enormous gas-guzzling Cadillacs, mariachi bands and flight. Lacking both narrative urgency and psychological realism, *Arizona Dream* has little forward movement and clearly would require careful handling to find an appreciative American audience.

In New York City, Axel Blackmar (Depp) is happy at his job counting and marking fish before returning them to the water, when he is approached by his cousin, Paul Leger (Vincent Gallo), gun in hand, asking him, not-too-politely, to return to Arizona for the wedding of his uncle, Leo Sweetie (Jerry Lewis). Leo is a Cadillac dealer who is marrying a young woman less than half his age, named Millie, played by model Paulina Porizkova. Unwillingly recruited to sell Cadillacs, Axel becomes involved with a beautiful, lecherous middle-aged woman named Elaine (Faye Dunaway) and her suicidal stepdaughter Grace (Lili Taylor). Although Axel is attracted to the older woman, the younger one falls in love with him.

The story, as it develops—or, more precisely, rambles around—involves a harebrained scheme by Axel and Elaine to build an airplane, only to have their attempts sabotaged by Grace. There is a lot of palaver about suicide, freedom and turtles. A mariachi band seems to appear everywhere. Uncle Leo passes on to his just reward. There is a party, and Grace finally manages to kill herself. Axel says he has lost faith in America and dreams of Uncle Leo and himself as Eskimos.

Although there are few reviews of *Arizona Dream*, Jonathan Rosenbaum, in his on-line commentary "Global Discoveries on DVD," opines that, as he "wrote many years ago for the *Chicago Reader* ... this film illustrates the truism that the biggest difference between European and American directors using America as a site for fantasies is that the Europeans are likelier to know what they're doing.... Combined with the cross-pollination of Johnny Depp, Faye Dunaway, Jerry Lewis, Lili Taylor, Paulina Porizkova, Michael J. Pollard, stacks of Cadillacs, homemade airplanes, and slices of Arizona landscape that call to mind Crazy Kat comic strips, this turns out to be a view of American madness that lingers like an acute form of clarity, if not exactly sanity" (<http://cinema-scope.com/cs26/col_rosenbaum_dvd.htm>; accessed July 20, 2008). As an attempt to drum up business for the film, this is acceptable criticism, but as considered analysis, it is weak stuff which is largely negated by a viewing of the picture itself.

Simply put, the film has no feeling for American iconography and legend. The huge automobile dealership is almost totally deserted; there is not a single Native American in sight; the only Hispanics are in a Mariachi band; and there is not a single reference to the westward movement, the desert, or any western films, including those of John Ford. Did they show any westerns in Yugoslavia when Kusturica was growing up?

Producer Ossard's comparison to Fellini is closer to the mark. Although the film lacks Fellini's strident boisterousness, it has something of his anything-goes spirit and will likely gain in appeal as the years pass. When viewed in segments, the faults of the film are minimized and its virtues become more apparent. It is safe to predict a long shelf-life on DVD and future formats for *Arizona Dream*.

Generically, *Arizona Dream* is an attempt to mediate the demands of European art-house cinema (appropriately, the DVD is published by ArtHaus) with Hollywood narrative cinema. Such films, whether originating in Europe or in Hollywood, have had, at best, only middling artistic and/or commercial success. During the post-war period, most of the great European filmmakers avoided Hollywood like the plague. Bergman and Fellini resisted the temptations, although Fellini attempted *Fred and Ginger* without leaving Cinecita. Only Antonioni went to England, scored a success with *Blowup* (1966), and came a cropper in Hollywood with *Zabriskie Point* (1967). The name refers to the lowest point in America, in Death Valley, but it might as well have referred to Antonioni's career.

It would, however, be wrong to assume that the Americans were not interested in art films. It is just that they wanted to make art films that made money. For example, Robert Altman, after the enormous commercial success of *M*A*S*H*, made *Brewster McCloud* (1970), the story of a young man who built up his body and designed a pair of wings to fly in the Astrodome, at that time the largest enclosed stadium in the world. Although generally ridiculed by the critics and ignored at the box office, the overriding imagery and purposeless ambition of the young man was quintessentially American and gives the film a coherence totally lacking in *Arizona Dream*.

The DVD version of *Arizona Dream* includes a fifteen-minute scene, minus a few seconds, cut from the theatrical print. The episode, which is complete in itself, occurs just before the conclusion and neatly encapsulates the entire movie. As the sequence begins, Axel (Johnny Depp), like a gunfighter in an old western movie, is walking down a wind-blown street. He is approached by a man dragging a door on his back. The man asks for a light, takes it, asks for a cigarette, takes it, lights up and then asks for Axel to buy the door. He says he has "brought this [the door] all the way from Milwaukee." When Axel twice refuses, the man turns sulkily away. A mariachi band follows Axel down the wind-blown street, caught somewhere between night and morning. (It is a nice critical question whether the shifting light is a matter of art or of incompetence.) Axel easily breaks open the door of his Uncle Leo Sweetie's automobile showroom and enters the largely empty and apparently deserted showroom. A cat is sleeping on the hood of one of the cars. In this scene, away from the distractions of the boisterousness of the rest of the film, Depp comes into his own as a seeker of the American dream. Where better than in a wind-blown, nearly deserted western street, and in the silence of a dusty nighttime Cadillac showroom? The scene is masterful.

In voice-over, Axel says that he "wasn't sure any discovery in America was possible any more." There is, however, nothing in the film to show that he had ever had any belief in American "discovery" to begin with. Certainly the movie does not demonstrate that he had. What the film has, courtesy of a stressed-out director, is a great deal of talk about suicide, some references to traditional classic Hollywood movies (*North by Northwest*, *Raging Bull* and *The Godfather 2*), a few memorable surrealistic images (a flying fish knifing through the air like a schooner, a man carrying a door cross-country on his back), and a memorable concluding scene in which Depp and Lewis, dressed as Eskimos, talk gibberish. The scene is hilarious; but at least, according to the subtitles and the DVD commentary, the language actually is Eskimo. It is perhaps beyond the nature of criticism to ask why here, and nowhere else, should there be a necessity for authenticity. The scene nonetheless shows clearly what the film might have been if the director had turned these two gifted actors loose against each earlier in the film and had done away with what seems like several hundred references to suicide. Nonetheless, Lewis, a clown if ever there was one, knows nonsense when he hears it, and Depp is happy to follow suit.

If nothing else, the history of the reception of the film, and Depp's participation in the DVD production years after the movie had tanked, shows the actor's loyalty to a project once he commits himself to it. Whatever any of the critics might think of a Depp film, or whatever Depp himself might think of it, he remains loyal to the project. This is an admirable quality that is not always found in leading actors, male or female.

1993 *Benny & Joon*

The Silent Clown

"You can't throw him out. I want him." (Joon, speaking of Sam)

Jeremiah Chechik's film *Benny & Joon* is a brave attempt to deal with the problems of mental illness. It is not a Jacobean tragicomedy in which almost everyone seems to try to do bad without ultimately succeeding. In *Benny & Joon* everyone tries to do good, and it works out, sort of. This may or may not work in real life, but it is usually a disaster in drama. Since there are no bad guys to beat up on, goodies must be rationed out among the deserving, a thankless job at best. Arguing that Chechik attempts to grab the dramatic baton by the wrong end, however, misses the point. As Henry James used to write rather grandly, an artist must be allowed his *donnée*— that is, his subject matter. He must, however, as James well knew, live with the results.

The main characters of *Benny & Joon* are Benny, a responsible, attractive man who runs a successful automobile repair shop; Joon, his younger sister, who suffers from a mental impairment; and Sam, a dyslexic young man who can barely read and write. Joon is a danger to herself and to others. She paints pictures and likes to set fires, including, apparently, the one which killed her parents. She wears a snorkeling outfit and directs traffic with a ping-pong paddle. Although she recognizes at some level that she has problems, she is unable to control her actions, and when she and Sam fall in love, they bring a long-simmering crisis to a boil. The best outcome is obvious from the beginning. Joon must be put in an institution where she can be constantly watched. Benny can have a normal life courtesy of a budding romance with Ruthie, who has indicated her liking for him. Although we are told that Joon and Sam have begun a sexual relationship, the film is silent, as well it might be, on whether children might ensue.

The situation, then, is close to Buffalo Bill's definition of "the show business" in Robert Altman's *Buffalo Bill and the Indians, or Sitting Bull's History Lesson* (1976): "It ain't all that much different from real life." The question then becomes: Does Chechik manage to take the curse off the material and make it work? The answer is: Yes, at least reasonably well, courtesy of skillful direction, a screenplay that manages to make light of the problems, and a cast of talented actors.

The reviews of *Benny & Joon* were respectful, but hardly enthusiastic. They were generally concerned about the unclear motivation of Sam and Joon. Peter Rainer, in the *Los Angeles Times*, grouped the film with *One Flew Over the Cuckoo's Nest* and *David and Lisa*. Aside from the fact that all three films deal in some way with mental illness, however, they have little in common. *Cuckoo's Nest* has a rebellious spirit, and *David and Lisa* is a serious and sober study of two damaged people. Rainer described Depp's Sam as "a holy fool — a redeemer ... a quirky, clownish spirit who idolizes Keaton and Chaplin," and Joon as wavering between "rational alertness and hyper-anxious loopiness."

Michael Medved, in the *New York Post*, described Sam as "a functional illiterate" with "an encyclopedic knowledge of old movies," and compared him to the "other-worldly misfits" Depp played in *Cry-Baby* and *Edward Scissorhands*, and (strangely) to one of the droogs in Kubrick's *A Clockwork Orange*. He characterized Sam as "totally predictable and utterly unconvincing." David Ansen, in *Newsweek*, did not much like the film and complained about the vagueness of Joon's condition. He did, however, like Johnny Depp — a lot. He wrote, "Depp plays [Sam] with such conviction that you can't take your eyes off him," and characterized Depp's Sam as having "a melancholic inner stillness that's positively Keatonesque."

Claire Monk, in *Sight and Sound*, saw the film in sociological terms and complained about the "low-risk liberal clichés of the American mental illness movie." While this unfairly criticizes the movie for being something it never pretended to be, Monk's description of the film as a "likeable but flawed magic realist script ... weighed down by unimaginative direction" was fair enough. She did admit, however, that "getting together with Johnny Depp" is probably more effective therapy for mental illness than "say, *Rain Man*'s vision of enforced contact with an autistic brother...."

The acting in *Benny & Joon* is generally excellent. Mary Stuart Masterson is perfect as Joon, all emotion and not quite coordinated movement, but capable of occasional stillness. She is creative and smears great swatches of paint on large canvases. At some level she is aware of her problems. When she is caught cheating at ping-pong, she huffs out, saying, "Don't underestimate the mentally ill."

Julianne Moore, plainly dressed but still sexy and likable, as Benny's girlfriend, has, of course, gone on to leading roles in many films, and provided memorable performances in such pictures as *The Big Lebowski* (1998), *Hannibal* (2001) and *Blindness* (2008). Oliver Pratt, who works in Benny's repair shop, has a memorable bit of business when he mouths, "Stoo-pid, stoo-pid," after Benny has turned down an offer from an attractive young woman to cook dinner for him. Perhaps Pratt's most notable performance, again under Chechik's direction, was as New York Yankees owner George Steinbrenner in the HBO miniseries *The Bronx Is Burning* (2007). CCH Pounder is an effective authority figure as the doctor who advises Benny to institutionalize Joon. Pounder played one of the good guys—there were not that many of them—in the long-running TV series *The Shield*. William H. Macy, unfortunately, has little to do except deliver what director Chechik helpfully tells us is the theme of the film: "What does it really mean to love somebody?"

As Benny, Aidan Quinn, an honorable and underrated actor, is the fulcrum on which the movie turns. There is not a single false moment in his performance. Knowing the terrible tragedy of the past, which the viewer learns only toward the end of the film, he subordinates his personal life to caring for Joon. In the process, he savages his own life. Quinn allows just enough of a tinge of self-pity into his performance to make his character believable. Indeed, the film's emphasis on Benny may be at least part of the problem. Jack Mathews in *Newsday* noted that Depp is now doing Keaton and Chaplin "imitations instead of ice sculptures," and complained that the Joon and Sam relationship is better written and more interesting than the Joon and Benny relationship, but that it gets "the most attention." This is exact. The film, as it now exists, has two faces.

This is not the result of the scene-stealing antics that so many actors attempt. Actors who have worked with Depp have seldom, if ever, complained about the actor's unfairness in his treatment of his fellow players. It seems, rather, that he was simply so good that he threw the film out of balance; his performance lightens the film and lifts it to another level. We first see him as a train chugs into town, holding a copy of *The Look of Buster Keaton*—a book of photographs by Robert Benayoun of the great silent clown—against the window for the world to see. While one might argue that Sam, who has a great admiration for Keaton's artistry, might have such a book, the image seems obtrusive, and the fact that it is played over the credits does not make it any less so.

John Schwartzman, the director of photography, said in his commentary on the lighting tests that Johnny Depp "spent a lot of time watching Buster Keaton films. In fact, he spent six weeks researching Buster Keaton and Charlie Chaplin, all the other great silent film stars

... to influence the way their stunts came off." The director's commentary also mentions Jacques Tati, the great French clown who did not, of course, make silent movies— although they might as well have been, since *Mon oncle* (1967) and *Playtime* (1968) are squarely in the tradition of the great silent comedies. Schwartzman points out that "the people were true circus performers," that Keaton "really did his stunts," and that the makers of *Benny & Joon* decided to experiment with film speeds to give Sam "a Keatonesque feature, a bit of extra margin." Eventually, however, they decided to shoot Depp at the usual sound speed of 24 fps. A deleted scene shows Depp's imitation of Chaplin's roll dance in *The Gold Rush.*

It would be unfair to compare Depp with Keaton and Chaplin. Both the comedians were nearly, if not actually, born on the stage, and both honed their skills as mimes professionally from childhood. It is fair to say that neither was much of an actor, and Keaton never pretended to be, but their comic routines required endless repetition and bruises. Before the ravages of cigarettes and booze took their toll, Keaton was beautiful. His small, strong, athletic body in motion was a sight to see, and his seemingly impassive face and searching gaze perfectly reflected his feelings.

Depp, of course, is a product of a later era and, perhaps, a lesser one. For his role, he practiced for hours with a circus performer. The film trades on his resemblance to Keaton, and while the routines in *Benny & Joon* seem to come from a better movie than the one we are watching, they are hardly equal to those of the master at his best. They are, however, good enough to toss the movie tail over tin-cup into another realm. The film ends with a perfect exhibition of comedic skills which seems at odds with the soberness of Benny that occupies so much of the film. Except for the shot of Sam on the train at the beginning of the movie, and a shot of Sam in a tree, we are nearly half an hour into the picture before he makes his magical appearance. The film then moves into another gear as the relationship between Sam and Joon heats up. And while Sam's late entrance into the action does not exactly ruin the film, it does give an indication of what might have been had the picture started with Sam rather than ended with him. Of course, we should not then have had the worthwhile moral lesson of the film. There is no indication, however, that Keaton ever felt he needed a moral lesson.

Chechik's professed hope for the film was that it would blend "a perceived sense of reality and a sense of romantic love." Unfortunately, the mixture proved elusive. The film did not get the first, but it did have Johnny Depp to provide the second in a performance which the director described as "so little said, so much expressed."

The last word may be reserved for Manohla Dargis. In her review, she admitted that "the cast is game," but believed that Depp was the only one who knew how "to pump up flat material." She described Depp as a "graceful physical comedian" who "never sinks into preciousness" and "takes the goo out of ... *Benny & Joon*'s movie madness."

1993 *What's Eating Gilbert Grape*

The Caregiver

"Way to go, Gilbert!" (Unidentified Voice)
"You're my knight in shimmering armor, you know that" (Momma)
"So, Gilbert, what's to become of you?" (Mrs. Carver)

What's Eating Gilbert Grape is yet another film about America from a European director, in this case Swedish director Lasse Hallström. The result is a strange movie which was apparently much better received overseas than in America. After a successful career in Sweden, highlighted by the international success of *My Life as a Dog* (1985), Hallström began making films in English. It is at least an open question whether he might have been better served artistically, if not financially, had he continued to make movies in Swedish.

What's Eating Gilbert Grape is a film about a dysfunctional family set in a town in Iowa named Endora (get it, End-ora?). Actually, as anyone who has driven through rural Texas will immediately recognize, the landscape and buildings are as purely Texan as anything in *The Last Picture Show*. For viewers to have any sympathy with the makers of the film, it is necessary for them to dismiss Iowa completely from their minds.

The Grape family consists of Gilbert, a young man in his early twenties, his retarded younger brother Arnie, who is about to turn eighteen, an older sister, Amy, who used to manage a school cafeteria before the school closed, a younger sister named Ellen, and their mother, "Momma," a tremendously overweight woman who has not been out of the house for years. The father abandoned the family seventeen years ago—that is, sometime right after the birth of Arnie, who is retarded and was not expected to live very long. The exact nature of the retardation has been the subject of some discussion on the IMDB.

The townspeople would be totally dysfunctional outside of Sherwood Anderson's Winesburg, Ohio, or William Faulkner's Mississippi. They include an undertaker who likes to talk about the desecration of corpses, an insurance salesman who is too stupid to realize that his wife is cheating on him with Gilbert (although everybody else in the town seems to know about it), and various others whose dreams of success mostly run to getting a job at the new Burger Barn franchise. Becky, a girl who lives with her grandmother in a mobile home outside town, becomes friends with Gilbert.

Gilbert, who works at the town's grocery store, which is in the process of being put out of business by a big-box store close to the interstate, is the chief caregiver for the family and gets blamed when anything goes wrong with Arnie, who requires constant attention. The story lurches forward and concludes with the death of Momma. When the authorities complain that they will need a crane to remove Momma's body from the house, Gilbert resents their tone, burns the house down, and leaves town.

The reviews for *Gilbert Grape* were genuinely mixed. Peter Rainer wrote that the film was "like an entire week of guests on Phil Donahue or Oprah Winfrey." The characters are "dysfunctionally functional — by all rights, their lives should be disastrous but somehow they turn out ok." Like other reviewers, he seemed fascinated by Darlene Cates, the tremendously overweight woman who had been chosen for her role in the film after appearing on a TV talk show about overweight women. The question of whether the film would have worked better with an actress in a fat suit might furnish an instructive debate. Rainer called Depp "the saint of the story," and rightly compared the role of Gilbert to that of Aidan Quinn's Benny in *Benny & Joon*. Both are caregivers for dysfunctional wards who require constant care. Rainer's characterization of Depp as "a pre–Raphaelite Fabian Forte" was one of the stranger of the many strange attempts to describe Depp. Forte, always billed simply as Fabian, was an enormously popular performer of the 1950s and early 60s who, although largely forgotten today, continues to perform.

Depp's performance as Gilbert was generally praised in muted and often satirical tones. John Powers wrote that Gilbert is "deftly played" by "the school girl's heartthrob" who has everything going for him for "adult stardom: warmth, good looks, physical grace, and a gift for playing generously off his fellow actors." Unfortunately, he also has a "seemingly incur-

Mid-American caregiver: Johnny Depp as the title character in *What's Eating Gilbert Grape.*

able taste for adolescent whimsy." It is unclear what — specifically — this last phrase refers to, at least as far as *What's Eating Gilbert Grape* is concerned.

John Anderson was unstinting in his praise of Depp. He called Gilbert "part enigma, part lost soul and something of an irritation for his lack of direction," but Anderson validated Depp's "considerable talent, which up to now has been overshadowed by his good looks." Having finally gotten a character unencumbered by mental deficiency (Sam) or hardware (Edward Scissorshands), Depp "gets inside Gilbert in a way that's cunning, almost reassuring."

There is much to praise here. Under the matchless eye of Sven Nyqvist, Ingmar Bergman's great cinematographer, the desolate landscape and buildings, which seem to have been left over from some earlier age, have never been more beautiful. The acting is generally excellent. Fresh from her breakthrough performance in Martin Scorsese's *Cape Fear*, Juliette Lewis is bright and new and not yet stereotyped. Crispin Glover is genuinely creepy as an undertaker, and John C. Reilly is convincing as the cheerleader for Burger Barn, a new hamburger franchise about to open in Endora. Mary Steenburgen, who began her career so wonderfully in Jack Nicholson's *Goin' South* (1978), but never managed to become the star she should have been, is believable and sympathetic as the unfaithful housewife who realizes that "nothing gold can stay," and who has no illusions about either herself or Gilbert. Her necessary but still generous relinquishment of Gilbert is genuinely moving. "He's all yours," she says to Becky as she goes out the door.

The world of the film, if not surrealistic, is certainly quixotic, and the scene in which the undertaker, a man acquainted with the ways of death, describes how Mr. Carver died, bending a spoon to illustrate how he fell and managed, so strangely, to drown himself, is straight out of an episode of *Alfred Hitchcock Presents*. It is, however, no more strange than the climax of the film, in which the police, after the death of Momma, make some unfeeling comments about having to use a crane to get her out of the house. Upset, Gilbert has the furniture moved out into the yard and sets fire to the house, with Momma's body inside. Strangely, the fire does not seem to attract any attention. The neighbors are not interested, and there is no evidence that the police ever investigate the matter.

The main difficulty of the film, illustrated by the final sequence, is the shifting among various modes of representation. Hallström seems to believe that he is giving a more or less realistic representation of American reality, and for the critic willing to accept that assumption, *Gilbert Grape* is a substantial achievement. Denis Meikle, in his biography of Johnny Depp, is unstinting in his praise. He praises the film's "observation of the nuances of small existence," its sympathetic understanding of its characters, its "immense heart and endless charm," and caps his praise by calling the film "a triumph" and "a great piece of American cinema, to boot" (Meikle 118).

The problem with this analysis is that none of the characters is anchored to any past. There are no Native Americans, no early settlers, no lovers of the land — absolutely no one to speak of any past whatsoever. Although too harsh in his condemnation, Michael Medved clearly made this point. He called the film "a miserable movie with no point and no plot — just the latest demonstration of Hollywood's tendency to confuse weirdness with artistry." Hallström, the director, gave "a Scandinavian intellectual's view of yukky yokels in middle America." Medved complained that the film, although supposedly set in lush Iowa, was actually shot in arid Texas, and compared it unfavorably to *The Last Picture Show*.

This is fair criticism. The chief problem with *Gilbert Grape*, as with Depp's earlier film *Arizona Dream*, is, quite simply, that the director did not know enough about America to make the film convincing. Larry McMurtry's novel *The Last Picture Show* is soaked in reality — in the dry, caked colors of Texas — and both his screenplay and Peter Bogdanovich's skilled direction rooted the characters firmly in their background and made them believable. In *Gilbert Grape* there is no one to speak for America, as Ben Johnson did in his Academy Award–winning performance in Bogdanovich's film. There are, everywhere in America, at least some people who have been there a long time. The characters in *Gilbert Grape* do not seem to belong anywhere, and while this does not necessarily ruin the film, it clearly moves it toward allegory. But what, if anything, the allegory could mean is an open question. Momma might be interpreted as a sacrificial victim — if it were clear that she represented anything, or that she, or anyone else, regarded her as in any sense sacrificial. "I was not always like this," she says, as if anyone believed that she were.

What are we left with? What many people thought they were left with was a wonderful performance from Leonardo DiCaprio, which won him a Golden Globe Award and an Academy Award nomination for Best Supporting Actor. Of course, the Academy has always been partial to nominations which privilege gaining and losing many pounds, or acting weird or ugly, and young DiCaprio certainly filled the bill. He is all tics, spasms, nervous energy, uncoordinated movement, and inappropriate remarks. He is clearly the male version of Joon from Depp's earlier film, and, like Joon, he needs Depp to calm him down. As usual, the scenechewer won the battle, but Depp won the war for the film's heart and soul. The film would not have worked on any level without him.

Critics generally regarded Depp's Gilbert as a rerun of what they saw as his "space-age" performances as *Edward Scissorhands* and Sam in *Benny & Joon*. Hindsight reveals his performance here as a carefully modulated response to the insanity around him. Depp's tendency, like that of many great actors, is to modulate his performance in response to the other actors in the film. Here, he is all alert attention, somewhat like that which we have so often seen in Buster Keaton. He is the only intelligence in the film, the only person capable of "taking it all in" and attempting, under difficult circumstances, to do the best he can. In a world composed of exhibitionists, he is the still center. It is unfair to say that he is in any sense without direction. Like Benny, in *Benny & Joon*, he spends so much time attending to the needs of his family, especially taking care of Arnie, that he has no time for anything else. It is doubtful that the film would have been better if the characters had been given better motivation. Without him, it would not have worked at all.

1994 *Ed Wood*
The Worst Director of All Time

"It's not the most uncomfortable coffin I've ever been in."
(Martin Landau as Bela Lugosi)
"Why spend your life making someone else's dream?"
(Vincent D'Onofrio as Orson Welles)

On an evening in May 1993, Johnny Depp received a telephone call from Tim Burton asking Depp to meet with him concerning a role in a new film he was directing. Depp was out of work. He had recently turned down roles in *Sliver* (accepted by William Baldwin), *Speed* (Keanu Reeves) and *Legends of the Fall* (Brad Pitt). Of these, *Sliver* was both a financial and artistic failure, *Speed* was enormously popular, and *Legends of the Fall*, based upon an American classic and directed by Robert Redford, was both a financial and artistic success. Burton asked Depp to star as Ed Wood, a role which John Waters, of the pencil-thin mustache, had been forced to turn down because of his commitment to his own film *Serial Mom* (Meikle 126–127).

The writers of the screenplay for *Ed Wood*, Scott Alexander and Larry Karaszewski, had been inspired by Michael Medved's *The Golden Turkeys Awards* to take a look at the life of Edward D. Wood via a book entitled *Nightmare of Ecstasy,* by Rudolph Grey. Denis Meikle vividly describes the book as "the result of a ten-year trawl through the Hollywood trash can," which "astringently captures the seedy, down-at-heels experiences of talentless filmmaking wannabes in a dog-eat-dog world on the fringes of Hollywood" (127). Tim Burton pulled out of filming *Mary Reilly*, a movie about Dr. Jekyll's housekeeper, to make his second film with Johnny Depp.

Ed Wood is an affectionately satiric biopic on the career of Ed Wood (1924–1978), who is almost universally referred to as "the worst director of all time." A cynic might ask how it is possible that such a nonentity should have such fame among the aficionados of cult movies, and why anyone would make a movie about his life. Tim Burton and Johnny Depp's answer to that question is a hoot.

The black and white film opens with a long graveyard sequence showing Jeffrey Jones speaking from a coffin, followed by the names of the makers of the film individually inscribed on tombstones. The story develops along two connected lines—the difficulties that Ed Wood has in raising money to make his sub–poverty row movies, and his friendship with Bela Lugosi, the once-famous star of Tod Browning's *Dracula* (1931) and some 120 other movies, whom Wood recruits as *his* "star." After some twenty years of morphine addiction, Lugosi is a miserable, unemployable wreck remembered only by a few fans.

Lugosi is a bravura role, played to the hilt by television star Martin Landau, who, although enormously popular on television, had never had a big Hollywood success. He and his then wife Barbara Bain had co-starred in the long-running television series *Mission: Impossible*, which began in 1961, lasted 171 episodes and was the inspiration for three movies starring Tom Cruise. Although Landau did not resemble Lugosi, he became the old ham courtesy of his talent, the film's crisp black and white photography, and Rick Baker's expert makeup. Both Landau and Baker won Academy Awards for their efforts.

The reviews of *Ed Wood* were thoughtful, and in general, extremely favorable. David Sterritt called the film "deeply solipsistic" and compared it to *Natural Born Killers,* where "the whole world is subsumed to the director's vision." While this judgment may be true, it does not necessarily follow that it is unfortunate. That judgment would, of course, depend upon the identity of the filmmaker.

Richard Corliss did not much like the movie's attitude, and did not consider Wood close to being the worst director of all time. True, his films had "floridly awful dialogue and actors

Johnny Depp as Ed Wood, and Martin Landau as Bela Lugosi.

who seemed terrified to be on camera," but he had passion and ambition and was a hetero-sexual who "enjoyed wearing women's clothes—a very chic identity crisis." Corliss notes that after Wood's death, his films were rediscovered, and he cites three films as evidence: *Ed Wood; Ed Wood: Look Back in Angora*; and a pornographic homage, *Plan 69 from Outer Space.* He writes suavely that Wood has now gone from being "a never-was" to a "brand name," attempts to define Wood's uniqueness, and asserts that Wood was both a "classic American optimist" and a "classic American loser." If this conclusion is just, and there is evidence in the film to support it, it would place him, generically at least, in exalted company, as a kind of comic version of F. Scott Fitzgerald's tragic Jay Gatsby.

As Corliss himself would probably admit, the term "worst director" is so general that without a specific (and highly judgmental) definition the phrase is meaningless. Clearly, how-ever, Ed Wood was a terrible director by any reasonable standard, and it is unclear whether he would be ashamed of the title. Wood, were he alive, would certainly respond like Captain Jack Sparrow: "Still, you have heard of me."

J. Hoberman noted perceptively that "the dank aroma of skid-row that clings to the Wood oeuvre evaporates in the simulated sunlight of a Hollywood biopic with a hot young cast," including Johnny Depp, Patricia Arquette and Sarah Jessica Parker, and concluded clev-erly that the film plays "both ends against the middlebrow." Todd McCarthy called *Ed Wood* "a fanciful, sweet-tempered biopic" about a man often described as the worst director of all time. While the film was "often dazzling in its technique," it was "a bit distended" and lacked "weight at its center." McCarthy praised Vincent D'Onofrio's performance as Orson Welles, but rightly considered Welles' jibe that he has been forced to take Charlton Heston as the lead actor in *Touch of Evil* unfair, since the film would not have been made without Heston's par-ticipation. McCarthy's verdict was that *Ed Wood* is "a cult film and a film buff's dream."

Kevin Lewis considered the film a success story showing "what an outsider will do to achieve his or her own immortality," and a portrait of America at a time when the counter-culture was emerging and "sexual neurosis was overtaking American society even in the sub-urbs." (It is, however, probable that "sexual neurosis" had been around "in the suburbs" since the beginning of the suburbs.) The film was a "triumph" that shows the cultural sensibility of the time "without creating a false hindsight sensibility." At its center is Johnny Depp as an untalented man of no shame, "an ingenuous Horatio Alger folk figure ... scratching his way along the Hollywood bottom." All of this "America" and "success" business was, of course, a heavy burden of criticism to place on so fragile a boat as a spectacularly untalented film director.

Film reviewers generally have had problems dealing with Tim Burton/Johnny Depp films. The reason, of course, is that Burton and Depp do not fit comfortably in any usual film category (but *Sweeney Todd*, with its dedicated homage to high art, might eventually shift the equation). In his choice of material and in its treatment, Burton is clearly a product of the Disney studio, although not perhaps quite the product it might prefer. Burton began as a Disney scholar and, although he was not always happy there, has always spoken highly of the experience. While he admits that he could not do animation in an accepted Disney style for Disney's then-current project *The Fox and the Hound*, he was allowed to work on his own projects, especially the short film *Vincent*. Although Disney himself yearned for the umbrella of high art, the financial failure of *Fantasia* soured his outlook, and after his death the stu-dio decided that high art and the bottom line did not meet in the middle. Even with the sub-versive Michael Keaton as Batman, Burton was not comfortable in the world of the super-hero, and he must have turned with relief to a modern fairy tale, *Ed Wood*.

Ed Wood is a film about low people, scum of the earth, bottom feeders, and it focuses on an untalented, stupid man who wears angora sweaters, and an old junkie has-been film actor whose best days were a caricature. How does Burton take the curse off his material? He does it by shooting the film in black and white and peopling it with characters done in the style of Theophrastus.

Characters, by Theophrastus of Lesbos (371–287 B.C.), was translated into Latin in 1592 by Isaac Casaubon, and into English by John Healey a year later. The character, as it was adopted into English, was a type (a conceited man, a blunt man), a social type (a braggart warrior, a self-absorbed teacher), or a type associated with a place (the people at the theaters or cockfights). Shakespeare's Falstaff is a character. Ben Jonson, Smollett and Dickens were masters of the use of characters; but realists with pretensions to seriousness disdained them — at the same time that they appropriated them. (See Cuddon 126–127.)

Tim Burton's characters have two chief characteristics: they are unable to change and they are guilt free. (It can be argued that Sweeney Todd is an exception.) It is possible, but not necessary, to argue that their freedom from guilt is the outgrowth of their inability to change. In terms of literary criticism, they are flat and not round. Of course, in some sense, the filmmaker must make us believe that they are real, and Burton allows reality to seep in around the edges of his film. The big studios rejected Ed Wood and made fun of him, and the only person that would allow him to make films admitted that the movies he made and sold were "crap." Ed's wife left him after declaring that all the people around him were "weirdos." But what is the opinion of all these small-minded people next to that of the great Orson Welles?

Ed Wood has worn well. Some fifteen years after the appearance of the film, David Thomson wrote perceptively in *Have You Seen...?* that the film is "lit up equally" by Tim Burton's belief that "passion is more than talent" and by Depp's "fabulous, wide-eyed absence of self-awareness" in the central role (254).

1995 *Don Juan DeMarco*
The Great Lover

> "I have been so great a lover: filled my days
> So proudly with the Splendour of Love's praise..."
> (Rupert Brooke, "The Great Lover")
> "The power of love of Don Juan is eternal and will not be denied."
> (Don Octavio de Florés)

After portraying Ed Wood, Depp's next film was a portrait of another dreamer, the psychotic, but harmless, Don Juan DeMarco, in the film of the same name. Originally called *Don Juan DeMarco and the Centerfold*, the film is a modern version of the story of the world's greatest lover, or of a young man who believes he is the world's greatest lover. Even if he does not deserve that august title, the film shows that the modern Don Juan's prowess is not to be sneezed at.

Director Jeremy Leven is a clinical psychologist who regularly incorporates insights gained from his practice into his films. He began his career as a fiction writer before moving into screenwriting and directing. Leven wrote the screenplay for *Don Juan De-Marco*, with a credited assist from Lord Byron, apparently from Byron's long poem *Don Juan*. It is, however, difficult to see what Leven might have borrowed from Byron's pica-resque poem. Byron's poem ranges from knockabout satire to burlesque, and if the film attempted to meet that standard, it failed. Byron's satire is much closer in tone to Richard Lester's *The Three Musketeers* (1973) than it is to *Don Juan DeMarco*, which pretends to be satiric but veers quickly toward the sentimental/romantic, which Byron avoided like the French pox, if indeed he did manage to avoid that.

Don Juan is an interesting but problematic film which Depp agreed to make on condition that Marlon Brando would play the psychiatrist who treats the title character. Depp's admiration for Brando is well known and culminated artistically in Brando's appear-

Three Icons: Johnny Depp (in costume), Faye Dunaway and Marlon Brando from *Don Juan DeMarco.*

ing in *The Brave*, the most heartfelt of all Depp's films. The personal relationship continued until the great actor's death in 2004.

After talking a young man named Don Juan DeMarco out of a suicide attempt, Dr. Jack Mickler, a psychiatrist about to retire after a distinguished career, takes him on as a last patient — against the strongly-stated advice of his supervisor. DeMarco is committed on a so-called "ten-day paper," which allows the authorities to hold a patient for ten days before deciding on commitment. Mickler is strongly opposed to giving the young man behavior-altering medications, the usual treatment for such a psychosis, at least until all other options have been exhausted.

The development of the plot could hardly be surprising to the dedicated — or, for that matter, even the occasional — filmgoer. Mickler becomes fascinated with, even enamored of, the young man's fanciful past and is changed during the process of his therapy, which has no effect upon Don Juan but which soon begins to change the psychiatrist's relationship with his wife. DeMarco's romanticism is contagious, as indeed it might be, considering the beautiful women and idyllic photography used to embroider the tale. Of course, it is at least possible that the visualization is that of the psychiatrist rather than of the neurotic dreamer.

Over the opening credits we see a beautiful young man carefully dressing himself for an evening's engagement. After applying cologne and checking his cufflinks, he pulls on an expensive pair of black leather gloves and finally dons a black mask. Now completely dressed, with a black felt hat and a cloak, he walks past an outdoor restaurant, attracting considerable admiring attention along the way, and enters an expensive hotel where the doorman recognizes him and greets him pleasantly. In a voice-over, the young man tells us that he is Don Juan DeMarco, "the world's greatest lover," that he is twenty-one years old, and that he has loved more than a thousand women, but that the one he loves most has rejected him, and he plans to kill himself. Before that final deed, however, he intends to make one last conquest.

In the hotel restaurant he sits down at a table where a beautiful red-haired woman tells him that she is expecting a friend. In a remarkable sequence he takes her up to her hotel room, seduces her and brings her back to the restaurant before her date arrives. Her cry of pleasure blends into the high note of a singer as the film cuts forward to the restaurant and to the glazed stare of the woman, whose unfortunate and uncomprehending date will presumably never know about the clandestine meeting. With a bow and a flourish of his cape as she glances toward him, the young man takes his leave to the knowing and approving glances of the restaurant's patrons.

The great lover is, of course, Johnny Depp, and it is difficult to imagine another actor who could successfully have convinced a skeptical audience of the plausibility of such a conquest. For the film to succeed, it must convince its audience, at least for the two hours of the movie's running time, to suspend its disbelief in the truthfulness of the psychotic young man who is its major character. It is one thing to make a film about an imaginary Don Juan and quite another to convince the audience that he might actually have seduced so many beautiful women. He himself admits, however, that although they were not always perfect physical specimens, he always saw them as perfect.

The reviews were generally respectful — even admiring — of the high quality of the acting, but worried about the plausibility of the film as a modern variation of the Don Juan story. Peter Rainer wrote that the film is a version of Peter Schaffer's play *Equus*, filmed in 1977 by Sidney Lumet, a movie about "the drudgery of normality and the romanticism of the deluded." In *Don Juan*, the psychiatrist, "burnt out by the unfeeling bureaucracies of his profession," attempts to persuade the boy that he is not a fraud, that he really is the masked lover. Presumably this means that the psychiatrist, in attempting to find some meaning in his own life, projects his own feelings upon the young man. The viewers are meant to regard the deluded boy in torment "as a liberating spirit, a holy innocent." This Don Juan does not exploit women; "he's God's gift to them." Brando is "pretty sunny," but exposes the dubiousness of the film's position. The scenes between Depp and Brando are "curious, tricky little duets." Rainer added perceptively that pain for the boy is not an issue since he does not have any. Depp's refusal to pass judgment on his character is, of course, characteristic of his portrayal of character. In this case, it takes away any satirical bite the film might have and turns it into a guilt-free fantasy.

Lizzie Francke attempted to fix the film in the context of Brando's career. Like a number of other critics, she noted Brando's first appearance "alongside a vast billboard" and concluded that the film "might be about reminding audiences that it was Brando who was once the most beautiful and the best," while now that title has gone to Depp. Other critics saw the scene as simply a way of acknowledging Brando's vast bulk and getting the issue out of the way from the beginning. The film reminds us of classical Hollywood idols (Rudolph Valentino, Douglas Fairbanks, Errol Flynn) "when gentlemen could be gentlemen before the likes of Brando came along to rough things up."

Philip Kent also emphasized the similarity of Depp's character to the swashbucklers of early film. Jack Mathews was ambivalent. He regarded the film as "a romantic fable ... a celebration of the ideals of romance and seduction," praised Brando as "engagingly playful" and Depp as "irresistibly sincere," and concluded that the viewer can "either surrender to it or die a slow death." Anthony Lane rightly considered the film an essentially comic tussle between Brando and Depp. The young actor and the old one fight the "rather flaccid script." Depp is "snug" in the role and "too smart to try and squeeze us for extra sympathy" as Don Juan recounts his younger life. Lane, unlike some reviewers, was generous in his recognition of Depp's importance to the film. In attempting to find an honorable place for the film in the downward arc of Brando's career, reviewers tended to take Depp for granted. Depp, as always, subordinated himself to what was needed to fulfill his conception of what the film should be, and, as a result, received somewhat less recognition than he deserved. Simply, the film could have succeeded without Marlon Brando, but not without Johnny Depp. Other actors could have successfully played the psychiatrist, but who could have played Don Juan? Sean Penn? Keanu Reeves? Brad Pitt?

Denis Meikle, Depp's best biographer, was hard on the film. He attacked Leven's direction as being "staged entirely in set-up from an apprentice's handbook ... a leaden by-the-numbers approach," and called the film "a dud, a florid, flaccid post-psychological panjandrum of a film, full of sound and fury signifying nothing of note." The result can only be attributed to the director's "lack of vision." According to Meikle, Brando's being enormously overweight and having problems with his "wayward son," then accused of murder, also contributed to the debacle. "Brando," he wrote, "is still Brando, but the magic is long gone." The film is "a psychobabble of clichés," and what "remains is a clever concept reduced by peculiarly American sensibility to simple platitude" (145–148). Much of what Meikle has to say is, of course, a matter of opinion, but it is harsh to call such a commercial film a "vanity project," and the slur on "American sensibility," whatever he may mean by the phrase, is gratuitous. Meikle gives a fairly detailed account of the tumultuous conflicts during filming, and knowledge of the difficulties encountered by the novice director during shooting may have soured his opinion of the project. Still, the film hardly deserves the opprobrium heaped upon it. According to Meikle, Depp's reading of the role is too harsh and heavy and leaves the viewer "cold on an emotional level — the opposite of what is intended" (146). Who says so? Intended by whom?

According to the "Trivia" section of the IMDB entry on *Don Juan*, Johnny Depp, in the Turner Classic Movies documentary on *Marlon Brando*, says that when he and Brando were discussing the inconsistencies in Don Juan's character, his lines were rewritten before shooting so that he had no time to memorize them. Brando talked to the director and the director of photography, figured out the camera angles, cut up Depp's lines, pasted them to the cup he was holding and held the cup where it could be seen by Depp without being picked up by the camera. This is probable. Brando, of course, privileged spontaneity above all else, but it is likely that cue words were used rather than actual lines.

The film, while hardly a top-liner, was not a flop. According to *Box Office Mojo*, on a budget of $25,000,000, *Don Juan* pulled $22,150,451 in domestic and $46,642,080 in foreign receipts, for a gross of $68,792,080. Admittedly, this put profit somewhere in the future, but with DVD, cable and television revenue yet to come, the situation was hardly hopeless. The package was considered to have all the necessary ingredients for success, but fell somewhat short of the hoped-for box-office take, and director Leven may have taken the fall. Apparently, his direction of *Don Juan DeMarco* was considered wooden, at least by the standards of big-budget filmmaking, and *Don Juan DeMarco* remains his only directorial credit. He has, however, continued a successful career as a screenwriter. His recent writing credits include *The Legend of Bagger Vance* (2000), *The Notebook* (2004) and *The Time Traveller's Wife* (2009).

Anecdotal evidence — a survey by the present writer — shows *Don Juan* to be a particular favorite among women. While the film is never likely to become the equal of *An Affair to Remember* or *Sleepless in Seattle,* it is hardly likely to go out of favor.

1995 *Dead Man*
The Voyage of Life of a Stupid White Man

"The tigers of wrath are wiser than the horses of instruction."
(William Blake, *The Marriage of Heaven and Hell*)
"Here's white man's metal next to your heart."
(Nobody)
"I haven't understood a single word since I met you, not one single word."
(William Blake)
"It's so strange that you don't remember any of your poetry."
(Nobody)

While Depp was filming *Ed Wood,* he was approached by independent filmmaker Jim Jarmusch about playing the lead in a western Jarmusch was trying to put together (Meikle 134). The resulting film, *Dead Man,* written and directed by Jarmusch, is an avant-garde film by an experimental filmmaker operating somewhere on the outskirts of big-budget commercial filmmaking. Produced at a time when few westerns were being made — much less black and white ones — *Dead Man* is unlikely to have been made without the participation of Johnny Depp. It certainly would not have been the great film that it is.

After its showing at Cannes, *Dead Man* was purchased by Miramax, which wanted Jarmusch to cut the film. Either because he was "contractually protected from any such interference," or for some other reason, he dithered. Eventually the film was cut and released in the U.S. to an indifferent box-office reception months after its release in many overseas markets. Jarmusch has claimed that his refusal to reedit the film led to its indifferent promotion by Miramax. Jonathan Rosenbaum believes that the cutting of some fourteen minutes from the film did not injure it (Rosenbaum, *Dead Man* 16). If, as the present writer believes, the deleted scenes on the DVD contain most, if not all, of the cut material, he would agree. And, of course, we may look forward to the director's cut in an upcoming DVD.

After a quotation from French poet Henri Michaux — "It is preferable not to travel with a dead man" — the film opens with a series of brief scenes, almost a montage, of a train moving westward across the varied landscapes of nineteenth-century America. William Blake, an extraordinarily attractive young man dressed in a fancy, store-bought suit and wearing round glasses, watches both the changing landscape and his fellow passengers, who change from rural to frontier types in buckskin as the miles pass. Obviously distraught, he clutches his canvas bag tightly. The train passes over mountains, through a tunnel, across prairies, through

Johnny Depp as William Blake in *Dead Man*. This is almost identical to the poster that comes to life in *LA Without a Map*.

Monument Valley (or what looks like it) and into what seems an endless frontier punctuated by wigwams and a broken Conestoga wagon. The mountain men shoot buffalo from the train windows.

Blake is approached by an inquisitive stranger whom we have seen earlier firing the locomotive. The fireman, who says that he is illiterate, but may be familiar with Rimbaud's "Drunken Boat," states: "And doesn't this remind you of when you were in the boat? And then later that night, you were lying looking up at the ceiling and the water in your head was not dissimilar from the landscape, and you think to yourself, 'Why is it that the landscape is moving but the boat is still?'" Blake says that he is heading west to a town called Machine at the end of the track on the promise of a job as an accountant. The job is guaranteed by a letter, which he promptly produces and which just as promptly is jeered at and rejected as worthless.

Viewers of a classical bent will notice the imagery of the journey, of death, and of the inferno of the train's engine, and conclude that the stoker is, in fact, Charon, the legendary classical ferryman who took passengers across the river Styx into the land of the dead. (This is not the only reference to Charon in a Depp film. At the conclusion of *From Hell*, Inspector Abberline leaves gold coins for the ferryman.) Whatever the future holds for William Blake, the viewer already knows with certainty that not getting the promised job will be the least of his problems. At the conclusion of the prologue, which runs more than eight minutes, the major credits scroll.

After arriving at Machine, a coarse frontier town in the mountains strangely dominated by what looks like one of engraver and poet William Blake's "dark satanic mills," the American Blake is summarily and coarsely rejected at gunpoint by the president of the Dickinson

Metal Company, a violent old man chewing on a cigar. When Blake befriends a beautiful young woman, Thel Russell, who is attempting to escape from prostitution by selling paper flowers in the muddy street, she takes him back to her room. The loving couple is interrupted by the sudden appearance of Charlie Dickinson, who, we learn later, is the son of the president of the Dickinson Metal Company. When Thel tells Charlie she never loved him, he shoots her, but the bullet passes through her and mortally wounds our protagonist, although it takes him the rest of the film to die. The film is unclear whether she is trying to protect Blake or simply avoid the bullet. Blake, however, turns out to be deadly with a gun, or lucky, and kills Charlie.

Not in a good mood to begin with, and understandably unhappy at the murder of his son, Charlie's father hires three killers and promises them huge rewards for William Blake, dead or alive — but preferably dead. The three killers, who look like scrofulous rejects from *The Wild Bunch*, include Eugene Byrd, who is called "the Kid" but looks at least thirty; Conway Twill, who talks without ceasing; and Cole Wilson, a killer who would shame anyone Ford or Peckinpah could offer. The deadly trio set out to kill Blake, but soon discover that since Dickinson has offered a large reward, which keeps getting larger as time passes, others are after him as well.

On the run, Blake is befriended by a Native American named Nobody, described by one critic as "a large and inscrutable native American outcast," who tells him that the bullet cannot be removed, but decides to look after him because he believes that he is a reincarnation of the English poet and engraver William Blake. On the road — or through the wilderness — Cole Wilson, the deadliest of the three pursuers, kills his two companions and eats one of them. To survive, Blake himself kills two United States marshals. Along the way, Blake, who

Jim Jarmusch on location for *Dead Man.*

previously had only a nodding acquaintance with guns, and who managed to kill Dickinson only with his third shot at point blank range, somehow manages, like Dustin Hoffman in *Straw Dogs*, to become the most efficient killer around.

After a series of deadly adventures on the road, Nobody takes Blake by river to an Indian settlement to prepare him for his "great journey." Drifting in and out of consciousness, Blake is pushed out into the great waters of the Pacific Ocean in a magnificent canoe built especially for the journey, while in the distant background Cole and Nobody kill each other. In the film's final shot, the small boat disappears into the ocean vastness, and presumably William Blake becomes one with the Great Spirit. The destinations of Nobody and Cole Wilson are left for the viewer to decide.

The followers of director Jim Jarmusch admired the film. Some others were admiring, but puzzled, while a few rejected it outright. Rather strangely, Johnny Depp received little comment. David Sterritt, in the *Christian Science Monitor*, wrote that *Dead Man* had occasioned a mixture of cheers and boos at Cannes some months earlier and had been trimmed of some fourteen minutes since then. According to Sterritt, the film is "less an ordinary horse opera than a dreamlike meditation on life, death, and the value of friendship in a violent world." All of this will be familiar to those acquainted with Jarmusch's earlier films, which Sterritt describes as "offbeat excursions ... through space and time with ... characters who're as perplexed by their experiences as the audience watching them." Blake and Nobody have a series of adventures that are "by turns comic, scary and so bizarre that it's impossible to pin them down with an adjective or two." Sterritt leaves open the question, as indeed the film does, of whether the original William Blake had any involvement with our hero's "inner self." The conclusion of the journey is, according to Sterritt, "at once poetic, melancholy and mystical."

Kent Jones, in *Cineaste*, wrote that *Dead Man* shows a landscape that "America the conqueror has emptied of its virtues and turned into a capitalist charnel house," and that the film is bluntly "dismissive of America's very existence." Although the meanings of these statements in context are clear enough, they seem to contradict each other. In his conclusion, Jones put his rhetoric into overdrive. *Dead Man* has the "superreal physical import of Murnau's flights into abstraction — the train ride in *Sunrise* or the final moments of *Tabu*. This may be the supreme cinematic compliment, but it's also accurate." Whether or not we agree with Jones' conclusion, his point is well taken. The film's literary references, the black and white photography, the dark satanic mills juxtaposed against the American West, and the deliberate ambiguity, beginning with Depp's impenetrability, add up to a serious film — and one subject to a variety of approaches.

In a philosophical mood, Ben Thompson argued that *Dead Man* lacks "the implicit humanism" of Jarmusch's earlier films, the comradeship of *Down by Law* and the romantic innocence of *Mystery Train*. Thompson concludes, however, that the movie "will not disappoint those who appreciate the languorous, elegiac pacing as a respite from Hollywood's eternal wham-bam-thank-you man [*sic*]." J. Hoberman wrote that *Dead Man*, although set in the 1870s and "filled with creepy details," suggests "an imaginary post apocalyptic 1970s, a wilderness populated by degenerate hippies and acid-ripped loners forever pulling guns on each other or else asking for tobacco." Hoberman's description of Depp as "game, but necessarily blank," is perceptive, but uncharitable and off the point. He concludes that *Dead Man* is the western Andrei Tarkovsky wanted to make: "This is a visionary film." Thelma Adams did not much like the picture, but, like everyone else, had only praise for Neil Young's music and Robby Muller's wonderful black and white photography.

Denis Meikle discusses the influence of the Belgian poet Henri Michaux, who furnishes the epigram at the beginning of the film: "It is preferable not to travel with a dead man." Michaux, like Blake, was a favorite of the Beat writers. According to Meikle, Michaux's "spiritual pessimism and ten-year employment of transcendental drugs" furnished an exemplar for the film, which he describes as "a long, slow, grueling and ultimately inexorable descent into the inferno" (Meikle 158). This is perhaps too harsh a judgment. Other critics, including Suárez, discussed the influence of Michaux upon the film in more detail (Suárez 106–111).

Since its appearance, *Dead Man* has received more serious critical attention than any other Depp film; indeed, outside the films of Quentin Tarantino, *Dead Man* may even lead the critical pack. In one way or another, it opens up a large number of critical approaches. It is, however, fair to say that little seems to have been settled. This is, of course, perfect for any work of art because it means that the critical discussion will continue. And if the critics should discover that the work is incoherent, they can at least study the author's disturbed psyche.

The alert viewer will already have noticed that *Dead Man*, although clearly a western, has significant differences from the typical remembered western. First, it is in black and white, and the last significant western in black and white was John Ford's *The Man Who Shot Liberty Valance* (1963). While the look and feel of the film seem to indicate an attempt at historical verisimilitude, the opening quotation from Michaux and the mysterious reference to Rimbaud's poem "Le Bateau ivre," which the stoker could not possibly have known, hint at a darker purpose, reinforced by his wonder at why William Blake would possibly have followed such a slim lead as a letter promising him a job "all the way out here to Hell."

Justus Nieland confidently asserts that the film takes place in the 1870s. The continental railroad was authorized by President Lincoln during the Civil War and was finished in 1869, but the events in *Dead Man* hardly take place in historical time. Nobody, the Native American teacher of William Blake, says that he was captured by British soldiers, taken to England, exhibited, and educated before escaping to return to America. It is hardly believable that British soldiers would have captured a Native American and have taken him back to England some twenty years earlier and put him on exhibit. This would have been believable a century or two earlier, but hardly around 1850. And even if he had learned to read, it is impossible to believe that he would have known the poetry of William Blake and would have appreciated it. Blake was a little-known poet who wrote obscure poems and engraved them. He died in 1827 and became known to a wider, but still small, public only with the publication of his biography by Andrew Gilchrist, which was published posthumously after its author's death in 1861. And the reference to Blake's *The Book of Thel* is equally obscure and improbable. Of course, "Thel" might simply be explained as a shortened form of "Thelma"; and the reference to "Nobody," the name Odysseus used to outwit Cyclops in Homer's *Odyssey,* is fair game and need not have been known to justify Nobody's name.

Despite Roger Ebert's jibe that his two-day journey across the Kalahari Desert was shorter than the opening sequence of *Dead Man*, the sequence is, or will become, a classic piece of cinema which will have a long life in film classes, if nowhere else. And Robby Muller's black and white cinematography deserves all praise and will look even better in high definition. It may, indeed, approach the benchmark beauty of Giuseppe Rotunno's black and white photography of Visconti's 1957 film *Le Notti bianche* (*White Nights*). Rotunno, however, had the advantage of shooting on a set.

The acting is top of the line throughout. The film is especially rich in so-called cameos— that is, roles which took only one or two days to film but which are important for pushing the narrative forward, explicating it, or, as it sometimes seems, muddling it up. These include: Crispin Glover's enigmatic stoker, whose face is begrimed and who seems to know more about William Blake's background than he does; Robert Mitchum, his face wonderfully scarred by age, booze and cigarettes, who worships a bear and who is certainly part savage himself; John Hurt, apparently deprived of all pleasure in life except sycophancy; Gabriel Byrne, turning on a dime from contrition to anger and deadly violence; Billy Bob Thornton as Big George, who gets shot in the foot and deserves it; Alfred Molina, a so-called missionary, all Bible-quoting violence, anger and greed; and, in an inside joke, Johnny Depp's friend Iggy Popp as a dress-and-bonnet-wearing killer billed as Sal Jenco, another of Johnny's buddies from *21 Jump Street.*

Dead Man is usually called a revisionist western, and, like all films aimed at a mainstream audience, it is more readily understood as a generic formulation. Its position in that formulation is, although clearly distinguished, open to debate. Historically, the western was an outgrowth of the tales of chivalry which originated and developed in America from the dime novels so popular with young people at the turn of the century, and from Owen Wister's novel *The Virginian*. It grew up with the growth of the movies and the idea of manifest destiny, which developed as a justification, or excuse, for the dispossession of the native peoples already in place. Of course, the westward movement represented the displacement of primitive peoples by a technologically advanced society and would have taken place with or without any attempt, written or spoken, to justify it.

John Ford's *The Iron Horse* (1924), about the building of the transcontinental railroad, was a stirring vindication of manifest destiny that justified the displacement of the Native Americans and at the same time argued for a new dispensation which would include, among others, the Irish and the Chinese. The western, in its various incarnations, was the most popular of all film stories until after World War II. The Civil War story, generically only an outgrowth of the western's great theme, the birth of a nation, introduced complex elements of racial equality which needed careful handling for a mass audience. Of course, the Indian — the Noble Savage, the Vanishing American — was not absent from the western, but he was easier to romanticize in an occasional film or simply as a noble figure outlined against the sky. The representations were seldom realistic and almost always lumped the Native American peoples together. The most realistic depictions of Native American life include Edward Curtis' *In the Land of the War Canoes* (1914) and George B. Seitz's *The Vanishing American* (1925). Indeed, the scenes of the Indian village at the conclusion of *Dead Man* could almost be mistaken for outtakes from the Curtis film.

After World War II, Commander John Ford continued the expansionist ethos in a number of films, including *My Darling Clementine* (1946), but began to question it in parts of the so-called "cavalry trilogy"—*Fort Apache* (1948), *She Wore a Yellow Ribbon* (1949) and *Rio Grande* (1950)—and launched a full-scale attack on it in *The Searchers* (1956) and *Cheyenne Autumn* (1965). The passing of the old order took center stage in the westerns of Sam Peckinpah, most powerfully in *Ride the High Country* (1962). Although a number of critics, including Ernest Callenbach, believed that the film heralded a revival of the traditional western, they were wrong. If Caravaggio came to destroy painting, Peckinpah came to destroy the western, and *The Wild Bunch* (1969) marked its demise. The makers of later westerns could perforce only scramble for ways to write in the margins of that elegiac masterpiece.

The revisionist western, the acid western, the dirty western, or whatever it happens to be called, never really replaced the traditional western, which continues in a much diminished role to the present time. *Lonesome Dove*, although made for television, is clearly a classic of the genre. Others of some distinction include *Wyatt Earp* (1994), *Tombstone*, (1993), *Dances with Wolves* (1990), *Open Range* (2003), *3:10 to Yuma* (2007) and *Appaloosa* (2008). Although outdistanced by the gangster film, which is a closer approximation of the way we live now, the traditional western obviously has some life left, at least allegorically.

Recent revisionist westerns, derived chiefly from Robert Altman's acute analysis of the vices of capitalism, *McCabe and Mrs. Miller* (1971), and from Alejandro Jodorowsky's *El Topo* (1970), have hardly fared as well. The revisionist western has been ignored by the commercial mainstream and survives almost entirely in low-budget films by native filmmakers. In short, the Spike Lee of Native American filmmakers has not yet emerged.

Jim Jarmusch's west has, apparently, not a single white man of any merit, only cretins rich and poor who poison the natural beauty of the land and mute it to black and white. None of the critics seems to think that this is unfair; instead they have emphasized peyote, tobacco, guns and violence. While these references are important in the film, they are hardly central to its meaning. Violence is the coin of art, and the references could be to any mind-altering substance. Tobacco has a bad name, and all of us of any age have seen its deadly ravages. Guns have always been a fetish in westerns, but almost all westerns have clearly indicated that only bad men are expert with them. The others use them only for necessary purposes, and the young are taught not "to take their guns to town." Shane's advice to young Joey is still the exemplar here.

There is no doubt that *Dead Man*, at some level, privileges what George Santayana called "the corrupt desire to be primitive," even, or always, at the cost of verisimilitude. For example, before Cole Wilson smashes the skull of a dead man into mush with his boot, he says that he "looks like a goddamn religious icon." Although Wilson can read, at least well enough to decipher a wanted poster, the chances that a cretin of Wilson's background would even know what a religious icon is, much less comment on it, approach zero.

It is characteristic of *Dead Man* that, whenever a signifier is mentioned, it is immediately defused, derided and laughed at. This is a characteristic of highly conventional and often bloody art, and is widely used in English Jacobean drama, for example. In the most famous exchange in *Dead Man*, Nobody tells William Blake that he is going back to where he came from, and Blake asks if he means Cleveland. Obviously, Blake has a ways to go to understand the infinite, but the response undercuts the mysticism lurking somewhere inside the film; it does, however, emphasize the sacrificial nature of his death.

Turn the sound off of *Dead Man*, or, better yet, listen only to Neil Young's great steel guitar score while watching the movie, and what you have is a totally different experience — and, it can be argued, a better one. Visually, the film might be a version of Cormac McCarthy's novel *Blood Meridian* (1985), or perhaps *The Road* (2006), with McCarthy's virtuoso gift of language standing in for Robby Muller's photography.

The concluding section of the film — roughly two-thirds of the whole — is a long journey toward William Blake's death. Although not strictly told from William Blake's point of view, the movie joins a list of small but distinguished feature films in which the main character has been mortally wounded at or near the beginning of the picture. The list includes Billy Wilder's *Double Indemnity* (1944), in which Fred MacMurray fesses up to a dictaphone while waiting for his boss Edward G. Robinson, and Rudolph Maté's *DOA* (1950), in which Edmond O'Brien sets out in a race against time to find the man who has poisoned him.

Ambrose Bierce's short story "An Occurrence at Owl Creek Bridge" (1891), which describes the hanging of a Confederate sympathizer during the American Civil War, is a variation on the Dead Man theme. The story takes place in the imagination of the man, if that is what it is, between the instant when the rope tightens around his neck and the second or two later when he loses consciousness. One of the most famous of American short stories, the story has been filmed several times, including a version presented on the fifth season of *Alfred Hitchcock Presents*, directed by old pro Robert Stevenson and starring James Coburn. The best-known version, helmed by Frenchman Robert Enrico as *La Rivière du Hibou* (1962), was shown in America on *The Twilight Zone* and is readily available on DVD. Since Bierce's story and Jarmusch's film share a similar theme, it would be interesting to know if Jarmusch knew it. Nobel Prize–winning English novelist William Golding developed the idea to book length in *Pincher Martin* (1956), published in America as *The Two Deaths of Christopher Martin*, but Golding's scoundrel ("pincher" is argot for "thief") has nothing in common with Depp/Blake's innocence.

Nobody speaks in riddles, and the cultural references in *Dead Man* are all over the map and cancel each other out. William Blake takes the classic road trip from East to West. By comparison, Nobody has a better sense of history, moving from West to East across the Great Waters and back again. He is the only person in the film with a sense of both Native American and European cultures. And yet Blake carries unknowingly within himself what both the film and Nobody believes is the meeting of the two cultures, East and West.

The canceling out of meaning pushes the film relentlessly toward allegory. Nobody is the bridge between the two worlds of experience, but he himself is not an innocent. It should be emphasized that the Native Americans in the movie, although privileged, are far from perfect. Nobody, the exemplar of wisdom in the film, is of mixed blood, and has been rejected by both the whites and the natives. He is called "He Who Talks Loud, Saying Nothing" by Native Americans, has been cast out of two tribes, or nations, and is forced to wander between the winds, so to speak. He has been exposed to the white man's culture, has read the poet and artist William Blake, regards him as a great seer, and sees the "new" William Blake as a man who can unite the two cultures. It would be interesting to know if the real William Blake had ever seen a Native American, and if he did, what he thought of him. While there is no evidence in the film that Nobody is willing to sacrifice himself, he clearly regards Blake as a man whose death will in some way if not unite, then at least bridge the chasm which tobacco and peyote have, for all their efficacy, failed to do.

Almost all critics have noticed the darkening of Depp's character, which begins with the shooting of Thel, who throws herself in front of William Blake either to protect herself, to attempt to protect him, or to ensure that they will be killed together. In terms of the film, Blake is already a dead man learning to kill others when he shoots Charlie Dickinson a second or two later. In the remainder of the film, Blake becomes, if not an angel of death, at least his lieutenant. Unlike Satan in Milton's *Paradise Lost*, however, his face does not darken, although he does allow Nobody to put tribal markings on it. Clearly, however, if the allegorical interpretation is correct, they would hardly have been appropriate.

The allegory of the book has now become clear. Nobody is the only person in the film with the knowledge of two worlds. But since he is an outcast from both, he is forced to find a mediator. William Blake is a pure innocent who may — or, more likely, may not — be a reincarnation of the famous poet. In a traditional western such as Robert Benton's *Bad Company* (1972), Jeff Bridges and Barry Brown, two young men looking for experience, are corrupted by what Shakespeare's Falstaff calls "base company" in the process of gaining it. William Blake, like his namesake, is not a usual innocent. He is a "sin eater" of Catholic tradition, a man who absorbs the sins of others; as such, he becomes, during his long day's dying, not only an efficient killer, but somehow through the instructions of Nobody a sacrifice for the sins of the white man. The balance of William Blake's *Songs of Innocence and Experience* is thus maintained. The new William Blake does not lie down with the lamb, but with the dead fawn.

What would the real William Blake have thought of *Dead Man*? He lived all of his life in the city and is never known to have used any mind-altering substances. He was, however, well versed in neo–Platonic mysticism, saw angels in the garden and knew how allegories worked. He was a mystic who saw this world as a mere shadow of the real world which existed just outside "the doors of perception" and could be perceived by adepts who knew how to lift the veil. He probably would have liked Nobody, and he may even have considered his namesake educable. Had he not passed from the world of innocence to the world of experience? The poet might even have approved of the death of the younger Blake as a mystical sacrifice.

He would not, however, have accepted any sacrifice in the name of organized religion, which he hated, and would have applauded Jarmusch's presentation of the evil missionary who sells diseased blankets to the Native Americans as simple truth. After all, he had written:

> And priests in black gowns
> Were walking their rounds
> And binding with briars
> My joys and desires.

Whatever Nobody is, he is not "a priest in a black gown," nor for the purpose of the allegory does he need to be. The Catholic mass represents Christ as the perfect sacrifice. While William Blake can never aspire to this perfection — there is no indication that he would even want to — he can take the sins of others with him, including, of course, those of both Nobody and Cole Wilson, who are killing each other in the distance.

Topics for discussion include the film's place in the independent film movement, its relationship to earlier so-called "revisionist westerns," its critique of America as a charnel house, the destruction of the American landscape, the relationship between European and American art films, and the depiction of Native American culture (religion, myth, attitudes toward tobacco, peyote and other drugs, the treatment of narrative). In *Dead Man*, naturalistic details, improbable characters, and events spun out against a fake historical chronology rub against each other. The problem is to decide what the rubbing means.

1995 *Nick of Time*

Barely

"I'd like to know what's going on." (Mr. Watson)
"This is going to prove to be one of the most bizarre stories of the year."
(Television broadcaster)

After a series of commercial flops, Johnny Depp realized that he needed a main-stream Hollywood film. He said, "I understand that you have to have a balance in this town, between commercial hits and smaller roles, and that balance is tricky to maintain.... But I like to experiment and try new things.... I thought it was a good time to make a change ... after being accused by everybody of playing weirdos" (Meikle 164–165). In other words, Depp was agreeing to make exactly the same kind of film he had repeatedly turned down in the past. The result, unfortunately, was not what either the studio or the star had hoped for.

Nick of Time was directed by John Badham, at that time still considered a top commercial director. After a promising start in commercial filmmaking, including the enormously popular *Saturday Night Fever* (1977), which made a star of John Travolta, and a modish *Drac-*

ula (1979), which had a wonderfully hammy performance by Laurence Olivier as Van Helsing, and Frank Langella reprising his Broadway triumph as the old bloodsucker, Badham seems to have lost his way and has recently been largely relegated to teaching and directing for television.

Like *High Noon*, *United 93*, and *16 Blocks*, *Nick of Time* is shot in so-called real time — that is, the running time of the movie approximates the ninety minutes of the events shown. Arriving in L.A.'s Union Station with his young daughter, Watson (Depp) is picked out of the crowd by "Mr. Smith" (Christopher Walken in a bad mood) to be an assassin after he had dealt effectively with a skate-boarding thug threatening his young daughter Lynn (Courtney Chase). Watson is given a gun, bullets, a photograph and a schedule of the Governor, the person to be assassinated (Marsha Mason). Lynn is held captive by "Ms. Jones" (Roma Mafia) while Smith follows Watson to make sure the assassination takes place. No viewer of the film expects for even a minute that all will not come well in the end, but does hope for some excitement along the way.

Nick of Time was widely and largely unfavorably reviewed. While some of the reviewers were willing to give the film a pass, most of them were unimpressed by the movie's gimmick and did not believe that it worked. Kevin Thomas admitted, "You might not be able to go along with it if you had time to think about it," but believed that it represented for Depp "a smart move into a genre that could expand his audience without diminishing his stature."

Michael Medved attacked not just *Nick of Time*, but the whole concept of dramatic films attempting real time, and argued that real time in movies means that every moment, such as a trip up an elevator, must deliver "some jolt of significance" to the plot, and concluded that the film was a "humorless, self-important paranoid project" which "loses all energy" before its time runs out. Medved's argument, however, is not precisely true, since, as Hitchcock well knew, the fact that nothing is happening does not mean that the story is not building suspense.

Kim Newman, in *Sight and Sound*, was severe with Depp. After savaging the "super-inflation" of recent thriller/action/genre films, he criticized Depp's "pretty-pretty looks and reliance on neurotic ticks," and wrote that he "delivers an early speech so intently that it's difficult on a plot level to work out whether his claim to a cab driver to have come from his wife's funeral is the literal truth or a made-up excuse to explain his distress." While Newman's statement is true, repeated viewings show that the ambiguity was clearly intended by the actor to show Mr. Watson's (Depp's) confused response to the desperation of his predicament.

Terry Gilliam, whom no one has ever accused of being unsympathetic to Depp, said in an interview that he thought the actor was miscast, and that it was his weakest performance. Janet Maslin, in the *New York Times*, wrote that Depp seemed "muted by a not very interesting role," noted that Marsha Mason resembled Diane Feinstein, and cited an improbable reference to John O'Hara's novel *Appointment in Samara*. Some writers rejected the film completely as having poor continuity, stilted dialogue and a ridiculous plot. Other exercised their cleverness: "Depp but no charge," "a little Depp 'ill do ya," "*Nick of Time* clocks out," and so on.

The problem was not just with the gimmick of real time versus movie time; it also had to do with the improbability of the plot. After all, Zinnemann's *High Noon* (1952) and Hitchcock's *Rope* (1948) had operated in real time, but their plots were much simpler, did not involve gross improbabilities — at least beyond those which were given — and allowed for respites for the suspense to build. Hitchcock's experimental film, however, was confined to a single room and long takes, and is generally considered a fascinating failure by a great filmmaker. It is, however, still admired for its homosexual subtext in a period of extreme prudery. And Fred Zinnemann's *High Noon* (1952) is tautly directed and admired for its perceived political courage during the McCarthy era. Neither film has the "gross and palpable" absurdities of *Nick of Time*. They include the apparent ability of Christopher Walken to appear wherever he wants to at will, the picking of a total stranger for such a complicated assassination, and the improbable motivation of the plotters, among others.

Still, the film is not totally without compensations. A cynic may revel in the ridiculousness of the plotting, characterization and action. At the climax of the film, Charles S. Dutton, an admirable actor and a good guy in the film, zaps a villain with what turns out to be his artificial limb. One can imagine Luis Buñuel — the great surrealist himself — nodding his head in admiration. And in *Once Upon a Time in Mexico*, Depp's CIA killer reprises the trick. Whether this reprise is homage or imitation is a delicate critical question.

In a final confrontation between Mr. Watson (Depp) and Mr. Smith (Walken), Smith sagely observes, just before being sent to his reward, "Mr. Watson, I told him I could make a killer out of you." This thoughtful statement clearly indicates that the viewer has moved into Sam Peckinpah territory; but *Nick of Time* is not *Straw Dogs*, and the observation has not been honestly earned.

Apparently, the television version ended with Depp, his daughter, Dutton, and the Governor "hanging out." While this could hardly have improved the film, the scene should be included on the next DVD version.

Johnny Depp should have turned this film down. *Nick of Time* was a flop at the box office and did nothing to improve his standing with the critics, the public, or the suits. According to *Box Office Mojo*, the film, released on November 22, 1995 — the 32nd anniversary of the assassination of President Kennedy — took in only $8,175,346 domestically.

What happened? Depp is the most thoughtful of actors, and it may be considered certain that he approached the role with a clear idea of how he would play an anxious father trying to save his daughter and himself in a life and death situation against dark forces. Depp's natural tendency against scenery-chewers such as Christopher Walken, who could have phoned in his performance and with whom Depp was to clash again in *Sleepy Hollow*, is to underplay. Unfortunately, here, as in *The Astronaut's Wife*, the strategy did not work.

1996 *The Brave*

"One Hour of Anything"

"You can stand one hour of anything, isn't that right."
(McCarthy)
"The depressed person is a radical, sullen atheist."
(Kristeva 5)
"Ah, but a man's reach should exceed his grasp,
Or what's a heaven for."
(Robert Browning, "Andrea Del Sarto")

A beautiful young Native-American man, long-haired and casually dressed, walks through the street of a slum town apparently built on a garbage dump. His stride is determined, fatalistic, and he wipes away what might be tears from his eyes. He tells the Priest that he wants him to make sure his family gets the money after his death. "You sold your soul," the Priest says. "No," he responds, "I sold my body like a whore." The priest takes the money. The young man gets on a bus and watches as a convoy of trucks move toward the shanty town to destroy it.

The walk down the middle of the street echoes a multitude of western movies. We all know that the "gunman's walk" is the middle of the street, but this young man is no gunman. The priest is a "whiskey priest," and we recognize him as a recurring type. He has appeared before in John Ford's *The Fugitive* (1947) in a version sanitized and purified from the Graham Greene novel *The Power and the Glory* (1940). In the Greene novel, the alcoholism is a personal failing. In *The Brave*, the priest's alcoholism is a badge of his authenticity, of his feeling and sympathy for the people. And the bulldozers we know from the destruction of the Joads' home in Ford's *The Grapes of Wrath* (1940) and in Sam Peckinpah's *Junior Bonner* (1972). In those films, the destruction signifies the end of a way of life. Here, the signifier is clear, but it has been largely leached of meaning by the lack of coherence of the film we are watching.

The Brave began life in 1991 as a novel by Gregory Mcdonald (incorrectly spelled McDonald on the Internet Movie Data Base and almost everywhere else), published by Barricade Books, a small, independent New York publisher. Mcdonald is best known as the author of the Fletch mystery series. Chevy Chase played Fletch in *Fletch* (1985) and *Fletch Lives* (1989), and the character was revived, with Joshua Jackson playing the detective, in *Fletch Won* (2009). Mcdonald's early novel *Running Scared* was filmed in 1972 under the direction of David Hemmings, who is, of course, now best remembered for playing the lead in Antonioni's famous countercultural film *Blow-Up* (or *Blowup*). The novel was, apparently, much better received in France than in America. According to Mcdonald's official website, the French translation, *Rafael, derniers jours*, a title which Mcdonald says he prefers, was voted Trophees 813 Award as the Best Foreign Novel for 1997, the year of its translation into French, garnering extravagant praise.

The film has an interesting backstory. The novel was purchased by Aziz Ghazal, a former film student and the producer of *Zombie High* (1987), who hired Carl McCudden to write the screenplay. The resulting script, according to Denis Meikle, was "as irreducibly dark in tone as its source, with a stark undertow of NC17 brutality which put it on the same level as Wes Craven's *Last House on the Left*" (Meikle 189). In 1993, Ghazal killed his wife and daughter and then himself. After floating around in the nether regions, the script eventually reached Johnny Depp, who decided to direct and star. According to Meikle, the actor's initial impression was highly unfavorable, but the script stuck in his mind: "In spite of everything, I found the idea very interesting—could you sacrifice your life for love?" (190).

Although differing in many details, the novel and film both begin with a young man offering to sacrifice himself for the sake of his family, and end with him going to the sacrifice. After learning about "a job," a young Native American, so specified in the film but not in the novel, offers himself as a candidate for the leading role, if that is what it may be called, in a snuff film. Rafael (Johnny Depp)—the correct spelling in both book and film—is totally uneducated, can barely write his name, is married, has three young children (two in the movie), has never held a job in his life, is a hopeless alcoholic and lives with his family in Morgantown, a dump city which is about to be demolished.

After learning that "a job" is available, Rafael meets "the uncle," McCarthy (Marlon Brando), a fat man in a wheelchair, in a cavernous warehouse room with a torture chair. In the eccentrically titled chapter "C" of the novel, McCarthy examines the young man's strength, health and physical attractiveness. (In a brief "Foreword," Mcdonald quite unnecessarily apologizes for the explicitness of the chapter, but defends it as necessary.) McCarthy does not stint on a description of the terrible death that Rafael will suffer, but says that it will last less than an hour. He offers Rafael $50,000 ($30,000 in the novel) as a down payment.

Rafael prepares carefully for his death. He gets a haircut (the barber refuses to cut his hair until he has washed it), opens a bank account, goes shopping, buys presents for his family (including an electronic keyboard which plays "Amazing Grace" and a frozen turkey), and clothes for himself. And he goes to confession.

Most of the few critics who wrote about the film savaged it both generally and specifically. Lisa Schwarzbaum, in *Entertainment Weekly*, fired a comprehensive salvo that would have sunk a much stronger vessel than *The Brave*. She wrote, "You haven't seen discreditable novice directing until you see *The Brave*," and called it "a pretentious misstep" which represented "movie-star indulgence gone amok." In the film, the generalized allegory of the novel becomes more specifically an allegory of the plight of Native Americans. Unfortunately, however, as the critics were quick to point out, the film lacks the specificity of detail of the culture of Native Americans which would have made the film more convincing. Godfrey Cheshire made the case clearly: "There's no specificity or authenticity to the characters; they're simply generic modern Indians." Cheshire called the film "a turgid and unbelievable neo-western," and accused it of bad faith for its lack of authenticity. Certainly, the vagueness of McCarthy's proposal and the pomposity and obliqueness of his soliloquy, which echo Brando's earlier speeches in *Last Tango in Paris* and *Apocalypse Now*, give the film an off-center quality and, at least on first viewing, make the viewer uncertain about what exactly is going on.

Although the technical aspects of the film, especially the photography, courtesy of Vilko Filac, are outstanding, *The Brave* never manages to settle on a single visual or narrative style. The result, as Godfrey

Paternal Love: Johnny Depp and Nicole Mancera in *The Brave*.

Cheshire noted, is that the film veers between what he called "Hollywoodesque unbelievability and Kusturica-like faux realism."

The latest biographer of Brando, Stefan Kanfer, who probably had not seen the movie, wrote that *The Brave* was "another of those movies undone by its good intentions." The problem, however, was not the film's good intentions, but the inadequacy of the script and the novice director's lack of experience. Still, *The Brave* was not totally without defenders. Jane B. Kaihatsu wrote that the film revealed a mystical side of Depp, and that Rafael "is much more complex than he appears." She concluded that the movie develops "an ordinary theme (love of family) but demands an extraordinary understanding that transcends the planes of visual comprehension and expectations." While this interpretation is certainly special pleading, it at least represents an approach that allows an entrance into a film that might otherwise be rejected out of hand.

Depp, who is said to be the great-grandson of a Cherokee chieftain, himself seems to have regarded the movie (and probably still does) as a way to pay homage to native peoples. "In a strange way, I thought it sort of paralleled what happened to the American Indians 100 or so years ago," the actor said, and cited President Jackson, "whose face is on the $20 bill," as a leader of the genocide. Present-day America has, he added, turned a blind eye to the survivors, who often live in miserable conditions.

The Brave was badly received at Cannes, where it was unfavorably compared to Gary Oldman's *Nil by Mouth*, a movie which seems to have gotten little or no circulation, at least in the United States. Martha Pickerell wrote in *Time* that Depp was on the receiving end of a noble tradition: "booing at the end of a crummy film." When the film broke halfway through the movie, many people walked out. Although the reviews were vicious, the press conference was an enormous hit, with many people being turned away. Depp himself is said to have made a positive but inarticulate plea for the film.

Depp has clearly been influenced by Jim Jarmusch and Emir Kusturica in his treatment of cultures in conflict, but there is a hodge-podge of other influences at work, especially of John Ford and Sam Peckinpah. Rafael's walk down the street echoes the long-lens shots of the Wild Bunch approaching their shootout with Mapache. At one point, Rafael, courtesy of Federico Fellini, quite impossibly constructs in a few hours a sort of miniature theme park with all sorts of games and displays and apparently an abundance of electricity.

There is also an air of free-floating religious symbolism, including Rafael's being stabbed through the hand, suggesting the stigmata. The injury seems to have been immediately forgotten, even though Rafael wears heavy bandages on both hands as he sets out on his gunman's walk to his execution. (It is, perhaps, worth noting in passing that Depp, as the sin eater in *Dead Man*, stabs the evil missionary through his hand.) There is also the alcoholic priest, well played by Clarence William III, who attempts unsuccessfully to dissuade Rafael from his sacrifice and is left to mourn with his family. Apparently, in Morgantown, his alcoholism is a badge of his concern for the people, to be one of them, to suffer with them.

In collaboration with his brother Dan, Depp rewrote the script. The problem, of course, is that both the novel and the McCudden script end with the leading character, Rafael, going literally to sacrifice himself for the money his family is to receive after he stars in a snuff film showing his own actual torture and execution. Such a film would, of course, be box-office poison. According to Christopher Heard, the shooting script gave Rafael a change of heart in which he refused to go through with the contract. McCarthy, the auteur, so to speak, of the snuff film, is a white supremacist. In the ensuing confrontation, Rafael shoots McCarthy with his own gun (Meikle 190).

After Marlon Brando arrived on the scene and began filming, the conception of McCarthy changed drastically over the course of shooting. Needless to say, this interpretation did not mesh with the existing script and required considerable adjustments in the film. An evaluation of the McCudden script, the shooting script and the finished film would be a nice study in the making of a motion picture.

Depp was, of course, a long-time admirer of Brando and had become friends with him while shooting *Don Juan DeMarco* and the abortive *Divine Rapture*, a film which was to have been shot in Ireland but which had been closed down after three weeks of filming. In the original *Brave* script, McCarthy had been what Meikle calls "a Mafia thug," but became, in the at least partly extemporized version of Brando, "a mystical and oddly sympathetic messenger of death, whose oblique philosophical musings shift the film into a higher plane" (Meikle 195). Other writers have not been so sympathetic. Blitz and Krasniewicz believe that Brando shaded the original character into "a more mysteriously sadistic man who happens to get satisfaction from killing others" (58).

Depp has said that he does not believe that anyone needs to direct Marlon Brando: "You just turn the camera on and capture and take what you can take. What he came in and did for me was above and beyond anything that I ever expected. He really dug inside." His importance is out of all proportion to his brief screen time. As noted above, his improvisation, if that is what it was, resulted in a reshaping of the film and a total revision of the ending. McCarthy is, in fact, a philosopher of death, and it is interesting to speculate how closely his views of death are to those of the great actor impersonating him, who certainly knew that his death could not be many months away. As he speaks in a conversational tone seated in his wheelchair, his vast bulk, as one critic writes, "heaves with creepiness." Because he is so close to death himself, both in his person and in the character he portrays, he alone in the film seems to understand fully Rafael's decision. The Priest knows what Rafael intends, but neither understands it intellectually nor approves. McCarthy both understands and approves, but not quite in the way Rafael does. What he suggests is that Rafael's reason is not the real one, that Rafael is "half in love" with a terrible death which would ennoble him in the process and would be equivalent to the terrible death which his ancestors had suffered at the hands of the pale-faces. But even that, he suggests, is not the real reason: the real reason is in the black heart of Rafael himself and the terrible romanticism which such a death represents. It is an analysis and performance which some in generations yet unborn will call "windy philosophizing" and others will analyze with admiration and despair.

Although *The Brave* has been recognized, at least in some sense, as political, it is not a political movie in the sense that some of the films of George Clooney or Oliver Stone, for example, are. It relates to—or attempts to relate to—the existential nature of man's choices, and not to, for example, issues of urban renewal or welfare for the poor. Rafael, like Tom Joad in *The Grapes of Wrath*, is motivated by concerns for his family rather than for society as a whole, and it is worthy of note that the scene in which the authorities in that movie talk about what they are doing to improve the plight of the workers is certainly the weakest in the whole film.

By any reasonable standard of judging motion pictures, *The Brave* is a terrible film. Its ambition is so great, its achievement so small that it seems impossible to defend. But we must, at least in some way, pay heed to its sacrificial ideal and to its union of two great actors taking turns at going one-on-one with death without flinching.

Booed at Cannes, and still nearly unseen and unknown ten years after filming, *The Brave* did nothing to further Depp's career; but it did not harm it either. By this point in his career, Johnny Depp's more perceptive critics were beginning to take heed. David Giammarco, in his review, may be cited as typical when he wrote that Johnny Depp had achieved enormous respect and industry clout without the benefit of box-office hits. That, of course, was written long before Depp's appearance in *Pirates of the Caribbean*.

The budget of *The Brave* was said to have been just under $10,000,000, and it racked up an excellent $800,000 in presales; but it was a flat-out failure with both the critics and the audience. Whatever Depp may have felt about the film, he has said that he would never direct again: "I think that is something to go through and run away from very quickly." In an improvised segment in *Cannes Man*, Johnny Depp, when asked what part he wants in a proposed movie project, says, "I want to direct." In context, this means that directing is the last thing he wants to do.

As of 2009, *The Brave* has never been released in the United States, either in theaters or on video.

1996 *Cannes Man*
Cameo Man

Cannes Man is what is usually called a "mockumentary"—that is, a film which mixes fictitious characters with real ones and leaves the viewer to separate one from the other. Although often practiced on a small scale as a form of humorous humiliation, the model for the large-scale mockumentary is probably Robert Altman's *Tanner "88,"* an HBO series which pitted a fake presidential candidate, Jack Tanner (played by Michael Murphy), and his attendants against real candidates during the 1988 presidential campaign. The results were often painful and only occasionally humorous.

Cannes Man is a low-budget film almost entirely filmed outdoors at Cannes during the yearly film festival held there. The movie begins in Hollywood with the outdoor funeral service of Sy Lerner (well played by Seymour Cassel), a small-time wheeler-dealer producer, before shifting to Cannes and Sy's earlier wheeling and dealing.

Lerner has no script, no money, and no actors. He recruits a wannabe writer named Frank Rhino (Francesco Quinn), a taxi driver who has never written anything in his life, and the two Cannes Men/Con Men go to Cannes to raise money. Ironically, the wheeler dealers at Cannes mostly go along with the ruse, or pretend to, since most of them are, or have been, con men themselves. The best story is perhaps producer Robert Evans' tale of going to Cannes to raise money for his film *The Cotton Club*. At the last moment, Sly Stallone, who was slated to star in the film, pulled out of the project, and Evans had no star and no director, only a huge poster which he used to raise $8,000,000 in a few hours.

The Cannes men are a blasé lot who, nevertheless, at some level want to believe in the project. John Malkovich's boredom is profound but courteous. Toward the end of the film, Johnny Depp and Jim Jarmusch are meditating and smoking on the grass, so to speak, when Lerner and Rhino approach them. Although they tell Lerner that they are floating "on another level," they eventually listen to his pitch. The ensuing improvised dialogue is moderately amusing, especially when Depp accuses Rhino, who has sat down next to him, of invading his space.

Although it has no narrative and the ending is predictable, *Cannes Man* is tolerable. Depp's cameo, however, although well done, is hardly up to his usual standard.

1997 *Donnie Brasco*
The Gangster Lover

"If Donnie calls...." (Lefty)
"The real city, one might say, produces only criminals;
the imaginary city produces the gangster: he is what
we want to be and what we are afraid we may become."
(Robert Warshow)

Baltimore filmmaker and producer Barry Levinson acquired the rights to *Donnie Brasco: My Undercover Life in the Mafia*, by Joseph Pistone, with Richard Woodley, and eventually took a producer's credit when the film was made. Coming as it did toward the end of a string of commercially successful gangster films, which included Martin Scorsese's *Goodfellas*, among others, the complex script by Paul Attanasio had been considered by some as an uncertain commercial project; although written in 1989, the project had languished in turnaround. Additionally, the choice of English director Mike Newell, best known for his hit comedy *Four Weddings and a Funeral* (1994), was regarded by many as an unusual choice for such a quintessentially American subject. Perceived as a stand-in for Martin Scorsese or Francis Coppola, Newell seemed unlikely to receive much sympathy from American reviewers. Hs careful research and immersion in his subject, however, eventually silenced much of the criticism.

Some twenty-five minutes into the film, Donnie Brasco (Johnny Depp), in reality the undercover FBI agent named Joseph Pistone, is having Christmas dinner with low-level mobster Lefty Ruggerio (Al Pacino). Donnie would rather be home with his wife and family, of whose existence, of course, Lefty is unaware; indeed, he would rather be almost anywhere else than where he is, and he hardly bothers to conceal his boredom. Depp's gaze is masked. His beautiful face, which is hardly more than shadowed by cigarettes and life — that is,

Inscrutable: the face of Johnny Depp as undercover operative Joseph Pistone in *Donnie Brasco.*

by "ruin's wasteful entrance" — does not change expression during the litany of woes that Lefty recounts: his lack of respect from the mob, his junkie son, and his horses that don't win races when he bets on them. Sandwiched between these woes is, "I've got cancer of the prick."

In what director Mike Newell calls "the longest reaction shot in film history," a full seven seconds pass while Donnie's consciousness slowly returns from the lassitude in which it is trapped. "You got cancer of the prick?" Donnie asks. Lefty responds that it's in the medical books and passes on. It is a precious moment. Depp's slow awakening is the work of a great comic artist. Keaton or Chaplin could not have done it better.

In his commentary on the DVD, Newell discusses the glory of Depp's performance. Most acting, either on stage or on camera, is devoted to showing more or less precisely how a character is feeling at any particular moment. Donnie, by contrast, is hiding his real self from the mob and initially from the audience. After the film's opening, the viewer is soon let in on the secret. A speaker on a featurette on the DVD talks of the "mask" of Joe Pistone, the original on which the Depp character is based, of his un-readability. The members of the mob are, of course, adepts at concealment and work ceaselessly during long periods of leisure at games of one-upmanship, alternately concealing and revealing.

The film has an absurdist element appropriate in a gangster film, where so much of what happens is beyond the range of ordinary experience. The irony here, of course, is that so much of what the gangsters talk about deals with the minutiae of their everyday lives. Lacking any intellectual interests except, apparently, gangster films, they taunt each other endlessly and rehash the same stories. They "call" Lefty, leading him to think that they are going to take him for a ride — that is, to murder him — and present him with a lion (a real, live lion) and humiliate him further by saying that he thought they were going to "wax" him. The mob, of course, comes to trust Donnie, but they do not believe he has nothing to hide; indeed, they would not trust a man who was not concealing something, perhaps a murder or two, or a wife or two left behind. They simply do not think his secret is the fact that he is a federal agent.

Donnie Brasco received a good deal of serious critical attention, most of it favorable. Almost all reviewers praised Pacino's performance, and gave Depp more modest praise. David Sterritt, in the *Christian Science Monitor*, called *Donnie Brasco* "a reasonably smart and involving gangster yarn" and lauded Depp as "a largely versatile actor," but believed that the screenplay would have been better directed by Coppola or Scorsese. John Anderson, in *Newsday*, echoed a popular idea when he called the film "a bit old hat."

Thomas Doherty, in a long and carefully considered review in *Cineaste*, noted that in classic crime films, the cop generally ingratiates himself with the gang boss and not, as here, with the underlings. He calls Pacino a "type A actor" whose natural tendency is toward exuberance. Here, he turns down his natural energy to register as "a lowly subaltern." He moderates his voice, his energy and his dress to play a born second-rater. Ultimately, Doherty sees the film as homage, not to the traditional gangster film which originated in Sicily and the Italian landscape, but to the 1960s. While this idea may appear dubious, Doherty may be correct in his belief that *Donnie Brasco* belongs to what he calls "the third wave" of gangster films. Doherty gives Depp full credit. His performance is "all reactive interiors, communicating with his eyes, alert, wary and fearful.... His is the controlling intelligence, the gaze that directs the vision of *Donnie Brasco*." Doherty contrasts in some detail the coolness and control of Donnie's undercover work with the trauma of his personal life.

Perhaps remembering Pacino's earlier triumphs, J. Hoberman wrote enthusiastically in *The Village Voice* that "the movie belongs to Pacino," and compared his performance here with his earlier outings as Michael Corleone and Scarface. Hoberman wrote that the film is full of "snappy tough-guy stuff," but "is founded on an active moral confusion." As evidence, he cited the trashing of the Japanese restaurant and Lefty wandering "morosely" around the FBI yacht in Florida while Pistone's daughter is receiving her first communion several hundred miles away. Unlike Lefty, Donnie is "definitively not lovable" and "becomes a regular little mob monster." This is unfair and is not even true. Pistone does not kill people nor peddle drugs and death. What is true is that Brasco-Pistone comes to like, even to love, Lefty, but he knows that he is doing what he must do and that it is, moreover, the right thing to do. There is no evidence at the conclusion of the film that he felt the recognition he would receive would be greater than a secret ceremony and a commendation, no matter what his family may have felt.

Kenneth Turan believed that the film has problems in both structure and casting, which leaves "the themes hanging," and that even the movie's talented director "can't make the film feel other than second-hand." Turan faulted Depp's performance. He wrote that the characters of Edward Scissorhands, Sam in *Benny & Joon,* and Ed Wood "called on Depp to be a cipher whose feelings are difficult to read." Unfortunately, this "bland, opaque quality is a disadvantage here." Turan concluded that "whatever this star is capable of making audiences feel is not at the top of his list." This makes the film "more one-sided than anticipated." By whom? Presumably this means that Depp should somehow have made Pistone's marital problems more sympathetic. Even if that were possible, it is difficult to see how that would have improved the film. It also assumes that Depp's supposed lack of expressiveness was somehow inappropriate for the role.

Since *Donnie Brasco* appeared, the difficulties of balancing the life of danger as a police officer, whether undercover or not, with a domestic life has become a staple of the television long form, particularly *The Wire* and *The Shield.* In the latter series, the solution has been to make Vic, the protagonist, a brute both at home and at work. In *Donnie Brasco,* Pistone's marital problems are hardly exaggerated, but rather the inevitable outcome of such tense work.

Donnie, of course, in some way becomes complicit with the violence of the mob. How could he not? David Denby praised Depp's acting in the scene in which Donnie, to avoid detection because he is carrying a wire, refuses to take off his shoes in a Japanese restaurant and watches the mobsters brutally beat a maître d'hôtel. With a "few glances," Depp conveyed the impression that he was enjoying the violence. Unlike Turan, Denby believed that Depp is saying adios to his old "gentle-flower act, which is a relief. This actor can move." He falls in love with the feeling of danger and excitement and turns "his family feeling to Lefty, who needs him."

David Ansen, the reviewer for *Newsweek,* recognized that "the love and trust" Lefty felt for Donnie is the fulcrum on which the film turns. It is not "playacting," and Pistone/Donnie is "pulled in by it.... As with most whose lives are a performance, his sense of his own identity is a slippery thing." This is a genuine insight, and it turns the film away from Lefty, "the observed of all observers," at least in the opinion of most of the critics, and makes the greatness of Depp's performance readily apparent.

After the usual praise of Pacino, John Wrathall, in *Sight and Sound,* wrote that Depp is equally "astutely cast," and that his "customarily blank, unknowable demeanor" is perfect for a man who "has to erase his own personality" in order to survive among killers. Wrathall cited Pistone's listening to his tape recording of the beating of the maître d'hôtel as evidence.

Donnie Brasco is, of course, a gangster film, but it is also a film about a platonic love affair. The heart of the film is the growing relationship between Donnie and Lefty.

A detective sets out to infiltrate a criminal gang but becomes ambiguously involved with a member of the gang. Indeed, Pacino had himself portrayed such a conflict in the politically incorrect and much maligned *Cruising.* In the earlier film, however, he had become enamored of the sadomasochistic life-style rather than with a specific individual.

The mystery of the film, and the secret of the greatness of Depp's performance, is that there would seem to be little for Depp to admire in Lefty, who absurdly overestimates his influence in the mob, which is indeed practically, if not actually, nonexistent, and who is constantly ridiculed by them. He is not particularly intelligent, has no money, and cadges—in effect, steals—from Donnie. His son is a drug addict. And unlike some of the other mobsters, he does not even dress well, although he believes he does. "Dress like me," he tells Donnie.

And yet we fall in love—if that is not too strong a word to describe such a resolutely non-sexual relationship—for largely unknowable reasons: a certain hesitation, a turn of the head, a way of speaking, a reciprocal affection, an admiration which we did not even know we possessed for a certain trait, even because we see ourselves, and not necessarily a better self, in the person we love. And Depp's performance makes all that believable, if not understandable. Without it, Al Pacino's performance is wasted and *Donnie Brasco* becomes simply another gangster film.

The first third of the film, which chronicles the growing friendship between Donne and Lefty as Donnie works his way into the mob, is its most convincing. After the mob moves to Florida, the cast of characters expands and the film becomes violent and theatrical. Although well done, the theatricality and staging of the violence can hardly compare with the best of Scorsese or Coppola. But the film's greatness does not rely upon the violence, and it is easy enough to imagine a chamber play with only Donnie and Lefty seated at a table talking while the violence resonates and escalates in the background.

Only the two main characters are delineated in any detail. The other characters in the

Lefty (Al Pacino) showing Donnie (Johnny Depp) how to carry his money.

film exist only in their relationship with them. Michael Madsen, in a patented but effective performance as an up-and-coming mobster, and Bruno Kirby, a mobster who prides himself on his ability as a dancer, and others, are involved in complicated schemes and shifting loyalties, all of which are peripheral to the film's main interest, the shifting semi-erotic dance between Lefty and Donnie. The spectacular operatic theatrics of Scorsese and Coppola are largely absent — indeed, to such an extent that the plot's shifting loyalties are difficult to follow at a first viewing. Anne Heche, as Donnie's wife and the mother of his three young girls, scores in a thankless role. The viewer keeps wondering why she has so little understanding of what her poor husband is going through.

In *Donnie Brasco*, as in the best films of Howard Hawks, the characters talk themselves into life. The greatness of the movie consists of the conversations between Lefty and Donnie, and Donnie's entrance into the confidence of the gangsters. Depp, by instinct and calculation, here becomes a totally reactive actor; and Pacino, hardly the most restrained of actors in the best of times, follows his lead and gives an understated performance which is arguably superior to the overstated performance which had just won him an Academy Award for *Scent of a Woman*.

Director Newell pays close attention to details, and his mobsters are both psychologically and visually convincing. Both he and/or screenwriter Paul Attanasio add touches of their own, the most notable of which is the "fugazy." Pistone, posing as a jewelry expert, tells Lefty that the jewel he is attempting to fence is a "fugazy." The name, which is presented as that of a certain type of fake gem, is made-up. It is, in fact, as director Newell tells us in his commentary, that of a limousine service in New York.

The airport scene, in which Pistone is addressed by an FBI agent who is too stupid to recognize that Pistone is working undercover (and is soundly clobbered as a reward), was added at the insistence of the studio, who wanted to show Pistone in danger. Whether it is improbable is open to question, but it seems somehow to belong to a different film. The business about the lion, although apparently more or less authentic, also seems out of place. The violence of the film, when measured against the *Godfather* films or *Goodfellas*, is infrequent and restrained.

It is probably fair to say that any number of actors could have played Lefty. In the argot of the tribe, he is a "made" man, but he is made only in a provisional sense. He is an aging mobster who has been "called" to "wax" twenty-six men, a total which we may take to be exaggerated. Although not overly smart, he is a trusted member of the crime family who will do what he is told but will never rise higher in the organization. At heart a simple person, he might, in other circumstances, have held a day job and not become a career criminal. He lacks the self-knowledge to be a tragic figure, but the scene in which he prepares for his death is remarkably moving. He takes his money, his billfold, his watch, his religious medal and rings, and puts them away in a drawer. He says, "If Donnie calls..." and adds, "If it had to be anybody, I'm glad it was him." The film cuts to Pistone firing away at a shooting gallery.

Joseph Pistone, known as Donnie Brasco to the mob, is more complex. He is young, intelligent and ambitious, a straight arrow who convincingly infiltrates the mob. To make the character work, the actor must make Donnie someone in whom the mob can believe. Donnie is bright and alert. Depp's most convincing characters have a hidden intellectual life, or, rather, believe they have one. *Donnie Brasco* is yet another version of a friendship betrayed, a kind of reversed gangster version of John Steinbeck's pastoral novel *Of Mice and Men* (1937). In Steinbeck's novel, George is dedicated to protecting the feeble-minded Lennie. Here, Donnie knows from the beginning that he must sacrifice Lefty; he just does not know that he will fall in love with him.

A large part of the subtlety of Depp's portrayal is the effectiveness with which he takes on the speech and mannerisms of the mobsters. The years that the real Pistone spent with the mob are, of course, collapsed in the film into an indeterminate period of time. Pistone infiltrates himself so deeply into the mob that he becomes one with them. He steals $300,000 of the mob's money and does not report it to the FBI. Indeed, he is saved from committing murder only by the split-second intervention of the FBI; and Pistone, knowing that if he is exposed as an FBI agent, Lefty will be killed, yells, "I'm not coming out." But, of course, he does. And the reward for such law work, as moviegoers know from Will Kane's tin star in *High Noon*, or Gil Westrum's two dollar watch in *Ride the High Country*, will be meager — in this case a $500 check and a medal presented at a secret ceremony in which the big-shot making the award mispronounces his name. The world has moved on since frontier times, and Donnie Brasco lives in a more complex and morally challenged society, but the payoff is still the same.

Depp's face is a battlefield of conflicting emotions, and Newell recognizes the power of that image. The film begins with a close-up of Pacino's eyes and ends with a close-up of Depp's eyes. These images, similar but different, neatly encapsulate the shifting of emotional response from one character to another in the journey the viewers have taken.

The theatrical version of *Donnie Brasco*, which runs 127 minutes, was released on DVD after the film's theatrical run, and followed later by the "extended" version, which runs 147 minutes. Significantly, the extended version is not called a "director's cut," and although it contains interesting material, including some hilarious antics by Bruno Kirby, it dissipates tension from the relationship between Donnie and Lefty and weakens the film. The extended version also omits director Newell's fascinating commentary about, among other subjects, the performances of Depp and Pacino.

1998 *Fear and Loathing in Las Vegas*

Gonzo Journalism

"And Hunter [S. Thompson] did something that none
of us had the guts to do — he led the kind of life that
secretly all of us would like to have had the guts to do.
(James Carville, Wenner 305)

"He liked good weed."
(Deborah Fuller, on Thompson, Wenner 223)

"The over-analyzed life is not worth living."
(Tim Gautreaux)

"This is a bitch of a movie."
(Hunter S. Thompson)

"This is bat country."
(Raoul Duke)

"Only a goddamn lunatic would write a thing
like this and then claim it was true."
(*Fear and Loathing* 210)

Although it was hardly clear at the time, the coming together of three major talents in different fields — Johnny Depp in acting, Terry Gilliam in directing, and Hunter S. Thompson in the so-called new journalism — represented a favorable alignment of the planets that would produce a unique work of art. Although *Fear and Loathing in Las Vegas* is now recognized as a classic film — as its inclusion in the prestigious Criterion Collection shows— it was poorly reviewed when it appeared and added another movie to Johnny Depp's list of box-office failures. (According to Nigel Goodall, the U.S. box office return was only $10,672,566 on a reported $19 or $20 million budget.) Like Tim Burton, Terry Gilliam is a risk-taking director, and, like Burton, he discovered a perfect collaborator in Johnny Depp. Together, Gilliam and Depp found in the work of Hunter S. Thompson the perfect subject for their skewed vision of reality. Although Depp was not the first actor to play the man whom he called "the good doctor," but whom most people, including most of those in journalism and filmmaking, more appropriately called "the mad doctor," he used his uncanny gift of mimicry— honed by months of close observation — to make drug-addled insanity appear not merely a plausible but a preferable reality. But no matter how skilled the actor, the film would hardly be the artistic triumph it is without Gilliam's superb visuals to reinforce the performance.

Hunter S. Thompson is almost always referred to as a "Gonzo" journalist, a term which he himself coined in an egocentric attempt to separate his writing from that of everyone else. He succeeded. The term is invariably identified only with Thompson himself, and was another form of self-aggrandizement for a man with an ego the size of a barn. Actually, Thompson was a proponent of the so-called "new journalism," a form of writing which became popular in the sixties and which differed from the "old" journalism in its propensity to make the journalist himself a part of the story.

Proponents of the new journalism would, of course, respond that the journalist himself had always been a part of the story, as indeed he had. Many important American writers had worked as journalists— Walt Whitman, Stephen Crane and Ernest Hemingway, among them — but they had generally been careful to keep themselves out of the story, or at least to pretend to. During World War II, however, Ernie Pyle, A. J. Liebling and others popularized the use of the first person pronoun, although keeping, or pretending to keep, an objective stance. During the same period, a few creative writers, most notably Henry Miller, added a large mixture of fiction to their ostensibly non-fiction works. In short, by the end of World War II, the boundaries between non-fiction and fiction, which had formerly, quite wrongly, been thought secure, were under attack from both sides.

Probably the most famous work of the new journalism was Truman Capote's *In Cold Blood,* which created a sensation when it appeared in *The New Yorker,* became a best seller and was turned into one of the last great black and white films. Capote, however, was not interested in being labeled a "new journalist," and claimed to have extensive personal documentation which would substantiate every word of his mesmerizing "non-fiction

Manic instruction in *Fear and Loathing in Las Vegas*: Johnny Depp as Duke and Benicio Del Toro as Gonzo.

novel" about murder and punishment in Kansas. Capote claimed to have combined all of the best techniques of the novel with the minute accuracy of the journalist. The claim of documentation, however, was shown to be a fabrication. The book was, in fact, largely the subjective reporting of a fiction writer of genius. Other writers less skillful than Capote were trapped in the vice of truth. For example, Forrest Carter's *The Education of Little Tree* (1976), a memoir of a child's relationship with his Scottish-Cherokee grandfather, used as a text in many sociology classes, was proven to be a fraud and was removed by Oprah Winfrey from her list of recommended books.

Other notable works of the new journalism were Norman Mailer's account of the first Frazier-Ali fight, "King of the Hill" (1971); *Of a Fire on the Moon* (1971), a story of the Moon landings; and *The Executioner's Song* (1979), an encyclopedic retelling of the killings by Gary Gilmore and his subsequent execution. And Tom Wolfe, more than any other writer, became perhaps the chief chronicler of his time with a series of books detailing the culture clashes of the period, roughly the last third of the 20th century. Subjects included the NASA pilots and their wives (*The Right Stuff*, 1979), modern art (*The Painted Word*, 1975), and a variety of liberal pretensions.

Unable to chain his apparently limitless ambition to reality, Wolfe turned to the writing of long, naturalistic novels in the manner of Zola about characteristic American institutions: *The Bonfire of the Vanities* (1987), *A Man in Full* (1998) and *I Am Charlotte Simmons* (2004). Wolfe's persona — well-dressed, sophisticated, urbane and unflappable — is in many respects the antithesis of that of the overheated Hunter S. Thompson. Both, however, were instantly recognizable tabloid fodder, and, like Faulkner and Hemingway, warily circled each other, damning with faint praise.

Hunter S. Thompson (1937–2005) was as much a child of his time as the postwar drug culture ever produced. He was, like Johnny Depp, a native Kentuckian; but unlike Depp, he showed a precocious talent — in his case, as a writer who began writing in high school and continued by penning a weekly sports column for his base newspaper during a two-year stint in the U.S. Air Force. Released from the service, he quickly found his vocation as a reporter and wrote for a variety of prestigious, and non-prestigious, periodicals, including the *New York Herald-Tribune*, *The Reporter*, *The Nation* and *Spyder* magazine, the voice of the so-called Free Speech movement in Berkeley. The phrase "Gonzo journalism" was apparently first used to describe an article by Thompson which injected the reporter, in a self-aggrandizing form, into a narrative. The tendency, if not the phrase, was hardly new. What *was* new was Gonzo journalism's emphasis on greater subjectivity, and its emphasis on the counterculture and drugs.

In the 1960s, television was cranking up, and some old-time reporters and pundits were beginning to make names for themselves in the new medium, but print journalists were still largely anonymous. The publication of *Hell's Angels* in 1967 changed that and gave Hunter the notoriety of a minor-league rock star. The book is an account of Hunter's experiences with America's most famous motorcycle gang, and is the work of a genuine, if overheated, reporter. The book ends with Hunter resolving to sever all connections with the gang after he is severely beaten. He writes that he does not know why he was beaten; however, the reader, like the gang, could give at least a dozen reasons.

Fear and Loathing in Las Vegas, by "Raoul Duke," first appeared in *Rolling Stone*, issue 95, November 11, 1971, and issue 96, November 25, 1971. Subtitled *A Savage Journey to the Heart of the American Dream*, it was an immediate critical and commercial success. *Fear and Loathing* has an outline which might suggest a plot, but little more than that. What it has is a lot of attitude. The book is a first-person account by Raoul Duke of his adventures in Las

Vegas at the end of the sixties, the era of "sex and drugs and rock and roll." Although Duke's ever-looming deadlines and his hallucinations pretty much rule out sex and rock and roll, he does ingest a cornucopia of illegal drugs and pays close attention to the cultural corruption around him, at least as much of it as he can puzzle out through his hallucinations. His straight-man, who is only slightly less addled than he, is Dr. Gonzo, a 300-pound Samoan civil rights lawyer (a stand-in for Oscar Acosta, Thompson's companion on his Las Vegas trip). Set in Las Vegas, "the dark heart of the American dream," Duke and Dr. Gonzo systematically, so they say, "degrade, abuse and destroy" the symbols of the excesses of a corrupt and decaying society. Whether their work is more demolition or celebration is still an open question.

Thompson destroys all barriers between himself and his protagonist. What is new is the way in which Duke, universally recognized as a double for Hunter himself, condemns the society in which he is a greedy participant while at the same time glorifying that excess. He manages this through the skillful use of the first-person narrative. In effect, he divides himself into two persons and in the end separates himself from Dr. Gonzo, whom he somehow regards as an extremist. Thompson has no interest in other characters, either male or female, except as objects of buffoonery and burlesque, and filters the world totally through his own drug-addled consciousness.

Fear and Loathing in Las Vegas is a permanent book, which may justly be regarded as a great novel of place, a kind of 20th century *Huckleberry Finn*, with Duke standing in as Huck's counterpart. If slavery is the difficulty with which Mark Twain had to deal, consumerism and the drug culture is Thompson's field. The romanticism of the drug culture, well documented in Althea Hayter's *Opium and the Romantic Imagination,* may be said to have originated in Thomas De Quincey's *Confessions of an English Opium Eater* (1822), and to have continued in any number of works, both pro and con, to the present day. De Quincey writes about the "pleasure" of opium before moving on to the "pains," and while later novels (*The Golden Spike, Cain's Book, The Man with the Golden Arm,* and a library of others) have emphasized the pains, the pleasures have always been the attraction for users, at least in the beginning. That Thompson romanticizes the drug culture is beyond question. The hallucinations which he describes are both truly terrifying and hilariously funny. Doubtless, many youngsters, and perhaps an oldster or two, might be tempted to take a trip or two.

Like Jack Kerouac's *On the Road* (1951), which, despite its fame, has never been filmed, *Fear and Loathing* was a difficult film project. *Where the Buffalo Roam* (1980), the first movie to be based on Thompson's skewed vision of reality, furnishes a useful example of the difficulties involved in making any film based, however loosely, on Thompson's life and works. Although more expansive than Terry Gilliam's later film, which takes place almost entirely in Las Vegas, *Buffalo* centers on the same two drug-addled central characters, a journalist and his lawyer.

Where the Buffalo Roam opens over Ralph Steadman's elegant credits with scenes of buffalo in a snow-covered landscape. Nearby, in his mountain home, Dr. Hunter S. Thompson is, as usual, attempting, with little success, to meet a deadline. The film evolves into a series of episodes concerning the Gonzo journalist (Bill Murray) and his sometime friend and lawyer Carl Lazlo (Peter Boyle) during the years of the Nixon administration. When a group of student demonstrators are arrested for possession of marijuana, Lazlo defends them belligerently, but ineptly, and they receive draconian sentences. When Lazlo loudly and physically protests, he is disbarred and given a prison sentence. When he next appears, he is involved with a bunch of crazy, dope-addled revolutionists captured by federal agents. And finally, he appears after Thompson has been kicked off the Nixon presidential campaign plane and attempts unsuccessfully to enlist him in his revolutionary cause by promising him guns, women and dope. Thompson refuses, and goes back to his mountain lair and his dog trained to attack a Nixon dummy on command.

Despite the fact that Boyle, rather strangely, is top-billed, his role is secondary to that of Thompson. After breaking out of a hospital with Lazlo's help, and being sent to cover the 1972 Super Bowl, Thompson gives his press tickets and hotel room reservations away, including nearly unlimited dining and boozing privileges, and heads for the open road. Wherever he goes he takes enormous amounts of booze and illegal substances, and creates chaos in hotels, hospitals and courtrooms. He even meets Richard Nixon in a restroom and accosts him there.

Admittedly, making a commercial film about Hunter S. Thompson is a tricky proposition, but *Where the Buffalo Roam* simply does not work. Bill Murray is an excellent comedian and occasionally a superb actor, and he does a commendable job struggling against a wrongheaded script. Writer Mitch Glazer put the matter bluntly: "Hunter's presence is so strong that it fucks actors up" (Wenner 227–228). Glazer noted that, years later, he saw Murray doing a Thompson imitation in *Scrooged*, a version of Dickens' *A Christmas Carol*. Glazer believed that at some level Murray withheld his "approval" of the character and did not go the whole way. Approval, of course, is the wrong word here. The character is the character, and it is not for the actor to approve or disapprove of him; the actor's job is to make him understandable. How he does this is up to him. He may be a classically trained actor, a method actor, a purely intuitive one, or a gorilla in disguise. The result is what counts. The actor may, of course, get too close to the flame and, like Heath Ledger, be forced to pay the price.

Buffalo was neither a commercial nor a critical success, and first-time producer and director Art Linson, although he continues to work as a writer, has not directed another film to date. He deserves better. *Buffalo* attempts to have its cake and eat it too. That is, Thompson is presented as a man with no limits who has limits. Unlike Lazlo, he is not a revolutionary, and he does not advocate the violent overthrow of the government. Nonetheless, the list of his trespasses is long and varied: he ingests an incredible variety of legal and illegal drugs, he drives drunk, he trashes hotel rooms and allows them to be trashed, he creates anarchy on airplanes, he collects large fees for his appearance on college campuses and arrives drunk, he drinks in court and sasses the judge (who would surely have found him in contempt), he keeps an arsenal and discharges guns carelessly when in his cups, he egregiously and feloniously assaults President Nixon in a restroom, and so on. It might be argued that he is an honorable man in a dishonorable time, but he seems to be advocating anarchy instead of reform.

One thing which *Buffalo* gets right is the use of Ralph Steadman's visuals, which were patterned after those on the cover of the book, as illustrations. Gilliam, himself an illustrator, sarcastically described by Thompson as a "cartoonist," recognizes graphic talent when he sees it and has used Steadman's concepts throughout his film to give his visuals a unified structure. Steadman's illustrations for *Fear and Loathing* are classics, or soon will be, and are likely to become as closely identified with the book as John Tenniel's illustrations are identified with *Alice in Wonderland*.

Happily, the failure of *Where the Buffalo Roam* did not lessen interest in Thompson's Las Vegas story, which retained its fascination. Director Alex Cox (*Syd and Nancy*) and Tod Davies wrote a screenplay for *Fear and Loathing*. Unfortunately, they quarreled with Thompson over the script; producer Laila Nebulsi signed Terry Gilliam to direct; and Gilliam and Tony Grisoni wrote a new screenplay (McKeen 236). Director Terry Gilliam was clearly the right man to project Thompson's skewed visuals, and Johnny Depp, with his deep interest in the drug culture and what it represented, was clearly the right man to play Hunter S. Thompson's stand-in, Raoul Duke. Benicio Del Toro ate sixteen donuts a day and gained many pounds to play Dr. Gonzo, and a number of famous actors, some of them unrecognizable, play supporting roles. They include Gary Busey, a pre–*Spider-Man* Tobey Maguire, Christina Ricci, Harry Dean Stanton, and Lyle Lovett. When Hunter S. Thompson himself actually shows up in the film at least twice, the movie becomes Kafkaesque and turns the whole cast into a projection of Thompson himself—which is, of course, what it has been all along.

Terry Gilliam, self-described as "one of nature's mutants," is a cartoonist by birth and training, and a film director by choice. Gilliam was born in Medicine Lake, Minnesota, on November 22, 1940. His family moved to Los Angeles in 1951, where, according to Gilliam's mother on the DVD supplements to *Tideland*, he was an outstanding and non-controversial student. After graduating from Occidental College in 1962, he moved to New York and worked on Harvey Kurtzman's *Help!* magazine, and briefly on *Mad*. After *Help!* folded in 1965, he moved to London, where he worked as a cartoonist and art director of *London Life* magazine, and as a television animator.

Gilliam's breakthrough came in 1969 when he began to do animation for the satirical television series *Monty Python's Flying Circus*, made by a group which included, in addition to Gilliam, Graham Chapman, Terry Jones, John Cleese, Eric Idle and Michael Palin. Gilliam's job, at least initially, was to link together, albeit loosely, the live segments. Gilliam was co-writer, animator, and performer for the first Monty Python film, *And Now for Something Completely Different* (1971). Ironically, this was the year in which *Fear and Loathing in Las Vegas* was published. The Flying Circus series continued for four seasons and led to *Monty Python and the Holy Grail* (1974), with Gilliam as co-writer, performer, and co-director with Terry Jones; *Jabberwocky* (1977), director, co-writer; *Monty Python's Life of Brian* (1977), designer, co-writer, performer, animator; *Time Bandits* (1981), director, writer, producer; and *Monty Python's The Meaning of Life* (1983), co-writer, performer, animator. Appropriately, *The Meaning of Life* was the last Monty Python film. Of the movies, only *Time Bandits* was a true Gilliam film; all the others had been closely identified with the Monty Python group. The group was getting old. Graham Chapman died one day before the twentieth anniversary of the first broadcast of the series, and some apparently half-hearted attempts to revive the group were unsuccessful. Terry Gilliam moved on to a full-time career in film directing, a move which some critics felt he should have taken earlier.

Based on the indifferent, if varied and occasionally successful, careers of the members of the Monty Python group after its breakup, it is interesting to speculate upon Gilliam's exact contribution. While the series was certainly a collaborative exercise, it was not an equal one. Just as nineteenth-and twentieth-century critics of what has been called "Shakespeare and Company" have spent an inordinate amount of time calculating, almost line by line, what each contributor wrote, so future critics, with nothing better to do, will likely argue which Monty Python man wrote what, where and when.

Terry Gilliam is anti-authoritarian in spirit, and opposed both the Viet Nam and Iraq conflicts. In *Brazil* (1985), the terrorists need war to survive. According to Gilliam, "If you want weirdness, reality delivers it." Gilliam's career, dogged by controversy and bad luck, has sometimes ground to a halt for years at a time. Examples include the enormous furor over *Brazil*, the cost overruns on *Baron Munchhausen*, the halting after shooting had begun on *The Man Who Killed Don Quixote*, and the death of his star before *The Imaginarium of Doctor Parnassus* was completed. Pretty much everything has happened to him that can befall a commercial, big-budget filmmaker. (He would, of course, with some justification, deny that he is a "big-budget" filmmaker and complain that his budgets have been only moderate, at best.) But, like the Timex watch, "He takes a licking and keeps on ticking."

The genesis of *Fear and Loathing* is byzantine and eventually led to a complex row about the credits for the film. Director Alex Cox (*Syd and Nancy*) initiated the project, purchased the rights, and wrote a screenplay with Tod Davies, which Gilliam says that he and co-writer Tony Grisoni did not see. One of the main reasons the Motion Picture Association of America's arbitration system was set up was to guarantee a fair shake for the writer or writers of a screenplay against the often spurious claims of the directors. Ray Bradbury harbored a forty-year grudge against John Huston, and even savaged him in a novel, when he claimed co-writing credit for Huston's *Moby Dick*. According to Bradbury, he had hundreds of pages of script, and Huston had only a copy of the screenplay with notes written in the margin. In any event, Terry Gilliam and Tony Grisoni were initially denied any credit, but eventually won top-line credit on appeal.

According to William McKeen, Depp met Thompson at Aspen in December 1995 at the Woody Creek Tavern (327). Thompson liked guns and explosions of all calibers and sizes, and back at Thompson's Owl Farm, they "set off a bomb, bonding over munitions" (328). In his DVD commentary, director Terry Gilliam says that after Alex Cox was dismissed from the project, the studio eventually called on him to take over the production and bring it in under $19,000,000. The actors had already been hired, and the project was an exercise "in seeing if one could work fast and cheaply again — really cheaply."

The reviews, which were mainly negative, tended toward the hyperbolic and generally condemned the film for its excesses. David Kronke called the movie "a spectacular wipeout, a visionary mess that is so unrelentingly dissolute that it may prove to be impenetrable for mass tastes ... simply a downer." Kronke praised Depp's performance, but surmised, probably correctly, that "someone that plastered [as Duke] probably doesn't have much of an emotional interior life to begin with." The real question, however, is not how much "emotional interior life" Duke had, but whether Gilliam found a visual equivalent for that life, or for whatever Duke thought that it was. The answer to that question would certainly have to be yes.

Rod Dreher thought that it was difficult to think of any director better suited to film Thompson's "freakedelic memoir" than Gilliam, but that the "livid movie" was a "fascinating disappointment." Dreher feared that "mainstream audiences" would be "viscerally repulsed" by the "assaultive intensity of certain scenes," and cited the bathroom sequences as evidence. Linda Ruth Williams, the feminist theoretician on pornography, speculated that Gilliam's multicultural background and his visual style had aided the project, and called the film "from bold word to excessive image ... a flamboyant adaptation." The movie attempted to see the present in terms of the past and to give it one more twist. Psychedelic drugs here became "the hand maidens of misanthropy." In her opinion, the film attempted to implicate everyone, and got bleaker "as it proceeds toward the humiliation of Ellen Barkin's waitress." This reading has the advantage of interpreting the film as Gilliam wanted it to be interpreted. Whether it is the best reading is still an open question.

A few reviewers hoped (vainly, as it turned out) that the film might serve as some sort of cinematic bridge between the oft-dismissed "'60s sensibility" and the cultural stagnation of today's youth. Unfortunately, this places a burden on the movie that few, if any, works of art, much less a motion picture, could support. A number of reviewers, J. Hoberman among them, compared *Fear and Loathing* to *Easy Rider*. Hoberman, whose sensibility certainly must have been toughened by watching Antonioni films, was probably alone in regarding the film as "lighter than one might expect," and characterized it as "at once prestigious literary adaptation and slapstick buddy flick."

Hunter S. Thompson, of course, complained about anything that came to mind, and threw stones at both Gilliam and Depp. When Depp improvised a bit throwing coins at the little people in the casino, Thompson complained that he would never have thrown coins at dwarves, and groused about the "renegade outlaw journalist" being "portrayed by a heart-throb." He derided Gilliam at every turn, and professed contempt at one time or another for everyone connected with the film. His most telling complaint, however, was delivered in one of his letters to Johnny Depp, cited in the Criterion DVD commentary. Thompson complained that the film had dumped the social commentary of his original, particularly the criticism of the Viet Nam war, for a movie about drugs. If the purpose of the change had been to aid the movie's prospects at the box office, it was not successful. It is, however, doubtful that more references to the Viet Nam conflict would have improved either the film or Thompson's disposition.

Artistically, the problem with *Fear and Loathing in Las Vegas* is that the movie starts at so high a pitch of insanity that it has nowhere to go. Gilliam attempts, with little success, to vary the insanity and move it toward some sort of reasonable climax. While there is some variation in movement, Duke's drug-induced stupor, no matter what its cause, produces striking hallucinogenic visuals that quickly exhaust viewers. Even a DVD viewer who has seen the film several times is likely to retire to a less exhausting Depp venue.

The customary way that artists deal with the problem of gaining sympathy for a weird protagonist is to begin with a narrator who seems to be normal, although he may be, in reality, as mad as a hatter. The narrators of Poe's tales pretend to a sanity they do not actually possess. The descent into madness begins on a gentle downward slope before speeding up and descending into the abyss. Both Thompson and Gilliam begin with the protagonist already far along in the process. Thompson maintained, and Gilliam agreed, that the insanity belonged to the world, that although the protagonist might be a bit addled by dope, the world was much more insane than he. Of course, Poe never fell for that ruse. "The terror of which I speak," he wrote, "is not of Germany but of the soul."

One might, of course, argue, as Duke essentially does, that the only way the malaise of the sixties can be fought is by burlesque, irony and a generous supply of dope. But the genuinely hilarious sallies of Duke so drolly delivered by Johnny Depp are at war with what the film's first audience perceived as Gilliam's brutally realistic visuals. The acceptance of these visuals is largely a matter of taste, and today's audience is much more likely to accept them. The extreme violence of Eurotrash cinema, Japanese horror films, and CGI mayhem has hardened the audience. (It does not necessarily follow, however, that it has made it more violent.) Gilliam abandoned the flatly visual one-dimensional Disney animation and substituted a harsher, more realistic style. He was, like Tim Burton, ahead of his time, but time has reeled them in, and Gilliam's animation now seems not so much shocking as post-modern.

Several reviewers of the film thought it should have condemned the drug culture. The movie, however, is not an endorsement of the drug culture—far from it; but even if it were, it should be given a pass. The terrors of hard drugs were not as dramatically apparent in the 1960s as they are today, when the terrors of addiction are vividly depicted in both non-fiction works and on television series, especially on *The Wire*. Gilliam himself is not a drug user, and his imagination needs no chemical stimulants. His visual projections are merely an elaboration into a darker realm of his Monty Python visuals. The first visualization, given at the start of the movie, is of "Bat Country," and shadows of bats fly around Duke's field of vision. As the film progresses, the visions become more grotesque, and finally nearly all-encompassing as the director conjures up a flooded hotel room which looks as if Lucifer has opened Hades and loosed all the demons. Gilliam has said that the ex-users to whom he showed the film approved of the visuals at the beginning of the movie, but became more and more unhappy with them as the film moved toward its climax.

In a scene originally intended to be the last in the film, but later consigned to the extras on the DVD, Duke bumps into the American dream "in reality" and is prevented by his cynicism from recognizing it. Leaving Las Vegas, Duke stops in the middle of the desert for gasoline and goes inside the gas station restaurant for refreshment. He is served a cold beer with a nice head of foam by an old man. When a beautiful young girl enters, greets her grandfather warmly, and kisses him on the cheek, Duke immediately sees an example of "back-country inbreeding," or at least some sort of perversion. Duke has become so corrupted that he cannot see "the real thing," as Henry James would put it, before his eyes. Terry Gilliam notes in his commentary that it is the only time Duke removes his glasses during the entire film. Gilliam says he removed the scene because tests showed that "the audience had been so corrupted by the film" that they thought the old man, wonderfully played by Ron Howard's father, was really having an incestuous relationship with his granddaughter and was indeed pimping for her. Gilliam thought this a failure by the audience. After two hours of debauchery, however funny, what else were they to think? It is more likely to have been a failure in the staging of the scene. Perhaps the film does not need this sequence, but it clearly needs a scene like it to show that the normal world exists outside the nightmare realm of Las Vegas. The nice touch added spontaneously by Depp during shooting when Duke leaves a guilty tip shows that the actor recognized the scene somehow needed to be clarified for the audience to understand it.

Whatever Hunter S. Thompson and his entourage may have thought of Gilliam's *Fear and Loathing in Las Vegas*, the director himself recognized its importance. In his preface to Bob McCabe's collection of his work entitled *Dark Knights and Holy Fools*, Gilliam wrote: "As I continued with that movie, it started to become clear to me that it was in many ways a culmination of many things for me, maybe even a natural end to one stage of my work" (Unpaged). He meant, apparently, that it was "a natural end" to the first part of his career in films, a part in which the "visual aspect" and animation were of paramount importance, and that he was now free to place a greater emphasis on other aspects of film, particularly drama. The jury is still out on whether that statement can be justified.

According to the Criterion DVD supplement, Depp spent a great deal of time with Thompson, observing him and "developing his character" for the film. In a DVD extra filmed in 2006, Depp reads some of his correspondence with Hunter on camera. He speaks of the Hunter S. Thompson Memorial Cell in the Jefferson County Jail — does this placard Depp mentions actually exist? — where the celebrated author was briefly imprisoned on a "bogus rape charge." The egotistical Thompson, always unhappy when attention was turned away from himself, abused Depp, but the actor was unrelenting and responded with a vulgarity. Depp told Thompson that if his portrayal was accurate, the public would likely hate him for the rest of his life. Although he claimed to be merely "an observer," Thompson clearly recognized the importance of publicity, and aided Depp with his choice of clothes for the movie.

Assisted by Gilliam's direction, Johnny Depp's portrait of Raoul Duke becomes the fulcrum on which the whole film turns; indeed, it can be argued that it turns the movie into a solipsistic portrayal of Thompson's mind — or, rather, his perceptions — to the exclusion of all else. Although Thompson was a large man and Depp a comparatively small one, the resemblance between them was uncanny, especially when Depp was in costume, wearing shorts, tennis shoes, pith helmet and tinted glasses, his head shaved and cigarette holder atilt. And Depp was much better at catching Thompson's pervasively ironic tone than the Gonzo journalist himself was. Thompson is Depp lite; Depp is "the real thing."

The book was always about Thompson himself. It has no plot, only a sequence of incidents, most of them ironic, and all of them filtered through Duke's addled consciousness.

While this has the perhaps unfortunate consequence of toning down the many cultural references of the film, it turns it into a dream in which everything becomes subservient to Depp's performance. The parade of gifted actors who appear in the film become shadows, faded aspects of Depp's Thompson. Gilliam has commented upon the fact that Depp's performance, honed by his native genius and by months of observing Thompson, quickly nailed his reading in one or two takes, while Del Toro had more difficulty and needed a number of takes. The fact that no two of Del Toro's takes were alike forced Gilliam into using wide-angled shots to include both actors so that the acting would be homogenous. The result is that Gonzo's character fades into the background and seems a mere projection of Duke's personality. Gonzo was needed to make Thompson look good, and it is even possible to argue that Depp should have played both roles.

Most of the minor characters are so briefly glimpsed and so heavily disguised that they hardly make an impression. And the ones who appear in longer scenes — Christina Ricci, Gary Busey, Ellen Barkin, and Tobey Maguire — seem more like leftovers from the Flying Fellinis shown in the circus act than any objective reality.

Indeed, *Fear and Loathing in Las Vegas* seems more like Fellini's evocation of the 1930s than an objective reconstruction of Las Vegas in any period. Like Fellini, Gilliam gives a series of pictures of the world but does nothing to move the narrative forward. The world is full of perverted people, the characters are skewed toward the grotesque, and monstrous lizards swim in slime in the hotel rooms. Gilliam finds useful work for the dwarves of *Time Bandits*, and Depp, much to Thompson's dismay, throws coins at them. Reality, always under stress in a Terry Gilliam film, recedes into the distance, and the briefly sketched shots of war and student protests seem like pictures from some ancient battlefield. As Gilliam himself has said:

> Thompson writes in this highly dramatic style: although often nothing is really happening, everything is dramatized. It's as if he's a war correspondent, but rather than going to Vietnam, he stayed in America and carpet-bombed his psyche with drugs [Christie 246].

Gilliam argues unconvincingly that Gonzo is Virgil, "not the nice pagan poet, but a pagan primal force," and that Depp's Duke is "the Christian, with a morality that he is testing, pushing to the limit" (246). The religious metaphor is, however, unconvincing. Based on the body of Gilliam's work, and comparing his films to those of great directors who have dealt with religious themes (notably, Fellini, Dreyer, Bresson, and Paul Schrader), it is difficult to regard *Fear and Loathing* as a religious film. Although the movies of these great directors deal with the secular life, their religious beliefs, unlike those of Gilliam, are genuine and permeate all aspects of their films. Duke, by contrast, has reduced the whole world to his own addled perceptions.

Depp spent a great deal of time observing Thompson closely and aping his mannerisms. Depp said: "The man should be sainted for putting up with my continual scratching away at the layers of his life.... He stuck it out like a champion and couldn't have been a better friend" (McKeen 328). It can be argued that Depp's Thompson, courtesy of Gilliam, is our tour guide through a modern Hades, and corresponds to Federico Fellini's Marcello in *La Dolce Vita*, but the comparison is unconvincing. Marcello Mastroianni's Marcello is bored, stoned, affectless and apparently oblivious to the moral decay around him, a reluctant but silent Virgil to Fellini's moralistic Dante. Depp's Thompson, by comparison, is an active participant in the world around him and, some would argue, looks out from the depths at a world which he believes, perhaps wrongly, is far more weird than he is or ever could be. Ultimately, however, Depp's portrait of Hunter S. Thompson is a role model for chaos, not for religion. The greatness of Depp's performance is that he observes Duke — and, by inevitable extension, Thompson — with a minute and understanding eye, and passes on. He makes no judgment on his character.

Although Depp's performance was praised, the reviewers generally seemed to take it for granted and were more fulsome in what they had to say about Del Toro, particularly about the amount of weight he gained for the role. After the premiere, which was hardly a roaring success, Thompson is said to have bombarded Gilliam and Depp with bags of popcorn. Depp asked: "Do you like me?" "Oh, no," Hunter railed, "It was like a live bugle call over a live battlefield" (McKeen 340). Thompson, of course, was a supreme egotist, and it is unlikely that he ever could have really liked anything, no matter how well done, if he were not the sole begetter.

Johnny Depp's attitude, however, was never in doubt. Although the pair were friends before the film was made, their friendship prospered during the making of the movie and remained strong until the journalist's death. After Thompson's suicide, Depp carried out Thompson's memorial fantasy. He spent $2,500,000 of his own money to build a 150 foot tower with a "double-thumbed fist" (which required clearance from the FAA) from which to shoot the ashes of the Gonzo journalist into space (McKeen 362–365).

1998 *LA Without a Map*
The Ghost of Johnny Depp

LA Without a Map is about a young British undertaker and aspiring writer (played by Richard Tennant) who follows a young American actress (played by Vanessa Shaw) to Los Angeles in search of love, fame and fortune. The film, directed by Finnish born Mika Kaurismäki, brother of the much more famous Aki, is generally considered a failure and has received only limited distribution in America.

Foreign filmmakers who have made movies in America have not been notably successful, and *LA Without a Map*, like *Arizona Dream* (filmed a decade earlier), suffers from the director's lack of first-hand knowledge of American culture. Unlike most famous American actors, Depp has attempted to assist international filmmakers who lack access to the opportunities of American filmmakers in finding an audience. In *LA Without a Map*, he makes another — or several — of these small but carefully calibrated appearances.

In this case, the appearances consist of a number of short scenes emanating from a poster of Jim Jarmusch's *Dead Man*, with Depp as William Blake pointing a gun straight at the viewer, followed by two longer, but still short, concluding scenes. In the movie, Richard (David Tennant), a Scottish undertaker, is a great lover of movies, particularly of *Dead Man*, and takes a poster with him to America after he falls in love with a beautiful American girl named Barbara (Vinessa Shaw) and follows her to Los Angeles. Before leaving the UK, he asks the poster for advice and gets a shrug in return. In LA he sees a huge billboard-sized advertisement of Johnny Depp starring in a movie entitled *Dangerous Curves*. Depp is dressed in full Errol Flynn mode, sporting a beret and a mustache. Later, Richard asks his poster for advice but again gets only a shrug in return. Indeed, the poster is not at all helpful, but it does express its disapproval by shaking its head in disgust after he quarrels with Barbara and she walks out on him.

Apparently in desperation, Richard looks for consolation in a graveyard—where else would an undertaker go?—and meets Johnny Depp, or the ghost of Johnny Depp, sitting on a bench. Depp helpfully tells the undertaker a shaggy dog story about food, which is not unlike the one he uses later in *Once Upon a Time in Mexico*, except that the food discussed here, apparently fried chicken, is hardly in the same class as the slow-cooked pork recipe in that later film. According to Depp, he was killed by a woman who left him for a man who owned a polo team. The ghost says that she attached a salt shaker to her right breast and a pepper shaker to her left breast and then killed him. The story is so unlikely that it is difficult to believe that even a person of low intelligence, such as Richard, would buy it, but apparently he does. Later he discovers Johnny Depp and the elegant Anouk Aimée watching a 16mm film being shown in a large room. The movie is a subtitled print of a film in which Aimée tells a really ugly man that she is going to America. The use of a wretched public domain print and the bare room clearly shows the low budget origin of *LA Without a Map*. After Richard greets the uncomprehending Depp effusively and leaves, Aimée asks Depp the identity of the stranger, and Depp responds that he has no idea. Aimée and Depp were to appear again together in *Happily Ever After*.

The story, told in increments, seems to have wandered in from some other, better movie. Whoever concocted it, it deals with the boundary between fame and reality, and might even be about the real, as opposed to the filmic, Johnny Depp. It is complete in itself and expanded, and courtesy of Roald Dahl or Robert Bloch, it might have served as a segment of *Alfred Hitchcock Presents* or Dahl's *Tales of the Unexpected*.

1999 *The Source*

Kerouac and Company

"Life is a cut-up."
(William Burroughs)

The Source is a non-fiction film by Chuck Workman about the Beats. "Beats" is a word referring to a loosely connected group which arose in opposition to the so-called "conformist" culture of the 1950s and 1960s. Their motto was, in the words of Timothy Leary: "Tune in, turn on, and drop out." They advocated resistance to war, use of mind- altering drugs (including LSD and peyote), and free love. Their poetic muse was Walt Whitman, their chief poetic form free verse, and their most famous poem Allen Ginsberg's "Howl." Their most famous novel was Jack Kerouac's *On the Road* (1951), a stream-of-consciousness hymn to the open road. Although the Beats advocated free love, they were generally male chauvinists, and *The Source* does not discuss a single female writer. The group evolved into the so-called "hippies" in the 1960s as members grew old and lost their enthusiasm. Not all stayed the course. Ken Kesey, the talented author of *One Flew Over the Cuckoo's Nest* (1962), decided that he liked farming better and dropped out. In the film, Kesey, standing by a straight-line interstate with the distant mountains behind him, says that "over those knolls" you thought you would find "something wonderful," but then you found out there "were just more knolls." Ginsberg, a tireless promoter, stayed the course and in the last three decades of the century profitably carried his fading message into classrooms and lecture halls.

Chuck Workman is a non-fiction filmmaker with an unerring eye for the telling detail. *The Source* is a skillful compilation of vintage clips detailing the history of the Beats. The movement apparently began with the meeting of William Burroughs, Jack Kerouac and Allen Ginsberg at Columbia in the late 1940s; came to maturity, if that is the right word, in the 1950s; and quickly declined. As usual, by the time Hollywood got around to it commercially with *Easy Rider* (1969), the movement was essentially over.

Presumably for commercial reasons, Workman decided to use actors to portray Jack Kerouac (Johnny Depp), Allen Ginsberg (John Turturro) and William Burroughs (Dennis Hopper). Whether the results represent "portrayals" is an open question. Turturro and Hopper do reasonable impersonations, if not particularly convincing ones. They look enough like the originals at different points of their lives to be believable. Hopper, a true heir of the Beats, is effective but too animated to be believable as the restrained Burroughs, and Turturro disappears in his role. Depp, by comparison, is too slight to resemble Kerouac even before he became the bloated, inarticulate drunkard shown in period television clips. But in the final passage recited by memory from Kerouac's *The Subterraneans*, Depp reaches a moment of emotional intimacy not found elsewhere in the film. The book concerns Kerouac's overheated but brief sexual relationship with a young woman. The passage recited by Depp, taken almost word for word from the book, concerns Kerouac's difficulty in finding the "essence," which is "located in the thighs" and to which he must return; in the meantime, he will have to "rush off" and construct for "nothing—for Baudelaire's poems" (Kerouac 17).

Summarized so briefly, the passage sounds both obscure and pretentious. While the exact meaning of the passage is obscure—if indeed it has an exact meaning—it deals at some level with the relationship between sexual feeling (or, indeed, feeling of any kind) and art, represented by Baudelaire's poetry. The passage may be read as a justification of the permanence of art as opposed to the briefness of life—that is, of sexual pleasure; or, conversely, of the idea that feeling is the only reality we possess, and that art is an illusion. Depp's reading is casual, almost slurred, but, as always, this great actor suggests another mind behind the one he mirrors, a buried life, real and genuine, if sometimes inarticulate.

Jack Kerouac would be proud to claim the reading as his own.

1999 *The Astronaut's Wife*

Inside Man

"He's hiding inside me."
(Mysterious Voice)

Johnny Depp's next career choice, after *Fear and Loathing in Las Vegas*, was, as usual, a surprising one, but it was one that he could hardly have benefited from in the end, at least artistically. For a reported $8,000,000, he accepted the leading male role in *The Astronaut's Wife*, by a novice director. Rand Ravich was—and still is—primarily known as a writer and producer. His only earlier credit as a filmmaker was a short, *Oink* (1995), which may or may not be about pigs.

The Astronaut's Wife is boiler-plate genre, the story of an astronaut who is taken over by an alien on a trip to outer space. As the critics pointed out, the film is a cross between Ridley Scott's *Alien* (1979) and Roman Polanski's *Rosemary's Baby* (1968), but without the thrills of the one or the suspense of the other.

The alien invasion story extends back to Hammer's horror film *The Quartermass Experiment* (1955, itself based on a BBC serial), Don Siegel's *Invasion of the Body Snatchers* (1956), and Howard Hawks' classic *The Thing* (1951). Over the years, the invasions became more aggressive and often involved hordes of malign creatures. In a generic subspecies dating from Robert Louis Stevenson's *Dr. Jekyll and Mr. Hyde* (1886), the evil creatures sprang from the evil inside homo sapiens itself, as in *Forbidden Planet* (1956), where, although audiences did not realize it at the time, the presence of Leslie Nielsen made the existence of the creatures more plausible. Indeed, the theme, in one form or another, was an expressionistic favorite dating back at least to the 1924 film *Orlacs Hände* (*The Hands of Orlac*). (*Hands* is available on a quality DVD from Kino on Video.) In the film, the hands which Orlac loses in a train wreck are replaced with the hands of a murderer. The unfortunate result is much the same as in *The Astronaut's Wife*, except that the earlier film, although it has a weak ending, offers more thrills.

In a move which always makes reviewers suspicious, New Line did not screen *The Astronaut's Wife* for the press. When the reviewers did finally get to see the film, they did not much like what they saw, but displayed a ho-hum attitude with no real hostility. Janet Maslin, in the *New York Times*, called the plot "ridiculously derivative," compared it unfavorably with Theron's earlier film *The Devil's Advocate*, and one-upped all the male critics by noting that Charlize Theron's hairdo aped that of Mia Farrow in *Rosemary's Baby*. John Brosnan called the movie "the ultimate feminist nightmare, that lurking behind the handsome façade of one's husband is a foul monster, whose only intent is the exploitation of the female body" (cited Harti). Joe Leydon called the film "an aggressively stylish but ultimately flaccid drama" which "tends to drift in a kind of dream state between dramatic highlights." The result, a kind of *Rosemary's Baby* in space, is "unremarkably generic."

The film has a classic structure: 1) the space flight, trouble and return; 2) the death of Alex Streck (Nick Cassavetes), the pilot who accompanied Spencer Armacost (Depp) into space; 3) Armacost's resignation from NASA and his new job; 4) the questioning by Armacost's wife Jillian (Charlize Theron); 5) a difficult pregnancy and the suspicions of Mr. Reese (Joe Morton), a NASA publicity agent who had been fired because of his suspicions; 6) the confrontation with the alien; and 7) a new marriage and a new beginning. Although *The Astronaut's Wife* was rated R ten years ago, if it were released today, it would either be slightly reedited to earn a PG13 or, more likely, juiced up to an R. Even by the standards of 1999, the film was sadly lacking in the thrills expected by most audiences, whose tastes were being hardened by more explicit Asian horror films. The producers may, perhaps, have thought that its appeal, courtesy of its two stars, would bring out a large audience of teenagers and women. If so, they were disappointed.

While science-fiction or science-horror films do not have to be new — indeed, it is inherent in genre films that the audience should, at least to some extent, be familiar with the story — they do have to juice up the formula in some way. In *The Astronaut's Wife*, nothing in the film is new, but the photography, special effects and acting are strong throughout. Charlize Theron is gorgeous but unconvincing as a NASA wife. At this point in her career she did not have the wide emotional range she later developed in her Academy Award–winning performance in *North Country* (2005), and one would have expected an astronaut's wife to be rather more of a good ol' girl than she turns out to be. The supporting cast, however, could hardly be better; Joe Morton, Samantha Eggar, Blair Brown and Clea DuVall are all solid and convincing.

Which leaves us with Johnny Depp. The reviewers generally gave him a pass, but not without an occasional witticism. Christopher Jones may be cited as typical. He wrote, "Depp's idea of being sinister is to smile." Although the money was certainly part of why Depp decided to take the part, other reasons also came into play. Perhaps Depp liked the idea of playing an alpha male space cowboy with a southern accent. Whatever his reasons for taking the role, he clearly decided to underplay it, presumably in the belief that that is what an alien would do. A more aggressive affect would have made a nice contrast to what we do see, and would certainly have made his characterization more convincing. How a man would act with an alien in command within him is, however, a delicate question, and one well worth a critic's attention. Most audiences would have wanted to see him to blow himself open at some point, or at least to speak like Hal in *2001: A Space Odyssey* (sinister good alien), or like the intruder in Friedkin's *The Exorcist* (sinister bad alien). Apparently an alternate ending shows that Jillian is not possessed by the alien, but that the children are.

1999 *Sleepy Hollow*

Heads Will Roll

BOY: "Is it dead yet?"
ICHABOD (helpfully): "That's the problem.
It was dead to begin with."

Washington Irving's "The Legend of Sleepy Hollow," one of the most famous American short stories of the nineteenth century, was first published in *The Sketch Book of Jeffrey Crayon, Gent.*, a collection of stories and sketches which appeared in seven paperbound numbers in both England and America in 1819–20. "Sleepy Hollow" and "Rip Van Winkle," which appeared in the same book, represent Irving's most famous contributions to American literature. Set in a sleepy hamlet in upstate New York, "Sleepy Hollow" is the story of a ridiculous and superstitious school teacher named Ichabod Crane who falls into disfavor with a village tough named Brom Bones when he courts a local village beauty named Katrina Van Tassel. Pretending to be the Headless Horseman, a legendary Hessian said to have returned from the dead to recover his head, Brom Bones chases Ichabod as he is returning from a dance one dark night and throws his head — in reality a pumpkin — at him and runs him out of Sleepy Hollow forever. Why the Hessian would have thrown his head, the very object of his eternal search, must remain a matter of conjecture.

At the time of the story's publication, gothic tales, designed to appeal to the lowest literary tastes of the emerging reading public, were enormously popular. Cheaply published, often as so-called "penny dreadfuls," gothic tales were frequently ridiculed by more sophisticated writers such as Irving. The best of such stories, the so-called "sportive gothic," managed at the same time to be both homage and parody. No one has ever managed this double task more adroitly than Washington Irving.

Both "The Legend of Sleepy Hollow" and "Rip Van Winkle" were favorites with early filmmakers. Both stories had characters which were immediately recognizable, and Joseph Jefferson, who had spent decades and made a fortune playing Rip on stage, made an early film version (1898). Will Rogers (1879–1935), the famous rodeo star, humorist, folk philosopher, columnist and movie star, starred as Ichabod Crane in a live-action version of the story, *The Headless Horseman* (1921, available in a public domain version from Grapevine Video). Rogers was miscast. He was too old for the role, and his public persona as a fast-thinking, slow-talking, country-wise man, used so successfully by John Ford a decade later in *Dr. Bull* (1933) and *Judge Priest* (1934), worked against his portrayal of the ridiculous and superstitious Ichabod. The most famous version of the story, at least before Tim Burton's film, was *The Adventures of Ichabod and Mr. Toad*, released in 1949. The old crooner himself, Bing Crosby, played Ichabod Crane.

The problem with Irving's story, at least so far as the movies are concerned, is that it does not contain enough material for a feature film. This is a problem that filmmakers have dealt with since they began making feature films around 1913. For *Sleepy Hollow*, the filmmakers began with a famous name and a famous story and had free rein, particularly important in a story with a horse named "Daredevil," to do what they wanted — except, of course, for the main incident, whatever it happened to be.

The credits for *Sleepy Hollow* credit the original story to Washington Irving, the screenplay to Andrew Kevin Walker, and the screenstory (whatever that is) to Andrew Kevin Walker and Kevin Yagher. Tom Stoppard also worked on the screenplay, but his particular contribution, although "not beyond all conjecture," remains unknown. His brilliance and his fame, however, are guaranteed to generate speculation upon the topic. The basic problem for the writers was to concoct a backstory to explain the headless horseman's decapitations. They (or he) did this by putting him under the control of a master criminal who had the horseman's head, controlled him and sent him on his evil errands. The working out of the complex — some would say *too* complex — plot involves a town in which the people are as inbred as those in an H. P. Lovecraft story, a wicked government, two little sister (one of whom eventually kills the other), and a dead Hessian mercenary who has teeth filed to a point like the title character in Murnau's *Nosferatu*, and whose sole purpose in death is to recover his head. Who better to solve the case than Ichabod Crane, a New York City constable who believes in the latest scientific methods and whose superiors want to get him out of town?

Reviews of the film were generally respectful, but many critics regarded the movie as somewhat strange and were restrained in their praise. Rob Lowing landed the beauty of the images and Depp's performance, but called the film "all production design and no content." He noted Burton's "twisted-beautiful images ... the elegantly menacing forest and the slightly skew-whiff town of Sleepy Hollow itself." He wrote that Depp puts his own spin on the role and is "genuinely funny," especially when he puts a small boy in front of him as a shield in a dangerous situation. His conclusion was that the film looked great but lacked direction.

Jonathan Ross wrote incorrectly that the film was based upon "one of the few genuine examples of American folklore." Even if we discount the numerous folktales and legends of Native Americans, the statement is incorrect since the story which Irving used is Germanic in origin. Ross, however, was correct is his assessment of the beauty of *Sleepy Hollow*. He called the movie "simply breathtaking ... one of the most beautiful films I have ever seen." He wrote that the film has blended "the classic look of the better known movies with the beautiful lighting effect of classic American art," and invoked the name of Andrew Wyeth. In this context it is useful to remember that Burton began his career working for Disney, and that the models for Sleepy Hollow include Disney's "The Old Mill" (1937), *Fantasia* (1940), and, beyond them, the masterpieces of German expressionism.

In an attempt to characterize the film, Peter Rainer, in *New York*, described *Sleepy Hollow* as closer to Gahan Wilson than to Washington Irving. Jonathan Foreman called the movie

Scientific investigation in *Sleepy Hollow*.

"a disappointment ... inspired by the kitschy Hammer horror films of the 1950s." Certainly the Hammer films were an influence, but hardly a major one, and Foreman's description of "the fog-shrouded village, the corpse-like scarecrows, the riders repeatedly silhouetted against a gloomy sky, the blood-spurting Tree of Death," for all its goriness, hardly sounds like a Hammer film.

Jeff Giles, like some others, praised the beauty of the film with a poisoned pen. He wrote that *Sleepy Hollow* is "the most gorgeous, sumptuous, painterly movie ever made about multiple decapitations." Burton, he said, can "make anything look beautiful — the picking of flowers, the exhuming of coffins, even the steady stream of heads that come rolling toward you through the leaves." Giles disliked "some lame Freudian imagery meant to evoke castration and the fear of sex," but did not cite the passage. He concluded that the film is inferior to *Edward Scissorhands* and *Beetle Juice*, but, at its best, "it's a marvel to behold." Janet Maslin's review objected to the violence of the film, and stated, "it is not unreasonable to admire Mr. Burton immensely without wanting to try to peer at the exposed brain stems of his characters."

Mike Clark described Depp's Ichabod as "rather avant-garde for his day," with a tendency to swoon and faint when the going got tough. "Cowardly" would be nearer the mark. Jack Mathews thought the film a "visual head trip that comes up empty," but liked Walken's "Nosferatu's beauty." Karen Schoemer thought the film "a tentative horror flick" which was not nearly as thrilling as she remembered Disney's "The Headless Horseman" to be. She may be remembering seeing that film many years ago when, in color on a big screen, the picture doubtlessly seemed to an enthralled youngster more thrilling that it looks today.

J. Hoberman waxed Freudian in his wonderful review. After praising Burton's repeated success in twisting studio resources "to his own dark and gibbering expressionistic purposes," he opined that the Horseman "serves as an all-purpose return of the Patriarchal repressed — a mutilated, yet potent, remnant of the American Revolution." Hoberman called the film "an act of historical hubris and symbolic regicide," and concluded triumphantly that the film is Disneyland "revised as rampantly Freudian — and historically resonant — Grand Guignol."

Anyone with even a passing interest in popular art will enjoy looking at *The Art of Sleepy Hollow*, which contains both the screenplay by Andrew Kevin Walker and a generous collection of the work of the numerous artists who toiled on the film.

Desson Howe, in his review, described Depp's Ichabod as a "superstitious goofball" and as "a cross between Buster Keaton and Tim Curry." He was at least half right.

2000 *The Ninth Gate*
Rare Book Man

"You mean the Devil won't show up."
(Dean Corso)

After playing leading roles in several films which any serious actor would be happy to claim, and another leading role in a film which he himself had directed, but which had been fairly judged as both an artistic and commercial failure (*The Brave*), Johnny Depp made a film with Roman Polanski, the famous Hollywood exile living in France whose best films, *Chinatown* (1974), from a screenplay by Robert Towne that is widely regarded as a masterpiece) and *Rosemary's Baby* (1968), were becoming distant memories. The resulting picture, although expensive, was a commercial success that received mixed reviews from critics who were more interested in Polanski's post-exile career than they were in Johnny Depp's performance.

Although major films directors, at least until recently, generally have had reputations as mavericks, Polanski's background and extra-curricular career brought sensationalism to a new creative level. His early years, recounted endlessly in the tabloids and his autobiography, were the stuff of legend. His parents were sent to the concentration camps, and his mother died at Auschwitz. He went to art school, and in 1955 to the Lodz Film School. He soon established himself as a gifted filmmaker who seemed to combine an art-house sensibility with mass-audience appeal. When Hollywood beckoned, he answered the call. His two best films, *Rosemary's Baby* and *Chinatown*, combined cinematic skill with an analysis of morbid psychology, extending outward, at least in the case of *Chinatown*, to society as a whole. Polanski's version of William Shakespeare's *Macbeth* (1971), financed by Hugh Hefner (of *Playboy* fame), was famous at the time for its violence and nude Weird Sisters (who were actually wearing body stockings); but it has not aged well. Polanski's own taste seemed to run to shaggy dog stories of lesser or greater seriousness (*Dance of the Vampires*, 1967; *The Tenant*, 1976).

No discussion of Polanski's films can ignore the two central events of his career — the murder of his wife Sharon Tate by the Manson family, and his conviction for the rape of a thirteen-year-old girl and his consequent flight to France in 1978, which turned into an exile that has long outlasted the vengeful judge. A careful account of the whole sordid business is given in John Sandford's excellent *Polanski: A Biography*. However justified the flight may have been, it was a terrible career move.

For an unknown reason or reasons—lack of access to top talent, inadequate funding, difficulty in obtaining rights, whatever—it is fair to say that Polanski's post-exile films have not achieved either the commercial or artistic success of the best of his earlier works. Only his holocaust narrative *The Pianist* (2002), which earned Polanski his only Oscar, may be judged an exception. *Tess* (1979) and *Oliver Twist* (2005) are staid literary adaptations, and *Pirates* (1986) and *Frantic* (1988) are dull by any standard. *Bitter Moon* (1988), however, is a dark fable with unusual verve which critics compared favorably to *Knife in the Water* (1962), the film that made Polanski famous.

Johnny Depp met Polanski in May 1997 at the Cannes festival when the actor was there publicizing *Donnie Brasco*. After the failure of *Death and the Maiden* (1985), Polanski was looking for a commercial project. He and Gérard Brach had written a script called *The Double* based on Arturo Pérez-Reverte's novel *El club Dumas* (1993, translated into English by Sonia Soto in 1996 as *The Dumas Club*). The novel's hot-house mixture of melodrama, antiquarianism and Satanism would seem to be suitable subject matter for the man who directed *Rosemary's Baby*. Polanski was slated to direct, and the film was to star John Travolta and Isabelle Adjani. According to Christopher Sandford, the project fell apart over Travolta's unhappiness with changes in the script and ended up in litigation (Sandford 319–320).

Arturo Pérez-Reverte is a Spanish journalist turned novelist whose action-filled novels, often written in the style of Alexandre Dumas, have achieved wide popularity around the world. His novels customarily mix intricate plots, romantic characters and, particularly in his period novels, stirring action sequences. *The Dumas Club* is a complex entertainment by a popular novelist who admires the nineteenth- and early-twentieth-century genre writers, especially Alexandre Dumas, Edgar Allan Poe and A. Conan Doyle, and attempts, quite successfully, to emulate them with sophisticated stories which often refer to them in a knowing, self-referential fashion. Pérez-Reverte's dream, of course, is to emulate their popularity, and while he may not quite have equaled them in this regard, he has come close. Contrary to what Polanski seems to think, his novels are not difficult to read. His series about the adventures of Captain Alatriste, a mercenary swordsman, have been particularly popular and have been turned into a film, *Alatriste,* starring Vigo Mortensen, which is, unfortunately, at the time of this writing not available in America.

El club Dumas is a complex novel dealing with two parallel plots: the search for the manuscript of a missing chapter from the celebrated novel by Alexandre Dumas, *The Three Musketeers*, and the search for variant copies of a rare book called *The Ninth Door* or *The Ninth Gate*. Polanski, who is apparently not much of a reader, considers *El club Dumas* only a little below James Joyce's *Finnegans Wake* in difficulty. Faced with such a complex work, the screenwriters jettisoned the Dumas plot, which had given the novel its name, and concentrated on the much more popular and cinematic story of the search for the key to the ninth gate into Hell. Considering the effectiveness with which Polanski handled the supernatural in *Rosemary's Baby*, this seemed a reasonable decision.

A man seated at a desk in what looks like a rare book room is writing a suicide note. The man is Andrew Telfer (Willy Holt), a rare-book dealer. He seals the note and hangs himself. The camera burrows into a cavern between two books as the credits appear and disappear time and again, and eventually disappear into a white light. This mirrors the ending and apparently represents the gate into Hell.

The film proper begins with a scene in New York in which Dean Corso (Johnny Depp), a rare-book dealer, is negotiating for the purchase of the library of a man who has apparently

Looking for the entrance to Hell in *The Ninth Gate*.

suffered a stroke. Unable to communicate, the man is still cognizant of his surroundings. As Depp purchases a valuable book for much less than it is worth, the man's eyes narrow and he attempts to clench his fist.

Boris Balkan (Frank Langella), a rich and unscrupulous collector of rare books who owns one of only three known copies of a rare book about the supernatural, Aristide Torchia's *The Nine Gates of the Kingdom of Shadows* (1666), hires Corso to examine the other two copies to discover if either of them is "authentic," and to procure them by legal means if possible, or by illegal means if necessary. Torchia's book had fallen into the hands of the Inquisition and been burnt, and its author had soon suffered the same fate. Corso, who operates in the best of times at the margins of legality, accepts the assignment for a large fee and the promise of more if he is successful. Strangely — and unbelievably — Balkan allows Corso to take his copy of *The Nine Gates* with him, which he says Telfer sold to him the day before he killed himself, to use as a standard of comparison.

Corso visits the widow of the hanged man, Liana Telfer (Lena Olin), who believes that the book Corso has is the copy that belonged to her husband, and which she believes (probably correctly) was stolen from his library. Later, Corso keeps running into a beautiful blonde called the Girl (Emmanuelle Seigner), even though she is middle-aged. She is a hippie who rides a motorbike and seems to have been in a time warp since the 1960s.

In a desperate attempt to recover *The Nine Gates*, Mrs. Telfer comes to Corso's apartment "to talk business." Although she successfully seduces Corso, she does not recover the book, which Corso has given Bernie (James Russo), a bookseller friend, to keep for him. Unfortunately, Bernie has been murdered; the book, however, has been hidden, and Corso recovers it. (Liana Telfer has a tattoo on her thigh which, we learn later, represents the Order of the Silver Serpent, a satanic cult, now apparently much degraded from its original, devoted to the cult of the Nine Gates.)

Corso flies to the Continent, and in a striking scene worthy of E. T. A. Hoffmann, visits the shop of two middle-aged brothers, identical twins named Ceniza, who restore books. (The twins are both played by the same actor, José López Rodero.) One twin smokes, the other does not; and the interplay between the two gives the exposition of the scene — a discussion of the possible symbolism of the nine engravings of the book, excluding the title page — a nice balance. As it turns out, not all of the engravings are identical. Some are signed "L.C.F.," which, the twins say, stands for Lucifer "because he wrote this book in collaboration with someone else." Or does he mean that Lucifer collaborated on the engravings? Of course, the secret, which is gradually revealed, is that the two sets of engravings contain a hidden message that will enable the enlightened to enter "the ninth gate" into Hell. The twins say that Telfer had bought the book at his wife's behest. The viewer is left to surmise that perhaps she wants to go to Hell too.

After a train ride in which Corso meets the Girl again, he visits Victor Fargas (Jack Taylor), a once-rich aristocrat who has been selling off his rare-book collection one volume at a time in order to survive, and now has only 834 volumes. Of course, as it turns out, Fargas' copy also has variations in the plates.

An attempted attack on Corso is foiled by the Girl. The attack, we learn later, was done at the command of Mrs. Liana Telfer. Later, the Girl wakes Corso and takes him back to Fargas' home, where they discover that Fargas has been murdered and his body thrown into a fish pool in the yard. Corso finds Fargas' copy of *The Nine Gates* partially burned in a grate, its plates torn out.

After flying back to Paris from Lisbon with the Girl, Corso goes to see Baroness Kessler (Barbara Jefford), whose collection includes the third (and final) volume of *The Nine Gates*. The Baroness, a rich, elegant old woman who has devoted her life to the study of Satan, is partially paralyzed, is confined to a motorized wheelchair, and has only a stump for a right hand. Corso surmises from what the Baroness says that Telfer may have committed suicide when he discovered his wife's promiscuity in connection with the rituals of the Order of the Silver Serpent. After the Baroness suspects that Corso is working for Boris Balkan, she summarily rejects Corso's request to examine her copy of *The Nine Gates*. That night Corso fends off an assault by Mrs. Telford's blonde-haired thug with the help of the Girl, who turns out, rather improbably, to be an adept in the martial arts.

The next day Corso inveigles his way into the Baroness's office, shows her reproductions of the plates in Balkan's book (which he had reproduced at his hotel), and convinces her to allow him to examine her book. Inside the volume, stuffed with various bits of paper, he finds a postcard from Balkan reading: "Sorry Frieda. Al saw it first." On the reverse is a reproduction of a painting which Corso had seen in Balkan's apartment showing a silhouette of several square towers photographed against a dramatically lighted sky. The photograph resembles the towers outlined in Fritz Lang's *The Death of Siegfried*. Before Corso completes his work, he is struck unconscious from behind. When he awakens, he discovers that the Baroness has been murdered, the library has been set on fire, and the Baroness' copy of *The Nine Gates* has been burned. When Corso returns to his hotel, he finds that Balkan's copy of *The Nine Gates* has been stolen by Liana Telfer.

Corso and the Girl track Mrs. Telfer to her hotel, only to discover that she and her blonde henchman are checking out of the hotel. Unable to find a cab, the Girl, a woman of resources, steals a car and follows the Telfer car to the Saint-Martin chateau. (Saint-Martin was Mrs. Telfer's maiden name.) They arrive in time to see the nude Mrs. Telfer don her satanic robes.

Corso's attempt to recover *The Nine Gates* is interrupted by the blonde bodyguard. In the ensuing fight, Corso beats him savagely to death. "I didn't know you had it in you," the Girl opines admiringly.

The satanic ritual is interrupted by the arrival of Boris Balkan. "Mumbo-jumbo," he announces, and ridicules the "orgies of aging flesh conducted in the master's name." In a struggle to the death, Balkan strangles Liana Telfer. The worshippers flee. The Girl tells Corso that the killings are over and that he's "off the hook." Corso finally comes to recognize what he should have figured out much earlier — namely, that she is working for Boris Balkan. Recognizing Corso's mixed feelings, the Girl responds, "Funny, I thought you were."

Later, fascinated by the towers in the postcard, Corso tracks down their location to a castle in the distant mountains (in Transylvania perhaps?). He arrives just in time to see Balkan arranging the nine engravings and invoking Satan: "To travel in silence by a long and circuitous route, to brave the arrows of misfortune, and to fear neither noose nor fire, to play the greatest of all games and win forgoing no expense is to mock the vicissitudes of fate and to gain at last the key that will unlock the Ninth Gate."

After a spirited confrontation with Corso, Balkan prepares himself to enter "the uncharted territory ... that leads to equality with God." He pours gasoline in a circle and invokes the power of Satan to "erase me from the book of life and inscribe me in the black book of death." Satan is apparently happy to do so and ignites Balkan. Corso saves the plates from the book and, at the last moment, shoots Balkan, either because he wants to speed him on his way or perhaps to take his place. While the fire is consuming Balkan, Corso has sex with the Girl, who has mysteriously appeared.

Later, in her automobile, the Girl tells Corso that he is not finished with the book and that one page used by Balkan was "a forgery." In context, this apparently means that it was not written or approved of by Satan himself. The Girl disappears but leaves a note behind directing Corso to the shop of the Ceniza brothers. The shop has closed and the twins have disappeared, but the plate which Corso is seeking mysteriously floats down from the top of a piece of furniture the workmen are moving. Apparently, Satan has accepted the book dealer as one of his own. At the conclusion of the film, Corso approaches the towers, and the film ends in a flare of light.

Reviews of *The Ninth Gate* were mixed. David Sterritt wrote of the film's "occasionally self-satirizing tone," and thought that it went on too long, but that the direction was "marvelously assured." J. Hoberman called the film "a tongue-in-cheek thriller ... stuffed with cheery blah-blah."

In an interesting review, Kenneth Turan labeled the film Polanski's second encounter with the devil, and liked Depp's portrayal of "an elegant, soulless weasel ... a protagonist so buttoned-down" that he was always difficult to read. He also thought the film lacked energy and drive, and speculated whether Johnny Depp was a contributing factor to this lethargy or found it to his liking. According to Turan, "The accumulation of clichés gives the film a peculiar dream quality," which he compared to that of *Eyes Wide Shut*, Stanley Kubrick's film that had recently appeared to largely unfavorable reviews. Both were "shaggy-dog stories about quests that cannot be fulfilled, including the viewer's own quest for a satisfying narrative conclusion." It is, however, unclear why a man who has sold his soul to the Devil and is going to claim his reward, or lack of it, should be an unsatisfying narrative conclusion, considering that Marlowe, Goethe, Thomas Mann and a multitude of other artists have considered it a perfectly satisfying one, whatever the protagonist may ultimately have thought. The discussion as to whether Corso may himself have been the Devil is a non-starter. Satan himself would hardly have found it necessary to have so destructive a self-immolation.

Jonathan Foreman called viewing the film "a painful experience," and also compared it to *Eyes Wide Shut*. Both movies were done by directors who have "been out of touch with popular culture for decades." Of course, this would not necessarily be a disadvantage artistically, although it certainly would be commercially. The consensus seemed to be that Polanski was selling out — if not to the audience, at least to the critics. Jonathan Romney wrote that "inept and archaic as the film seems, you feel that Polanski knows it perfectly well, and is simply mocking our indulgence."

The makers of *The Ninth Gate* were either ignorant, deliberately misleading, or, perhaps, both in their depiction of the rare book trade. The author of the novel, Arturo Pérez-Reverte, knows about the rare book trade, but, for narrative purposes, was deliberately misleading. The film, however, seems both ignorant and stupid. Corso uses a fountain pen and smokes cigarettes when taking notes, no-nos for which he would be immediately chastised by any rare-book owner or librarian. Smoking, which only the Baroness complains of, would not only pollute the air, but sparks and bits of ash could easily injure the book. The Baroness has yellowed bits of paper stuffed between the pages of her rare copy of *The Ninth Gate* — another no-no, since the acid in the cheap modern paper would quickly contaminate the pure rag paper of the original. No one mentions paper or watermarks as important guides to the age of books. Early paper was "laid" — that is, hand-made and not mass-produced by machine — as indeed were all books from the period, and customarily had watermarks identifying the maker of the paper. And it is absolutely unbelievable that Boris Balkan would give Corso a rare and valuable book to take with him to use as a check to ascertain the "originality" of other copies when a Xeroxed copy would have done just as well. Most early books had wood engravings with crude outlines which, lacking the subtle details of copper engravings, would

Ersatz bibliographical expertise in *The Ninth Gate.*

reproduce well. As for the watermarks, Corso could easily remember them or write them down on a sheet of paper.

None of the talk about "forgeries" makes any sense. When faced with copies of early printed books that are identical except for small differences in the wood engravings, the expert would not assume that some of the copies were forgeries, but that they represented early or later states of the wood engravings and (perhaps, but not necessarily) the text. Indeed, surviving copies of early books almost always contain significant differences, at least if more than a few are still extant. In the First Folio of Shakespeare's plays (1623), nearly every known copy that has been studied in detail — more than a hundred — reveals a number of significant variations due to proofreading and printing, including variations regarding corrections made in the course of printing and in the engraved portrait of the author in the front of the book. It is extremely unlikely that anyone would forge a copy of a book as rare and obscure as *The Ninth Gate*. Even if it had been reprinted and pirated at an early date, which was not uncommon when the book's content was controversial, the forgery would not have been a forgery in the modern sense, but merely an unauthorized reprinting with no attempt to reproduce the accidentals of the original. If all of the copies of *The Nine Gates* were identical except for the illustrations, it would not follow that any of them were forgeries in the modern sense. What was common, of course, were books printed with incorrect dates or publishers to disguise their origins, usually from fear of persecution. Modern crooks generally manufacture a provenance for a desirable book which might exist, say, a privately printed copy of Mrs. Browning's *Sonnets from the Portuguese*). and then manufacture the book. Such a book is not a forgery, although the attempt clearly is to deceive, creating a puzzle to be solved by the initiated. While manuscript forgeries were and are common, there were few, if any, exact forgeries, contemporary or modern, of authentic early books.

It might, of course, be argued that the rare book gimmick is simply a Hitchcockian "McGuffin" — that is, merely an instrument for setting the plot in motion. A McGuffin, however, does not depend upon real knowledge which the viewer, or anyone else, for that matter, might have. It is simply an idea — a formula for blowing up the world, an atomic secret, anything of great value — which depends only upon a suspension of disbelief to be accepted. It does not, as here, expect viewers to suspend belief about a trade with which they are, or might be, familiar.

In his commentary, Polanski says that European actors often lack experience. By contrast, English actors usually have had a great deal of experience and are generally well-prepared. He praises Barbara Jefford's performance as Baroness Kessler. American actors, according to Polanski, are generally influenced by method acting and like to experiment. Polanski, of course, does not like such experimentation.

The numerous process shots, praised by some reviewers, vitiate against realism, and the film does not have the gothic feeling which would have made it more effective. The terror by daylight, which was effective in *Rosemary's Baby*, is out of place amid so much process photography, and both the character and the acting of the hippie girl seems to have wandered in from some other movie. Vanessa Paradis (who was, of course, to become Johnny Depp's longtime companion and the mother of his children) auditioned for the role of the Girl, but was rejected in favor of Polanski's wife Emmanuelle Seigner, who is unconvincing and much too old for the role.

Although there can be little doubt that Polanski's personal experiences, including his traumatic childhood during the holocaust and the Manson murders in Hollywood, influences his choice of films and his treatment of material, the exact nature of that influence is speculative and unknowable, probably even to the director himself. Thematically, *The Ninth Gate* fits easily into Polanski's films somewhere between *Chinatown* and *Rosemary's Baby*. Whether exemplified in the dark heart of man or in the reality of Satan, evil exists. While *The Ninth Gate* will never achieve the reputation of Polanski's two earlier classics, repeated viewings are likely to enhance its reputation.

Although Depp was eager to work with Polanski, Polanski was hesitant at first, believing that Depp was not quite right for the role of Dean Corso, the unscrupulous rare-book dealer. According to Polanski's DVD commentary, Depp plays the role "somehow straight and flat," which was not the way the director had originally imagined it. A few days of shooting, however, gave the role a "different aspect" from what he had anticipated. The actor himself said that he wanted to start out with a character which the audience would not like at the beginning, but which they would come to like by the end of the film, even though he had become a much darker character by then. He thought the change in Corso would be an interesting concept, with all the "strange and funny secondary characters around him." Polanski says that Depp is a quick study, alert to suggestions, and easy to get along with.

It is hardly fair to consider the director of *Rosemary's Baby* to be selling out. *The Ninth Gate* is extremely well acted throughout, and has, especially upon repeated viewings, an unsettling ambiance typical of Polanski's best work. What *The Ninth Gate* does not have is the visual unity that Terry Gilliam or Tim Burton would have given it, or a screenplay that makes any particular sense. It is certainly lacking in the thrills of the latest Hong Kong actioner, whatever that may be. Without either the visual or motivational context that would have given the viewer some motivation for Coleridge's willing suspension of disbelief, the film seems trivial.

Roman Polanski's literary adaptations—of William Shakespeare (*Macbeth*), Thomas Hardy (*Tess of the d'Urbervilles*), and Charles Dickens (*Oliver Twist*)—are oddly uninformed of cultural references and seem to be wandering around in a cultural vacuum. By comparison, Akira Kurosawa's *Throne of Blood* (1957), for all of its Japanese references, is much closer in spirit to Shakespeare's play than is Polanski's film. And *Oliver Twist*, for all its top talent and big budget, cannot compare to David Lean's 1949 film, described by David Thomson as "ravishing still: magnificent in its period recreation, its rank city and its evil ... greedily edited and ravishingly designed ... and shot in greedy shadows and imperiled light, with great performances" (*Dictionary*). It does not even compare favorably with the best of the recent British adaptations—with the Andrew Davies scripted *Bleak House*, for example.

Peter Rainer, in his review in *New York*, speculated that Polanski's exile from Hollywood took away the "armature" and "commercialism" of the studio system, and "reined in his excesses." Although his later films "are still the work of a distinctive talent," they are less fully realized. If Rainer's conclusion is true, and there is considerable evidence to support it, it is, as Rainer admits, an unusual fate for an émigré director.

What, then, are we to make of Polanski's films? Unlike the great directors of the past, who studied film art and European cultural traditions, and often affected appropriate personae, Polanski is empty. Even the surrealists, with whom he might have been expected to have aligned himself, are absent from his résumé. Whenever he makes a film, he surrounds himself with experts, but the result almost invariably appears second-hand, and only *The Pianist* appears to have activated him emotionally.

In his discussion of *The Ninth Gate*, Christopher Sandford speculated that the movie may have been done in by its lavish budget. Certainly Polanski is hardly at home in the world of big-budget special effects. Sandford quotes a perceptive comment by Polanski about "older filmmakers: "I do observe in older filmmakers a phenomenon that's quite irritating, almost obscene. It happens to certain artists who realize that everything going on around them is changing and moving further away from what they're doing.... So they end up performing somersaults which, for them, is quite undignified. Something odd always happens to older artists." (Sandford 325). This is acutely observed and can be seen clearly in the late films of John Ford and Billy Wilder, among others. In *Cheyenne Autumn*, for example, the greatness of John Ford seems to be disintegrating before our eyes. What is more interesting is that the cultural referents necessary for great filmmaking seem to have been absent in Polanski's films from the beginning. Without Hollywood's technical expertise and the quintessential Americanism of Robert Towne's brilliant script, *Chinatown* would hardly be the great film it is.

Whatever is wrong with *The Ninth Gate*, it is certainly not Johnny Depp. Expensively but shabbily dressed, mustachioed, chain-smoking, toting a canvas bag in which he can quickly stow rare books, he is a legitimate expert on rare books, knows where he can find them, and operates on the edge of legality. Polanski calls him a "complete mercenary" in his commentary, but he is not a fraud, and the people he sells his books to, although deeply concerned with the authenticity of their purchases, know that they are being over-charged but do not believe they are being cheated.

The unknowing, however, are a different story. As illustrated at the beginning of the film, Corso uses a bait-and-switch technique. When confronted with a library of old books and an owner who knows little of their worth, he praises the value of the books as a whole, admires and overvalues some items, and stows the most valuable piece away in his bag after purchasing it for a nominal sum.

As usual, the performance of Depp has a hidden layer. Although Corso spends his life dealing with rare books, there is no evidence that he is a collector himself. The chase is what interests him. Apparently, at some point he has become interested in the supernatural world of demons and witches depicted in many of the books he buys and sells, and his apparently instantaneous transformation into a true believer in the book *The Nine Gates* is not as sudden as it appears. Depp's performances, when required, always allow for the possibility of change, and that is the case here.

2000 *Chocolat*

Rowing in Eden

"Wild Nights! Wild Nights!
Were I with thee,
Wild Nights should be
Our luxury."
(Emily Dickinson)

"I'll bet he's the Captain." (Anouk Rocher)

"I'll come around some time and
get that squeak out of your drawer."
(Roux)

Chocolat, Johnny Depp's second film with Swedish director Lasse Hallström after *What's Eating Gilbert Grape*, is the story of a mysterious woman named Vianne Rocher, well played by Juliette Binoche, who arrives in a small, extremely conservative French village during lent with her young daughter Anouk (Victoire Thivisol) and sets herself up as a chocolatier. An object of curiosity among the villagers, she is resented by the Count Paul de Reynaud, who uses his considerable influence to attempt to turn the villagers against her and drive her out of town. Vianne's secret weapon in the struggle is her chocolate, which seems to be an all-purpose medicine that serves as both an aphrodisiac, when appropriate, and a friendship medicine which vanquishes the enmities of the village, many of which are of long standing, and unites the people, including, of course, the malicious Count.

Judi Dench, the current reigning queen of British actresses, plays a grandmother who is estranged from her daughter and is not allowed to see her grandson. Brought together in the coffee shop, the boy and his granny provide a powerful argument for family unity, and the mother eventually caves in to the maudlin assault. The cast is uniformly strong, particularly in the female roles. The beautiful Juliette Binoche makes an impossible role almost believable. Alfred Molina, who had played an evil trader with the Indians in *Dead Man*, is again appropriately villainous, but much smoother, and Lena Olin is as sympathetic here as she was villainous in *The Ninth Gate*. And the great Leslie Caron, fifty years after *An American in Paris*, makes an appearance.

Lance Lee, in *The Death and Life of Drama*, distinguishes between raw and cooked emotional response: "The 'cooked' refers to emotion expressed through some degree of emotional formalization, the 'raw' to its direct, unvarnished expression" (71).

Although Lee recognizes that the classification resembles the old distinction between round and flat characters, he argues that *Chocolat* is not what he calls "slice of life or cinéma vérité," but "magic realism" (71). In the film, the Count, superbly portrayed by Alfred Molina, is our old friend the religious hypocrite, a type which can be edged toward either comedy or tragedy. In the popular novel by Joanne Harris, the prime mover against Vianne is the Priest, but in the film his perfidies have, for purposes of political correctness, been largely switched to the Count. The film, however, is unlikely ever to be a favorite of the church. The priest, a weak

River Man: Johnny Depp as Roux, the Great Lover, in *Chocolat.*

young man, allows the Count to write his homilies for him. Envious of the influence of Vianne's chocolates upon the simple people of the village, the Count begins a brutal campaign against her.

Lance Lee argues that an ambiguous ending in a film such as *Chocolat*, where such an ending might not be expected, gives the film "shades of ambiguity" typical of film noir (*Death* 47). Perhaps, but such an ending need not generically disqualify a film as a comedy. Shakespeare's plays often have a character, such as Malvolio in *Twelfth Night*, who says, in effect, "count me out" and does not take part in the general merrymaking. The Count is a despicable character who would seem to be outside the pale of humanity when he urges Serge, his imbecilic disciple, to commit outrage, but is appalled when he burns the gypsy camp. (In our politically correct times, the river rats are not identified as gypsies in the film, as they are in Jane Austen's novels, for example; but that is exactly what they are generically — bad guys who can be counted on when someone is needed to perform a reprehensible deed.) Shakespeare again furnishes an example: in *Richard II*, when the new King Bolingbroke wishes fervently that the old King, Richard II, were dead, Sir Pierce of Exton takes him literally, kills Richard and is exiled for his loyalty.

In the end, after the Count understands what he has caused, he collapses into what Lee called "a chocolate-eating frenzy" (*Death* 47). The ending is a clear victory for Vianne. Presumably, Lee's "shades of ambiguity" means ignoring the destruction of the gypsy flotilla, the loss of property, the possible loss of life, and Vianne's own insensitivity to her young daughter's desire to quit moving from one town to another and settle down. Apparently, the solution for all of the town's problems was to get the Count to eat chocolate.

Chocolat was widely praised and, in spite of some spirited opposition, was nominated for Academy Awards for Best Picture, for Best Actress (Juliette Binoche), for Best Supporting Actress (Judi Dench), and for Best Adapted Screenplay (Robert Nelson Jacobs), but was shut out on Oscar night. Although some reviewers had reservations, the reviews for *Chocolat* were generally sympathetic. The most enthusiastic was probably Kevin Thomas, who called the film "a splendid work in the good humanist tradition of the classic cinema of France, where it takes place," and compared it to the films of Jean Renoir. This seems a stretch for a movie in English, based on a novel in English, with a Swedish director, a largely English and American cast, and a banal script. Thomas noted the "downright pagan" subversive quality of chocolate in the film. He called the movie a "human quality in the form of a fairy tale," approved its portrayal of "religious practice that condemns rather than forgives," and summed it up as "a work of artistry and craftsmanship at the highest level."

Lou Lumenick called the film "a bittersweet confection that few holiday filmgoers will be able to resist," and praised the actors, particularly Alfred Molina's Count. Lumenick described the Count as "massively repressed," and called Molina's portrayal an "inventive comic masterpiece." David Ansen straddled the fence. He labeled *Chocolat* "a seriocomic plea for tolerance, gift-wrapped in the baby blue colors of a fairy tale and served up with a sybaritic smile." He admitted that, although the film has a "moral argument" which is "pat and predictable," it disarms the viewer with its charm and craftsmanship. By comparison, Richard Schickel found little to praise. He cited the film's relentless "predictability," "tasteful vulgarity," "humanistically healing banality, the life-crushing behavioral cliché," and its "sugary sentimentality."

John Mount, in *Sight and Sound*, damned the film with faint praise as "soft-centered entertainment with marvelous acting," and called Binoche's Vianne "a slightly racy version of Mary Poppins." John Anderson's interesting review saw the movie as primarily a typical Miramax concoction served up by the Weinstein brothers, and cited as its predecessors *Cin-*

ema Paradiso, *Like Water for Chocolate*, and *Life Is Beautiful*. These films represent "a kind of Foreign Films Lite — the type of movie that makes audiences feel both sated and intelligent, the way a diner does after three éclairs and a coffee with Sweet 'n Low." Anderson concluded that the film is "a feminist fable, more simplistic than most, perhaps, but well meaning enough."

None of the reviewers paid much attention to Johnny Depp's gypsy, Roux. Meikle wrote that few actors at Depp's stage of their careers would have accepted so "rewarding and underwritten" a role, and suggested that the audience was expecting him to come in on a white horse and somehow set things right. Meikle wrote that Depp is "a romantic lead," and romantic leads "need to have their features seen." (The precise meaning here is unclear.) He criticized Roux's improbability and his thinness of characterization, and concluded that he is "merely ... Prince Charming, whose kiss awakens the sleeping beauty" (280).

It is unlikely that either the writer, the director or the star intended Roux to be plausible. He is the gypsy Davy of song, a guilt-free sex fantasy, a transient who has sex with a beautiful woman on a river boat and disappears, only to reappear when her problems have all been worked out. He is an exemplar of the perfect sexual experience; paradoxically, however, he also provides the safe harbor Emily Dickinson writes about:

> Rowing in Eden,
> Ah! the sea!
> Might I but moor
> Tonight in thee!

The same character, differently attired, is going to turn up on horseback in *The Man Who Cried*, and on an elevator in *Happily Ever After*.

2000 *The Man Who Cried*

Romance on Horseback

"O, happy horse to bear the weight of Antony."
(Shakespeare, *Antony and Cleopatra*)

After the funding for Terry Gilliam's Don Quixote film dried up — and not for the last time, either — Johnny Depp signed on to star in Sally Potter's *The Man Who Cried*. Sally Potter is an English filmmaker (b. 1949) attracted to feminist themes. Her best-known film, *Orlando* (1992), based upon Virginia Woolf's classic 1928 gender-bending novel, is a breakthrough feminist movie which achieved a measure of critical and commercial success that her other films have not equaled. Potter is a complete filmmaker — screenwriter, dancer, composer, sometime actor, and director — but her insistence upon complete control of the artistic project sometimes leads her into difficulties which might have been avoided.

The Man Who Cried begins with a short episode set in the USSR in 1927 (cited as Russia in the film) in which a young Jewish girl named Fegele (Christina Ricci) is caught up in the persecution of the Jews and the gypsies, and separated from her father. She is left with only his picture. The gypsies, of course, were always outside the pale and had been presented as villains by many earlier writers, including Jane Austen. Fegele miraculously escapes to England where she is raised by unsympathetic foster parents who forbid her to speak her native Yiddish. Fortunately, she turns out to have an excellent voice, which gets her a job in a Paris opera house.

The long central portion of the film takes place in Paris just before the German occupation, where Fegele, now known as Suzie, rooms with Lola (Cate Blanchett), a Russian émigré who takes her under her wing and makes a fruitless attempt to teach her to use her budding sexuality to better her life. Lola, always after the main chance, flatters and makes love to a talented but vain, horny, and obnoxious Italian opera singer named Dante Dominio, superbly played by John Turturro. Suzie, meanwhile, has fallen in love with a gypsy horse trainer named Cesar (Johnny Depp), whose horse makes the mistake of defecating on the stage during a performance, antagonizing the egotistical star, whose lecherous gaze has turned toward Suzie. These minor problems are displaced by major ones when the Germans enter the city. After an improbable series of adventures, Suzie escapes to America.

In the concluding episode, the flip side of the opening one, Suzie, now grown, has traced her father to Hollywood, where he has been working in the motion picture business. In the final scene, which occasioned some sarcasm from reviewers, Suzie shows her father her picture, and daughter and father are reunited.

Faced with a complex but unsatisfactory film, the more erudite reviewers were interested but unimpressed. Jan Stuart was dismissive, and savaged the film's conclusion uniting

Johnny Depp as Cesar, contemplating destruction in *The Man Who Cried*.

father and daughter as a "lachrymal flood." He believed that Ricci was miscast, and that both she and Depp were "essentially reactive" actors, as much victims of underwriting as they are of persecution. Jonathan Foreman thought the film "crude and mechanical, despite considerable visual and musical virtuosity"; said that it was "spotted with historical inaccuracies and groaning with dialogue so dreadful that it makes a fine cast look ridiculous again and again"; and called it "mysteriously titled" for good measure. Certainly the film does not even hint at, much less make clear, who the title refers to.

In an attempt to categorize the movie, some reviewers compared it to quality films of the past. J. Hoberman believed that "the film attempts to reanimate a passé genre: the multistar romantic epics of the 1950s," downsized from the great romantic stars of Taylor, Brando, Monroe and Kirk Douglas. Like those films, *The Man Who Cried* is rich with inadvertent anachronisms. Ultimately, Hoberman regarded the film as camp, a ludicrous "Yiddish generational tearjerker." Perhaps in an attempt to salvage something from his carnage, Hoberman wrote that the picture "gives bad movies a good name," and cited Edgar G. Ulmer in support. The comparison, however, is not apt. Ulmer gave style and distinction to films with miniscule budgets and impossible scripts. Potter, however, has a substantial budget and top-of-the-line actors.

Sally Potter has admitted that "the original impulse" for the film "came from music." It did not, however, come from a single source, but from many, including "opera, gypsy music and klezmer," a species of secular Jewish folk music. The musical organization evolved from the script, and the "visual starting points" came from Henri Cartier-Bresson's period photographs of Paris in the years covered by the film, and from Josef Koudelka's photographs of gypsies in Eastern Europe. The seven weeks shooting in the Opéra Comique also suggested important visual elements.

Ginette Vincendeau was correct in stating that the film has "an operatic sensibility," and in calling it "a sensual, colorful, excessive melodrama" about a young Jewish girl's search for her father and her lost identity, "with broad strokes, boldly defined characters and superb music." The film deals with the relationship between life and art, a theme that Potter had treated earlier in *The Tango Lesson*. Certainly the movie has a large political agenda, including anti–Semitism, fascism, the oppression of gypsies and Jews, and the devastation of war. Vincendeau believed, probably correctly, that these themes could be better treated in a more experimental film.

Vincendeau and others cited the movie's historical accuracies without exploring their significance. The list would certainly be long. In reality, the official attitude — the "general line"— toward the Jews during the mid–1920s was one of toleration and understanding, and it was not until some four or five years later that the persecution against them began in earnest. In 1925, Aleksandr Granovsky's *Jewish Luck* gave a wonderfully detailed and sympathetic portrayal of Jewish life in the Soviet Union. A year later, Vladimir Vilmer's film *Benya Krik*, from a magnificent screenplay by Isaac Babel, was suppressed by the Soviet authorities for its unfavorable portrayal of a Jewish gangster. (Both films have been carefully restored and are available for purchase or rental from the National Center for Jewish Films.) And occupied Paris is sadly under-populated with a solitary horseman, who surely would have been shot on sight, roaming the streets at night — perfect for lovers probably, but highly improbable for the film.

The movie has neither a logical visual style nor a coherent narrative. More seriously it makes implicit historical claims that it cannot support. It need not have done so.

2000 *Before Night Falls*

Bon-Bon and Victor

"...highly skilled queers called 'porterettes'" (Reinaldo Arenas)

The director of *Before Night Falls*, Julian Schnabel (b. 1951), has been described by Derrick R. Cartwright in *The Dictionary of Art* as "[p]robably the most exhibited, financially successful and aggressively self-promoting American artist of his generation." He produces large-scale prints and paintings with garish colors and obscure textual references, and is primarily famous for his textured use of a variety of surfaces, including crockery, animal hides and tarpaulin. Although his art remains controversial, his financial success has enabled him personally to finance a second career as a filmmaker.

His first film, *Basquiat* (1996), was a biopic about Jean-Michel Basquiat, a talented young artist whose financial and critical success was undercut by his drug addiction. Basquiat, who was famously said by Australian art critic Robert Hughes to have been one of the most fashionable painters in the world for about fifteen minutes, died at the age of twenty-seven of a heroin overdose. Although *Basquiat* was praised for the performance of Jeffrey Wright in the title role, the film received generally poor reviews for its use of unconvincing cameos by famous film personalities, and for its genius-against-society stereotypes. In retrospect, the movie may clearly be seen as the work of a talented but neophyte director who deserves praise for, among other reasons, his convincing portrayal of the New York art milieu. Unhappy with the distribution of the film by Miramax, Schnabel chose Fine-Line for the distribution of his second film, *Before Night Falls*.

Cuban novelist and poet Reinaldo Arenas (1943–1990) was an enthusiastic early supporter of Fidel Castro and the Cuban revolution, but soon soured on it because of its restrictions on artistic expression and its persecution of gays. Constantly in trouble with the authorities because of his stridently gay lifestyle and the publication of his novels and poems abroad, he was in and out of jails and prisons before he was allowed to leave for the United States during the so-called Mariel Boatlift in 1980 as a so-called "passive" homosexual. He said that he lied so that the authorities would consider him less dangerous than an "active" homosexual. In New York he continued to work for liberal causes, but his failing health soon restricted his activities. Suffering from an advanced case of AIDS, he committed suicide in 1990. In his introduction to his memoir, *Before Night Falls*, published in 1992 after his death, he wrote movingly of his physical deterioration.

Generically, *Before Night Falls* is a biopic of the life of the Cuban novelist. The episodic and impressionistic film is divided into three unequal parts. The first depicts the life of the novelist from his birth in 1943 in Oriente province to his arrival in Havana during the early days of the revolution. The second segment details his part in the Cuban revolution and his growing disenchantment with Fidel's Castro's revolution, and particularly with his persecution of homosexuals. And the third, and shortest, part delineates his exile to America and his death of AIDS in New York City in 1990.

Before Night Falls is a remarkable film which, politics and themes aside, any major film director would be proud to acknowledge. Aesthetically, Julian Schnabel came to filmmaking fully formed: he had simply not completely mastered the medium, the means of expression. He clearly learned from *Basquiat*; and, for the most part, he did not repeat its errors. Arenas' memoir is not an experimental work; it is, for the most part, a straightforward autobiography whose main interest is in detailing the terrors of a totalitarian and repressive regime. Its subtext is a celebration of male homosexuality and a plea for tolerance. The problem for any director would be to take the curse off the material so that the viewer would not simply be subjected to two hours of suffering.

Schnabel does this by successfully tilting the film toward so-called "magical realism." The term is usually associated with the "boom" in Latin American literature, and particularly with Gabriel García Márquez's *One Hundred Years of Solitude* (1967, tr. 1970). The novel, which is almost universally regarded as one of the greatest of the century, blends together imagined and historical events into a colorful and artistic tapestry. Schnabel understands how images work, and he uses color, camera angles, and the devil's own eye for both beautiful and dirty-drab details (indeed, often a combination of both). For example, the unsuccessful and ultimately deadly attempt to escape from Cuba by a hot-air balloon is at once exhilarating to watch and sobering in its denouement.

Before Night Falls received generally outstanding reviews. Kenneth Turan described the film as a "florid examination of an artist's coming of age, of cultures in collision and conflict" that "is difficult to resist." Jay Clark wrote that the contradictions in Cuban society of the period were "embodied daringly by Johnny Depp in a double performance. In one role, he plays a defiant transvestite smuggler; in another, he appears as a repressive military officer who can't quite conceal his own homoerotic urges as he puts pressure on Arenas." Jan Stuart, in the *Advocate*, wrote that Schnabel "has made something gloriously visual and grippingly cinematic" from the life of Arenas, and presents "a harrowing portrait of what it meant for a writer to be gay and out" during the heyday of the revolution. Like others, Stuart praised the two cameo performances by Depp.

A few mainstream critics hated the film. Howard Rosenman, co-producer of *Buffy the Vampire Slayer, Father of the Bride* (1995), *Shining Through* and *Stranger Than Us*, called the film "a small, arty, pretentious movie," and added that he thought it would find an audience in New York "from people who like to wear black — they'll love it" (Cited Fink). Obviously, "arty" and "pretentious" are subjective terms, but it is difficult to see how such an ambitious film covering decades in the life of a country could fairly be called "small." Gary Arnold criticized what he called the film's "ramshackle story construction, inconsistencies on the soundtrack, [and] linguistic hodgepodge," and concluded that Schnabel lacked the "cinematic experience and assurance needed to sustain dramatic interest in a feature-length film." Certainly, the mixture of English and Spanish would limit the film's mainstream audience, especially in America, but the movie has a clear structure. It does not have a romance, unless Arenas' relationship with his mother is considered to fulfill that function, and it is generally lyrical rather than dramatic and realistic. In other words, it is not a mainstream Hollywood film and was never intended to be.

Some critics thought the movie aided in the demonization of Cuba. Experts in Hispanic studies, however, suggested that Arenas would have had problems no matter where he lived because of the intolerance against gay people from the '50s through the '80s. Arenas' extreme promiscuity, which apparently involved hundreds of partners, might be difficult for many people, gay or straight, to accept even today. And there were certainly enough reasons to demonize Cuba outside of the victimization of homosexuals.

The question of the relationship between Arenas' sexuality and his creativity is complex. The three films by Schnabel to date, including *The Diving Bell and the Butterfly*, stubbornly insist upon his belief that the artist, including the person who does not know that he is one, is in some sense an outsider who has to struggle against the pricks of orthodox society. In context, it hardly seems cricket for Arenas to complain about the unfairness of American society (difficulties with agents, problems with hospital care, and so on), but it is probable that, even if he had been rich and in perfect health, he would have found something to complain about. It is part of the greatness of Schnabel's film that he recognizes that fact. Although *Before Night Falls* was essentially an art house film, it was seen and appreciated, and the performance of Javier Bardem in the leading role was much admired. The Academy Award is often a make-up award, and the Academy Award which Bardem won for *No Country for Old Men* was clearly a make-up call for the one he could have won earlier for *Before Night Falls*.

Arenas described his incarceration in Havana's notorious El Morro prison in detail. If only half of what he wrote is true, a season in hell would be preferable to his stay in El Morro Castle. He was imprisoned not for homosexuality, although that was a crime, and the people accused of it were the worst treated in the prison, but for a variety of unspecified charges, and he arrived with a reputation as a rapist, a murderer and a CIA agent. The actual crime, of course, was the publication of his novels and poems abroad without government permission; the other charges were fabricated. There were no secrets in El Morro, and it quickly became known that he was a writer. Among so many illiterate men, writing was a useful commodity, and Arenas wrote letters for the prisoners to send to their loved ones. They paid him in cigarettes, the common coin of the prison, and he used the cigarettes to buy paper and pencils and to smuggle what he had written out of prison.

According to Arenas, what he calls "a group of highly skilled queers called 'porterettes'" were adept at concealing all sorts of objects in their capacious anuses and smuggling them into prison. Once or twice a month, the prisoners were taken outside and the homosexuals put on a show. Arenas is silent about any of the specific individuals involved, but the film is not. Courtesy of Johnny Depp, the film shows us the star of the show," Bon-Bon, the "observed of all observers."

The "heart-throb of the prison," Bon-Bon is so glamorous that, according to the voice-over, she makes the inmates "feel like they were in the movies." Bon-Bon wears a boa around her neck, which is tied down in the back. She is tattooed, wears a blond wig and bandeau, a garter belt, stockings and panties. She wears lipstick, with lip liner, heavy makeup, and eye shadow. She has a bare midriff and a sarong tied around her waist, and strides through her adoring worshippers like Cleopatra on parade. When she bends over, the viewer gets a medium close-up of her haunch. She is, in short, a wonder to behold. No girl would want to wear the same outfit twice, and there are some slight differences between her dress in the character's two different appearances in the film.

The expression on Depp's face when the exchange—four tightly wrapped and greased packages—is made beggars all description. His face shows first pride, then difficulty that reaches toward but does not quite achieve pain, then a combination of both, and finally a glorious pride.

Bon-Bon does not appear in the autobiography, and she is probably a figment of the screenwriters' vivid imagination (or even, perhaps, of Depp's). Smuggling objects out of prison was probably easier than smuggling them in, since almost all of the traffic was going in and the security was not as tight. But real or not, Bon-Bon is a memorable character—as is the military officer, also played by Depp, who interrogates Arenas and forces him to make a written statement renouncing all of his published works.

The military officer, identified as Lieutenant Victor, accuses Arenas of "counter-revolutionary poop." He is neatly dressed in a khaki military uniform and sports a mustache. In his autobiography, Arenas speculates that the officer knew he was gay and scratched his testicles as proof of his manliness, as if "stating that he was the only man there." Arenas adds, as if in proof of his own manhood, that, after he returned to his cell, he masturbated while

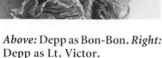

Above: Depp as Bon-Bon. *Right:*
Depp as Lt. Victor.

having a "pleasant fantasy" about Lt. Victor (Arenas 199). Depending upon one's point of view, this will strike the reader as either courageous or sick, or perhaps a bit of both.

In the film, Arenas (Bardem) says in a voice-over about the five minutes he had been given to make up his mind about writing his confession: "It might take a queer more than five minutes to make up his mind while watching the handsome lieutenant stroke his magnificent organ." While Lieutenant Victor is an interesting character, he might convincingly have been played by any alpha male actor. Sean Penn, who also has a cameo in *Before Night Falls*, would have been excellent in the role, but he could hardly have played Bon-Bon successfully.

In his commentary, Schnabel, who does not mention Depp by name, sees the double roles, as in some sense, representing aspects of the same person. Certainly the fact that one role follows the other might indicate that; but the analogy should not be pushed too far, lest any sense of moral distance between the torturer and his victim be eradicated. They are already too close for the comfort of many, both in the book and the film.

As Lieutenant Victor, Depp makes a pass, so to speak, at his genitals, but there is absolutely no evidence that Depp is "packing"—that is, stuffing his trousers with cloth or papers to make his genitals appear larger than they are. This base canard has been following Depp at least since the commentary by Peter DeLuise on *21 Jump Street*. It is totally without support and should be dismissed out of hand.

Depp's Bon-Bon cameo is one of the great moments of film history and will be so regarded in years to come. It is absolutely transparent. There is nothing to show that the actor feels anything but admiration for the character. His graceful movements, lovingly followed by the camera, reflect her pride, her self assurance. Bon-Bon is not like some of the performances in, say, Japanese silent films, in which a man successfully pretends—that is, acts—to become a woman. Bon-Bon is a strange creature, knows it, and would not be anything else. There is no condescending, no pointing out, in Richard III fashion, her weirdness. In perhaps three minutes of screen time, Johnny Depp has made Bon-Bon immortal.

Depp's performance in *Before Night Falls* will not be forgotten. In a letter to the International Edition of *Newsweek,* Hugh Harrison wrote of Depp:

> He is rapidly becoming the actor on whom younger, upcoming actors strive to model their careers, as he did with his own icon Marlon Brando. While his dual performance in Julian Schnabel's *Before Night Falls* is not mentioned in your article [on *Pirates of the Caribbean*], it's amazing how many young performers rank it right up there with Depp's performance as Jack Sparrow, Edward Scissorhands, Ed Wood and Don Juan DeMarco. Fans especially admire his performance as the transvestite prostitute in the same movie (for which, amazingly, he received no billing), awed by his total commitment to the role and his complete truth without one false moment. This, indeed, should have been his first Oscar nomination and, in my opinion, should have won. It was absolutely superb work from our most unafraid, original and inventive actor.

It should be noted that, whatever Depp's billing may have been in the film's original release, both he and Sean Penn receive billing on the American DVD version of the film.

2001 *Blow*

The Entrepreneur

"Who the hell's Johnny Depp?" (George Jung)
"Johnny Depp blew my mind. He became me." (George Jung)

Ted Demme's *Blow* is an episodic story covering some twenty-five years in the life of George Jung, a big-time drug dealer. Based, as they say, on a true story, *Blow* was the second major film within a few months to deal seriously with the problem of drug trafficking. To say that it is less ambitious than Steven Soderbergh's much praised *Traffic* is merely to characterize *Blow*, not to judge it. Concentrating on a single character, especially when that character is played by Johnny Depp, gives *Blow* a dramatic advantage *Traffic* does not have. Unfortunately, that was the only advantage.

Blow opens with a montage of scenes showing the growing of coca, its transformation into heroin, and its loading into a plane for transportation to the United States. The film then shifts to the childhood of George Jung, his mother's unhappiness at the lack of money, and his father's bankruptcy. Jung moves to California during a period of "happy rebellion." Nobody works, the girls are all beautiful and claim they are stewardesses, and drugs are everywhere: "It was paradise." Jung moves effortlessly into the selling of pot and then hard drugs, first in California and then coast to coast. Ever looking for new opportunities, Jung goes to Columbia and becomes Pablo Escobar's main man in America. In and out of jail along the way, Jung acquires a drug habit, a beautiful young wife (also with a habit), a child, and a first-hand knowledge of the American penal system.

The California scenes clearly define a period when drug-induced happiness seemed the answer to the world's problems, and are the best in the movie. The remainder of the film defines Jung's inevitable descent into drug addiction, major criminality, ruin in his family and romantic life, and terms in prison. "I'm great at what I do, Dad," he tells his father, but his mother turns him in to the authorities. The remainder of the film is a sometimes funny descent into hell. At the end of the movie, he is serving a long prison sentence and hoping to build a relationship with his son. The moral, according to Jung: "My ambition far exceeded my talent." It is, however, unclear if more talent would have improved his lot, but it might have made the movie more exciting. The film ends with a shot of the real George Jung.

Coming as it did on the heels of Steven Soderbergh's *Traffic*, a much more ambitious film, *Blow* was not well received. Most reviewers compared *Blow* to *Traffic*—and always, or nearly always, unfavorably. Stephen Rea was typical. He wrote that *Blow* is directed in a "linear but unimaginative fashion.... The tone is flat, the scenes are a series of clichéd mini-dramas that echo ... any number of other films featuring drug-fueled freaks, fools, crooks and party girls." He also criticized Depp's appearance and wrote that he aged unconvincingly. The last half of this analysis, courtesy of a poor make-up job, is clearly true. Rea thought that Depp brought "a degree of playfulness to the role" but was hampered by a poor script. Jack Mathews believed the film was too long and detailed, and that Depp did not age convincingly. He concluded, "Depp can be as charming an actor as any around and his empathy with Jung suggests that he is playing him as a far more romantic figure than we can believe he actually was." If this statement is true, the fault was more likely that of the director than of the actor. As an actor, Depp has never been afraid of going dark.

By the time *Blow* appeared, Depp's performances were finally beginning to attract the attention they deserved. For example, Joe Morgenstern wrote that the film received a boost from Depp's performance, despite an addled script. David Sterritt wrote that the actor "lends a touch of class to this inherently stale stuff by playing Jung with his trademarked understatement, evoking psychological depth and emotional power with less showiness than many of his peers would have brought to the part." Sterritt praised the subtlety of Depp's acting and concluded that he was "a gifted star who deserves more-impressive cinema vehicles."

Peter Travers was unusual for liking both the film and Depp's performance. He wrote that if *Goodfellas* and *Traffic* were "the class bookends" of the last ten years of drug films, *Blow* "scorches the screen with a badass bravado all its own. Smart, sexy and dangerous, this high wire act is a movie and a half." Travers seems to have been alone in his opinion.

When appropriate, Johnny Depp has always been a style leader, and Lou Lumenick wrote that Depp gives the "performance of his career" while wearing "hilarious wigs and period fashions." Charlotte Raven thought that Depp's performance was limited to "several different versions of staring," that the film attempted "to have it both ways," and that the conclusion in which Jung receives a long prison sentence is depicted as "bad luck rather than a moral consequence of the life he has chosen to lead." Admittedly, psychological analysis is not the film's strength, but Raven's assessment is harsh and largely negated by the movie itself. Certainly, competition among the so-called "dope opera films" is severe, and the film's achievement hardly measures up to its ambition.

In one form or another, anti-drug films go back to the beginning of movies, but the attitudes toward individual drugs have changed over time. Silent films reflected a variety of attitudes toward alcohol and other drugs, ranging from the tragic and censorious (Seastrom's *The Phantom Chariot*, Griffith's *Broken Blossoms*) to the comic, sometimes both in the same film. Chaplin worked both sides of the street in his two-reelers (again, sometimes in the same film)—the comic in *One A.M.*, and the comic/censorious in *Easy Street*, where the anarchist is clearly represented as addicted to the needle. Charlie, however, has it both ways by sitting down on the needle. After the death of Wallace Reid, one of the most popular film stars of the post–World War I period, of addiction to morphine in 1923, his wife, Dorothy Davenport, produced a film, *Human Wreckage*, exposing the prescription use of the drug. The film is now lost.

Because of the restrictions of the Hollywood code, there were few treatments of drugs in mainstream films in the third of a century following its inception in 1935. Honorable exceptions include Billy Wilder's *The Lost Weekend* (1945), with Ray Milland as an alcoholic, and Otto Preminger's *The Man with the Golden Arm* (1955), with Frank Sinatra as a heroin addict. The 1960s and Woodstock softened the attitude towards drugs, but widespread publicity of the horrors of drugs and the desolation of crack cocaine darkened them once again. Viewers who have watched the destruction depicted in the television series *The Wire* might be hard pressed to defend the legalization of hard drugs, however uncertain they might be about ways to suppress the drug traffic.

Depp, wearing a wig and using a variety of prosthetic devices as he ages, is in nearly every scene and carries off the difficult role with his usual flair. Jung's father and mother, well played by Ray Liotta and Rachel Griffiths, appear from time to time to complicate his life. His father is understanding, but his mother turns him over to the police when he jumps bail — and then chews him out in the bargain. Penelope Cruz (*All the Pretty Horses*) plays the beautiful Columbian whom Jung marries, but her drug addiction and their daughter are complicating factors in an already confused and dangerous life. Paul Reubens, aka Pee-Wee Herman, is weirdly convincing as a California drug dealer.

Blow is as non-judgmental as a police report. Some reviewers have stated that Jung was not very smart or he would not have ended up in jail so many times. He was, however, in a dangerous business, and the Columbians and junkies he dealt with were not exactly stable people. Reviewers have also noted that the movie is not *The Godfather*, or *Goodfellas*, or whatever. And it is certainly not *Traffic*. It reads like an off-beat version of the great American success story, sort of Horatio Alger sells dope and goes to hell.

The price Jung pays is high. He is shot, jailed frequently (for ever longer periods of time), and makes a fortune and loses it. He is betrayed more than once by his friends and confederates, develops an enormous habit, is betrayed by his wife, and estranged from the only person he has ever really loved, his daughter.

Jung is now in jail, where he will remain until 2015, if he lives that long, dreaming about his daughter, who is now grown and has never visited him. At the end of the film we are rewarded, if that is the word, with a picture of the real George Jung, who looks like death warmed over.

Director Ted Demme (1964–2001) was the nephew of the much better-known Jonathan Demme, who began as a genre director (*Crazed Heat*, 1974; *Crazy Mama*, 1975) and moved toward mainstream big-budget Hollywood filmmaking, most successfully with *The Silence of the Lambs* (1991) and *Philadelphia* (1993). By comparison, Ted began with small-budget and independent films, and had only recently moved into the Hollywood mainstream when he helmed *Blow*. Ironically, he died soon after the release of *Blow*, after being stricken while playing basketball. According to newspaper reports, the autopsy found cocaine in his system.

To say that it was an ironic ending for a man who could make a film which portrayed the ravages of cocaine as horrendously as *Blow* does is an understatement, especially considering the extras on the DVD in which Demme was an active participant. These include a graphic non-fiction film about the violence and chaos in Columbia occasioned by the enormous shipments of drugs to America (but especially to California) in the late 1960s, and Ted Demme's conversations with Jung about his life and the making of *Blow* (filmed at the Ottisville Correctional Institute, where Jung is imprisoned). Jung talks objectively and dispassionately about the devastation which drugs caused in his own life. His actions were, he says, "totally unexplicable [*sic*] to anyone, even myself." The only explanation he can offer is to blame California: "The day I went to California was the day I went bad." Ah, the sunshine, the beaches, the nakedness of the women, their immorality, the prevalence of drugs and the ease of procuring and selling them — doubtless, the combination was overwhelming.

And I'll bet he never really looked like Johnny Depp either. Or was half as charismatic.

2001 *From Hell*

Pipe Dreams

"From Hell. Well, at least they got the address right." (Sergeant Peter Godley)

From Hell began life as the enormous graphic novel *From Hell*, written by Alan Moore and illustrated by Eddie Campbell. The complex plot pivots on the attempt to cover up the birth of a child fathered by the dissolute, syphilitic and probably retarded Prince Albert with a prostitute. Sir William Gull, a famous surgeon and, as it turns out, sadistic murderer, is ordered by Queen Victoria to take care of the matter. Gull operates on the woman to impair her sanity, and becomes both royal protector and serial killer, aka Jack the Ripper, when he sets out to murder the women who knew about the baby and the Prince's marriage to the prostitute. Of course, Gull is only one of a multitude of men who have been proposed as the Ripper, but since the film does not pretend to be true, at least in any literal sense, it is hardly fair of Denis Meikle to write that, since Gull had been disproved to be the killer, the film "was thus bound to an outmoded convention before the first frame of film had ever passed through the gate of the camera" (284). Indeed, it is unlikely that even one out of a hundred viewers of the film could name one of the possible Ripper candidates.

The graphic novel is a vast historical drama in which many of the characters are based on real people. A few of them, including Inspector Abberline and Queen Victoria, play major roles in the labyrinthine drama, but many other historical characters play more or less probable minor roles. These include: Walter Sickert (the painter whom a popular crime novelist, Patricia Cornwell, "proved" to be Jack the Ripper in her 2002 book *Portrait of a Killer*), William Blake, William Butler Yeats, Richard Mansfield (a celebrated actor then [1888] playing Dr. Jekyll and Mr. Hyde on the London stage), James McNeil Whistler, William Morris, Buffalo Bill Cody, Oscar Wilde, Aleister Crowley, Karl Marx, George Bernard Shaw and Joseph Merrick (the Elephant Man), among others less well-known, including those involved in the enormous newspaper circus surrounding the Ripper murders.

Moore began with the idea that, in order to solve a crime holistically, one would need to understand the entire society it occurred in and to depict the murders as "a consequence of the politics and economics of the time." While *From Hell* is almost certainly the first comic book or graphic novel to develop the idea, at least in such detail, it is hardly new and has been around for centuries in more or less explicit form. The literary work which *From Hell* most closely resembles is perhaps Charles Dickens' *Bleak House* (1853), with the Court of Chancery and the case of Jarndyce and Jarndyce metaphorically playing the Jack the Ripper role. The sordid interactions between the various levels of society and the corruption of the aristocracy, the dirt and grime of the great city, and the complex plot are similar. Of course, Moore's sexual explicitness and the involvement of the Queen are beyond Dickens' grasp, but it is hardly clear that *From Hell* is superior for that.

From Hell would make a wonderful eight-hour miniseries, but it is too sprawling and complex for a two-hour film. Screenwriters Terry Hayes and Rafael Yglesias simplified the plot and made the film a kind of historical police procedural. In the graphic novel, the identification of the murderer is known almost from the beginning, but in the movie it is withheld until near the end, presumably to build suspense. Except for an occasional mention, most of the famous cast of the novel is omitted, although John Merrick, the Elephant Man, does make an appearance. The commentary on the DVD clearly shows that much ingenuity was spent attempting to keep the viewers guessing as to the identity of the Ripper. However, since

Mean Streets: Depp as Inspector Abberline in *From Hell*.

it is clear almost from the beginning that the Ripper was not one of the Nichols gang harrying the Whitechapel prostitutes—the gang did not travel in carriages, and the conventions of the genre require an up-scale murderer—the possibilities are strictly limited to the moneyed class, and the viewer, who is more interested in the excitement of the series of events than the solution, is unlikely to care who the murderer is.

The film provides motivation for the murders—Dr. Gull has been infected by a prostitute—but his apocalyptic visions have been omitted, or, rather, down-sized and shifted to Inspector Abberline. In the novel, Gull is a human monster fueled by sadism. His science is soaked in blood and the intricacies of dark rituals. The film, however, reduces him to a sadistic murderer. Like Iago in Shakespeare's *Othello*, Moore's monster needs no motivation. His hatred is comprehensive.

Johnny Depp's Inspector Fred Abberline is a far cry from Moore's original. In the novel, Abberline is a heavy-set man in early middle-age. He has a black mustache and wears a bowler hat. He is not a drug addict and is, by the standards of the times, only a moderate drinker. According to Moore, Abberline was married, and his interest in the Ripper murders and the prostitutes involved disrupted his home life. There is a hint on the last page of the novel that he intended to join the Pinkertons, but neither the prologue nor the epilogue, both of which take place in 1923, mentions either his wife or the Pinkertons. In his apocalyptic final vision, dated 1904 or 1905, Gull sees an Irish mother calling in her children and telling Gull to return to Hell. The woman may or may not be Mary Kelly, who may or may not be Emma, the prostitute to whom Abberline gave money and with whom he was apparently infatuated. Moore writes that he gives this information "just in case that helps." Of course, it does not, nor does Moore believe that it would.

In the film, Abberline is given second sight. His opium dreams furnish visions of murders yet to come, which the authorities find useful enough that he is allowed to stay on the force, even though they know he is an addict. He has been married, but his wife died delivering a still-born baby. He falls in love with Mary, or Marie, Kelly, a beautiful red-haired prostitute. In the film, both Mary and her daughter are allowed to survive; and there is an idyllic portrait of Mary raising her daughter in an Irish seaside cottage. In the novel, only the child survives, and Abberline dies of an overdose.

The reviews of *From Hell* found the film interesting for a variety of reasons, but generally ignored Depp's performance as Abberline. Phillip Kerr's review in the *New Statesman* was, however, genuinely savage. Kerr noted that although Depp was hailed for his performance in *Donnie Brasco*, he had made "some spectacularly bad career choices," singled out *Don Juan DeMarco, Fear and Loathing in Las Vegas* and *Sleepy Hollow*, and concluded that it is "difficult to see why anyone should note him at all." In full Swiftian mode, Kerr labeled the Hughes brothers and Terry Hayes—"an Australian screenwriter of expert mediocrity"—as the Three Stooges ,and, for good measure, added Depp to the list. He described Depp as "[b]owler-hatted, sparsely mustachioed and looking more than a little like Charlie Chan." Peter Rainer, in *New York*, was also hard on Depp and wrote, in the wry tone of a truth-teller, "Whether he's gypsy or gent, Depp never seems to be taking part in his movies. Most of the time, he looks glazed over with soulful blah." Or, in this case, with laudanum.

Lou Lumenick believed, certainly correctly, that the film was heavily influenced by the Hammer horror movies of the 1960s. The film lays out "an elaborate conspiracy theory ... against an eye-popping (and blood-spattered) re-creation of gaslight-era London that suggests an unlikely collaboration of Tim Burton and Oliver Stone." Whatever other influences may have been at work in the movie, its chief source is the brutal and enormously complex graphic novel on which it is based.

The most overheated praise came from Carl Bromley. Writing in the aftermath of the destruction of the World Trade Center disaster, Bromley called the film an "infernal postcard postmarked Victorian London, a ghostly premonition of things to come," and opined, "The horrors of September 11 might have ended something Jack the Ripper started in Whitechapel, East London, in 1888." Apparently carried away by the emotions of the moment, Bromley wrote that the film "is a witches' brew, an absinthe-laced fever dream, a Hammer horror ... a paranoid conspiracy thriller" and "a detour through the mother of all conspiracies, which swoops down devastatingly on the London poor." To be fair, Bromley admitted that despite all the directors brought in to aid the project, he does not believe that any film could measure up to the greatness of Moore's original. Clearly, however, Bromley's pain is a heavy burden to put on any film, especially one as crudely made and replete with historical inaccuracies as *From Hell*. By modern standards of butchery, Ripper Jack was, at best, a small-timer who managed to slaughter, even by the most optimistic standard—if that is the phrase—fewer than a dozen women, and those among the most wretched of a great city.

Of chief interest to the reviewers was the status of the Hughes brothers as minority artists. Twin-brothers Albert and Allen Hughes, although bi-racial, are usually identified as black, and, at least until *From Hell*, were associated with themes of identity and racial conflict. *Menace to Society* (1993) is an unsparing look at black violence and is generally regarded as superior to John Singleton's *Boyz n the Hood* (1991). *Dead Presidents* (1995)—that is, those presidents pictured on American money—is a much more ambitious film which chronicles a group of black friends before, during and after Viet Nam. *American Pimp* (1999) is a non-fiction film about pimps, a colorful and charismatic group of men, always black in the movie, who commandeer working girls and take a part of their earnings. Despite its dreary subject, the film has many humorous moments and is constantly entertaining.

It is apparent from the often bitter commentary on the DVD that the suits kept a tight rein on the Hughes brothers and oversaw every frame of the film. Apparently, much attention was given to the motivation of the characters and to the working out of the plot. Nonetheless, the continuity is murky, and the editing is defective. The graphic-novel storyboarding, so commonplace in filmmaking these days — and often to the films' detriment — detracts from the character development in *From Hell*. For example, the murders might have been shot as classical montage, but instead we see only a dark canvas and slashes of red. All the scenes are developed more or less at the same pace so that there is no beginning or end, just a cutting from one scene to the next.

From Hell is very much a studio film which gives the appearance of having been written and shot by committee. The Hughes brothers, who had done excellent work in smaller films, were apparently overwhelmed by the complexity of the undertaking and also, to some extent, by a lack of knowledge of the period. Hemmed in by the studio and shackled by a script which seems to have been in a process of constant change, they produced an interesting film which cannot, however, be considered a success by any standard and which did nothing to further their careers.

Among the cast, Robbie Coltrane (*Cracker*) is a standout as Shakespeare-loving Sergeant Peter Godley, who understands Inspector Abberline's opium addiction and tolerates it because of his genius at using his "visions" for crime-solving. Godley cites not only the most famous plays (*Hamlet, Othello, Romeo and Juliet*), but also the lesser-known *Measure for Measure*, which a Victorian was hardly likely to have seen performed or even to have read: "Ay, but to die.... / To lie in cold obstruction and to rot."

The prostitutes, or "unfortunates," in the film are generally unconvincing compared with those in the novel. The exploitation of the prostitutes by both the aristocracy and the lower-class thugs would be readily apparent without the emphasis placed upon it in the film. The actors seem uncomfortable with the obscenities and vulgarities they are required to recite. The disgust they register when their lesbian member kisses another woman passionately on the mouth is unbelievable coming as it does from women who nightly perform a variety of sexual acts in alleyways. Presumably the distaste has to do with the publicity of the kiss, its lesbian nature, or the idea that prostitutes kiss only those they love — but none of the reasons is convincing.

The English actors, both upscale and down, are generally superior to the Americans, but Ian Holm is miscast as Gull. According to the commentary, Nigel Hawthorne was originally cast as Gull, but a recurrence of the cancer which eventually killed him forced him out at the last moment, and Holm was chosen. Holm, a small man, has the intelligence, but lacks the egocentricity and force of character the role demands. He was more successful as J. M. Barrie in the TV miniseries *The Lost Boys* (1978), a character which Depp was to play some fifteen years later in *Finding Neverland*. Jason Flemyng's portrayal of the coachman and lookout for the Ripper is especially memorable, a classic performance in a role which has few lines.

According to the DVD commentary, the studio fretted about Johnny Depp — strangely enough, not about his talent but his choice of roles; I assume because they feared it might have weakened his star power. (In retrospect, this hardly seems to have been a problem.) The commentary praises his acting ability, particularly his mastery of accents. He is said to have mastered three English accents: a Northern accent, a Liverpool accent, and a Cockney accent. Indeed, the role of Abberline seems to have been written to appeal to Deep. The drugged and depressed protagonist, the period setting, the man who appears to be an outsider working at an insider's job, the only person in the film whose dress does not show his class, and the occasionally brilliant repartee: When Jack tells Abberline that men will one day "look back" and say he "gave birth to the twentieth century," Abberline cleverly responds that Jack was "not going to see the twentieth century."

While not a failure, *From Hell* was not the financial success Fox had hoped for. With a production budget of $35,000,000, it generated box-office receipts of approximately $31,000,000 domestically and $42,000,000 foreign. While the film did not injure Johnny Depp's career, its relative lack of success seems to have put the career of the Hughes brothers into at least a temporary turnaround. Their outspoken criticism of the suits on the DVD commentary could not have helped.

In a striking scene, unfortunately (but rightly) cut from the film, Abberline is given a more exotic death, dying of an overdose in a Chinese opium den peopled by, among others, three beautiful native women in a large sunken bath. Apparently, he has carefully prepared for his own death, and the oriental caretaker closes Abberline's eyes and places two coins over them for the ferryman.

2003 *Once Upon a Time in Mexico*

The Man with Three Arms

"Are you a Mexi-can or a Mexi-can't?" (Agent Sands)

Once Upon a Time in Mexico is the third film in director Robert Rodriguez's Mexican trilogy. According to Rodriguez, the name had been suggested some five years earlier by Quentin Tarantino as appropriate for the third film in the series, following *El Mariachi* (1992) and *Desperado* (1995). The name echoes and emulates both Italian director Sergio Leone's *Once Upon a Time in the West* and his so-called "Dollars" trilogy, *A Fistful of Dollars, For a Few Dollars More* and *The Good, the Bad and the Ugly*. The reference to Leone's films, which have canonical status among many aficionados, suggests both a bravura style and a kind of bravura free-wheeling artistic integrity operating in a popular tradition. And just as Leone was an Italian director making films in the tradition of American westerns, American director Robert Rodriguez, albeit of Hispanic background, was making Hollywood films more influenced by Leone's westerns than by any native Hollywood tradition. Such, at any rate, was the intention.

Critics generally found the film disappointing. Chris Pryke noted that the movie was "high on explosive action, but a little threadbare when it comes to plot and logic." Ray Conlogue called the plot endless, and then attempted (with only moderate success) to summarize it. He wrote that the film contains "too much stuff and the cast lost their energy early on." Although the first part of this statement is clearly true, the second part is dubious, considering the fact that the movie was shot catch-as-catch-can out of sequence, with little regard for continuity. The end result is "over cooking a taco-spaghetti western rehash." Claudia Puig called the film "a swaggering fantasy that pays homage to spaghetti westerns" such as *The Good, the Bad and the Ugly*. Brendan Walls grouped Rodriguez with Quentin Tarantino and wrote that the picture appropriates "old plots, old shots and old characters from old films."

There is, of course, nothing wrong with that, but comparisons to Sergio Leone's trilogy, although encouraged by the film's title, are misleading. Leone's leisurely story-telling, mastery of wide-screen cinematography, and studied aestheticism have little in common with Rodriguez's slam-bam-thank-you-man approach. Rodriguez is a shoot first and ask questions later director, and the film was shot in a brisk seven weeks. Selma Hayek was available for only the last week of shooting. Johnny Depp worked only nine days on the film and was apparently surprised to find himself the star.

Johnny Depp, as Sands, a hired killer for the CIA, approaches El Mariachi (Antonio Banderas) in a downscale Mexican restaurant. Sands tells "El," as he prefers to call him, that he has quite a price on his head. Puerco pibil is served, apparently without anyone ordering it. Sands says that he orders the dish with tequila and lime wherever he goes in Mexico, that the dish here is "as good as it's ever been anywhere," and that it is "so good" that when it is finished, he will go to the kitchen and shoot the cook. Sands tells El that he needs him to kill someone to restore the balance in "this country." "You want me to shoot the cook?" El asks reasonably. Sands responds that his car is parked out back — this presumably means that shooting the cook will not inconvenience him — and that he wants him to kill General Marquez after he has killed the president. Apparently, this is similar to killing the cook, and will, according to Sands, restore the balance to the country. In a wonderful tracking shot, Sands then goes into the kitchen and shoots the cook himself.

The joke here is that puerco pibil is a wonderful dish whose recipe is included as an extra on the DVD, and that, while mastery of the recipe could not reasonably justify killing the cook, it might at least justify taking him hostage. Indeed, killing him makes no sense. The mixture of off-the-wall dialogue and senseless action which subverts the humor is typical of the film.

The three-arms joke is another elaborate put-on. In a conversation with the sleezy Belini (Cheech Marin) in a restaurant, Sands is shown pointing a gun at him under the table. When the waitress spills coffee on the table, she apologizes profusely and makes the mistake of wiping off Sands' fake arm. Sands shoots both of them, takes Belini's body out, stuffs it in his car, takes it out into the country, parks the car by a river, and searches the body. He thoughtfully lifts Belini's eye-patch, and takes out a small wrapped package apparently containing drugs.

It is worthy of note that detached body parts, a sure source of humor, tend to move around a lot in Johnny Depp films. A whole essay could be written about the phenomenon in Tim Burton's movies, but the contagion seems to have spread. Eyes are particularly abused. In *Pirates of the Caribbean: Dead Man's Chest*, Ragetti's detached glass eye rolls around the deck before being retrieved and replaced — after, of course, being "cleaned" by the mouth of its owner. And Sands is blinded by having his eye sockets reamed out with what looks like a roto-rooter left over from David Cronenberg's 1988 film *Dead Ringers*.

Like Oedipus, Sands feels betrayed by fate: "I set them up. I see them fall." Nonetheless, he soldiers on blindly. Although he lacks both the talent and finesse of Zatoichi, the famous blind swordsman of a multitude of Japanese films, he manages, with the aid of a small boy acting as his eyes, to survive for a time. Eva Mendes, as Ajedrez, revives him briefly with a kiss and throws away his artificial arm, presumably to show that he no longer needs it; but even her marvelous restorative powers eventually run out, and he meets his death with the same noble words Randolph Scott used to say adios to Joel McCrea in Sam Peckinpah's *Ride the High Country*: "See ya later."

The film contains lots of explosions, numerous bloody jokes and a really complicated plot. Perhaps the best way to enjoy it is to put your mind on hold, appreciate the many jokes, most of which seem to have been made up on the spot, and go along for the ride.

Oedipus in Mexico (and ticked off): Johnny Depp in *Once Upon a Time in Mexico*.

2003 *Pirates of the Caribbean: The Curse of the Black Pearl*

The Pirate King

"For I am a Pirate king!
And it is, it is a glorious thing
To be a Pirate King."
(Gilbert and Sullivan, *The Pirates of Penzance*)
"It's remarkable how often those two traits [madness and brilliance] coincide."
(Captain Jack Sparrow)
"It was never in the deepest, darkest recesses of my brain to do this kind of thing.
I'm just an actor who thought that at least I could always do a roaring
rendition of 'My Way' and believe it was true." (Johnny Depp)

The first question everyone seemed concerned about was: Why did Johnny Depp, after turning down an enormous number of big-budget films over the years, agree to do *Pirates of the Caribbean*? As a quick tour of the internet clearly shows, the public currently has a greater interest in Depp than in any other film personality. There is, however, no reason not to take him at his word:

> When I became a dad for the first time, it was like a veil being lifted.... I've always loved the process of acting, but I didn't find the occupational hazard particularly rewarding ... there was a long period of confusion and dissatisfaction, because I didn't understand any of it. There was no purpose to it. I was never terribly self-obsessed or wrapped in my own weirdness, but when my daughter was born, suddenly there was clarity. I wasn't angry anymore, suddenly there was clarity. It was like a veil being lifted [Smith, Dead Man's Chest, *Newsweek*].

The *Pirates of the Caribbean* series began as an unlikely alliance between Walt Disney Productions and producer Jerry Bruckheimer. Disney, of course, is known for family-oriented films and theme parks. In an interview with *Rolling Stone*, Johnny Depp said that he had a meeting with the Disney producers and told them that he had been watching Disney cartoons with his three-year-old daughter, and that he would like to do a voice-over for a family film. Disney then asked if he was familiar with their theme parks and said that they were thinking of doing a Pirates of the Caribbean film based on their theme park exhibition. To the shock of his agent, who was also in the room, Depp said: "I'm in." He said that he was a little shocked himself (*Rolling Stone* website). The project was fast-tracked and went from treatment to completed film in a year. This may well be a record for such an enormous production. The result is the stuff of legend, a blockbuster that spawned two sequels (with more to come) and an avalanche of Disney products. After carefully watching the first film, *Pirates of the Caribbean: The Curse of the Black Pearl*, and attempting to explain its enormous popularity, the only reason viewers, pundits, reviewers and wise men could come up with was Johnny Depp.

Pirates have long had a romantic hold on the popular imagination. *A General History of the Robberies and Murders of the Most Notorious Pyrates* was published in 1724 and was so popular that it led to a second volume four years later. The books are commonly referred to as "Johnson's Pirates" because the author's name was given as Captain Charles Johnson; but the tomes are now universally attributed to Daniel Defoe. The first volume, dealing with contemporary pirates, is accurate enough, at least by the standards of the time, but the accounts given in the second volume are mostly, or in some cases entirely, fictional.

Defoe was essentially a journalist who trafficked on the border between fiction and reality, and pirates were grist for his mill. Generically, they belonged to rogue literature, which had been around forever in songs and tales, and which became even more popular with the invention of printing and the expansion of the reading public. During the Elizabethan and Jacobean period, Robert Greene and others of his fly-by-night ilk piously warned their readers of the thieves and murderers lurking behind every hedgerow, while at the same time making their livings (albeit usually poor ones) from writing about them.

The pirate story, which combined (or could combine) love, action, adventure, sex, scandal and satire, simmered in the public consciousness and became a perfect storm with the appearance of W. S. Gilbert and Arthur Sullivan's *The Pirates of Penzance* (1879) and Robert Louis Stevenson's *Treasure Island* (1885). The cheerful tunes and broad satire of the comic opera said that all Englishmen were, after all, pirates of one sort or another; and Stevenson's one-legged rogue and plucky English boy showed adventure and good writing were still alive and well in the empire.

Generically, the pirate movie may be considered a subheading of the adventure film. Although not as clearly defined as, for example, the submarine movie or the bullfight movie, the pirate movie has produced several of the most popular films of all time. It also has produced a number of duds, perhaps most notably Roman Polanski's *Pirates* (1986) and Renny Harlin's *Cutthroat Island* (1995), the former a washout and the latter a megaton detonation which poisoned the atmosphere for more than a decade.

Robert Louis Stevenson's *Treasure Island*, filmed as early as 1912, has long been a favorite for filmmakers and influenced, in one way or another, all the early pirate movies. The 1934 MGM version is a clinker, with Wallace Beery hamming it up as Long John Silver. Two versions are particularly memorable for their portrayals of the old cutthroat. Robert Newton effectively chews the island scenery in Byron Haskin's 1950 film which, as the Disney studios point out, was their first all-live-action feature film; and Orson Welles is genuinely evil in John Hough's underrated 1972 version. Disney's *Peter Pan* (1953) is not usually considered one of the best of Disney's animated films. Bobby Driscoll, who had played Jim Hawkins in Disney's *Treasure Island* three years earlier, supplied the voice of Peter Pan, and Hans Conried played Captain Hook and Mr. Darling.

Douglas Fairbanks' *The Black Pirate* (1926), the only great pirate movie of the silent period, shows the silent swashbuckler at the top of his game. The third of only three silent films shot entirely in two-strip Technicolor, the movie has been beautifully restored and is available in a quality version on DVD. As always in a Fairbanks film, the action scenes are effectively staged, and Fairbanks projects a purely physical joy in filmmaking unmatched in the entire silent period. Perhaps because of the problems involved in the color shooting, however, the film is not quite up to Fairbanks' best.

Aside from Robert Louis Stevenson, the two men who did the most for the pirate genre were probably illustrator Howard Pyle (1853–1911) and Italian adventure writer Rafael Sabatini (1875–1950). Pyle's illustrations for *Howard Pyle's Book of Pirates* and other works clearly show that, in the words of one writer, "Howard Pyle owns the subject of pirates." Indeed, Captain Jack perched on the crow's nest at the opening of *The Curse of the Black Pearl* could, aside from its more flamboyant coloring, have come straight out of a Pyle illustration. And Sabatini's adventure stories had been favorites since the silent period.

Fairbanks always treated romance in a perfunctory fashion, but later films generally emphasized it. The most popular pirate movies of Hollywood's golden years were probably *Captain Blood* (1935) and *The Black Swan* (1942), both based on novels by Sabatini. The romance between hang-loose Errol Flynn and up-tight Olivia de Havilland in *Captain Blood*

"You Have Heard of Me": Johnny Depp as Captain Jack Sparrow in *Pirates of the Caribbean: The Curse of the Black Pearl.*

generates some heat. *The Black Swan*, directed by veteran helmsman Henry King, and starring Tyrone Power and Maureen O'Hara (ably supported by Laird Cregar, Thomas Mitchell, George Sanders, a young Anthony Quinn, and Leon Shamroy's Technicolor photography), is even better. Among later pirate films, Robert Siodmak's *The Crimson Pirate* (1952) easily takes the prize, courtesy of the dazzling acrobatics of Burt Lancaster and his ex-circus partner Nick Cravat. However, the athletic ex-circus performer turned star was ambitious, moved on to more prestigious projects, and largely neglected the adventure films for which he was so well-suited — or unsuited, as it were.

Long John Silver aside, the competition between the so-called "strappers" of the pirate film is severe. The contenders— Douglas Fairbanks, Errol Flynn, Tyrone Power and Burt Lancaster — have set a high standard of super-masculinity which would certainly be difficult to equal, much less surpass. Adding to the difficulty of recent pirate films is the problem of CGI, which removes any shred of the illusion of reality which settled comfortably over the shoulders of the earlier stars.

The *Pirates of the Caribbean* franchise had an interesting genesis. Anyone intrigued by the subject may safely be directed to Jason Surrell's *"Pirates of the Caribbean": From the Magic Kingdom to the Movies*, and to Michael Singer's account of the making of the films, *Bring Me That Horizon*. The books, although done as part of the media blitz connected with the films, contain beautiful illustrations and a substantial amount of accurate information about both pirate movies in general and the three *Caribbean* films in particular. Singer has the advantage of covering all three films, and his volume is more comprehensive.

The original Pirates of the Caribbean theme park attraction opened in Disneyland on

March 10, 1967, three months after the death of Walt Disney. As usual, Disney had actively participated in the design and execution of the project. Passengers on an indoor boat ride were actively assaulted by a series of pirate adventures projected through state-of-the-art audio and animatronic figures, including the song "A Pirate's Life for Me," composed and written by George Burns (the Disney animator, not the ventriloquist) and X Atencio. Later versions opened in Tokyo Disneyland and Disneyland Paris.

The chief characteristics of Walt Disney as an artist and entrepreneur were creative/constant innovation and synergism — that is, his constant effort to combine new technology and old. For example, he moved into television — and color television at that — at a time when the film studios were jealously keeping their movies *off* television because he realized that he could use the new medium to publicize his new movies, old movies and theme parks. For the Disney Corporation of today, the idea of the supernatural pirate film was not precisely new, but it was new enough. After all, Disney had made an animated film, *Treasure Planet* (2002), which retold Stevenson's *Treasure Island* in outer space. While that picture had hardly been a success by Disney standards, a science-fiction pirate was not precisely a supernatural pirate.

Yesterday's state-of-the-art is today's old hat, or chapeau, as the French might say, and the idea was to make a popular film — hopefully, a *very* popular film — which would also make a pot full of pirate booty, create many Disney spinoffs, and attract hordes of people to the new state-of-the-art theme park attraction. In order to achieve these worthwhile objectives, the movie would have to be carefully scripted to blend together the old and the new — that is, to appear cutting edge while at the same time repackaging old ideas with new technology. What better way to do this than with a supernatural pirate movie? And what better man to produce the film than Jerry Bruckheimer?

Producer Jerry Bruckheimer (b. 1945) is the most commercially successful film producer in the world today. His early successes included both artistic triumphs (Paul Schrader's *American Gigolo* and *Cat People*) and, in association with Don Simpson enormous commercial hits (*Cat People, Beverly Hills Cop, Top Gun*, and *Days of Thunder*). When Simpson died of a drug overdose, Bruckheimer continued with a long string of commercially successful films, including the *National Treasure* series, and, more recently, television series, including *CSI: Crime Scene Investigation*, *CSI: NY* and *CSI: Miami*.

After the death of Walt Disney, the company had gone through a period of transition before moving into PG films, but the use of all those pirate skeletons dripping gore, which would surely give the film an MPAA rating of PG13, must have seemed a bit daunting. Bruckheimer, however, with his canny sense of audience expectations, was reassuring. After all, he was, with Simpson, the man who had made *Flashdance*, a film which, despite its R rating, had become a blockbuster. Bruckheimer knew that children today are bombarded daily on network television — forget about cable — with images more disturbing than anything *Pirates of the Caribbean* would show them.

Bruckheimer's choice for director was Gore Verbinski (b. 1965). Although a relative newcomer to big-budget filmmaking, Verbinski had begun his career by making music videos and brand-name commercials, and knew how to deliver movies with immediate visual impact. After completing a short film entitled *The Ritual*, he began his feature career with *Mouse Hunt* (1997), a live-action film starring Nathan Lane done in the style of a cartoon. *The Mexican* (2002), starring Brad Pitt and Julia Roberts, showed that Verbinski could deliver a star-driven commercial vehicle at a reasonable price. *The Ring* (2002), a remake of a Japanese horror film, showed that he could also deliver thrills on demand without grossing out the mainstream audience.

The Curse of the Black Pearl was an important movie for Disney, Bruckheimer and Verbinski. Except for the films made by Pixar during its contentious on-again, off-again relationship with Disney, Disney's recent slate of feature films had enjoyed, at least by Disney's standards, only relative success. If Bruckheimer could deliver the goods, he would open up a whole new arm — or, in the case of the *Pirates* films, a lucrative tentacle — for future productions to go along with his feature films and television series. And if Verbinski could bring in the $150,000,000 project successfully, his future would be assured. By comparison, Johnny Depp had little to lose. He was not considered a big-budget box-office draw and could always go back to the kind of movies he had been making for the past twenty years.

The recipe for the film included supernatural pirates, lots of shape-shifting forms and special effects, a romantic hero and heroine for the young audience to identify with, gifted actors in supporting roles, colorful supporting characters, and — oh yes — what used to be called a "sidekick" in the old cowboy movies to supply comic relief.

We first see Captain Jack Sparrow (Johnny Depp) standing, posed heroically, in a crow's nest. He is handsomely dressed in full pirate regalia. He has a battered tri-corn on his head, a braided beard, a mustache, thrift-shop earrings, a smattering of gold teeth, and, as critics have gleefully pointed out, a full load of eye-shadow. Alas, the heroic pose is a fraud. He is not on a large, square-rigged ship, but on a small boat which is rapidly sinking. He maintains his noble posture and, just as the boat is about to go under, steps nimbly onto the pier. The gag is from Buster Keaton's *The Boat*, except, of course, that Keaton goes all the way down with his boat.

Our beautiful heroine, Elizabeth Swan (Keira Knightley), who has been introduced to us earlier as a child, has very improbably fallen from the battlements of the fort at Port Royal into the sea. Captain Jack acts quite out of character and nobly rescues her. His good deed is immediately punished when he is condemned as a pirate, sentenced to hang, and imprisoned. There, having nothing better to do before escaping, he has a vigorous fight with our handsome young hero, Will Turner (Orlando Bloom), a sword-maker by profession, who has been in love with Elizabeth Swann since childhood. Five years earlier, after the boy Will had been rescued from the sea, Elizabeth, fearing that the medallion made of Aztec gold which he was wearing had been stolen, and that he might be executed as a pirate, had taken the medallion from him and kept it. Later, the harbor is attacked by the *Black Pearl*, a pirate ship manned by ghosts and captained by the fiendish Captain Barbossa (Geoffrey Rush), who takes Elizabeth Swann prisoner and seizes her medallion.

The backstory is explained in increments. Captain Jack Sparrow's consuming motivation is to recapture his ship, the *Black Pearl*, which has been stolen from him by Barbossa, the captain of a crew which morphs into skeletons during battle (or whenever the plot calls for it). Barbossa has taken the ship from Jack and marooned him on a deserted island, from which he had escaped on the small boat with which he entered Port Royal at the beginning of the film. Barbossa's motivation — and what Hitchcock would have called the McGuffin of the three films — is to regain the "final" medallion made of Aztec gold and join it to the other pieces he has "recaptured" after he and his men had squandered them in dissipation after stealing them from Davy Jones' locker. Jones, understandably displeased by the theft, had somehow changed the pirates into undead skeletons and apparently made them impervious to death.

It is unclear why the pirates would want to become mortal again, although their desire for women may have had something to do with it; but they are, of course, constantly thwarted in their quest. Without this motivation, all three films would have had to do without fighting skeletons. From the studio's point of view, of course, that would not have been acceptable. Whenever the pirates get close to success, they are thwarted at the last moment by some demand or other. In the first instance, the pirates produce Elizabeth Swann as the daughter of Bootstrap Bill Turner to satisfy the demanded blood requirement — only to discover that, although she has the medallion, she is *not* the daughter of Bootstrap Bill Turner. And so it goes, through three long films.

The filmmakers were faced with the difficulty of putting a large number of characters in a feature film. The *Pirates of the Caribbean* series would have worked better as a series of episodes which would tell the same story (with, of course, a few different characters in every episode) over and over in incremental fashion, adding or subtracting a bit each time, or sometimes doing both in the same episode. In most television series, the problem (or problems) is never solved, just postponed until the series is canceled (and sometimes not even then). After all, a revival is always a possibility.

Television past and present furnishes many examples. J. D. Cannon's Peter Clifford treats Dennis Weaver's McCloud, a cowboy detective in the big city, as an idiot every week; and in every episode he shows clearly that he is not. House, and Monk, and Cracker have a variety of personal failings, and are in danger of being fired in almost every episode but continue to solve crimes successfully.

The television series, as it has developed over the past sixty years, has two stories to tell. The first story has to do with the protagonist's problems and difficulties. He, or she, has family problems, is an alcoholic, is in love with an ex-wife or husband, gets no respect from his superiors, has difficulty with authority figures, or whatever. These problems may be alleviated, but generally come back in an altered form and must be dealt with again. A few early series, such as *Perry Mason*, had only one story to tell and omitted any reference to family or professional difficulties. The second problem, usually a crime of some sort, is solved in every episode (although occasionally, especially in the last episode or episodes, the solution may be postponed to build suspense for the next season). The series can begin almost anywhere and end almost anywhere, and the protagonist's problem may be endlessly altered or postponed. The problem with a movie, of course, is that the audience expects some sort of resolution, even if, in the so-called franchise movies, the audience knows that it will not last. Unfortunately, the skeletal pirates and the large cast of supporting players, being anchored, as it were, to the theme park, must be retained.

Fortunately, they are an appealing lot, played by talented actors, many of them familiar from other films. Perhaps the most important of them, Captain Hector Barbossa, is played by the talented Geoffrey Rush, who won the 2000 Academy Award for Best Actor for *Quills*. According to Michael Singer, Rush invented an elaborate backstory for what director Gore Verbinski calls "the quintessential villain" (71). Whether the biographical details of the captain of skeletons were necessary may be a matter of debate, but it is typical of the actor's careful attention to details. His larger-than-life performance plays off nicely against Johnny Depp's even more skewed performance of Captain Jack. The scene of the two men peering through their telescopes is a hoot (illustrated Singer 72). Barbossa's telescope looks as if it might actually work, while that of Captain Jack, curved as it is, could, at best, present only a skewed vision of the world.

Jonathan Pryce's Governor Swann is hardly a flashy role, but Pryce gives it his full attention. Pryce is a gifted player who has done outstanding work in films ranging from Shakespeare to Ray Bradbury to Terry Gilliam. He played the leading role in the BBC version of the master's *Timon of Athens* (1981), was wonderful as the appropriately named Mr. Dark in Jack Clayton's marvelous version of Bradbury's *Something Wicked This Way Comes* (1883), and played Sam Lowry in Terry Gilliam's *Brazil* (1985).

The comic relief in *Black Pearl*, if that is what it is in a film which abounds in slapstick, is supplied by two teams and a number of gifted singles. Giles New (Murtogg) and Angus Barnett (Mullroy) score as klutzy Royal Marine guards easily outwitted by Jack Sparrow. Lee Arenberg (Pintel) and Mackenzie Crook (Ragetti) have extended comic routines in each of the three films. Ragetti's eyeball sequence, in which the dislocated wooden orb is chased around before being rescued and restored to its socket, is a highlight. Some producer ought to sign these guys up for a comedy series. It would be interesting to know what the Disney suits thought about the sequence when they read the script (or, for that matter, about other bits of business—for example, the sequence in which Johnny Depp uses the leg of a skeleton to row a floating coffin). They likely regarded such sequences with the same skepticism Walter Brennan initially had for Howard Hawks' idea that he would lose his false teeth to an Indian in a card game in *Red River* (1948). By the time the role won Brennan his second Academy Award for Best Supporting Actor, he had revised his opinion. David Bailie (Cotton), as a man who has had his tongue cut out and has taught his parrot to speak for him, also has some excellent moments. Of course, the fact that the parrot knows only a few traditional parrot phrases allows for some difference in interpretation.

The romantic leads, Orlando Bloom and Keira Knightley, do decent work, but received little praise from the reviewers. Bloom, the more experienced of the pair, had appeared in the *Lord of the Rings* trilogy and in Ridley Scott's *Black Hawk Down*, and was to follow *Black Pearl* with the lead in Scott's *Kingdom of Heaven*. Despite Scott's elegant direction, Bloom was, however, the weak link in that epic film. In a role which Charlton Heston or Russell Crowe would have eaten alive, he seemed undersized and lost. Fortunately, he fares better in the three *Pirates* movies in a less demanding role in which he is not required to carry the film. Knightley fares even better. Although she was only seventeen when she made *Black Pearl*, she was already a veteran of film and television. She is beautiful and game, and when she realized who the real star of the films was, she came alive in her scenes with Johnny Depp in *Dead Man's Chest*.

It is difficult to think of another project of such size whose success became so identified with one actor. Children everywhere identified with Captain Jack and imitated him; however, any detailed analysis of *The Curse of the Black Pearl* is likely to find the character of Captain Jack Sparrow unfocused, at least in the early sections of the film. The much-bruited discussion of the early controversy over how the character should be interpreted may indicate that the screenplay may not have been clear. Of course, this may not have been the fault of the writers. If we accept veteran scripter William Goldman's dictum that "one size fits all" as far as the leading characters are concerned, the decision may simply have been left to be decided later. It is clearly probable that no one had imagined a character as weird as Depp's Captain Jack.

The Black Pearl begins with Captain Jack heroically rescuing Elizabeth Swann from drowning. He is immediately punished for this heroic exploit by being imprisoned and sentenced to be hanged. The deed is so out of keeping with the character he shows throughout the three films that it awakens a suspicion that the character may not have been completely formed in the minds of the writers—at least, that is, in the way Depp portrays him. If the character was to be interpreted as what Anthony Lane calls "a strapper"—that is, a Douglas Fairbanks type—it is difficult to see why he would not get the girl or why the film might need Orlando Bloom. Of course, the characters are figures of romance, not of tragedy. In Shakespearean terms, they belong to the world of comedy and romance, that is, to the world of *A Midsummer Night's Dream*, and not to the world of tragedy (that is, of *Hamlet* or *Othello*). They are generically incapable of growth. Depp takes the character of Captain Jack Sparrow by the throat, so to speak, and strangles the life into him. Careful analysis of Falstaff in *Henry IV* has shown how the character grew rapidly in Shakespeare's mind. From the simple braggart warrior of Roman comedy, the fat rogue grew into a universal type involving, at least to some extent, nearly all the contradictions of perfidious man.

Johnny Depp has famously said that he patterned Captain Jack after Keith Richards, the craggy-faced guitarist, composer, Rolling Stones vocalist and world-class substance abuser. Of course, since Richards appears as Captain Teague in *At World's End*, and since his image is readily available all over the internet, the viewers may judge for themselves the extent of the influence. As students of his films know, Depp is a great mimic and a tireless student of behavioral tics. There is no doubt that Depp's Hunter S. Thompson was more real than Thompson's impersonation. As Captain Barbossa might say, "being, as it were, more precise."

The reviews were generally favorable, and in the case of Johnny Depp, outstandingly so. Dan Etherington, in *Sight and Sound*, called the film the "most satisfying of the summer's blockbusters," and wrote that it was "lively, humorous and well cast," despite being inspired "by a theme-park attraction and released by franchise-minded Disney." Peter Travers was impressed by Depp, but not by the movie. "Johnny Depp in eye shadow and dreads" is "comic dynamite" and has "a scene-stealing gusto unseen since Marlon Brando in *Mutiny on the Bounty*." The Brando reference is interesting, but seems out of place since the two films have little in common except that they are both in some sense sea movies. Perhaps the reference shows a reviewer, who probably knows about Depp's admiration for Brando, attempting with no great success to find a comparable performance. While both performances are certainly over-the-top, Brando was in the process of sabotaging his film while Depp was in the process of saving his.

Reviewers admired Depp's sartorial elegance and beauty. Richard Corliss called him "America's most beautiful serious actor," and noted ironically that Gore Verbinski's prior artistic achievement was Budweiser beer commercials. Others dissed the low origins of the film. David Ansen opined that the movie is better than any movie "based on a theme park ride has any right to be," fretted about the probability of building "life-or-death suspense with characters who can't die," and cited *The Matrix Reloaded*, a film then currently in release, as another example of this perhaps unfortunate trend. Depp, he wrote, "steals every scene in the movie."

John Waters, director of *Cry-Baby* and *Hairspray*, and long-time friend of Johnny Depp, said of Depp's performance as Captain Jack: "First of all, Johnny is a pirate in real life. It's the closest part he's ever played to his real self, but the fact that he played it kind of nelly was a big risk.... If only gay pirates were that much fun" (Smith).

2003 *Lost in La Mancha*

The Great Storm

"It was a great Biblical storm.... I'm cleansed, I'm free at last.... [*Lost in La Mancha* is] the only postcard we've got on what happened." (Terry Gilliam)

"Poor naked wretches, wheresoe'er you are
That bide the pelting of his pitiless storm...." (*King Lear*)

Terry Gilliam had long been fascinated by Miguel de Cervantes' *Don Quixote de la Mancha* (tr. Thomas Shelton, 1612), often called the first and, in the opinion of many, the greatest of all novels. Gilliam identifies with Don Quixote as a visionary who seeks to do the impossible — that is, to force reality to conform to his own vision of it. The film was to be a modern version loosely based on Cervantes' crazed knight, entitled *The Man Who Killed Don Quixote*, and was to star Johnny Depp, French actor Jean Rochefort and Depp's companion Vanessa Paradis, who was to play Dulcinea. Paradis does not appear in any of the film that was shot, although there is a shot of her double riding away on a horse (*Interviews* 211).

Although it would be too strong to write that the novel has a curse on it, at least so far as filming it is concerned, the many past attempts do not inspire confidence. The problem with the novel is that it is all conversation, mostly between Don Quixote and his squire, and has little in the way of plot or even incident — excepting, of course, the famous attack on the windmills which Quixote mistakes for dragons. The great Orson Welles spent decades attempting to film his version, only to have his leading man die and he himself pass on to his reward without finishing it. He left behind a series of magnificent fragments for batteries of lawyers to fight over. Perhaps the most mysterious version of Cervantes' novel is *Don Peyote*, described "as a hipster take on Cervantes," made by the novelist H. L. Humes, author of *The Underground City* (1958). The film, which stars Ojo de Vidrio, described as "an expressive actor who bears a resemblance to Johnny Depp in *Don Juan de Marco*," is an attempt to capture "the zeitgeist of bohemian Manhattan in the 1960s" (Carlaw 15). The film, as it exists, is a silent movie without the Ornette Coleman score or the narrative by Lord Buckley. If we ignore the hopelessly sentimental Broadway musical *Man of La Mancha* and its 1972 Hollywood clone, the only reasonably effective version of *Don Quixote* is Russian director Grigori Koz-

Before the storm: Johnny Depp and Terry Gilliam in Spain filming *Lost in La Mancha*.

intsev's 1957 film. No doubt inspired by the worldwide success of his movie, Kozintsev went on to make famous versions of *King Lear* and *Hamlet* before his untimely death.

Gilliam, frustrated by his inability to put a project together after the troubled *Adventures of Baron Munchausen* (1988), called Jake Eberts, the executive producer of *Munchausen*, and said that he had two names—"one's Quixote, one's Gilliam"—and that he needed $20,000,000. Eberts read the book, but found no plot and thought the book impossible to condense. Eventually, the offer "tumbled into nothingness," and Gilliam decided that the best thing would be to add a modern story for context, somewhat in the manner of Mark Twain's *A Connecticut Yankee in King Arthur's Court*. Depp would become Don Quixote's squire.

After reading Cervantes' novel and writing several drafts of a screenplay with regular collaborator Charles McKeown, Gilliam scouted locations in Spain, "post Ridley Scott's *1492*." Since no one has ever accused Ridley Scott of not having a good eye for locations, it is hardly surprising that Gilliam ended up picking some of the same sites for filming. Although Gilliam admitted that the character of Don Quixote might end up being too much like the characters of Munchausen in *The Adventures of Baron Munchausen* and Parry in *The Fisher King*, he thought he could make it as a western — "outside, lots of sun and horses." Eventually, Gilliam resurrected the project with Terry Grisoni as co-writer under the title of *The Man Who Killed Don Quixote* (McCabe 185).

According to Johnny Depp, the actor had discussed two or three projects with Gilliam while filming *Fear and Loathing in Las Vegas*. A year or so later, Gilliam sent him a screenplay. Depp had admired "the creative process" and the "energy" of working with Gilliam on the Hunter S. Thompson film and agreed to star in Gilliam's new movie. Depp's character was a modern scoundrel sent back in time to serve as Don Quixote's squire in place of Sancho Panza.

The $40,000,000 budget, said to be the largest for any film ever made in Europe, was raised independently, and pre-production on *The Man Who Killed Don Quixote* began in June 2000. Production designs, based on Terry Gilliam's sketches, were impressive in number, size and scale, and clearly indicate what the finished film might have looked like. Shooting began in September 2000, but stopped after only five days of filming. Negotiations to resume filming began, but the completion bond company intervened and put a permanent stop to the project.

Everything went wrong. Although Gilliam knew that the company was filming close to a NATO air base, he had been told the flights would be limited; such, alas, was not the case. The flights were constant. Their aging star, Jean Rochefort (b. 1930), who was perfectly cast as Don Quixote, suffered a double disc hernia, was in constant pain, barely able to sit on a horse, and would be unable to continue for an unknown period. Although the film was shooting in a desert area in which rain was rare, the skies opened and an enormous storm destroyed nearly all the location film equipment, and, as an extra blow, turned the landscape from brown to green overnight. Terry Gilliam stood in the midst of the storm, raging against the elements like Shakespeare's King Lear, being purged, like Lear, of vanity and ambition, but not apparently of all hope of eventually making the movie. Depp later described Gilliam's failure: "Slowly but surely you see him [Gilliam] shrink and you see a different human being. He transforms into this other thing, this beaten man.... It's very funny and very tragic and all horribly true."

Johnny Depp has said that, while watching *Lost in La Mancha*, he was amazed by how much material had been shot in so brief a time. Much of the material shows the pre-production of the film, including building of sets, storyboards, costumes, casting and so forth. The most interesting segments are scenes of a fiesta shown at the beginning, and Gilliam's prepping the so-called Three Giants for their scenes. Of course, the insurers, who took an enormous hit when the film closed down, owned the rights to the few scenes actually shot for the film.

Originally, Keith Fulton and Louis Pepe were picked from a group of film students to make a non-fiction film about the shooting of *12 Monkeys* (1995). Gilliam gave the pair a camera, tape, access and a promise not to interfere. The director defined this as "maybe a kind of narcissism to see what the truth is" and "maybe learn something." Gilliam admits that part of his motivation was to show himself as a responsible filmmaker and not the out-of-control maverick he was often depicted as being after the filming of *Adventures of Baron von Munchausen*, and he even hoped that the documentary film might help him get employment in the future. Despite the fact that the outcome was hardly one that Gilliam might have hoped for, the decision was a fortunate one. Fulton said they shot about 100 hours of film. Of course, only a fraction of this was shot on location during actual filming. The resulting non-fiction film, *Lost in La Mancha*, stands as a permanent record of what was, and suggests the greatness of what might have been. It is a wonderful film, not just for fans of Johnny Depp and Terry Gilliam, but for anyone interested in the nitty-gritty of creative, big-budget filmmaking. Whether *Lost in La Mancha* is cinema vérité, as its makers allege, is a delicate question that need not concern us here.

The reviewers were numerous, horrified and brief. They used phrases such as "a horror film," "a train wreck," "a no-fault catastrophe," compared Terry Gilliam to Don Quixote, and quickly turned their eyes away, preferring to watch the latest slasher film rather that a tragedy of such magnitude. In a later interview with the *London Daily Observer*, Gilliam described the disaster as "so cruelly absurd, so surreal and disturbing it still has a grip on me," adding that he hopes to buy the film back from the moneymen: "The film is in my head. I've watched it there thousands of times. I just want to get it out. All my efforts are concentrated toward that."

What Vladimir Nabokov called McFate was not finished with Terry Gilliam. As the world knows, Heath Ledger, the star of Gilliam's *The Imaginarium of Dr. Parnassus*, died of a drug overdose before finishing the film. Johnny Depp, Colin Farrell and Jude Law agreed to fill in the missing scenes. Needless to say, having four different actors play the same character in a narrative film would hardly be possible in most movies, but would hardly be surprising in a Terry Gilliam film.

On August 4, 2008, Terry Gilliam announced plans to revive his Don Quixote project as soon as Johnny Depp became available. "We're just talking about dates to film," the director said. Gilliam is not a man to concede defeat easily.

2004 *Finding Neverland*
The Boys of Summer

"Nothing Gold Can Stay." (Robert Frost)
"I see the boys of summer in their ruin…" (Dylan Thomas)
"This is the land of lost content,
I see it shining plain,
The happy hours where I went,
And cannot go Again." (A. E. Housman)

Although the character of Peter Pan has a complicated textual history, he is best known from the play *Peter Pan* (1904, and later revisions). The play, which opened at the Duke of York's Theatre in London on December 27, 1904, was an immediate and enormous success, and has been successfully performed on the stage, television and the big screen for more than a century. Although given two names of unquestionable male potency, the role has from the beginning always— or almost always— been played by mature women. Notable versions available on video include Betty Bronson in Herbert Brenon's beautifully restored silent film (1924), Mary Martin (1954) and Sandy Duncan (1980).

Although the popularity of the play continues unabated, critical attention has moved away from the play to its author, J. M. Barrie, an enormously successful novelist and playwright, and to the so-called five "lost boys" whom he adopted after their parents' deaths. This interest, which had been simmering for some time, came to a boil with the three-part BBC series *The Lost Boys*, written by Andrew Birkin and directed by Rodney Bennett (1978), and continues to the present time. Birken's later biography, an outgrowth of the research he had done for the BBC series, was written, he says, in three months, and published as *J. M. Barrie and the Lost Boys* (1979). This essentially Freudian interpretation of Barrie, although not without garnering some skepticism, has become standard and, unless dramatic new biographical evidence is uncovered (an unlikely event in any case), is likely to remain so.

Why was Johnny Depp interested in playing so introverted a man? Aside from the fact that Depp may have been interested in making a family film, the role gave him a chance to practice his Scots accent, and the character's hidden life interested him. According to Depp: "We see tidbits of information that inspired it [*Peter Pan*], and there was always some speculation about Barrie that maybe there was some kind of paedophilia going on, which I actually don't think there was. What I do believe is that he was an incredibly dark figure, really depressed ... morose" (Meikle 317).

After the critical and commercial success of *Monster's Ball* (2000), which won Halle Berry an Academy Award, German-born director Marc Forster scored another commercial success with *Finding Neverland*. Forster's later films include *The Kite Runner* (2007), based upon an enormously popular novel, and *Quantum of Solace* (2008), the strangely-titled James Bond film starring Daniel Craig.

Unlike most biopics, which deal with the whole, or at least a major portion, of a person's life, *Finding Neverland* covers only a limited period of time. The film begins with the failure of Barrie's earlier play *Little Mary* and ends with the triumphal opening of *Peter Pan*. Unhappily married to a beautiful young woman, Mary (Radha Mitchell), who does not understand him and his total lack of interest in marital relations, Barrie befriends and plays childish games in the park with the four young sons of a beautiful widow, Sylvia Llewelyn Davies (Kate Winslet). As Barrie's affection for the boys deepens, tension with his wife increases, and the boys' grandmother (Julie Christie), who both distrusts and envies Barrie's relationship with her grandsons, and blames him for blighting her daughter's prospects for a lucrative second marriage, vainly attempts to destroy Barrie's relationship with her grandsons.

The title of the play which opens the film, *Little Mary*, may be glimpsed in the newspaper clipping cut out by the Barries' maid; later, Barrie first sees the boys when he peers through the opening in the newspaper which Barrie reads as he sits in Kensington Park. This symbolism, although obvious, is effective in context. Barrie teaches the children fantasy, convincing them that the dog Porthos is a bear performing in a circus ring. When Barrie's wife, Mary, discovers what has happened, she invites the family to supper. After the meal, which has been a fiasco, Mary and Barrie climb the stairs to their separate bedrooms. Mary pauses, her right hand on the door knob; tells Barrie despairingly that if he cannot devote more time to being

J. M. Barrie (Johnny Depp) confronts a rebellious Peter Llewelyn Davies (Freddie Highmore) in *Finding Neverland*.

with her, "then we must end this"; and enters her dark room. In the film's best moment, Barrie then opens his door into a sunlit outdoor scene. The sequence's unspoken subtext — that she has no children and no hope of having any since he has no interest in normal marital relations — is vividly expressed.

After helping Peter fly a kite in the park, Barrie takes the children to their home, only to be confronted by Mrs. DuMaurier, who tells him that his attentions are unwanted. Barrie images her as a witch, and she turns up transgendered into Captain Hook: "Not one of you will escape." As time passes, Barrie continues to play with the children and to transmute his experiences into the world of the play he is writing. The film develops considerable humor from the experiences of the actors who have been retained by producer Charles Frohman, as they adapt themselves to acting characters in a play more suited to vaudevillians than to actors trained in classical theater. Although the other children accept Barrie, after Sylvia becomes ill, Peter begins to resent him and to rebel against his authority. He believes, quite rightly, that Barrie is not telling him the truth about his mother's health. As the film progresses, Barrie's relationships with the boys and his wife Mary deteriorate, and his relationship with the boys' grandmother, strained from the beginning, develops into open warfare.

Both grandmother and wife have a case to make against Barrie, and it is a credit to the film that both are allowed to make it honestly (even if, in context, the film does not allow the viewer any sympathy — or very little — for their characters). After reading her husband's journal, Mary says that she was "very naïve" when she got married: "I imagined that brilliant people disappeared into some secret place where good ideas floated around like leaves in autumn.... And I'm sure the Davies will adore the world you've created for them. I only wish I were part of it." When George becomes concerned about his mother's health, Barrie tells the boy that he must grow up — indeed has grown up "during the last thirty seconds" — and deal with the situation himself. When George injures his arm experimenting with the flying apparatus of the play, he refuses to allow his arm to be set until his mother agrees to a medical examination. Of course, all comes well on opening night. The eventual largely-tragic maturity of the so-called "lost boys" is hardly in question in the obligatory happy ending of both the play and the film.

Martin Erickson, in the *Journal of Feminist Family Therapy*, examines the film's personal dynamics, focusing on the movie's ideas "about gender, gender roles, masculinity, historical time period, Hollywood realism, and the like." While he admits to "a lot of compassion" for this "lonely man," he makes the valid point that Barrie's attention to the boys "may have kept him from his responsibilities to the people in his life," and that he depended upon women to do the hard work of parenting the boys. In *Peter Pan*, the late Victorian gender roles are "completely requisitioned" and segregated to their appropriate duties and responsibilities. While everything that Erickson says is true, the situation is not as dire as he seems to think. If the story and play had not somehow enforced the traditional roles, it could hardly have achieved its enormous popularity among parents. Also, the traditional casting of a girl/woman as Peter Pan took the curse off the material, and if there is any residual curse left today, an androgynous Johnny Depp easily carries it away. As for the rest, Erickson's concern for Barrie the man, long dead and artistically celebrated, is pure sentimentality.

The reviews of *Finding Neverland* were mixed. Although many critics thought that the story was weak, most found something to praise about the film. There was a general unhappiness about what was perceived as an inadequacy in the movie's presentation of J. M. Barrie. The writers who liked the film generally agreed with David Ansen that Barrie's "awareness of lost innocence" infused the picture with "echoes both sprightly and melancholic," and that it was made "more passionate by restraint." As usual with biopics, there was considerable carping about what was left out. Among what was left out was one of the five brothers and a husband, said to have died in the film, who was still alive when Barrie met the children. Still, there does not seem to have been a lack of brothers in the film, and a living husband would simply have been an impediment to an already complicated story. The husband's presence might, however, have made the story more plausible. Stanley Kauffmann, in the *New Republic*, noted that his absence makes Barrie's completely asexual friendship with their attractive mother rather more improbable, at least by Edwardian standards. Stephen Dalton complained that the director and his team overlooked "a few inconvenient truths, erasing Winslet's husband and youngest child to sweeten a tale of adultery and tragedy into a fable of fantasy and imagination."

Anthony Lane's review noted that, in the film, Barrie treats the boys as "ideal spirits made flesh," and opined that "no child should be freighted with such an embarrassing burden." He concluded, however, that the movie "skims across the bright surface of the story, blithely oblivious to its darker undercurrents," and that Depp is "charmingly innocent of guile." Perhaps Ty Burr's analysis of Barrie is as close to the mark as any. He called Barrie an "asexual aesthete" trapped in his own dream of childhood innocence.

The screenplay for *Finding Neverland* is based upon a play of the same name by Allan Knee. Wisely, the filmmakers decided to limit the scope of the film to the childhood of the boys, and not to carry their story into adulthood. In a sentimental event in the movie which has no basis in reality, Barrie asks Frohman to reserve twenty-five seats on opening night for orphans to be brought in, presumably because he feels they will be a good audience. Sylvia's mysterious illness, which endangers her attendance on opening night, is another invention. In reality, Llewelyn Davies was not a widow; her husband was alive and, by all accounts, bitterly resentful of Barrie's intrusion into his sons' lives. The couple had five, not four, boys, but the youngest, "Nico" (Nicolas), was omitted from the film. American producer Charles Frohman was not present at the opening of *Peter Pan*; he was in New York and received news of the play's success in an understated telegram from his London manager: "PETER PAN ALL RIGHT. LOOKS LIKE A BIG SUCCESS" (Birkin 115).

The performances are uniformly strong. Dustin Hoffman scores as American producer Charles Frohman, a man dedicated to artistic freedom but not unconcerned about costs—in fact, pretty much as the evidence in *J. M. Barrie and the Lost Boys* shows him to have been. The strapping Kate Winslet would seem to have been miscast as the tubercular heroine, but she shows a sure maternal instinct and is perfectly convincing as a mother concerned about the welfare of her children beyond all else. In the unsympathetic role of Barrie's wife, Radha Mitchell is believable. Young, beautiful, wanting children of her own, she has little sympathy and understanding for a child/man who is more interested in other people's sons than in any potential son she might bear. And the great Julie Christie, decades after Schlesinger's *Darling* and Altman's *McCabe and Mrs. Miller*, attempts to fight off the intruder from what she considers her own domain, and at the climax of the film is given a moment of respite when she leads the applause attesting to the audience's belief in the reality of fairies.

J. M. Barrie seems to have had much in common with a group of talented Victorian and Edwardian introverts who made permanent contributions to literature. The group included John Ruskin (*The King of the Golden River, The Stones of Venice*), Lewis Carroll (*Alice in Wonderland*), A. E. Housman (*A Shropshire Lad*) and, of course, Barrie. Whatever their sexualities may have been, they cracked under the relentless pressures of the sexual mores of the times and turned inward toward a more-or-less physical idealization of the beauty of children and young men. It is, however, improbable that Barrie was the monster depicted in Peter Dudgeon's recent biography, *Captivated: J. M. Barrie, the Du Mauriers and the Dark Side of Neverland*. Whatever else Barrie may have been, he came to the writing of *Peter Pan* fully prepared. "Intellectually," he was, in the words of Allison Lurie, "anyone's equal" (121). He was a successful, if underrated, novelist and playwright. For the early years of the century, two of his works, although now relegated to the dust bin of literary has-beens, nearly equaled *Peter Pan* in popularity. Barrie's play *The Admirable Crichton* (1902) was a great favorite. It was filmed in 1913 as *Shipwrecked*, with Anna Q. Nilsson; in 1918 under the original name; and as *Male and Female*, by Cecil B. DeMille a year later. A desert island story in which the social roles are reversed, *Male and Female* is generally regarded as one of DeMille's best efforts and is available on DVD.

Barrie was also the author of the popular novel *The Little Minister* (1891), and the 1897 play based upon that novel was his first dramatic success. It was filmed in 1913 by the then enormously popular Clara Kimball Young in a version directed by her husband. Other versions appeared in 1915, 1921, 1922, 1934 (with Katharine Hepburn), 1950 (TV), and 1975. The last version, produced by the BBC and starring Helen Mirren and Ian Oglivy, beautifully produced, acted and preserved, is available on DVD in the *Helen Mirren at the BBC* boxed set.

Unfortunately, many of the qualities that made Barrie popular during his lifetime have worked against his reputation. Both the sentimentality and the sexualizing of childhood so pervasive in his novels and plays have made Barrie little more than a literary footnote. Only *Peter Pan* seems to have escaped. Whatever J. M. Barrie may have thought about himself, the film is quite aware of the differences between childhood and adulthood. If childhood is regarded as a perfect state, it is natural enough to want to stay there permanently — without the specters of sex, wage-earning, marriage and career. But we no longer believe that. Even as *Peter Pan* appeared in 1904, Sigmund Freud was sexualizing childhood. Ironically, in an age in which we no longer believe in sexual perversion — but pass laws against it — the violation of children is one of the last perverse acts. The film knows this — and shows it — in the casting of Freddie Highmore as the young Peter. Noticeably less attractive than his brothers, he alone resists the authority of Barrie, at first only tentatively and then with open rebellion. He may have passed through Neverland, but he does not intend to stay there.

John C. Tibbetts began his review with the dubious assumption that Peter Pan may be the most famous person that never lived. He has perhaps forgotten Hamlet, Don Quixote,

Scrooge and half-a-hundred others. Tibbetts traced the development of the character of Peter Pan and compared *Finding Neverland* unfavorably to the four-and-a-half-hour BBC miniseries *The Lost Boys*. Tibbetts concluded that the movie is "pathetic and uninspired," and delineates a character who could declare, in the words Barrie put in the mouth of the character of Tommy Sandys in his novel *Tommy and Grizel*: "I think I am rather a fine fellow when I am flying." The problem with this is that it raises, in the last sentence, the issue of homosexuality, which Tibbets has not discussed in his review. Although the term "flying" is not customarily used today to describe exaggerated and stereotypical homosexual mannerisms, it was so used during the lifetime of Barrie. (See Foster Hirsch's biography of Otto Preminger for the use of the term in the argument over the choice of Clifton Webb to play the male lead in the 1944 Otto Preminger classic, *Laura*.)

The three-part BBC series *The Lost Boys* is long, detailed, and much more accurate in family details than *Neverland*. It also covers a much longer period of time, shows the horrors of the Great War, the desolation of the boys—including death in war and an apparent double suicide (perhaps because of an unhappy gay love affair) and their attempts to throw off what they perceive as the malign influence of their generous benefactor. It is indeed a sad story. Of course, Hollywood would have nothing to do with such a prolonged run of sadness and chose, probably rightly, to end with the triumph of *Peter Pan*. The series is dull but affecting, and contains a justly celebrated performance by Holm. When the miniseries was made in 1978, Nico, the only one of the brothers still alive, praised both Ian Holm's look and the authenticity of his performance. More than twenty years later, Sir Ian was to appear in another, much darker turn-of-the-century tale—that of Jack the Ripper, with Johnny Depp tracking him down in *From Hell*.

Denis Meikle cited substantial evidence to show that Depp perceived himself as moving from the margins of commercial filmmaking to mainstream family films (314–315). Inevitably, the transition grew more difficult as the public taste expanded and/or (depending upon your point of view) coarsened. The Disney template has been defined by Janet Wasko as: individualism and optimism; escape, fantasy, magic, imagination; innocence; romance and happiness; and good triumphing over evil. And indeed, *Finding Neverland* was produced by Miramax and aimed directly at a mainstream audience. According to Jennifer Geer's analysis of the marketing of the film, Miramax, then a subsidiary of Disney, advertised *Finding Neverland* as a "child-centered fantastic spectacle that supports wish-fulfillment and firmly excludes death or unhappiness." Although Geer admitted that this "template fits clumsily," the "blatant reinterpretation inadvertently reveals key features of Disney/Miramax's marketing strategies for family films."

Finding Neverland was a commercial success. It cost approximately $25,000,000, and grossed $51,680,613 domestically and $65,085,943 foreign for a total of $116,766,556. Despite mixed reviews, *Finding Neverland* was nominated for 7 Academy Awards, including Johnny Depp's first nomination for Best Actor, but won only for Best Original Score (Jan A. P. Kaczmarek). Other nominations included Best Picture, Best Adapted Screenplay, Best Costume Design, Best Editing, and Best Art Direction.

That it was successful in finding a family audience need not blind us to the darkness in Depp's portrayal of Barrie. It is interesting to compare Depp's performance with that of Ian Holm's. Holm's is more plausible. He looks like Barrie and effectively portrays his sly humor and his love for "his boys," and most audiences and critics would probably see his portrayal as superior to Depp's. The chief difference is that Holm's character lacks self-knowledge, while Depp's has looked into the abyss and, whether pedophile or not, knows exactly what kind of character he is. He knows that he is outside the pale, a kind of monster, but he does not pass judgment upon himself. Nor, typically, does Depp pass judgment upon him, and he does not allow the audience to do so either. And that is the mark of the greatness of his performance.

Although a satisfying movie, *Finding Neverland* is hardly the great movie it might have been if the producers had had the foresight to cast Johnny Depp in a second role in addition to that of J. M. Barrie — that of his evil doppelganger, Captain Hook. Perhaps Miramax thought the role too close to that of another famous pirate captain.

2004 *Secret Window*
Again the Double

"It's the most important part of the story, the ending." (Mort Rainey)
"I told them things so you wouldn't have to." (John Shooter)
"You have no idea what you're doing." (John Shooter)

Secret Window opens with a shot of a haggard Mort Rainey (Johnny Depp) looking straight at the viewer through an automobile window. He is wearing a knit cap, and his gaze is fixed and unswerving. It is sleeting, and he tells himself to go home, but we know that he will not go. Instead, he pilfers a motel key and surprises his wife, Amy (Maria Bello), and her lover, Ted Milner (Timothy Hutton), in bed.

As the story proper opens, Rainey is separated from his wife, and the divorce papers have been agreed upon but have not yet been signed. Rainey, a well-known writer of horror and crime fiction, is suffering from a severe case of writer's block and spends most of his time dozing, smoking and lounging around in his home in the woods. One day a Southern hick named John Shooter (John Turturro) arrives and accuses Rainey of plagiarizing one of his stories word for word, and gives him what he claims to be the original manuscript to substantiate his claim. Eventually, Rainey sets out to prove that he could not have plagiarized the story because it had been published in *Ellery Queen's Mystery Magazine* before Shooter wrote it. Of course, as it turns out, Shooter is a product of Rainey's all too vivid imagination, and ends up killing people and burying them in his "secret garden."

Stephen King, one of the world's most popular and prolific writers, has had more than one hundred films based (both closely and distantly) upon his novels and stories, and this does not even count the individual television episodes and miniseries. A few of the films are classics — Stanley Kubrick's *The Shining*, Frank Darabont's *The Shawshank Redemption*, and Brian De Palma's *Carrie* — many are entertaining, and a substantial number are poor, or worse. But then not all of the films based on Shakespeare's plays are wonders either.

Secret Window has impeccable cinematic credentials. Like *The Shawshank Redemption* (the film version of which is, at the time of this writing, ridiculously ranked number 1 on the IMDB fan ranking of the best 250 films of all time), *Secret Window* is based on one of four novellas, or short novels, in Stephen King's collection *Four Before Midnight*. The original title, *Secret Window, Secret Garden*, was shortened because the filmmakers feared confusion with the numerous film versions of the children's classic *The Secret Garden*.

David Koepp, the director of *Secret Window*, began his career as a writer of screenplays, and has written (alone or with others) some of the most popular films ever made, including

The Paranoid Self: *Secret Window.*

Jurassic Park, Mission Impossible, Spider-Man and *Indiana Jones and the Kingdom of the Crystal Skull.* His less numerous directorial credits include *Ghost Town* and the highly regarded *Stir of Echoes.*

The gifted John Turturro, who plays John Shooter, had, of course, worked with Johnny Depp before, as the conceited opera singer in *The Man Who Cried.* Whatever else may be wrong with *Secret Window*, it is not Turturro's performance. He is the very personification of a certain type of Southern redneck, with his flat-brimmed hat, his buttoned down work shirt and his hillbilly accent. Literate but poorly read, he has aspirations as a writer, and in a day when everyone believes he or she can write fiction worth millions of dollars, he is out to get his share. In retrospect, after all has been revealed, he can plausibly be seen as an evil doppelganger of Mort Rainey's addled mind. The other cast members, although well cast and efficient, are little more than the means of moving the plot along.

The classic theme of the horror story as it developed from Edgar Allan Poe was the fragmentation of the personality and the descent into madness. His stories concern the descent of the soul — that is, of the individual segments of a personality — into insanity brought on by drunkenness, drugs, incest, defective heredity, or sheer cussedness (which he called "perversity," and which his great contemporary, Nathaniel Hawthorne, and the preachers called "original sin").

Stories of the double, which are nearly always horror stories, are generally short stories or novellas. Other well-known examples include Fyodor Dostoevsky's *The Double*, Guy de

Maupassant's "The Horla," and Robert Bloch's "Yours Truly Jack the Ripper." The list could be extended indefinitely. In film, the classic embodiment of the fragmented personality is Dr. Caligari in Robert Wiene's *The Cabinet of Dr. Caligari* (1920). In *Caligari*, the concept of the individual personality — indeed, of truth itself — is under attack. Alfred Hitchcock's chronological analysis, the "voyeur trilogy" (*Rear Window*, *Vertigo* and *Psycho*) carefully delineates the stages of the descent into madness of a particular type of insanity. *Secret Window*, like most stories of the double, turns in upon itself. According to the film, the story "The Other Man" was published in *Ellery Queen's Mystery Magazine* and is, of course, the story we have been watching (although the ending, "the most important thing," may or may not be the same). And in another irony, Jim Hutton, the father of Timothy Hutton, who portrays Mort Rainey's rival in love, played fictional detective Ellery Queen on television. And in another twist, the name "Ellery Queen" itself was a pseudonym for the two men who wrote the novels.

Stephen King has earned particular praise for his understanding of the zeitgeist, particularly its popular culture, where so much of the paranoia of the late twentieth century has been engendered. King understands both the pleasure and problems of being a famous writer. The devotion of crazed fans has been an abiding interest, and the crazed fan so memorably personified by Kathy Bates in *Misery* may well be a definitive personification of any popular writer's worst nightmare. Of course, the flip side of being a famous popular writer is that you can spend a lot of time looking at a blank computer monitor. And while there is absolutely no evidence that King has ever suffered from writer's block, he understands its terrors. King knows that depression and writers go together like ham and eggs, and that self-destruction, or worse (the destruction of others), often follows in its wake.

It is probable that the poor reviews the film received were based, partly at least, upon expectations the viewers brought with them when they saw the film. The reviews were mixed, with the majority leaning toward the unfavorable. Most reviewers regarded it as a Stephen King movie, compared it to *The Shining* and other King movies, and pronounced it predictable and lacking in thrills. Stephen Rea compared Mort Rainey to Jack Torrance in *The Shining* as "a guy stewing in the juices of his own cracked psyche." Peter Howell agreed with other critics that the film was a predictable entry in a "well-worn genre." Nigel Kendall called the movie "a tired Stephen King adaptation." And so on.

Reviewers who were not bothered by the familiarity of the story were sympathetic to Depp's performance, and a number of critics who did not particularly like the film admired Depp's portrayal. John Griffin, for example, described Mort Rainey as "the very model of a smart man holding on to reality by the slimmest of threads," and praised Depp as being "a great, generous and genuinely eccentric actor" who "now elevates everything he's in."

Another problem was the film's PG13 rating. Jane Horowitz, who writes about family films and pays close attention to ratings, enumerated the many examples of bloodletting and mayhem in the film, and concluded that *Secret Window* is "another in the new breed of darker, more graphically violent PG13s." Indeed, it is probable that the movie's depiction of graphic violence was calibrated almost to the frame to earn a PG13 rating. Moviegoers accustomed to the more graphic violence of *The Shining*, and more recent slasher and Asian horror films, probably expected more explicit mayhem than *Secret Window* provides. Still, whether a more graphic presentation would have improved the box office take is an open question.

Secret Window is a story of indirection. Depp has said that he was attracted to the project because most of the film takes place within the mind of the protagonist, a writer suffering from what is apparently a classic case of depression brought on by writer's block. The script was about "a man not doing things," and had "fourteen pages of phone calls." Such scenes, with no one to react against, are generally not favored by actors. The trick, as Depp saw it, was to fool the viewer as long as possible — in other words, to deceive the viewer into thinking that John Shooter was a real person. The effectiveness of Depp's performance would be measured by how long he would be able to maintain the deception that he was not Norman Bates with a writer's block.

Although the evaluation of a performance is, of necessity, subjective, the evaluation that depends upon the trust of the audience is particularly so. All audiences have a sense of expectation that must be satisfied, and there are tattletales everywhere ready to give away the secret. There are, nevertheless, ways to achieve this goal. When making a horror film, one of the ways is to take an actor who has always been a nice guy and turn him into an axe murderer. You cannot turn Jack Palance into an axe murderer; the audience already knows that he is one. Michael Caine, however, is another story; and Johnny Depp is a third. Although the audience is disposed to like Depp, he has played some unstable characters in the past and is not totally to be trusted. As a persona, he is completely neutral, a switch hitter who can bat from both sides of the plate.

Even if you know how the story ends — and remember, the ending is the most important part of the story — put the DVD in the player and watch the film carefully to see at what point Depp gives the game away. The answer may surprise you.

2004 *The Libertine*

Rake Rochester

"I know he is a Devil, but he has something of an Angel
yet undefac'd in him." (George Etheredge on Rochester)
"He who makes a beast of himself gets rid of the
pain of being a man." (Dr. Johnson)

Considering Johnny Depp's attraction to ambiguous characters, John Wilmot, Second Earl of Rochester, would have an obvious appeal. After completing the filming of the first *Pirates of the Caribbean* movie, Depp was approached by John Malkovich to star in a film based upon the life of Rochester. The movie was adapted by Stephen Jeffreys from his play of the same name, which had starred Malkovich in the title role. For the film version, helmed by first-time director Laurence Dunmore, Depp starred as Rochester and Malkovich played King Charles. Two years after making the movie, the producers were able to catch up with the busy Johnny Depp to make "Filming *The Libertine*," a thirty-five-minute documentary (included as an extra on the DVD) about the difficulties of making the film on a limited budget. After years of preparation, and within days of shooting, the British government, because of alleged corruption in the film industry, suddenly changed the rules for film subsidies and in the process did away with a third of *The Libertine*'s budget. The producers had to scramble to cut the budget and refinance the film. The task was made even more difficult because of the tightness of Johnny Depp's schedule, which allowed him only a limited time to work on the picture. Finally, a deal was arranged to shoot the film on the Isle of Man, which was able to provide incentives not available in England. (Even through it was set in Washington, D.C., Paul Schrader's excellent film *The Walker* was also shot on the Isle of Man for similar reasons.) Additionally, much of the film was shot in smoke and fog to conceal the bareness of the location shooting. The movie was shot in a brisk forty-five days.

The Libertine is a biopic covering the last years of the life of John Wilmot, Earl of Rochester. On July 26, 1680, the dissolute Earl died at the age of thirty-three. Heir to one of the greatest names in England, Rochester was a court wit and the author of a variety of witty, profane, obscene and atheistic poems. He was attended on his death bed by Gilbert Burnet, later Bishop of Salisbury, who wrote a celebrated account of the Earl's death-bed conversion to orthodox Christianity — which, according to the skeptical account given in a recent biography, elevated the celebrated libertine almost to sainthood (James William Johnson 340). Burnet's enormously popular story of the deathbed conversion, although probably true in the essentials, was certainly embroidered in the details. Still, Burnet's stark account of the Earl's dissolution, quoted by Johnson, is enough to bring even the most hardened sinner to heel (342–343).

Before his early and painful death from a perfect storm of venereal diseases, the Earl had become famous both for his quick wit and his dissipation. Described by one critic as "socially and culturally potent," he is remembered today for his poetry, which is traditional in versification, obscene, blasphemous, ironic and often difficult to interpret. Completely unpublished during his lifetime, at least under his own name, his poetry provided useful work for a battery of scholars during the twentieth century who sorted out Rochester's authentic works from a multitude of manuscripts and early editions. Although Rochester completely lacks Shakespeare's variety, he has at least one great characteristic of the master: it is almost impossible to tell what his attitude is toward the material he presents. Admired by some — but by no means all — of his best contemporaries, including Dryden, Swift and Pope, he was largely banned by the moralists of the later periods of English literature. The revival of metaphysical poetry in the twentieth century brought him back, at least to some extent, into critical favor, but his obscenity and his apparent atheism have limited his popularity both with the public and with some modern schools of criticism. The New Critics of the twentieth century, who admired wit and paradox, might have been expected to like Rochester's poetry, but they were religious and cultural conservatives, and so ignored him.

At the beginning of the film, a restoration rake, the great Lord Rochester himself, looks directly into the camera and tells us that we will not like him. And indeed we do not, either then or later. The Earl looks terrible: he is prematurely aged and apparently near death, but still mysteriously defiant. He reappears again at the end of the film to tell us, in effect, that he told us so.

Although the chronology is muddled, the period covered is roughly the last three or four years of Rochester's life. In the film the King says that Rochester came to the court when he was eighteen years old, and Rochester says that was ten years ago. At the beginning of the movie, King Charles II allows Rochester to return from a year's banishment from court after only three months. Chronologically, this is hardly possible since the incident depicted is almost certainly the Earl's banishment in late 1676, and is followed by Rochester's introduction to the actress Elizabeth Barry, which in reality had occurred some time earlier. Obviously, chronology is not the film's strong suit.

The film deals with Rochester's belated attempt, during the last period of his life, to rehabilitate himself. At the beginning of the movie, King Charles, who is obviously fond of Rochester, allows him to return to court, but tells him that he expects a great play from him that will rival Shakespeare. Rochester becomes reacquainted with his old drinking buddies, including Sir George Etherege (Tom Hollander), remembered today as the author of *The Man of Mode* (which contains a memorable portrait of Rochester as Dorimant). Rochester takes

Marital strife in *The Libertine*: Samantha Morton and Johnny Depp.

on Alcock, a thug and criminal, as "his man," presumably because Alcock represents more vices in one man than Rochester has been able to find elsewhere. For mysterious reasons, Rochester undertakes the tutelage of Elizabeth Barry, a struggling young actress who has been hissed off the stage and fired for having neither the cadence nor the posture for the heroic roles she aspires to play. Because of Rochester's instruction — at least according to the movie — Barry becomes the most celebrated tragic actress of the era. According to Rochester, the theater is a temple, if a pagan one, while real life is uncertain and deceitful.

At the request of King Charles, Rochester agrees to write an important play which will vanquish the French culturally. After Barry becomes a great actress, the King enlists her to spy on Rochester and help him produce a work of sublime thoughts and immense philosophy. She fails miserably in this endeavor, and his "sordid little play," a pornographic celebration of the dildo, offends everyone, including the King. Spurned by his King, Rochester goes into hiding, posing as a fraud named Dr. Bendo. Deathly ill, Rochester goes home to die, but is drawn back to London to speak in the House of Lords for a law protecting the succession. He hobbles about with two canes and wears a silver nose like that of drunken gunfighter Kid Shelleen's double in *Cat Ballou*. The speech is celebrated, and Rochester dies in the arms of the church he has so long maligned.

In the film, John Malkovich, as King Charles II, seems a kind of reverse image of Depp's Rochester. This is hardly surprising since a large number of knowledgeable people, when asked which actor Johnny Depp most resembles in ability and choice of roles, have responded with the name of Malkovich. Although Malkovich (b. 1953) became famous for a sympathetic role in *Places in the Heart* (1984), which earned him an Academy Award nomination for Best Supporting Actor, he can turn on a dime and has generally worked the dark side. He was memorable as Steinbeck's Lennie in *Of Mice and Men* (1982), as Valmont in *Dangerous Liaisons*

(1988), and, although too old and apparently miscast, as Patricia Highsmith's Ripley in *Ripley's Game* (2002). Malkovich has recently turned to producing and directing. Malkovich's film persona has been the subject of considerable creative speculation, as Spike Jonze's *Being John Malkovich* (1999) clearly shows.

It is unfortunate that Depp and Malkovich do not have more scenes together. Tilt the story a bit to one side — and it certainly needed to be tilted one way or another — and Malkovich becomes a father figure, so that the film takes on an edge it does not have. In the movie that exists, the King likes "Johnny," as he calls him, and has no moral objection to the way he acts; he merely wants to rein him in a bit so that he will not cause too much trouble. Although Malkovich is hardly more than a subordinate player, the scenes between the two great actors are the best in the film.

Elizabeth Barry (1658–1713), played by Samantha Morton, was, by all accounts, one of the best actresses of the period. She was Rochester's mistress for a time and, as the film tells us, bore his child in London while Rochester was dying at his estate. With her eye on the main chance, she saved Rochester's letters. The exact influence that Rochester had on her career may be argued, but she was certainly slow to develop as an actress. James Nokes, who saw Barry in her full maturity, wrote that she was past "the short life of beauty" before she developed into "a complete actress," and cited her as an example of the difficulty of judging with certainty "from the first trials" whether young actors "will ever make a great figure on a theatre." He added that she was discharged at the end of her first year as "a useless expense" and speculated that the problem was "in her manner of pronouncing" (Cole 111).

Barry's firing is, of course, depicted in the film, but Nokes was quiet on the question of Rochester's tutelage. Whatever Barry's particular accent was is an open question, but certainly pronunciation had been standardized for serious roles, and the regional and lower-class accents were suitable only for comic roles. Nokes praised Barry's "elevated diction, her mien and emotion superb, and gracefully majestic; her voice clear and strong, so that no violence of passion could be too much for her; and when distress, or tenderness possessed her, she subsided into the most affecting melody and softness." He concluded: "In the art of exciting pity, she had a power beyond all the actresses I have seen, or what your imagination can conceive" (111). This description must, of course, be taken on faith, and Samantha Morton's scenes are so abbreviated, it is no criticism of her that she can hardly do more than suggest Barry's greatness.

Stephen Jeffreys' screenplay cleverly brings together a variety of scenes illustrating Rochester's low opinion of mankind, most notably those involving Rochester's man Alcock, his disciple in vice, and those showing Rochester's monkey. Richard Coyle's Alcock is a total rogue, apparently hired by Rochester because he thinks that he has a suitable name for a man without a single redeeming characteristic (unless, of course, one counts his eventual affection for Rochester, apparently based solely on the opportunities for vice Rochester provides for him). Alcock is Lord Rochester's monkey, a creature unbounded by morality and fueled by caprice. In actuality, Rochester had a man named Alcock, and although he was probably no better than he should have been, there is no evidence that he was the monster depicted in the film. Jeffreys— and Rochester — must have liked the obscene pun in his name, but he can hardly compare with the real monkey shown in Jacob Huysman's portrait of Rochester.

In the portrait, Rochester holds a laurel wreath over the monkey's head while the monkey offers him a poem. As a pre–Darwinian putdown of mankind, the idea could hardly be bettered, and the disapproval shown by Rochester's wife when he wished to include the monkey in the family portrait is certainly plausible. It should, perhaps, be pointed out that the painting shows no high opinion of poetry either.

In what may be his best poem, "A Satire Against Reason and Mankind," Rochester antic-
ipates Darwin, and even does him one better by preferring the monkey to mankind:

> Were I (who to my cost already am
> One of those strange, prodigious creatures, man)
> A spirit free to choose, for my own share,
> What case of flesh and blood I pleased to wear,
> I'd be a dog, a monkey, or a bear,
> Or anything but that vain animal
> Who is so proud of being rational.

The poem is ultimately nihilistic. Rochester, having no belief in religion, and having attacked
reason itself, had nothing left except, one supposes, the temporary and destructive respite of
the senses through alcohol and profligacy.

The Libertine is a complex and interesting film. The photography, courtesy of Alexander Melman, is dark, brown, and full of smoke, rain, fog, and candlelight. Even the scenes
in the country, which might have been expected to brighten the palette, are brown and muddy.
According to the commentary, this was at least in part an attempt to conceal the bareness of
the location scenes. The interior sequences, comprising the larger portion of the film, are uniformly dirty-drab. While the dark photography, it might be argued, is used for the purposes
of unifying the film and giving it a greater realism, it has the unfortunate effect of making
the viewers feel that they are slogging through two hours of mud and grime.

The set designs and music for the "Signior Dildo" numbers are inventive and clever, and
the scenes, although obscene by any standards, bring the dour film to vivid life. A dwarf riding "a phallus the size of Britain" on what looks like a gun carriage is worthy of Fellini on his
best day, although there may also be some influence of Lang's *Dr. Mabuse* (1922), which
appeared on DVD about the time the film was shot. The "Signior Dildo" words are, of course,
Rochester's and may be read on: *http://andromeda.rutgers.edu/~jlynch/Texts/dildo.html*. The
dildo, of course, was (at least according to the English) the evil invention of either the French
or the Italians. It is unlikely, but possible, that Rochester knew Thomas Nashe's celebration,
The Choice of Valentines, or *Nashe, His Dildo*, written nearly a hundred years earlier. At any
rate, Nashe's jovial poem has a cheerful obscenity and lacks the obscene meanness in which
Rochester specialized. Nashe's poem may be read in Wikisource: *http://en.wikisource.org/wiki/
The_Choise_of_Valentines*.

Released some two years after it was filmed, *The Libertine* received little criticism, and
that mostly unfavorable. Owen Gleiberman, in *Entertainment Weekly*, wrote that Depp played
Rochester as "a cross between Casanova and Richard III," looked like "a debauched rock-star
musketeer," and starred in what is probably "the most sexless film about a seducer ever made."
Manohla Dargis, in *The New York Times*, believed that "Mr. Depp's beauty and talent do not
lend themselves to our displeasure and neither does his stardom, which is probably why he
was cast." While these comments are certainly true, they are also beside the point. The real
question is: why does the film not work better than it does?

David Stratton may be taken as typical: "Depp inhabits the role with brio," and "it's
hard not to embrace Depp, especially when he displays such glee in tackling the strangest of
characters." Stratton's conclusion was, however, largely negative. He was disappointed that
the film did not explore a wider canvas depicting "the tumultuous, social, cultural and political events" of the period. Stratton was, of course, asking for a totally different film from the
character study the movie attempts, and at least partly achieves.

Australian critic Rob Lowing wrote that the preview audience at the showing he attended
arrived "expecting larrikin laughs" but was quickly "muted by the bawdy, adults only lan-

guage and oppressive tone." Nonetheless, he concluded that Depp was "hypnotically good," and that the film was "a perfect, provocative, refreshing alternative to the usual pastel biographies." Anthony Lane, in *The New Yorker*, suggested sagely that if you "blend together Hunter S. Thompson, Jack Sparrow and Willie Wonka, you could hardly come up with anyone as highly seasoned as 'His Lordship,' who speaks from a gloom that might as well be the nether depths of Hell," which might be the "most plausible place to look for him." Indeed. Peter Travers called Rochester "a raunchy wonder," and wrote that Wonkaphiles who can't endure watching the "dazzlingly debauched" Earl's nose fall off from syphilis are just "wussies."

The film looks as if it were shot in a mud puddle; the acting is lugubrious and solemn; the talk, delivered in smirks, is all about swiving and dildos; and the motivation of the main character is a mystery. And yet the film has genuine merits and might have worked. The play by Stephen Jeffreys upon which the film is based must certainly have worked better than the movie, since the theater is a less realistic and more stylized medium than film. All of the evidence indicates that Rochester, at least until the last few years of his short life, was an extremely witty man, full of paradox and quick repartee, who could, as Shakespeare wrote, "set the tavern in a roar."

The earliest recorded performance of Sir George Etherege's play *The Man of Mode* was at the Duke's Theatre in Dorset Garden on March 11, 1676. Jeffreys certainly knows the play; in the film, Etherege quotes from it the description of Dorimant/ Rochester cited at the beginning of this chapter. The Rochester represented in the play is, therefore, the Rochester of an earlier period before venereal disease and alcoholism inaugurated the last miserable phase of his life.

In fact, the darkening of Rochester's character in the film is only an intensification of characteristics apparent in Etherege's Dorimant. These include his indulgent treatment of servants (shown in a corrupt form in his treatment of Alcock), his impulsive libertinism, his pretended good nature (which at that time may not have been completely pretended), and his deeply held conviction that society really hides its true self in sexual and religious hypocrisy. Satire takes extreme forms, and it is unlikely that Rochester's daily pronouncements, except perhaps in the last year or two, took such extreme forms as are indicated in his poetry. The fact that almost every obscene poem of the period was long attributed to Rochester obscured our knowledge of his development as a poet. Graham Greene's *Lord Rochester's Monkey*, whatever its lack of scholarly rigor, makes Rochester's development as a poet more plausible and understandable.

The DVD of *The Libertine* includes scenes filmed but not included in the release print. When he had just turned eighteen, Rochester performed heroic service at the battle of Burgen in 1665. According to Bishop Burnet's account, Rochester, knowing that a great battle would occur the next day, entered into a compact with George Windham (or Wyndham), the brother of one of his classmates, that if one were killed he would reappear to the other. The compact, according to Burnet, was "a solemn pact, not without ceremonies of religion, that if either of them died, he should appear, and give the other notice of a future state, if there was any" (Greene 49, Johnson 73). While it is unclear exactly what "ceremonies of religion" might mean, it certainly included a solemn oath of a type forbidden by the church. A third man, named Montague, refused to enter into the compact. Both Windham and Montague were killed together the next day, but Rochester was spared, and his bravery during the battle was the most celebrated event of his life. However, according to Burnet, "that gentleman's never appearing to him was a great snare to him, during the rest of his life" (Greene 50).

While the event is certainly true, it is hardly unusual for dying men to review the dramatic incidents of their lives. It may even be true that the event influenced Rochester's turn toward atheism and debauchery. Brief scenes depicting the battle and the death of Montague were shot, but, for whatever reason, were cut from the released version of the film. Shorn of other context, the scenes are hardly enough in themselves to serve as motivation for a ruined life and were properly discarded.

Although it is probable that the film was compromised at the screenplay stage, it is possible that it might have been salvaged with some hints of Rochester's promise as a youngster. There is no hint either of his brilliant start as a young classical scholar or of the attractive personality and wit that Etherege delineated so well in *The Man of Mode*. This might have been done by including short, brilliantly lighted scenes of happiness to relieve the horror, as Mel Gibson did so memorably in another dark film, *The Passion of the Christ*. The attractive romanticism of the youngster who carried off his future bride only to have the pair hauled back and his intended bride taken from him might have been shown in the film. The beginning of the movie shows us that even much later his wife cannot resist the sarcastic, diseased rake in a carriage, but it never shows us, as Etherege does, the personality which attracted her in the first place.

The story is one which Billy Wilder would have changed and eaten up. His rake would likely have been, at least philosophically, a sophisticated and better educated version of the William Holden character in *Stalag* 17 — sarcastic, cynical and quick with a quip. *That* Rochester would not have been essentially different from the Rochester of *The Libertine*, but he would have been more plausible.

And Johnny Depp could have played that figure superbly too. The only point of having one of the most popular and charismatic actors in the world tell the audience at the beginning of the film that we will not like him is to have us prove him wrong. Of course, we do not prove him wrong, but the character we do not like is the film's Rochester, not Johnny Depp. The purpose of art is not to make the tragic figure likable, but to make him plausible and make his fall meaningful. Who could like King Lear or Macbeth? And there is a great tragic figure in *The Libertine* who almost emerges.

Depp's performance is spot on psychologically. Depp himself has noted that, in today's language, Rochester was clinically depressed, medicated himself with alcohol, and quickly became an alcoholic. He told Bishop Burnet that he went for a full five-year period without ever being totally sober a single day. Of course, depressives look for reasons to justify their bleak visions of life. Reasons enough abounded in the perfidiousness of mankind's sexual depravity, in the corruption of the court of the "merry monarch," and in the hypocrisy of religion. Was not all this foretold by the classical writers Rochester so much admired, Juvenal and Ovid, among others.

Rochester, although an aristocrat by birth, was a democrat by inclination. Although the nobility might be better educated, he knew that they were no better than Alcock, whose straightforward villainy amused his master, Rochester supported Alcock by giving him money and did not even expect him to do what he is supposed to do. When Alcock comes to the city after being asked to stay in the country, Rochester hardly notices. Alcock is a mere bundle of needs, sexual and otherwise — as, or so Rochester would respond, are we all.

Rochester's conversion during his hellishly painful death was hardly surprising and, as portrayed by Depp, is totally convincing. Rochester, a conservative in his literary tastes and his verse forms, was extreme only in his life. He was a satirist and, like Juvenal and Ovid, the great satirists he admired, a creature of the city. He returned to his country estate only when forced by necessity or finally to die. Andrew Marvell's "The Garden," with its images of repose and classical purity, was beyond him psychologically and emotionally.

The darkness of the film and its sameness have obscured the greatness of Depp's performance, but an even darker one, that of the Demon Barber of Fleet Street, was on the way.

2005 *Charlie and the Chocolate Factory*
Dracula on the Verge of a Sex Change

"Don't touch that squirrel's nuts. It'll make him crazy." (Willy Wonka)

Although the pairing of Johnny Depp and Tim Burton may never become as famous as that of John Wayne and John Ford, it is clearly a relationship made in heaven. Both Depp and Burton are attracted to highly visual stories populated by offbeat and eccentric protagonists. Roald Dahl's acclaimed fantasy *Charlie and the Chocolate Factory* (1964) seems almost to have been written for them.

Roald Dahl (1916–1990) is remembered today as a writer of some of the best children's books of the century, and some of the most sophisticated adult stories. The bitter edge of his adult tales shaded off into whimsy for his children's books, but lost little of its force. What someone is alleged to have said of Billy Wilder — that he had a mind full of old razor blades — might equally have been applied to the English writer. Dahl is an astringent author, and his works — and occasionally the author himself — have continued to receive criticism, often severe, over the years. Critics are often particularly sensitive to perceived imperfections, particularly of a moral kind, in literature addressed to young people, and the author of "Switch Bitch" and "The Man from the South" was, and remains, an open target. Although his stories are clearly not to everyone's taste, his reputation continues to grow. His *Collected Stories* appeared in Everyman's Library (2006). Among twentieth-century writers of whimsy, perhaps only John Collier, although lacking Dahl's astringency, is his equal.

The novel may be briefly summarized. Willy Wonka, the eccentric owner of a chocolate factory, sponsors a contest in which five children, the finders of a Golden Ticket, will be his guests and given a tour of his factory (which has been closed for years, although it somehow manages to turn out truckloads of the enormously popular chocolate). The winners are Violet Beauregarde, who is intent on setting a world record for gum chewing; Augustus Gloop, a fat glutton; Mike Teavee, whose only interest in life is watching television; Veruca Salt, a selfish rich girl; and Charlie Bucket, the hero of the story and the sole custodian of two pair of grandparents who never get out of their beds.

Eventually, after winning one of the five tickets, Charlie rouses his Grandfather Joe from his bed and, along with the other four winners, shows his Golden Ticket to gain admittance to the wonders of the chocolate factory. The mysterious factory, described as a "gigantic rabbit warren," is run by Oompa-Loompas, a group of little men who all look alike. (Originally pygmies from Africa, the men were changed in the 1986 revision to an imaginary group of starving chocolate lovers who are apparently happy to work as slaves and subsist only on chocolate.) One by one, four of the children are eliminated and, after being sufficiently degraded and humiliated, are then resurrected. Only Charlie, an average boy who has managed to escape Willy Wonka's wrath, is spared and eventually carries the day. Willy Wonka gives Charlie control of the chocolate factory and takes the whole family group, bed included, with him to the magical factory in the Great Glass Elevator, which was to furnish the title to the sequel, *Charlie and the Great Glass Elevator.*

The subversive quality of the novel, apparent in even a brief summary, had derailed its appearance in America when Virginie Fowler, A. A. Knopf's editor for children's books (who apparently regarded all children's books basically as Victorian fantasies), criticized it severely and wanted extensive revisions, which Dahl refused to make. Ironically, especially since the book appeared during the depths of the civil rights movement, she did not criticize the African pygmies, the very problem which led to Dahl's revision of the story more than two decades later.

When Hollywood arrived, the title was changed to *Willy Wonka and the Chocolate Factory* (1971), and Dahl was enlisted to write the screenplay. According to Dahl's widow, Liccy Dahl, the author had wanted the then well-known English comedian Spike Milligan to play Willy, but the studio turned him down in favor of Gene Wilder. The film's director, Mel Stuart, unhappy with certain aspects of the screenplay, hired David Seltzer for revisions without consulting the prickly author. Apparently, the main changes were to darken a minor character, Slugworth, so that the film would have a definite villain, and to change the ending. Although Seltzer did not receive a screen credit, he cites the film as the real beginning of his career, which includes sole writing credit for *The Omen* (1976) and other notable films.

Although clearly a product of its time and not a financial success when it appeared, *Willy Wonka* continues to be popular a third of a century after its original appearance. It furnished Gene Wilder with one of his best roles, and he says in his DVD commentary (2002) that he is still recognized by children as Willy Wonka. When first seen as the factory gate opens, he limps toward the camera using a cane, then does a tumble and comes up waiting for applause. Wilder says that he insisted on the opening as a condition of taking the role to show that Willy Wonka was a trickster and not the evil man he pretended to be. The exteriors of the film were shot in Munich, but most of the movie was filmed on an enormous interior set. *Willy Wonka* has an outstanding score by Leslie Bricusse and Anthony Newley, and "Candyman" became the theme song of Sammie Davis, Jr.

Gene Wilder was unhappy with the very idea of a remake and is reported to have said that he did not see the point of "doing it over again." Dahl's widow Liccy, who had final approval of the script, director and star, had no difficulty with approving Tim Burton as the director after he told her that, when he was in the third grade, he had written a letter to Dahl and had received a postcard in return. Obviously, Burton and Depp were the men for the job.

For the most part, Tim Burton's film, which returns to the original title of the book, *Charlie and the Chocolate Factory* (2005), follows the book closely, with the notable exception of a new character, Dr. Wonka, the father of Willy Wonka, portrayed by Christopher Lee. As it turns out, Dr. Wonka, a dentist, has a deadly fear of cavities and considers chocolate the sum of all fears. In a flashback, the young Willy is shown wearing some sort of fiendish contraption attached to his teeth and anchored to his head. Doubtlessly designed by Tim Burton and looking like an instrument of torture left over from *Sleepy Hollow*, it is intended to keep Willy from eating chocolate. In all probability, it would have prevented him from eating anything. In the end, Willy is reconciled with his father, befriends Charlie and his family, and gives Charlie the chocolate factory.

Whether the Dr. Wonka story is necessary and/or improves the movie is a matter of dispute. The reconciliation at the end of the film would seem to be the type of happy resolution that Burton had complained about in the past. In a contrarian mood, the director may have felt that the simple story needed a greater complexity to hold the viewers' interest for two hours. Conversely, the darkening of Willy Wonka's character could hardly have made the studio happy. Burton's films, except for *Sweeney Todd*, are generally strong on one-dimensional characters, but short on the dramatic intensity and character growth and resolution which develop from plot. Even Sweeney Todd may hardly be said to have developed as a character; he merely became focused. Clearly, the suits wanted to end the film on a happy note after all the children, except, of course, for Charlie, had been brutalized.

Tim Burton darkens the whimsical treatment of character in the earlier film into the grotesque. The four evil children and their parents, hardly models of deportment in the earlier picture, here become totally despicable, and are cheerfully and appropriately savaged and dispatched by a grumpy Willy Wonka, who decries any responsibility. When told that Charlie is the only one of the children left, Wonka asks brightly what happened to the others. Later, Willy Wonka allows all of the children to return, but only in mutilated and abbreviated forms. It is unclear whether they have learned anything from the experience. Their parents, however, clearly have.

With the exception of Mike Teavee, the interests of the evil children are basically unchanged from the earlier film; but Mike, who was earlier depicted as a slave to television, has now expanded his domain to computers, video games and all sorts of interactive playthings. Ironically, as earlier critics had pointed out, Dahl, who had been very hard on television in his novel and the original film, had not been slow in having his stories adapted to television in *Tales of the Unexpected* (now on DVD), and even in introducing them himself in the manner of Alfred Hitchcock.

Reviews of *Charlie and the Chocolate Factory* were mixed, and some of them may have been influenced by the fact that Burton's film appeared during the 2005 Michael Jackson trial for child molestation. Several reviewers wrote that Depp's Willy Wonka looked like Jackson and aped his mannerisms. Burton, however, denied the accusation. He said that the two characters were not alike at all, that Michael Jackson loved children, but that Willy Wonka hated them. In his review, Anthony Lane wrote that Johnny Depp "dresses like Oscar Wilde, smiles like Michael Jackson, enunciates like Tootsie, and wears purple gloves to keep away the germs." He compared him to Macbeth's "cream-faced loon," and wrote that he is more of a child than the children around him. And indeed he is. Lane, in a speculative mode, noted the changing of stereotypes from Dahl to Burton, neither of whom had heard of "political correctness," and called the remaining plot "an infantilized version of Agatha Christie." Apparently, what he means is that Burton, after being forced to change Dahl's old politically incorrect characters, transformed them into equally incorrect new ones.

Of course, Dahl and Burton are always subversive and are caught in a trap. The very qualities which define them as artists work against vast popularity. Like Billy Wilder and other contrarian directors, they walk a fine line that can bring great popular success, but can also quickly turn the public against them. Attempts to walk that line can also make the critics unhappy. For example, Richard Schickel wrote that the film has "a distance, a detachment" and "lacks passion." He believed that Burton's movie never fully explores the dark side of the story, and that children can handle "deeper scares than the film offers." Every day they face kids in school who are much worse than the ones in the movie, and they deserve "edgier, more suspenseful storytelling than it provides."

Part of the problem which Schickel worried over may be that the huge central portion of the film — an extravaganza of music and top-of-the-line special effects orchestrated by Willy Wonka and presided over by thousands of computer generated Deep Roys — overwhelms the conclusion of the film. The sequence occupies a disproportionate amount of screen time without significantly advancing the narrative. It does, however, give Deep Roy the largest number of supporting roles in film history. Whether he is an advance over the pygmies of

Dahl's original or their counterparts in early Disney cartoons must still remain a matter of conjecture.

The musical numbers, according to Peter Travers, seemed "to have been choreographed by Busby Berkeley on crack." The result, it is fair to say, is like the hung-over morning after in Shakespeare's *A Midsummer Night's Dream* or Bergman's *Smiles of a Summer Night.* Those people, however, knew that they had had a great time. It is not clear that the characters in *Charlie and the Chocolate Factory* knew that they had.

In an interesting and provocative review, Ryan Gilbey, in *Sight and Sound*, argued that the production design for the film was old hat and made the movie seem familiar, particularly in the scenes inside the factory. He did, however, praise the designs of the external scenes of the town and factory. To the present writer, the endless duplication of Deep Roy took away any familiarity the scenes inside the factory may have had; by comparison, the exteriors are completely expressionistic and could have been transferred from a Fritz Lang silent film. Gilbey believed that the flashback scenes evoke "quiet misery" because they "revisit" the parental tensions of Burton's earlier films, *Batman, Edward Scissorhands* and *Big Fish*, and that Depp portrayed Willy Wonka as deranged as the "wee terrors who have won a day in his company."

We need not believe Gilbey's Freudianism to accept his description of Johnny Depp's Willy Wonka as "both flamboyant and reserved with eerily translucent skin and a shiny bob." And we need not believe the "rigor mortis grin" to be a "hangover from his childhood," as Gilbey does, to agree that Depp's choicest acting is reserved for his eyes. Depending upon what is appropriate, he can be plaintive simply by lowering his gaze, or hilarious by registering "silent panic" as he is given a bowl of caterpillars.

Owen Gleiberman's review memorably described Depp's Willy Wonka as "a milky-skinned misanthrope who's like Dracula on the verge of a sex change." His performance "is a put-on laced with perverse sincerity." This is perceptive. Most actors know exactly how they want the audience to respond to the characters they play, and act accordingly. Depp says to the audience, in effect: "Willy Wonka is what he is. It is not my place to judge him. You're the audience. That's your job."

Numerous studies of adolescent males have pointed out that most — some would say all — try on personalities as if they were suits of clothes, attempting to find one that fits. The period of indecision is a way station on the road to maturity. The protagonists of Tim Burton's films, however, are permanent adolescents, completely happy with the personalities they have. Children must learn that the world is an unjust place, and Willy Wonka is just the man to teach them. Willy Wonka wants them to change — or pretends to want to — but he is not about to change himself. During the shortages of the first world war, Erika, the first born and the favorite of the great German novelist Thomas Mann, remembered her father dividing the food and, having only one fig left, giving it to her and announcing to the others, sententiously and with emphasis: "One should get the children used to injustice early" (Tóibín). Willy Wonka knows that the world is unjust; whether the film knows it, however, is another question.

David Thomson reported that his two young companions who were with him when he saw the movie did not have much good to say about it. Thomson opined that Dahl's book did not have much in the way of story, and lamented the lack of narrative thrust which "leaves the ingenuity of Burton's visual imagination and Depp's shoddy aplomb a little stranded." At the close of his review, expressing some disappointment with Johnny Depp and Tim Burton, both of whom he believed to have gone astray, Thomson concluded presciently that "talent has its own standards. And I think the ultimate measure of both Burton and Depp may be creating a modern fairy story in which they frighten the life out of us."

Sweeney Todd was on the way.

2005 *Tim Burton's Corpse Bride*
Migratory Body Parts

"I've got a dwarf and I'm not afraid to use him." (Victor Van Dort)

Tim Burton's Corpse Bride appeared when the world was preoccupied during the holiday season with other films. Though well received by the public, considering the fame of its director and star, it received little attention from the media. The fact that it was created using puppets photographed in stop motion made it an anachronism at a time when almost all of the animated films were produced on computers, and may or may not have contributed to its being lost in the holiday shuffle.

Tim Burton made the early sketches for the characters, and Carlos Grangel helped to develop them. Johnny Depp, Helena Bonham Carter and Christopher Lee moonlighted on the voices of the film while working on *Charlie and the Chocolate Factory*. *Corpse Bride* was Burton's fifth movie with Johnny Depp and his twelfth with composer Danny Elfman. Depp is said to have developed a persona for Victor, the protagonist of the film, in a single grilling session with Burton. The curious might ask if there is any significance to the fact that the sadistic, sexually voracious guard Depp played in *Before Night Falls* is also named Victor.

Johnny Depp and Tim Burton during the making of *Sweeney Todd.*

The plot of *Corpse Bride* is simple enough to fit neatly into some seventy minutes, minus the credits. Victor Van Dort, voiced by Johnny Depp, flunks the wedding rehearsal the day before his wedding, wanders into the world of the dead and somehow puts a wedding ring on a "corpse bride" and marries her. (The film is said to be based loosely upon a nineteenth-century Russian legend of a young Jewish bride said to have been murdered on the way to her wedding.) Of course, all comes well — or does it?— in the end when he has a "real" wedding with his human bride, the beautiful Victoria.

Almost everyone praised the nice contrast between the grey Victorian cityscape surrounding the living, and the flamboyant characters, bright colors and clever antics of the dead characters, with their body parts that break apart, mingle promiscuously and reassemble in whole or in part(s). The amiable hi-jinks, which James Christopher called "the clubby carnival atmosphere ... of the rotting brethren," include a drunken soldier with a cannonball hole through his ribcage and a head waiter with a skull mounted upon an army of scarab beetles. The skeletons, doubtless in homage to Disney's 1929 short *The Skeleton Dance*, tend to burst into song and dance together. Christopher concluded that the film is "an animated marvel, a fabulously painted Gothic fantasy."

Owen Gleiberman described the movie as "a ghoulishly witty crackpot puppet show." The Victorian buildings he described as having forbidding shadows and architecture that made "Count Orlock's castle in *Nosferatu* (1922) look like a well-lit condo." Stuart Klawans regarded the film as a return to form after *Charlie and the Chocolate Factory*. Actually, the two were made concurrently, with Burton devoting most of his creative energies to *Charlie*. According to Klawans, "[E]very river of chocolate [in *Charlie*] had its undertow for the unwary; every child's downfall is celebrated in psychedelic song," In *Corpse Bride*, however, Burton "plays jump-rope with the borders ... between desire and revulsion ... and Depp does most of the jumping." The heroine of the film, the beautiful Corpse Bride, Klawans described as "a beautiful, blue-skinned, truly dead femme fatale with a shapely set of femurs, a nose like Michael Jackson's unbandaged, a decayed hole in the cheek through which you can glimpse her molars, and an eyeball that pops right out." And Klawans did not even mention the wisecracking maggot in her rotting skull or her leg that keeps falling off.

Of course, migrating body parts have always been a rich source of humor, but until the coming of animation, their migrating was perforce limited. The earliest animators, from Méliès on, recognized the potential, and the interested student may be referred to the nearly complete recent DVD collection of the cinematic pioneer's extant films for many early examples: *Georges Méliès: First Wizard of Cinema (1896–1913)*.

Eric Hynes wrote that *Corpse Bride* "explores and conflates desire and death in spectral shades of black and grey, with sallow stock figures humanized by doll eyes and familiar voices." The situation is, however, more complicated than that. Jack Mathews, in his review, stated Victor's dilemma clearly: "Either give up his mortal life for an endless party among the dead or find a way to get back to sweet Victoria and have a traditional, if wholly ill-conceived marriage." A number of critics expressed some uneasiness with the film, but were not quite sure why. M. K. Terrell wrote that it "feels unfinished."

The film's chief problem started at the script stage. Certainly the suits would have wanted to lighten up the picture. Although the film's living celebrants need never have achieved the rambunctiousness of the celebrants of the dead zone, it could have ended with some sort of vision of a better world. Old-school Disney animators would have finessed the problem by surrounding Victoria with birds, flowers and talking animals shown in brilliant Technicolor. They might have started the film with dirty-drab colors, but they would have ended it in splendor.

As the movie exists, the only sensible solution would have been a marriage between Victor and the Corpse Bride. It would be interesting to know if Burton ever considered that ending. That would have been a hoot. It would almost certainly have necessitated an R rating, but it would have been a better film than the present one.

The voices are in excellent form. Albert Finney and Helena Bonham Carter do splendid work in the major roles, and Christopher Lee does his best Christopher Lee voice as Parson Galswells. Richard E. Grant is superb as the villainous Barkus Bittern, the old lecher who wants to marry the saintly Victoria. (The name Barkus echoes that of a character in Dickens' *David Copperfield*, who announces his proposal to his beloved by way of a third party by saying, "Barkis is willing.")

Ironically, as any number of reviewers pointed out, Depp's hero, trapped between the world of the living and the world of the dead, represents the only voice of sanity in the film. Depp's reading of the bemused protagonist is wonderful. The voice of sanity looks out upon a crazy world — and then another crazy world — and attempts to make sense of what he sees. It would be interesting to know what Victor would have thought of the script.

2006 *Happily Ever After*

Elevator Ride

"An instant of all but union." (James Joyce)
"And then that elevator starts its ride...." (Harold Arlen, "That Old Black Magic")

Yvan Attal (b. 1965) is a French actor and director born of Algerian Jewish parents who established himself as an actor before turning to writing and directing. He has had a long-term relationship with Charlotte Gainsbourg, his co-star in *Happily Every After*. The movie's French title, *Ils se marièrent et eurent beaucoup d'enfants*, may be roughly translated as "They Got Married and Had Many Children." On a short film on the DVD, Attal says that he became aware at some point that most of the people roughly his age had married, had children, and then divorced. He apparently referred to successful professional people on either side of forty who were balancing, or attempting to balance, relationships with their ex-wives, their children and their hit-or-miss sex lives. Of course, the sexes being what they are, the men and women had different objectives. Everyone, however, still regarded the ideal as including a perfect sex life within the confines of a permanent marriage, several children and two successful careers. Robert Browning opined that "a man's reach should exceed his grasp, or what's a heaven for." But another great philosopher expressed a divergent point of view: "A man's gotta know his limitations."

In a short film on the DVD, director Attal says that Gainsbourg, who knew Johnny Depp, arranged to have a copy of the script sent to the actor. Depp liked the script, and the director and his co-star visited the actor's home in the South of France, had a long discussion with him about the "very small part," and ended by staying the night.

Depp, who is billed as "L'inconnu" ("The Unknown One") in the credits, appears in only two scenes, one some fifteen minutes into the film and the other at the end. Gabrielle (Charlotte Gainsbourg), an unfulfilled married woman in her thirties, is browsing in a Virgin mega store. She is attractive, has long hair and is casually but smartly dressed. She puts on headphones and listens to a CD. A man (L'inconnu) comes into focus moving toward the camera. She turns toward him. He is slender, smartly dressed, wears glasses and has a loose tie. He is chewing gum. They evaluate each other. He listens to a record, takes off his earphones, smiles and walks away. She watches him disappear, evaluates what has been lost, and rushes after him. She loses him but finds him again. They show each other their CDs— they are identical — and separate.

Gabrielle is a real estate agent, and, of course, they meet again. She has made an appointment to meet a man about an apartment on an upper floor of a large downtown building. The man, of course, is L'inconnu. When they meet outside the building it is not immediately apparent whether they remember each other. They get on a small elevator and begin the ride. He says he feels as if he has met her before. "Peut-être," she lies. As the elevator rises, their relationship blossoms, the skies open and they travel unimpeded to the heavens. The camera circles the elevator and the music surges. A door opens to the perfect sexual experience and the credits begin to roll.

Although Depp's role is only a small one, it is difficult to think of another actor who could have played it so well. In the midst of the middle-aged men and women moiling and churning around in a generally vain attempt to find some sort of satisfaction in their lives, it suggests— the cynic might say too sentimentally — that the genuine experience is waiting somewhere, perhaps even on the next elevator ride.

2006 *Pirates of the Caribbean: Dead Man's Chest*

The Return of the King

"Once you've sworn an oath to the Dutchman, there's no leaving it." (Davy Jones)

After a wait which was much too long for the millions of fans of Captain Jack Sparrow, the pirate captain returned in the summer of 2006. The fans were still loyal to the new film, but the critics were getting a bit grumpy. While the old favorites were back, Captain Barbossa, although scarcely to be seen, was threatening to return for the third film. As compensation, the movie offered two interesting new characters, Bootstrap Bill Turner, the father of Will Turner, and Davy Jones, custodian of the famous locker. Both characters suffered from interesting facial deformities. Bootstrap Bill, darkly lit and apparently suffering from depression, had what appeared to be barnacles eating away one side of his face, and Davy Jones was all tentacly, with what looked like spare parts from an octopus bank attached to his face.

Stellan Skarsgård, the well-known Swedish actor who played Bootstrap Bill, assumed his facial deformity would be computer-generated; but eventually, with the aid of some four-and-a-half hours a day in the make-up chair, he was able to play the character, progressively deteriorating before the eyes of the viewers without CGI assistance (Singer 76). In the more important role of Davy Jones, skipper of the *Flying Dutchman* and keeper of the locker for miscreants, Bill Nighy was praised and would probably have won an Academy Award nomination if the reviewers could have figured out whether to nominate him or his tentacles. What is beyond question is that Nighy has shown himself to be a superb actor in a variety of roles, both fore and aft (as a sailor might say) of the *Pirates of the Caribbean*. He is particularly effective in the film *Love Actually* and the British miniseries *State of Play* (both 2003). His portrayal of Davy Jones aided his career and has helped him to obtain better roles.

Playing Davy Jones was Nighy's first experience with computer animation. He described the process as requiring "an act of faith and a bit of leap of the imagination." The finished product looked like a man with big octopus suckers of some sort attached to his face and moving around vigorously. He could hardly be seen at all behind such scene stealers, and he still somehow managed to create a vivid character. Davy Jones is a philosopher of sorts, and his aphorisms of the pirate's life tend toward the dark side. "Life is cruel," he opines. "Why should the afterlife be any different?" Anthony Lane described Nighy as "properly mean beneath his suckers and blubber" (83). Indeed, no actor has so successfully overcome such odds since Lee Marvin won an Academy Award for *Cat Ballou* and thanked an old horse grazing in the valley for its assistance. Certainly Nighy owes a similar debt to his friends in CGI for their superb work on his tentacles.

In order to save Elizabeth Swann (don't ask why), Will Turner is sent to find Captain Jack. Meanwhile, the cowardly Captain Jack has been captured by cannibals and taken to their village, where he is treated like a God. Always an optimist, Jack is disillusioned when he learns that the cannibals are going to roast him. There is also a great to-do about Will's search for his father, Bootstrap Bill, and the "beating heart of Davy Jones," which is concealed in his famous chest and which Captain Jack purloins.

Reviewers generally found themselves perplexed by the storyline, if they could figure it out, but Anthony Lane of the *New Yorker* is helpful in this regard. Will Turner and Elizabeth Swann are arrested for aiding Captain Jack Sparrow, who is wanted "for falsely impersonating a Rolling Stone." Davy Jones is captain of the *Flying Dutchman*, described by Lane as "a ship constructed largely of rag and bone, which can dive and surface like a submarine" and which is manned by skeletal pirates. (As an actor, Johnny Depp is perfectly at home in fighting the undead, although not in such numbers. Had he not vanquished the headless horseman a few years earlier?) Even the dauntless Lane, however, confessed himself confused and in need of assistance when the action "zipped from beach to crag to poop deck." Various mysteries include exactly what Davy Jones keeps in his chest, how Jack's magic compass operates, and why Elizabeth Swann betrays Jack Sparrow. Lane notes that the gender-bending scene in which Keira Knightley "smooches" Depp in order to betray him is a relief from the "invertebrate" Orlando Bloom.

After complaining that the first two *Pirates of the Caribbean* movies are "pure Disney products ... culled initially from a ride at Disneyland," Anthony Lane wrote that the films "were always going to be Depp's baby," and compares them to the 1952 Robert Siodmak film *The Crimson Pirate*, starring Burt Lancaster, "the leading strapper of his time." The comparison is trenchant. Lancaster, a former trapeze artist, and his former acrobatic partner Nick Cravat, give both *Pirate* and *The Flame and the Arrow* of two years earlier "an exuberant athletic energy which all the digital effects of *Pirates of the Caribbean* cannot match." By comparison, Johnny Depp, "as if pursuing a whim, or honoring a drunken bet, chose to float them into our eyes and ears as his own personal prank ... the latest in a singular cinematic breed, the effeminate leading man." Lane describes Depp as representing "the joy of irresponsibility." Elizabeth tells Jack that he will one day accept responsibility to do a worthwhile and honorable deed: "I love those moments," he responds. "I love to wave at them as they pass by."

Reviewers were beginning to bail out, but they still liked Johnny Depp. Peter Travers thought that *Dead Man's Chest* was better than *Black Pearl* in every way because "it pumps out the bilge and offers a fresh start." The writers and the director have learned from Depp "how to play fast and loose with the material." He described Captain Jack memorably as "a bi-sexual narcissist with a devilish glint that suggests he'll never tell you where he stashed his drug kit." David Ansen, in *Newsweek*, praised Depp's "hilariously fey, tipsy pirate" who turned what was "otherwise a solid but unremarkable adventure movie into a larkish blockbuster," but lamented that the second movie can't recapture the subversive thrill and surprise of the first. He concluded that the filmmakers attempted to outdo the original film by pouring on the special effects and making everything bigger, louder, and more expensive. The result, he wrote, is a movie that is "cluttered, hard to follow, and hard to care about."

A. O. Scott, the *New York Times* reviewer, saw Captain Jack, or at least Depp's portrayal of him, as a product of the 1960s: "It was about this time [1969, the year of *Easy Rider* and *The Wild Bunch*] when Mr. [Mick] Jagger and his bandmates began affecting eyeliner and the dazzling earrings that would ultimately provide Johnny Depp with the visual cues for the character Jack Sparrow, his Pirates of the Caribbean homage to Keith Richards-as-dandy, a characterization that helped make a multimillion-dollar franchise out of a dull cinematic cartoon." Between the fighting skeletons of the *Flying Dutchman*, the Kraken — an enormous sea monster which looks suspiciously like an octopus — and the wiles of Elizabeth Swann attempting to assist her sweetie, Captain Jack has a hard time of it and is dispatched to Davy Jones' locker, waiting to be rescued in the third film. Confronted with such riches, Scott concludes that the film is "a glistening, sushi-grade chunk of franchise entertainment," and comments that the movie "dispenses with an ending — it's pretty much all middle."

Obviously, if the filmmakers had wanted an ending, they would have given it one.

2007 *Pirates of the Caribbean: At World's End*

Straining Credulity

"There's never a guarantee of coming back." (Captain Barbossa)
"Gentlemen, I wash my hands of this weirdness." (Captain Jack Sparrow)

As the film begins, all "English rights" have been suspended, and a large number of men, women and children are about to be executed. Will Turner has been caught stealing navigational charts "to the most distant gate" (whatever that is), and the Brethren court (whatever that is) is to be convened. Sao Feng (Yun-Fat Chow), the Pirate Lord of Singapore, is searching for Jack Sparrow. Jack Sparrow has one of the nine pieces of eight and must be rescued from Davy Jones' locker. This long, dull opening-sequence certainly poisoned the critics against the film even before Captain Jack appeared. If the sequence had been drastically shortened — or, better yet, consigned to the DVD — *World's End* would probably have been regarded as the best film of the series. Apparently, since the aim of the moviemakers was to entice everyone in the world to see it, they thoughtfully included a clichéd version of every ethnic

Geoffrey Rush, Keira Knightley and Johnny Depp in *Pirates of the Caribbean: At World's End.*

group they could think of and had them mumble at and threaten each other while the filmmakers worked out something for Johnny Depp to do.

At least it was worth waiting for when it came. We are a full thirty-three minutes into the film before we get our first look at Captain Jack Sparrow — or, rather, a host of Captain Jack Sparrows. The CGI experts have attempted to identify the major ingredients of the redoubtable Captain and have turned him into a Jack of all nautical trades — or, rather, of a ship's tackle and trim. Captain Sparrow is attempting to dine upon a large peanut when he is shot and apparently killed by a more elaborately dressed Captain. Having dined, the real — or reel, or pretended Jack — commands his crew, and they jump eagerly to work. He angrily runs through one of the "feculent maggots" who has mishandled a tack line. Unfortunately, he has killed one Jack too many and finds himself trapped in the doldrums. He awakens, alone, trapped with his ship in Davy Jones' locker, which is apparently a large beach with the *Black Pearl* sunk in the sand. In a scene which would have delighted the surrealists, Jack manages to escape from the island. Although he fails miserably in his attempt to pull his ship from the sands, he discovers help near at hand — or under foot, as it happens. An army of land crabs, if that is what they are, having nothing better to do, allow themselves to be ground to bits in the sand in order to float the ship. The sequence is brilliant, with its free-floating anarchy and lack of logic reminiscent of the best Disney cartoons of the early 1930s. Of course, surrealist films and cartoons were short and made no pretense of giving a select audience two-and-a-half hours of narrative, and *World's End* stumbles along from pillar to post attempting to justify its plot.

The third *Pirates of the Caribbean* film is longer, louder, noisier and filled with more spectacular computer-generated-imaging than the first two. The reviewers, already hostile from the second film, were in high dudgeon. As if the producers had been fully aware of the possibility of a rebellion this time around, the two gifted screenwriters, Ted Elliott and Terry Rossio, had been shanghaied and were apparently kept on board for salvage operations on the script during most, if not all, of the shooting of the last two films. Many of their lines were unquestionably clever. Two of the best were "Full bore into the abyss," and "Nobody moves; I dropped the brain."

Reviewers generally were so angry that they did not give the film credit for its brilliant passages. Mike Clark called *Dead Man's Chest* "drearily paced" and a "bloated mishmash," and added that "a now-bored Johnny Depp ... is subordinate to the romance between Keira Knightley and facially immobile Orlando Bloom — just what everybody wants." Clark added charitably: "For the record, I had the 2003 original on my 10-best list, back when the concept seemed cheeky instead of asleep in the deep."

Reviewers alternated between trying to make some sense out of the plot and vilifying it, often in the same sentence. Christian Toto, in *The Washington Times*, spoke for the consensus in a review entitled "Lost at Sea": "Just describing the first half-hour is exhausting, and we've got another two-plus hours to endure." He complained about the loud soundtrack and the characters all running "hither and yon ... as if they stepped on tacks," and "drawing guns on each other." He noted a huge set-piece toward the end of the film in which two ships fight each other during a hurricane is "awkwardly framed," but added guiltily that it is "a wonder to behold."

David Ansen in *Newsweek* called the film "loud, cluttered and confusing," and complained that the plot "is not only hard to follow, [but] there seems to be nothing real at stake." There are "swordfights with dead people who can't be killed with swords," and the love story between the two romantic leads is "running on dead batteries." The result is "just business."

As usual, female reviewers were more likely to praise the Depp style. Jeannette Catsoulis noted that when we first see Jack Sparrow hallucinating in Davy Jones' locker, which she described as "an arid limbo of rolling dunes and raging heat," he is impeccably attired. According to Catsoulis, the film's "real love affair has always been between Jack and his mirror." She particularly admired "the army of merry clones in kohl eyeliner and fancy head scarves." She is, however, unclear about the question of where Captain Sparrow may have acquired his fashionable accoutrements.

And what is an objective viewer supposed to make of these three enormous movies? Are they defensible as anything but a crassly-designed, huge money-making machine? Certainly, by the usual standards of criticism, they leave much to be desired. The characters are flat and have no verisimilitude, psychological or otherwise. Motivation is, in any real sense, absent. Captain Jack wants to get his ship back, and that is the end of it. Barbossa wants to redeem himself and his crew and become human, but often seems to want only to raise hell. The plot, if that is what it is, circles around and goes nowhere.

The films are postmodern in at least one sense. They are often self-referential. If the viewers are having difficulty figuring out what is going on, the writers are willing to help. Toward the end of *Dead Man's Chest*, when Norrington, Jack and Elizabeth are sword-fighting on the beach, Elizabeth threatens *in media res* to give up pirating forever. Pintel and Rigetti, lagging behind, observe the proceedings, and Pintel helpfully explains that each of them wants the so-called "dead man's chest." Norrington is attempting to regain his honor, Jack wants to swap the chest to save himself, and Turner is attempting to finish up some business concerning his father. Having decided to their own satisfaction that they know what is going on, Pintel and Rigetti decide to run off with the chest themselves and remove temptation.

Later, Elizabeth appeals to Jack's carnal instincts and chains him to the ship. In order to save Will Turner, she gives him a small carnal reward, a kiss, and a promissory note of greater rewards to come. In effect, she seduces him and sends him to Davy Jones' locker forever, or for at least the next hundred years. The rules in such matters are vague. Later she agrees to rescue Jack, and all is forgiven. As in a soap opera, alliances shift constantly, and the characters can change sides in an instant.

The two romantic leads hardly exist as personalities; they are merely blanks for presumably young viewers to fill in. One could make a case that Will Turner's motivation is a classic search for a father, but that is forgotten for long periods and seems to emerge only when needed — as Wild Bill Elliott's search for the man who killed his brother, or father, or whomever, did in his B films of the 1930s.

The *Pirates of the Caribbean* films are perhaps best regarded as generic formulations for a DVD age. They are designed to be seen in the theaters, to make people go to the Disney theme park rides, to appear on pay television, to appear between blocks of advertisements on network and cable television, and, perfectly, to be watched endlessly at home by youngsters on DVD. They are the modern-day equivalent of the romances of the past, of the stories that unhinged Don Quixote, and no one is better equipped to embody their crazy characters than the Walt Disney Corporation and Johnny Depp.

The medieval romances, whose origins may be traced back to the *The Arabian Nights*, were fantastic tales of romance, adventure and the supernatural which could start anywhere, ramble around for hundreds of thousands of words, digress at will and stop almost anywhere, only to be continued by a later hand if so desired. Some of the romances, such as Sir Philip Sidney's *Arcadia* (pub. 1590), were sophisticated products of a courtly society, but most of them were merely stories of love and the fantastic — of the type which drove Don Quixote mad. Like the fairy tale, which was a favorite of the Disney studio during their early years, the romance was a perfect template for a young DVD or television audience.

It may be argued that the *Lord of the Rings* and *Harry Potter* franchises are superior — they have distinguished literary genealogies — but their greater sophistication is an illusion; and in their variety of incidents, humor, burlesque, and appeal to the young, the *Pirates of the Caribbean* films clearly carry the day. The theory may easily be tested by showing the movies consecutively to any group of youngsters of twelve or under. Since the plots make no particular sense, the films need not be shown in order and may be started at any place and stopped at any place. Although the movies may be lacking in variety, they are alive — and often devilishly clever — in the moment. And the moment is what children are interested in.

At the end of *At World's End*, Elizabeth Swann and Will Turner are finally united, although they face an uncertain future. Captain Jack Sparrow, having regained his ship, is celebrating in port with two doxies. When he decides to show them his ship, he discovers that Barbossa has hijacked it once again and sets out after him in what looks like a revamped version of the small boat we saw submerge at the beginning of *The Curse of the Black Pearl*. The Captain is underway as the credits roll. The classic ending, which promises an endless series of adventures, is also used in Peter Weir's far more serious ocean adventure, *Master and Commander: The Far Side of the World* (2003).

There is an additional scene which takes place some ten years after the credits (which seem to have lasted ten years themselves) that many people — including most, if not all, of the critics — missed when they first saw the movie. Elizabeth Swann and her young son, who is perhaps eight or so, welcome an incoming ship, with Will Turner greeting his family heroically, albeit from so great a distance that they could hardly have seen him. What this tells us, and what people in the know have confirmed, is that Swann and Turner, who have found what we presume to be marital happiness, will not be back in the next *Pirates of the Caribbean*.

Captain Jack, however, will be.

2007 *Sweeney Todd*

The Demon Barber of Fleet Street

"And he will have his revenge." (Sweeney Todd, speaking of himself)
"Blood was its Avatar and its seal — the redness and horror of blood."
(Edgar Allan Poe, "The Masque of the Red Death")
"Because the law worketh wrath: for where no law is, there is
no transgression." (Romans 4:15, King James Version)
"A face folded in sorrow." (John Webster, *The Duchess of Malfi*)

After the Herculean labors of the three *Pirates of the Caribbean* movies, Depp went back to the safe haven of Tim Burton, and in collaboration with him produced their most daring film. As if to show the world that "the masters of weird" had not lost their nerve, they filmed a brilliant cinematic reworking of a classic postmodern work, Stephen Sondheim's 1979 musical *Sweeney Todd: The Demon Barber of Fleet Street*. R-rated and steeped in blood, the film was released four days before Christmas 2007 as an insolent alternative to all the cheerful family films of the period.

Barbers in general have not had a good reputation, and Christopher Benfey provides a helpful anecdotal history from Cicero to the present. Cicero writes of a Roman general who taught his daughters to shave him so as not to place himself in the hands of his numerous enemies. The most artistic presentation, at least until *Sweeney Todd*, is in Melville's novella, *Benito Cereno*, where the shaving of Captain Delano is a threat of instant death by the leader of a slave revolt aboard the captain's ship (Benfey, "Barber"). Recent barbers, however, have had a reputation more for gregariousness than for violence, as Ring Lardner's once-famous story "Haircut" reminds us. Perhaps the coming of the safety razor has had a chastening effect.

Although the story of Sweeney Todd has never become a part of American popular culture in the way that the stories of Frankenstein and Dracula have, Sweeney Todd had already appeared in novels, films and a highly successful musical. Sweeney Todd began life in 1846–47 at absolutely the lowest rung of the literary ladder, the penny dreadful. Published anonymously in eighteen weekly parts under the title *A* [or *The*] *String of Pearls: A Romance*, the serial celebrated, if that is the word, the appearance of Sweeney Todd, the barber, and his confederate, the pie-baking Margery Lovett, or Lovet, and their friends and enemies. The growth of literacy among the lower classes and advances in printing had made sensational stories a delight which even the poorest people could afford. For a penny they could buy a weekly installment of a sensational story with one or more illustrations.

Although Thomas Peckett Prest is listed as the author of *String of Pearls* in Mark Salisbury's authorized book on the film, the authorship question remains unsettled and is likely to remain so (Mack xvi). The story may even have been written by more than one author. The writers of the penny dreadfuls lived from hand to mouth, and such Grub Street collaborations were not unknown. Without any convincing evidence, Peter Haining's claim in *Sweeney Todd: The Real Story of the Demon Barber of Fleet Street* (1993) that Sweeney Todd was an actual person may be discounted. But no matter how the story originated or who wrote it, there can be little doubt of its popularity. The tale was presented on the stage in a version by George Dibdin Pitt even before serial publication had ended. In 1850, an enormously expanded — and inferior — version of *String of Pearls*, now subtitled *The Barber of*

Fleet Street, a Domestic Romance, appeared in book form, after being published in weekly form for an astonishing 89 weeks (Mack xxxi).

Since its low beginning, the story of the Demon Barber has entered into the kind of anything-goes, free-fall adaptations characteristic of enormously popular works, and will doubtlessly continue to do so in the future. The first film version, now lost, was a short made in 1926 by British pioneer filmmaker George Dewhurst. According to Mack, the first extant version appeared two years later and featured "the well-known actor Moore Marriott as Todd" (Mack xxxii). A 1936 British film version directed by the now-forgotten George King, who has a long list of films on the IMDB, starred the appropriately named Tod Slaughter as Sweeney. (Clips from this film, excellently restored, are included on Disc 2 of the Tim Burton film version.) King's film clearly and cleverly shows that Sweeney had not one, but two chairs, one right side up and one right side down, and the instant that he hit the switch, the victim was sent to his reward and the chairs were reversed. Apparently, Tod Slaughter (1885–1956), called by the IMDB the "last of the British barnstormers," played Sweeney Todd on stage for many years.

Television versions include the 1998 John Schlesinger-helmed drama *The Tale of Sweeney Todd*, starring Ben Kingsley and Campbell Scott, and the 2006 BBC film starring Ray Winstone (*Beowulf*), which retells the story as a straight horror film. By 1998, Schlesinger, the famed director of *Midnight Cowboy* and *Marathon Man*, had been reduced to working for television. Especially worthy of note is the DVD of a 2001 concert performance starring George Hearn as Sweeney and Patti LaPone as Mrs. Lovett, which, whatever its deficiencies as drama, furnishes a benchmark standard for the singing.

The witch's brew of ingredients that had been simmering for more than a century in popular culture finally came to a boil in 1979 in *Sweeney Todd, The Demon Barber of Fleet Street: A Musical Thriller*, with music and lyrics by Stephen Sondheim and a book by Hugh Wheeler. The critically acclaimed work, which starred Len Cariou and Angela Lansbury, won both the Tony and the Drama Critics Circle Award, and has since been successfully staged in a variety of venues, including a 1982 version filmed for television and now available on DVD (with Angela Lansbury reprising her role as Mrs. Lovett, but with George Hearn replacing Len Cariou). (For an excellent *Sweeney* chronology, see Mack xxxi–xxxvii.)

The huge Broadway production featured enormous sets which were being constantly moved around, not always unobtrusively, by stagehands. Action was continuous for three hours, except for a break between the two acts. Action took place in the streets, in an asylum, in Sweeney's upstairs barber shop, in the basement where Mrs. Lovett's pies are prepared, in the shop where they are sold, and occasionally in an indeterminate space. The most striking bit of stage magic represented Sweeney's hydraulic chair, in which he slits the throat of a customer, customarily the last of the day, before tripping an apparatus that slides the poor devil down a chute to his reward in the basement — Mrs. Sweeney chopping the body into chunks before grinding him up, cooking him, and serving him as the major ingredient of her increasingly popular meat pies.

While it is hardly fair to compare a videotaped version of a highly successful and acclaimed Broadway musical to a Hollywood film version of that musical, the comparison may suggest something of the strengths of, and differences between, the two types of artistic presentations, and between the two versions of the same story. The play's book by Hugh Wheeler is based upon a play by Christopher Bond; the music and lyrics are by Stephen Sondheim. The video version is efficiently directed by Terry Hughes. The music was re-mastered and the DVD was re-released to coincide with the DVD publication of Tim Burton's film.

The time is 1846. The play opens with a musical montage by the chorus suggesting the

Sweeney Todd (Johnny Depp) working on Judge Turpin (Alan Rickman) in *Sweeney Todd: The Demon Barber of Fleet Street.*

tone and content of the play. A body is thrown into a furnace over the jovial but macabre lyrics which set the plot in motion. Benjamin Baxter returns to London, accompanied by Anthony, a young man who has rescued him from the sea. Although the details are sketchy, Baxter had been "transported," apparently to Australia, on order of the despicable Judge Turpin, "a pious vulture of the law." As Baxter discovers later, Turpin has taken Baxter's beautiful daughter Johana (spelled Johanna in the movie) as his "ward" after raping and debauching Baxter's wife before leaving her to roam the streets as an alcoholic whore whom Baxter does not even recognize when she accosts him bawdily in the street.

Returning to his old hangout, Fleet Street, Baxter, now calling himself Sweeney Todd, falls in with the jovial Mrs. Lovett, who cheerfully admits to selling "the worst pies in London." Mrs. Lovett agrees to let Sweeney, a barber by trade, take over the top floor of her establishment and gives him an expensive set of straight razors which had originally belonged to him, and which she had found and saved. He greets them as "my friends." (Although the usage is not given in the *Oxford English Dictionary*, "Sweeney" is said to be a colloquial term for a barber.) Meanwhile, Anthony hears Johana singing to her birds, and the young couple immediately fall in love. Learning of the budding romance, the Judge has Johana put in an asylum. Anthony eventually learns of her whereabouts and rescues her by pretending to be interested in buying beautiful blonde hair for wigs.

The working out of the plot could hardly have been surprising, even to the play's first audience a third of a century ago, but its ferocity might have been, and its tone, perhaps somewhere between comedy and dark burlesque, certainly was. Sweeney sets up his barber shop with its special chair on the upper floor of Mrs. Lovett's shop and opens for business. The "real business," of course, is reserved for the last customer of the day, whose fate is similar to that of the famous "four and twenty blackbirds" of song.

Retribution inevitably follows, and the slaughter begins. At the conclusion, Sweeney successively slits the throat of Beadle Bamford; Lucy, his wife (Mrs. Lovett knows her identity but has not told him); Judge Turpin; and, finally, Mrs. Lovett. Toby, or Tobias, the young boy befriended by Mrs. Lovett and solaced with her gin, discovers too late the truth about the pies and slits the barber's throat. The play ends abruptly, perhaps cynically. Toby is left for the law, the two young lovers are left to fend for themselves, and the company is left for a reprise.

The problem for the gifted John Logan, who wrote the screenplays for Scorsese's *The Aviator* and Zwick's *The Last Samurai*, was to condense the discursive, nearly three-hour musical into a movie lasting approximately two hours. Dramatic musical films tend to be long and generally privilege the music at the expense of the drama. The decision was made to use the music almost entirely for dramatic, as opposed to lyric, effect, and to privilege the drama — that is, to make a musical horror film. *The Phantom of the Opera*, the recent film version of Andrew Lloyd Webber's famous musical (2004), had been a financial success, but had been indifferently received by the critics. The film had turned *Phantom* into a mood piece which privileged the music and slighted the drama. For the Burton film, Logan, in collaboration with Burton and Stephen Sondheim, cut approximately half the music and put the drama on steroids. The result, aided by Burton's direction, is tensely dramatic and moves like the wind.

Although it can hardly have been a secret that *Sweeney Todd* was a musical based upon a famous Broadway play, neither the previews nor the publicity drew attention to the fact. Generically, the film was without precedent — a bloody, big-budget, R-rated musical drama. The rating was genuine; *Sweeney* was not a PG13 gussied up with a vulgarity or two, but, as the reviewers dutifully noted, a film with enough blood, gore and body parts to appeal to fans of *Saw*, *Friday the 13th* and others of that low-budget but highly profitable genre. And opening some five days before Christmas, it faced an uncertain future at the box office. The fears proved unfounded. While the domestic box-office take was a perhaps disappointing $52,898,073, the foreign receipts totaled a remarkable $99,624,734. In other words, the foreign box-office tally was twice that of the American. While the domestic audience may have regarded the film as a musical, foreign audiences apparently appreciated it as a distinctive horror film with music, perhaps akin to *The Phantom of the Opera*, but better. Of course, television and DVD profits would be added to the total.

The critics found little to dislike. Claudia Puig called Depp "undeniably one of the best actors of his generation"; found the film bloody but "mesmerizing and highly entertaining"; and thought that "unlike more realistic violent fare, the gore in this gloomy Gothic marvel feels exaggeratedly theatrical and a vital part of the melodramatic mayhem." Puig also praised the effectiveness of both the acting and the singing, opined that Sacha Cohen as Pirelli nearly steals the show," and noted that Mrs. Lovett's song about her "inedible meat pies," performed while swatting away large roaches, "is a hoot." Puig's conclusion: "Burton's fascination with the macabre and the mischievous has found a perfect outlet in this lavish Grand Guignol slaughterfest." Roger Ebert, in his four-star review in the *Chicago Sun-Times*, wrote: "The bloodiest musical in stage history, it now becomes the bloodiest in film history, and it isn't a jolly romp, either." A. O. Scott called the movie "as dark and terrifying as any motion picture in recent memory ... as much a horror film as a musical ... cruel in its effects and radical in its misanthropy, expressing a breathtaking, rigorously pessimistic view of human nature. It is also something close to a masterpiece: a work of extreme — I am tempted to say evil —

genius." Peter Marks went all out: "With oceans of gore, streams of luscious musicality and a performance by Johnny Depp redolent of malevolence and magnetism, Burton brings Sondheim's 1979 musical to the screen with a bravura musical style thrillingly in touch with the timelessly depraved delights of Grand Guignol."

Gregory Dart believed that, except for "a few spectacular throat slittings and one dramatic fling into the furnace," the film is "restrained and classical." Dart interprets the film as dramatizing "the mysterious alchemical power of nineteenth-century factory production, its extraordinary capacity effecting unseen transformations." The film then becomes a "mini-allegory of modern capitalism, with its penchant for suppressing the link between production and consumption, obscure raw material and final pristine commodity ... an apparently sourceless commodity, cannibalized from lots of different bodies of material."

Anthony Lane made the negative case in *The New Yorker*. After chiding the advertising people for attempting to conceal the fact that the film is a musical, he called Sondheim's musical a "hell brew" which needed, somehow, to be rescued from "absurdity." He believed that Sondheim managed it while Burton did not. Sondheim's play had sophistication, which Lane apparently predicated not so much on the play itself as on regarding it as a musical way station to Sondheim's masterpiece of some seven years later, *Into the Woods*. While the point is valid enough, it should not be used as a stick to beat Burton over the head with. Lane is talking about the film that he believes Burton should have made instead of the one he did. To show that he is fair, he ended his review by praising the performance of young Ed Sanders as the last man — or, in this case, boy — left standing, and by disparaging Johnny Depp for no longer being Edward Scissorhands.

Lane attacked the movie's gore for not being repulsive — that is, for not being realistic enough. But it was, of course, not intended to be realistic; and the film, like Burton's earlier *Sleepy Hollow*, was generally praised for what might be called its tasteful excess. This excess may be more precisely regarded simply as one of the many ways in which Burton successfully integrated the gore into the fabric or atmosphere of the film. Some writers, to prove they were critics who thought for themselves, allowed the throat slashing but condemned some other aspect of the film — the plummet of the victims down the chute, the oven (which looked more like a furnace than anything else), or the bucket of body parts.

Although the gore of *Sweeney Todd* is both too extensive and too realistic for many filmgoers, it is hardly excessive, either by Tim Burton's standards or by the standards of modern horror films, such as the *Saw* series. For example, Burton speaks favorably of *The Brain That Wouldn't Die*, in which "the guy gets his arm ripped off and rubs the bloody stump along the wall before he dies," a scene which, the director opines, would be too violent to be shown on television today. Burton's violence is so artistically photographed and so beguiling that, while it might not be food for the general public, it would certainly be caviar for many of the sophisticated.

In a critical review of recent movies in *USA Today*, film critic Thomas S. Hischak rated *Sweeney Todd* at the top of the list, giving it an A+ as a film. Stage critic William Wolf, however, gave the film only a B. Although he praised Depp's acting and the visuals of the film, he believed that the singing was not up to the quality of the material, and that Burton's penchant for bloodletting injures the movie. Certainly *Sweeney Todd* is not a classical Hollywood musical in which each scene is choreographed and set off like a little jewel. It more nearly resembles an abbreviated opera with the arias shortened.

David Thomson includes *Sweeney Todd* in his massive compendium of 1000 film reviews, *Have You Seen...?* He makes the usual arguments against the film, chiefly that the singing is not good enough and that the violence is too graphic. Thomson, however, has no taste for, or understanding of, Asian horror films, and does not include a single one among his 1000 films. A viewing of several might have increased his understanding of *Sweeney Todd*. Fortunately, he is capable of learning. For decades he has been grousing about what he considers John Ford's inflated reputation, but although still grousing, he has included a generous number of Ford's films in his magnum opus.

Since *Sweeney Todd* is a story about a barber who slits men's throats and has them dismembered and baked into meat pies, the subject would hardly be appropriate for a G or PG rating. Considering the highly technical, some would say hypocritical, nature of the ratings system, a PG13 rating might have been possible with careful editing. Although a PG13 rating would likely have made the movie more popular at the box office, it would surely have compromised its integrity as a horror film. The director of *Sleepy Hollow* would hardly be likely to agree to such a compromise. The film that *Sweeney Todd* most resembled, at least in the minds of the suits, was *The Phantom of the Opera*, a more expensive horror movie based upon a musical. The relatively small number of musicals produced recently by Hollywood is due, at least partially, to the fact that musicals do not generally perform well overseas, and overseas box-office receipts are an important element of a film's revenue. It is fair to say that Lloyd Webber's musical was much better known than Sondheim's. Anecdotal evidence supports the belief that the majority of the moviegoing public was not even aware that Burton's film was a musical before it opened. Whether this bait and switch advertising ploy had any effect, one way or another, upon the movie's first-week box-office take is an open question. *Sweeney Todd* would likely have been a difficult sell, at least domestically, under any circumstances.

Walter Scott, in *Parade*, a magazine supplement included with many Sunday newspapers, answered a reader's query about why Tim Burton made the film so bloody with the statement that Burton "apparently decided that the only way to attract moviegoers to Stephen Sondheim's musical was to accentuate the gore." This is both unfair and untrue. The assumption is that gore would make the movie more popular, but the assumption is true only of low-budget films which have a limited downside, not of a film with one of the world's most charismatic actors. Burton could easily have toned down the gore and accentuated the comedy, as the Broadway version had done. The resulting film would have been closer to the Broadway version than to the movie Burton actually made.

Sweeney Todd was nominated for four Golden Globe Awards: Best Musical or Comedy; Best Actress in a Musical or Comedy (Helena Bonham Carter); Best Actor in a Musical or Comedy (Johnny Depp); and Best Director of a Musical or Comedy (Tim Burton). Both Depp and Burton were announced as winners in a presentation which substituted for the show eliminated by the writers' strike. *Sweeney Todd* was nominated for three Academy Awards: Best Actor (Johnny Depp), Art Direction–Set Decoration, and Costume Design, but won only one award, for Dante Ferretti's art direction and Francesca Lo Schiavo's set decorations.

Sweeney Todd is strongly cast and superbly acted. Sacha Baron Cohen, best known for his impersonation of Borat in the vulgar but enormously popular 2007 film *Borat: Cultural Learnings of America Make for Benefit of Glorious Nation of Kazakhstan*, plays Signor Adolfo Pirelli, a mountebank who appears in only two scenes. Magnificently dressed in a gray suit, with a pink cape, a pretentious top hat, a white neckerchief and gloves, and affecting an Italian accent, he is a wonder to behold. In the first and longer scene, he loses a public shaving contest to Sweeney Todd. In the second and shorter scene, he is summarily dispatched by the sharpest razor around. Cohen's performance is memorable, magnificent, and permanent.

Alan Rickman, who plays Judge Turpin, is a man of many talents, a man who can both sing and act, play evil or play nice. His characteristic concern can suddenly darken into villainy or lighten into genuine solicitude. He is affectionately remembered by Jane Austen

The Barber and the Fraud: Sweeney Todd (Johnny Depp) confronts Pirelli (Sacha Baron Cohen).

aficionados for his sympathetic portrayal of Col. Brandon in Ang Lee's *Sense and Sensibility* (1995), but has recently moved toward the dark side as Serverus Snipe in the Harry Potter movies. He portrays Turpin as a sexual predator who hypocritically believes that his "ward" is in love with him and has her placed in an asylum when she disillusions him. Turpin is a role that Vincent Price would have loved, but Price would have been more maniacal, and would, in some sense, have shown that he was playing at evil; but Rickman will have none of that. He is not only evil in himself, but the cause of evil in others, and what he cannot destroy he corrupts.

The minor roles are less flamboyant but no less artfully performed. Timothy Spall is appropriately conceited and sycophantic as Beadle Bamford. The gifted Stall has also made notable appearances in the Harry Potter movies and in the 2007 BBC production of *Oliver Twist*. Young Ed Sanders is genuinely moving as Toby, or Tobias, the boy who appreciates the kindness—and the gin—Mrs. Lovett gives him, but is appalled when he discovers her deadly secret. The ingénue roles, often the least appreciated roles in plays and films, are capably performed by Jayne Wisener as Johanna and Jamie Campbell Bower as Anthony. Laura Michelle Kelly, who has played Mary Poppins and Eliza Doolittle, is memorable as the alcoholic and debauched Lucy.

The most notable change from the play comes in the character of Mrs. Lovett. Angela Lansbury—no angel she, at least not in this play—plays Mrs. Lovett as a character of high comedy. Lansbury (b. 1925), a versatile performer, made her mark in Hollywood early with notable performances in *Gaslight* (1944) and *The Picture of Dorian Gray* (1945). In the latter film she plays Sibyl Vane, a night club singer done in by Dorian Gray; her singing of "Goodbye, Little Yellow Bird" is a classic bit of cinema. Unfortunately, her less than classic beauty limited her Hollywood roles, and she turned successfully to the theater and later to television, where her performance in the enormously popular series *Murder, She Wrote* reportedly earned her $400,000 an episode.

Lansbury's Mrs. Lovett is a hoot. She is a fun-loving woman down on her luck and forced to survive by selling "the worst pies in London." Sweeney offers her a way out. A traditionalist, she believes in solid middle-class values and is willing to do whatever it takes to get them. She exudes fun, murders only out of necessity, and never feels guilty about it. All she wants is a happy carefree life with Sweeney. And even in her late fifties, Lansbury can cut a caper with the best of them. Since George Hearn's Sweeney is so dour, she is the only character left to root for. Her vitality twists the play and turns her into the central character. Her carefree lack of morality is the pivot on which Lansbury turns Sondheim's great play toward postmodernism.

Helena Bonham Carter's performance as Mrs. Lovett has been almost universally praised. More in keeping with Burton's darker vision of the play, it is a quieter and less showy portrayal than Lansbury's—so much so that when she and Sweeney do a dance step or two together, the scene seems almost to belong to some other movie. British-born Bonham Carter showed herself an actress of note with a series of performances in upscale English films, notably *A Room with a View* (1985), *Howard's End* (1992), and *The Wings of the Dove* (1997), for which she received an Academy Award nomination. Her association with Tim Burton began in 2001 when she starred in the Burton-helmed version of *Planet of the Apes* (2001). Like seemingly every other British actor of note, she has appeared in the Harry Potter series (*Harry Potter and the Order of the Phoenix* and *Harry Potter and the Half-Blood Prince*).

Helena Bonham Carter's Mrs. Lovett is gaunt, frizzy haired, with heavily shaded deep black eyes and wears expensive clothes that look as if they had just been picked up on the street as rejects from Paris Hilton's Halloween party. She is, in fantasy (and presumably in reality), Burton's ideal woman. She has complained that her pregnancy during the shooting of *Sweeney Todd* altered her appearance, especially since the scenes were, of course, not shot in sequence. She never convinces the audience, and possibly neither she nor Burton ever intended to convince us, that she would be comfortable, much less at home, in the idyllic paradise that the film briefly shows us. By comparison, Angela Lansbury, a city girl to the core, can easily be imagined as perfectly at home at Coney Island or another of the seaside resorts which became enormously popular playgrounds for the burgeoning middle class at the turn of the twentieth century, and which are vividly illustrated in the films of Mitchell/Kenyon in the early years of the twentieth century. Bonham Carter's singing is adequate, if no better, and she is, as might be expected from her long association with the director, totally at home in Burton's dark world.

Tim Burton's direction has never been more assured. *Sweeney Todd* is the complete film. Generically, it is the first masterpiece of a nascent genre: the musical horror film. Other films have moved, in one way or another, toward that form, from the silent version *The Phantom of the Opera* starring Lon Chaney, to the 2004 version directed by Joel Schumacher; from the high road of opera to the low road of *The Rocky Horror Picture Show*, a popular midnight movie of the late seventies; from the "Night on Bald Mountain" section of Disney's *Fantasia* (1940) to Burton's own *Corpse Bride* (2005). And, of course, this listing does not even include such oddities as *The Abominable Dr. Phibes* (1971), *The Phantom of the Paradise* (1974), and others of their ilk.

Knowledge of genre is essential for getting big-budget films financed, and most successful directors specialize in one or two types of films. Burton's movies may be characterized as fantasies of one form or another, ranging from science-fiction (*Planet of the Apes*) or sci-fi fantasy (*Mars Attacks*) to the sportive Gothic (*Sleepy Hollow*) to the real Gothic (*Sweeney Todd*). Some of them, like *Charlie and the Chocolate Factory*, are perched in a way station somewhere between. Samuel Taylor Coleridge said that every work of art contains in itself the reason why it is so and not otherwise. By this standard, *Sweeney Todd* is a perfect film. It is what it is, it does not want to be anything else, and it must be accepted or rejected on its own terms.

Like a Shakespearean play, Sondheim's great musical travels light. It can support different interpretations, and many different films could be made from it. It is no criticism of Burton's film to say that the intricate games of Brecht or Beckett do not interest him. The hardening of the character of Mrs. Lovett, as portrayed by Lansbury in the play, darkens Burton's film, narrows its confines, turns its focus directly upon Sweeney Todd, and hardens it into a drama of revenge run amok. Sweeney becomes a sort of dark Edmond Dantes who does not know when to stop. Unlike the Count of Monte Cristo, who sails away with a beautiful woman who loves him, Sweeney meets a death which is no different from that of the many people whose throats he slit.

Nevertheless, the film need not be interpreted as the mere bloodletter most of the critics and audiences seem to have considered it, and repeated viewings moderate its horrors and emphasize its humor. Indeed, much of the humor is more traditional than a first viewing might suggest. For example, Cohen's Pirelli turns out to be a fraud in more ways than one; he was even accused by one critic, who will remain anonymous here, of packing—that is, of using padding of some sort to augment the manly portion of his skintight outfit. Traditional comics wore baggy trousers which were, according to Eric Segal, "an acknowledged symbol of sexual incapacity" (432). In marked contrast to Sweeney's modest apparel, Pirelli's dress and demeanor loudly proclaim his super-masculinity. Together the pair represent the fundamental comic conflict between what Segal calls "the blusterer and the ironic man" (433). That the relationship between the pair is a dark one is beyond question; how dark is a matter of the artistic treatment and of the individual interpretation of both the audience and the critics.

In a fascinating essay on the making of *Sweeney Todd*, Estelle Shay has written about Tim Burton's evolving conception of the role of special effects in the film. While there is no doubt that the movie is, at least by most definitions, "a special effects film," the scope of the special effects changed somewhat to allow the actors greater freedom. Shay's essay discusses Burton's changing relationship with visual effects supervisor Chas Jarrett. During preproduction the "look" of the London exteriors was decided upon through the close collaboration of Jarrett and Academy Award–winning production designer Dante Ferretti. During shooting, Burton thought the so-called greenscreen, where the actors act only against each other without any background, was too limiting, "a bit too impersonal," and moved toward "more intimate environments" to give the actors more scope and something "to connect with and play off of" (25).

Sweeney is logically the role that Johnny Depp has been moving towards in the best of his earlier film roles. Depp, more than any other film actor of the sound period, has provided a scapegoat for the audience. His characters, at least until Sweeney, have been guilt-free. He has accepted the burden of the sins of the viewing public. Of course, all acting does that to some extent, but in nearly all films there is a sense in which the great actor knows that he is a fraud, that there is a distance between him and the role he plays, whether it is Olivier's Hamlet or Brando's Terry Malloy. Admittedly, the function of the Actor's Studio and method acting is to narrow that difference. Depp's function as an artist is to obliterate it.

Actors generally want to be loved. They want their characters to be sympathetic, or, when they are not, they want the audience to know, at least at some level, that they are only playing at being bad. An actor loses, or gains, weight, uglies up or down, plays a largely unsympathetic role, and the Academy Award people come to call. Depp's monsters are guilt-free; at least they have been previously. With *Sweeney Todd*, Depp puts in all his chips.

Simply put, *Sweeney Todd* could not be the great film it is without him. For the first time, Depp has allowed the audience in. The actor himself has said that his face "is a rictus of pain" in the movie, and that he "can't watch it." It is interesting, but totally unnecessary, to speculate whether the illness of Depp's daughter, which necessitated the actor's three weeks' absence from the shooting of the film, darkened his performance. (Fortunately, the young girl made a complete recovery.)

Depp is a small man, and like all great actors, he uses his body to his advantage. (We may disregard his tattoos, even that of his mother over his heart.) Look at the photograph of Depp, as Sweeney, walking away from us down a dark street (Salisbury 175). His body is stiff, frail, determined; his jacket too long. He does not ask for our sympathy, but we give it without hesitation. Now in his forties, his face has darkened and he might resemble one of the fallen angels of Milton's *Paradise Lost*. His hair is long, with a streak of white running down one side, as if blasted in the fall from Paradise. He seems too frail to match wits with such a physically imposing and talented blowhard as Pirelli. In the act of execution, for that is how Sweeney regards the slitting of throats, his face is composed, but he takes on a growing ferocity as he discovers how much he likes it, and his ultimate ferociousness as he slashes Judge Turpin's throat is almost beyond belief, his razor raised in a triumph of rage, his face a blood-spattered grimace of hatred.

2009 *Public Enemies*

Number One

"Early *Public Enemies* reviews hint
Johnny Depp might be proficient actor." (Gawker)
"Surprise, surprise." (Gomer Pyle)

On Wednesday, July 1, 2009, at the height of the summer season, Johnny Depp's first movie in eighteen months opened on the screens of America. Depp took center stage as John Dillinger in Michael Mann's high-powered gangster thriller *Public Enemies*. The film, which has been long in gestation, was based upon Bryan Burrough's work of popular history *Public Enemies: America's Greatest Crime Wave and the Birth of the FBI, 1933–34* (2004). Richly anecdotal, simply written, and carefully researched, the book is a fascinating read. Burrough apparently traveled around the country visiting many of the original crime sites, copied six full filing cabinets of FBI files (at a cost of ten cents a page) and mastered a ton of secondary material. Although the present writer built up some incredulity about the many verbatim quotations from seventy-five years ago, some of which are of considerable length, the result is mesmerizing.

Burrough's thesis, although hardly new, has never been examined in such detail. Simply put, a small number of criminals headed by John Dillinger enabled J. Edgar Hoover to build the FBI into a powerful crime fighting organization. Hoover's later life, when he led the organization into gross violations of the rights of American citizens, is mentioned, but is beyond the scope of *Public Enemies*. Although the subject matter would have a built-in appeal for Hollywood, the book was not an obvious candidate for filming. Covering a broad canvas and containing a large number of albeit very colorful characters, some of whom never meet each other, it would obviously require careful pruning to produce a successful film. Originally conceived as a mini-series, which would have allowed each of the three protagonists to take center-stage separately, the project eventually ended up with Michael Mann. According to Mark Harris, Mann had long contemplated a gangster film dealing with Melvin Purvis (the man who got John Dillinger and was denied all credit by the egotistical J. Edgar Hoover) and the ascendency of the FBI, and the Burrough book appealed to him.

The interested reader may trace the byzantine trail by which the project came together in Harris's careful account. The complex character of John Dillinger, with its suggestive mixture of complex social forces, individual perversity, pop culture and the growth of the FBI, would have an obvious appeal for Johnny Depp. To date, Depp's outsiders had always been at the edge of the American dream. With *Public Enemies*, he moved toward dead center.

Career criminals have been important both to filmmakers and their audience from the early years of film. Whether D. W. Griffith's *The Musketeers of Pig Alley* (1912) is the first gangster film may be open to question, but it is fair to say that the Great Depression, the coming of sound, and the enormous publicity given to a few criminals by sensational stories in the newspapers and on the radio made gangster films popular in the early 1930s. Robert Warshow, in two influential essays collected in *The Immediate Experience* (1962), compared the gangster and the cowboy. The essential differences were that the gangster was a city boy who was amoral, ambitious and interested in expensive women and conspicuous consumption. The cowboy, by comparison, was a loner who lived by a stern moral code and who needed only a horse, a gun and the ability to shoot straight and to hold his countenance in the face of death. Scarface and Little Caesar died in shootouts and the cowboy either rode away into the hills alone or settled down on a ranch with a little house on the bend of a river. The moral ambiguity of the gangster gave him possibilities as a tragic hero lacking the cowboy.

Except perhaps for Scarface Al Capone, the most famous gangster of the period was country boy John Dillinger. His country boy satellites, Bonnie and Clyde, Pretty Boy Floyd, and a few lesser lights, followed some distance behind. Although the city boys attracted attention from major filmmakers who made some of the greatest of all American films, including the first two Godfather films, the country gangsters had little popular success to boast of, at least in films, until after World War II. Poverty-row Monogram's *Dillinger* (1945) and would-be tough-guy auteur John Milius's film of the same name (1973), with *Wild Bunch* graduate Warren Oates in the title role, never made much of an impression. Only Arthur Penn's early assault on the Hollywood production code *Bonnie and Clyde* (1967), with star turns by Warren Beatty and Faye Dunaway, caught the attention of the public and the critics. Forty years on, however, the film seems all bang-bang and bloviation.

The two best Depression crime movies are probably Nicolas Ray's *They Live by Night* (1948) and Robert Altman's *Thieves Like Us* (1974), both based on Edward Anderson's 1937 novel *Thieves Like Us*, which was included in the prestigious Library of America. Ray's film is pure film noir on California roads, but Altman took his talented French cinematographer Jean Boffety to Mississippi and found authentic Depression settings for his doomed lovers, superbly played by Keith Carradine and Shelley Duvall. Except for *An American Tragedy*, no other American novel has produced two classic films from directors of such distinction.

Judging by the amount of critical attention — or rather the lack of it — Michael Mann (b. 1943) is currently the most underrated big-budget film director in Hollywood. Whatever else may be said about him, he makes films that are strongly narrative driven and visually distinctive. A whole beautiful book could be written and illustrated showing the evolution of his always distinctive visual style.

After working at a variety of jobs in the motion picture field, including directing a successful television movie, *The Jericho Mile* (1979), Mann achieved fame as the producer of *Miami Vice* (1984–89), which, as has often been noted, made a star of Don Johnson and his wardrobe. The series, although short on character development, was strong on action sequences and unsurpassed for its clean, well-lighted pastel visuals, which set a new standard for television and shortly thereafter for motion pictures.

When Mann graduated to big budget mainstream Hollywood films, he brought his visual aesthetics with him, and when supported by strong screenplays, he did outstanding work. *Manhunter* (1986), the first Hannibal Lecter film, although a box-office failure, looks better every year, and his updated version of James Fenimore Cooper's *The Last of the Mohicans* (1992), filmed in the mountains of North Carolina, is one of the best versions of any classic American novel. Mann, however, is best known for his crime films, especially *Thief* (1981), *Heat* (1995), *Collateral* (2004) and *Miami Vice* (2006), a darker but no more convincing version of the television show.

Anthony Lane, in *Nobody's Perfect*, perceptively cites David Lean and Michael Mann as directors who like to "paint pictures in watercolors" and who "have to fight hardest to prevent their characters from shrinking into the landscape" (327). Clive James, in a superb — but too brief — essay on Mann's films in *Cultural Amnesia*, writes that "the atmospherics" of Mann's *Heat* has affected the look of every crime film in the past decade either positively, if that is the word, toward glamour or negatively toward grunge. Like his contemporary Ridley Scott, Mann is a creature of the interregnum between film and the digital revolution, and like Scott, he has changed his aesthetics with the changing technology. If Mann is a romantic who likes the complex but well defined visuals of romanticism, Scott is baroque, and his visual field is cluttered, but like Mann, he privileges the look of the film above all else. Both Mann and Scott make what are essentially silent movies in which, as James recognizes, language is simply another form of sound. Arguably, the best way to watch a Mann movie is to turn your DVD to some language you do not understand and regard the dialogue as just another part of the film package.

The problem, of course, is that films need writers and that Mann is often betrayed by his, the chief of whom is generally himself. Smack in the middle of *Heat*, there is what Clive James calls "a hamming contest" between Al Pacino and Robert De Niro in which each actor attempts to out-yell the other. Sam Peckinpah and John Ford, who understood such conflict, would have had their actors talk calmly about something other than the matter at hand, whatever that might happen to be: people they used to know, family problems, the good old days, the value of Ford over Chevrolet, whatever. After all, the two men have not met to have a flyting (bragging contest), but to measure each other and calculate the odds.

Burrough's book has three classic characters—J. Edgar Hoover, the Godfather; Melvin Purvis, the straight-arrow; and John Dillinger, the gangster — and, appropriately adapted to film, might well have equaled *The Godfather* for scope, drama and intensity. Faced with limited funds after the comparative failure of the enormously expensive *Miami Vice* and such a complex source as the Burrough's narrative, the writers sensibly decided to slice away most of the Hoover material and that of the minor gangsters and to concentrate upon Melvin Purvis' relentless pursuit of Dillinger, that is, to make a Michael Mann film. The character of Hoover was essentially dropped and Purvis was darkened nearly to insanity. The original title was maintained even though it was now hardly appropriate.

When the film opened, the reviewers were grumpy. They praised Johnny Depp's performance and that of co-star Marion Cotillard, but groused about the many unbelievable shootouts—as if that were a surprise in a Michael Mann film — and the absence not only of commentary but an almost total lack of social consciousness in a film about the Great Depression, which was, after all, a period in many respects much like our own. Few writers had anything good to say about Christian Bale's clenched-teeth performance as Purvis. The supporting players do not seem to have made much of an impression and were largely ignored.

Most of the critics, including apparently star Johnny Depp, did not like the HD in which *Public Enemies* was shot. Both *Miami Vice* and *Public Enemies* were shot in HD, and while much of the discussion of Mann's use of the newest technology has been negative, Mann's justification is clear enough. Digital is where movies are going and HD at least has the advantage of giving the director final — if perhaps only temporary—control of the look of his film. The director argues that the darker look of *Miami Vice* was appropriate because of the use of crack cocaine and the darkening of the drug culture since the days of the television series. Mann admires the deep focus which HD allows, where all objects can be kept in perfect focus to infinity, provided of course that you can get that far. This belief is, of course, pure romanticism. The classic cinematographers knew that the public wanted to see Garbo's face and believed that the rest should be indistinct.

A minority of reviewers were happy just to accept Depp's star-power and to go along for the ride. Rex Reed called the film "thrilling, glamorous, richly textured and breathlessly action-packed" (*New York Observer*). Roger Moore, of the *Orlando Sentinel*, called the film "riveting, rousing entertainment." In praise cited on film posters, Peter Travers was even more enthusiastic, citing Depp's "towering performance" and the way in which "Mann uses color, design, editing, score and Dante Spinotti's expressionistic camerawork to take you there." This is fair praise whether you agree with it or not; it at least gives the viewer a way to get into the movie.

At least one critic, Constance Droganes, took what is generally taken to be the greatest limitation of the movie, its lack of an adequate vocabulary to supplement its elegant visuals, to be its strength. Dillinger tells Billie Frechette, well-played by Academy Award winner Marion Cotillard, that he likes "baseball, good clothes, fast cars ... and you," and then adds as a kicker, "I rob banks" (CTA.ca). (Of course, we have heard a similar line delivered more than forty years ago by Warren Beatty with much greater emphasis and a cocky smirk as big as all outdoors.) Dillinger says that is "all you need to know." According to Droganes, what you see in *Public Enemies* is what you get.

As in the *Pirates of the Caribbean* series, the female lead knows who the star of the film is, and their scenes together generate real heat. It would, however, be a mistake to believe that Dillinger's statements are adequate to explain his motivation. Audiences, lacking anything else in the film that would explain Dillinger's motivation, seem to be willing to accept Dillinger's simplistic pronouncements at face value. Dillinger, however, does not know what motivates him, and neither, for that matter, does Johnny Depp. Neither do you and I know what motivates us. Beyond the violence and the visual elegance of *Public Enemies*, the characters are clueless. The absence of any directorial authority allows them to wander in the orbit of the great actor at the center, who as always has a secret life he is willing to share with the viewers if they will attend carefully to him.

Filmography

Unless noted, release dates are for the United States.

1984

A Nightmare on Elm Street (November 16, 1984) New Line Cinema

Director/Writer: Wes Craven *Producer:* Robert Shaye *Associate Producer:* John Burrows *Executive Producers:* Stanley Dudelson, Joseph Wolf *Music:* Charles Bernstein *Song: "Nightmare:"* Steve Karshner, Martin Kent, Michael Schung *Photography:* Jacques Haitkin *Production Design:* Greg Fonseca *Editors:* Pat McMahon, Rick Shaine *Sound Mixer:* James LaRue *Production Manager:* John Burrows *Make-up:* Kathy Logan *Special Make-up Effects:* David Miller, Louis Lazzara *Hair Stylist:* RaMona *Costumes:* Dana Lyman.

CAST: John Saxon (Lt. Thompson), Ronee Blakley (Marge Thompson), Heather Langenkamp (Nancy Thompson), Amanda Wyss (Tina Grey), Nick Corri (Rod Lane), Johnny Depp (Glen Lantz), Richard Englund (Freddy Krueger), Charles Fleischer (Dr. King), Joseph Whipp (Sgt. Parker), Lin Shaye (Teacher) Joe Unger (Sgt. Garcia), Mimi Craven (Nurse), Jack Shea (Minister), Ed Call (Mr. Lantz) Sandy Lipton (Mrs. Lantz), David Andrews (Foreman), Jeff Levine (Coroner), Donna Woodrum (Tina's Mom), Shashawnee Hall (Cop), Brian Reise (Cop), Carol Pritkin (Cop), Ash Adams (Surfer), Don Hannah (Surfer).

Running Time: 91 minutes *MPAA Rating:* R.

1985

Private Resort (May 3, 1985) TRISTAR

Director: George Bowers *Story:* Gordon Mitchell, Ken Segall, Alan Wenkus *Screenplay:* Gordon Mitch-ell *Producers:* R. B. Efraim, Don Enright *Photography:* Adam Greenberg *Editor:* Samuel D. Pollard.

CAST: Rob Morrow (Ben), Johnny Depp (Jack), Emily Longstreth (Patti), Hector Elizondo (The Maestro), Karyn O'Bryan (Dana), Dody Goodman (Mrs. Rawlings), Tony Azito (Reeves), Hilary Shapiro (Shirley), Leslie Easterbrook (Bobbie Sue), Michael Bowen (Scott), Lisa London (Alice), Andrew Dice Clay (Curt), Ron House (the Barber).

Running Time: 82 minutes (DVD) *MPAA Rating:* R.

Lady Blue "Birds of Prey" (October 10, 1985), Episode 4 of the television series *Lady Blue.*

CAST: Jamie Rose (Lady Blue), Danny Aiello, Ron Dean, Johnny Depp, Lorenzo Clemens, Terry Ferman, David Oliver.

1986

Slow Burn (Made for TV 1986) Castles Burning Prod., MCA Pay TV

Director/Writer: Matthew Chapman, based upon the novel *Castles Burning,* by Arthur Lyons *Casting:* Kimba Hills *Costumes:* Gale Parker-Smith *Music:* Loek Dikker *Editor:* T. Battle Davis *Visual Consultant:* Bo Welch *Photography:* Tim Suhrstedt *Executive Producers:* Joel Schumacher, Stefanie Staffin Kowal, Mark Levinson.

CAST: Eric Roberts (Jacob Asch), Beverly D'Angelo (Laine Fleischer), Dennis Lipscomb (Ron Mc-Donald), Raymond J. Barry (Gerald McMurtry), Ann Schedeen (Mona), Emily Longstreth (Pam Draper), Johnny Depp (Donnie Fleischer), Henry

Gibson (Robert), Dan Hedaya (Simon Fleischer), Frank Schuller (Norton), Victoria Catlin (Erica), Edward Bunker (George), Ruth Richards (Mrs. Poulson).

Running Time: 92 minutes *MPAA Rating:* None. *Slow Burn* was made for pay television and is unrated. Because of drug usage, nudity, language and violence, it would unquestionably have been rated R.

Platoon (December 24, 1986) Hemdale, Orion

Director/Writer: Oliver Stone *Producer:* Arnold Kopelson *Co-Producer:* A. Kitman Ho *Executive Producers:* John Daly, Derek Gibson *Photography:* Robert Richardson *Editor Original Music:* Georges Delerue, *Editor:* Claire Simpson, *Production Design:* Bruno Rubeo, *Art Directors:* Rodell Cruz, Sherman Williams, *Special Effects:* Yves de Bono.

CAST: Tom Berenger (Staff Sgt. Bob Barnes), Willem Dafoe (Sgt. Elias Grodin), Charlie Sheen (Pvt. Chris Taylor), Forest Whitaker (Big Harold), Francesco Quinn (Rhah), John C. McGinley (Sgt. Red O'Neill), Richard Edson (Sal), Kevin Dillon (Bunny), Reggie Johnson (Junior Martin), Keith David (King), Johnny Depp (Pvt. Gator Lerner), David Neidorf (Tex), Mark Moses (Lt. Wolfe), Chris Pedersen (Crawford), Tony Todd (Sgt. Warren), Corkey Ford (Manny), Ivan Kane (Tony Hoyt).

Running Time: 120 minutes. *MPAA Rating:* R *Academy Awards:* Best Picture (Arnold Kopelson); Best Direction (Oliver Stone); Best Sound (John Wilkinson, Richard D. Rogers, Charles Grenzbach, Simon Kaye); Best Film Editing (Claire Simpson). *Academy Award Nominations:* Best Supporting Actor (Tom Berenger; Willem Dafoe). Numerous other awards worldwide.

1987

Hotel (TV Series) "Unfinished Business" (Season 4, Episode 15, Broadcast February 4, 1987) Johnny Depp (Rob Cameron).

1987–1991

21 Jump Street (Made for TV 1987–1991) The series ran five seasons, 103 episodes, although Johnny Depp did not appear during the final season. The IMDB gives much helpful information, but contains many errors and does not give the names of the directors. Directors and writers are listed in this book in the main entry.

1990

Cry-Baby (April 6, 1990) Imagine Entertainment, Universal

Writer/Director: John Waters *Producer:* Rachel Talalay *Executive Producers:* Jim Abrahams, Brian Grazer, Pat Moran *Photography:* David Insley *Editor:* Janice Hampton *Original Music:* Patrick Williams *Production Design:* Vincent Peranio *Art Direction:* Delores Deluxe *Set Decoration:* Virginia Nichols, Chester Overlock *Costume Design:* Van Smith.

CAST: Johnny Depp (Wade "Cry-Baby" Walker), Amy Locane (Allison Vernon-Williams), Susan Tyrrell (Ramona Rickettes), Polly Bergen (Mrs. Vernon-Williams), Ricki Lake (Pepper Walker), Traci Lords (Wanda Woodward), Kim McGuire (Hatchet-Face), Darren E. Burrows (Milton Hackett), Stephen Mailer (Baldwin, Allison's Boyfriend), Kim Webb (Lenora Frigid), Alan J. Wendl (Toe-Joe Jackson), Troy Donahue (Hatchet's Father), Mink Stole (Hatchet's Mother), Joe Dallesandro (Milton's Father), Joey Heatherton (Milton's Mother), David Nelson (Wanda's Father), Patricia Hearst (Wanda's Mother), Willem Dafoe (Hateful Guard at Training School), Iggy Pop (Uncle Belvedere Rickettes), Jonathan Benya (Snare-Drum, Pepper Walker's Son), Steve Aronson (Mean Guard), Kelly Goldberg (Pepper's baby), James Intveld (Cry-Baby's singing voice).

Running Time: 85 minutes, DVD *Director's Cut* 92 minutes *MPAA Rating:* R.

Edward Scissorhands (December 14, 1990) 20th Century–Fox

Director: Tim Burton *Producers:* Tim Burton, Caroline Thompson. *Executive Producer:* Richard Hashimoto *Writer:* Caroline Thompson *Story:* Tim Burton & Caroline Thompson *Music:* Danny Elfman *Casting:* Victoria Thomas *Costume Design:* Colleen Atwood *Special Effects:* Stan Winston *Editor:* Richard Halsey *Production Design:* Bo Welch *Director of Photography:* Stefan Czapsky.

CAST: Johnny Depp (Edward), Winona Ryder (Kim), Dianne Wiest (Peg), Anthony Michael Hall (Jim), Kathy Baker (Joyce), Conchata Ferrell (Helen), Robert Oliveri (Kim), Caroline Aaron (Marge), Dick Anthony Williams (Officer Allen), O-Lan Jones (Esmeralda), Vincent Price (the Inventor), Alan Arkin (Bill).

Running Time: 105 minutes *MPAA Rating:* PG13.

1991

Freddy's Dead: The Final Nightmare (Released September 13, 1991) New Line Cinema

Director: Rachel Talalay *Writer:* Michael De Luca *from characters by* Wes Craven *and story by* Rachel Talalay *Producers* Robert Shaye, Aaron Warner *Associate Producer:* Michael Knue *Executive Producer:* Michael De Luca *Original Music:* Brian May *Photography:* Declan Quinn *Editor:* Janice Hampton.

CAST: Robert Englund (Freddy Krueger), Lisa Zane (Dr. Maggie Burroughs, Katherine Krueger), Shon Greenblatt (John Doe), Leslie Deane (Tracy), Ricky Dean Logan (Carlos), Breckin Meyer (Logan Spence), Yaphet Kotto (Doc), Roseanne Barr (Childless Woman), Tom Arnold (Childless Man), Elinor Donahue (Orphanage Woman), Johnny Depp (Teen on TV), Cassandra Rachel Friel (Little Maggie), David Dunard (Rachel Frel Kelly), Marilyn Rockafellow (Mrs. Burroughs), Virginia Peters (Woman in Plane), Stella Hall (Stewardess), Angelina Estrada (Carlos' Mother), Peter Spellos (Tracy's Father).

Running Time: 96 minutes *MPAA Rating:* R.

1992

Arizona Dream (*The Arrowtooth Waltz*) (Filmed 1992, Limited USA Release September 9, 1994) Constellation, Hachette Première, Le Studio Canal+, Union Générale

Director: Emir Kusturica *Writers:* Emir Kusturica and David Atkins *Producers:* Claudie Ossard, Yves Marmion *Photography:* Vilko Filac *Original Music:* Goran Bregovic, *Editor:* Andrija Zafranovic *Costumes:* Jill M. Ohanneson.

CAST: Johnny Depp (Axel), Jerry Lewis (Leo Sweetie), Faye Dunaway (Elaine Stalker), Lili Taylor (Grace Stalker), Vincent Gallo (Paul), Paulina Porizkova (Millie), Michael J. Pollard (Fabian), Candyce Mason (Blanche), Alexia Rane (Angie), Polly Noonan (Betty), Ann Schulman (Carla), Patricia O'Grady (Master of Ceremonies), James R. Wilson (Lawyer).

Running Time: 142 minutes *MPAA Rating:* R.

1993

Benny & Joon (April 16, 1993) Metro-Goldwyn-Mayer

Director: Jeremiah S. Chechik *Story:* Barry Berman and Lesley McNeil *Writer:* Barry Berman *Producers:* Susan Arnold, Donna Roth *Executive Producer:* Bill Badalato *Associate Producer:* Leslie McNeil *Original Music:* Rachel Portman *Director of Photography:* John Schwartzman *Editor:* Carol Littleton *Production Designer:* Neil Spisak *Casting:* Risa Bramon, Heidi Levitt *Costume Designer:* Aggie Guerard Rodgers.

CAST: Johnny Depp (Sam), Mary Stuart Masterson (Joon), Aidan Quinn (Benny Pearl), Julianne Moore (Ruthie), Oliver Platt (Eric), CCH Pounder (Dr. Garvey), Dan Hedaya (Thomas), Joe Grifasi (Mike), William H. Macy (Randy Burch), Liane Alexandra Curtis (Claudia), Eileen Ryan (Mrs. Smail), Don Hamilton (UPS Man), Waldo Larson (Waldo), Irvin Johnson (Orderly), Shane Nilsson (Orderly), Leslie Laursen (Admitting Nurse), Faye Killebrew (Video Customer), Ramsin Amirkhas (Video Clerk), Lynette Walden (Customer), Amy Alizabeth Sanford (Young Joon), Brian Keevy (Young Benny), John Grant Phillips (Policeman), Tony Lincoln (Local), Noon Orsatti (Patron), Dan Kamin (Patron).

Running Time: 98 minutes *MPAA Rating:* PG.

What's Eating Gilbert Grape (Released December 25, 1993) J & M Entertainment, Paramount

Director: Lasse Hallström *Writer:* Peter Hedges, based on his novel *Photography:* Sven Nykvist *Executive Producers:* Alan C. Blomquist, Lasse Hallström *Producers:* David Matalon, Berlil Ohlsson, Meir Teper *Original Music:* Bjorn Isfalt, Alan Parker *Editor:* Andrew Mondshein *Casting:* Gail Levin *Production Design:* Bernt Capra *Art Direction:* John Myhre *Costume Design:* Reneé Ehrlich Kalfus.

CAST: Leonardo Di Caprio (Arnie Grape), Johnny Depp (Gilbert Grape), Juliette Lewis (Becky), Mary Steenburgen (Betty Carver), Darlene Cates (Bonnie Grape), Laura Harrington (Amy Grape), Mary Kate Schellhardt (Ellen Grape), Kevin Tighe (Ken Carver), John C. Reilly (Tucker Van Dyke), Crispin Glover (Bobby McBurney), Penelope Branning (Becky's Grandmother), Tim Green (Mr. Lamson), Susan Loughran (Mrs. Lamson), Robert B. Hedges (Minister), Mark Jordan (Toddy Carver), Cameron Finley (Doug Carver), Brady Corman (Sheriff Farrel), Tim Simek (Deputy), Nicholas Stojanovich (Boy), Libby Villari (Waitress), Kay Bower (Police Secretary).

Running Time: 118 minutes *MPAA Rating:* PG13.

1994

Ed Wood (September 28, 1994) Touchstone Pictures

Director: Tim Burton *Producers:* Denise DiNovi, Tim Burton *Writers:* Scott Alexander, Larry Karaszewski, based on the book *Nightmare of Ecstasy,* by Rudolph Grey *Music:* Ray Evans, Jay Livingston, and Howard Shore *Costume Design:* Colleen Atwood *Editor:* Chris Lebenzon *Production Design:* Tom Duffield

Photography: Stefan Czapsky *Co-Producer:* Michael Flynn *Executive Producer:* Michal Lehmann *Casting:* Victoria A. Thomas.

CAST: Johnny Depp (Ed Wood), Martin Landau (Bela Lugosi), Sarah Jessica Parker (Dolores Fuller), Jeffrey Jones (Criswell), G. D. Spradlin (Reverend Lemon), Vincent D'Onofrio (Orson Welles), Bill Murray (Bunny Breckinridge), Patricia Arquette (Kathy O'Hara), Mike Starr (Georgie Weiss), Max Casella (Paul Marco), Brent Hinkley (Conrad Brooks), Lisa Marie (Vampira), George "the Animal" Steele (Tor Johnson), Juliet Landau (Loretta King), Ned Bellamy (Dr. Tom Mason), Danny Dayton (Sound Man), John Ross (Camera Assistant), Bill Cusack (Tom McCoy), Aaron Nelms (Teenager), Biff Yeager (Rude Boss), Joseph Gannascoli (Security Guard), Carmen Filpi (Old Crusty Man), Lisa Malkiewicz (Secretary No. 1), Melora Walters (Secretary No. 2), Conrad Brooks (Bartender), Don Amendolia (Salesman), Tommy Betelsen (Tough Boy), Reid Cruickshanks (Stage Guard), Stanley Desantis (Mr. Feldman).

Running Time: 127 minutes *MPAA Rating:* R.

1995

Don Juan DeMarco (*Don Juan DeMarco and the Centerfold*) (April 7, 1995) New Line Cinema, American Zoetrope

Director/Writer: Jeremy Leven *Producers:* Francis Ford Coppola, Fred Fuchs, Patrick Palmer *Executive Producers:* Michael De Luca, Ruth Vitale *Music:* Michael Kamen, Robert John Lange *Cinematography* Ralf Bode *Art Director:* Jeff Knipp *Editor:* Tony Gibbs *Sound Mixer:* Richard Lightstone *Production Manager:* Patrick Palmer *Costumes:* Kirsten Everberg *Special Effects:* James Fredburg *Stunt Coordinator:* Victor Paul.

CAST: Johnny Depp (Don Juan DeMarco), Marlon Brando (Dr. Jack Mickler), Faye Dunaway (Marilyn Mickler), Bob Dishy (Dr. Paul Showalter), Geraldine Pailhas (Dona Ana), Talisa Soto (Dona Julia), Rachel Ticotin (Dona Inez), Richard C. Serafian (Detective Sy Tobias), Marita Geraghty (Woman in Restaurant), Tresa Hughes (Grandmother DeMarco), Stephen Singer (Dr. Bill Dunsmore), Franz Luz (Don Antonio), Carmen Argenziano (Don Alfonzo), Jo Champa (Sultana Gulbeyaz), Esther Scott (Nurse Alvira), Nada Despotovich (Nurse Gloria), Gilbert Lewis (Judge Ryland), "Tiny" Lister, Jr. (Rocco Compton), Tom Mardirosian (Baba, the Eunuch), Al Corley (Woman's Date), Nick La Tour (Nicholas), Bill Capizza (Sultan).

Running Time: 97 minutes *MPAA Rating:* PG13.

Nick of Time (November 22, 1995) Paramount

Director/Producer: John Badham *Writer:* Patrick Sheane Duncan *Photography:* Roy H. Wagner *Casting:* Carol Lewis *Music:* Arthur B. Rubinstein *Costume Design:* Mary E. Vogt *Editors:* Frank Morriss, Kevin Stitt *Production Design:* Philip Harrison *Executive Producer:* D. J. Caruso.

CAST: Johnny Depp (Gene Watson), Christopher Walken (Mr. Smith), Roma Maffia (Ms. Jones), Charles Dutton (Huey), Marsha Mason (Eleanor Grant), Peter Strauss (Mr. Grant), Gloria Reuben (Krista Brooks), Courtney Chase (Lynn Watson), G. D. Spradlin (Mystery Man), Bill Smitrovich (Officer Trust), Yul Vazquez (Gustino, Guest Services), Edith Diaz (Irene, Guest Services), Armando Ortega (Hector, Guest Services).

Running Time: 88 minutes *MPAA Rating:* R.

Cannes Man (1995, apparently never released in theaters) Cult DVD, Rocket Pictures Home Video

Director: Richard Martini *Writers:* Deric Haddad, Richard Martini, Irwin Rappaport, Susan Shapiro *Photography:* Denise Brassard, Dean Lent *Editor:* Richard Currie *Music:* Richard Martini.

CAST: Seymour Cassell (Sy Lerner), Francesco Quinn (Frank "Rhino" Rhinoslavsky), Rebecca Broussard (Rebecca Lerner), *And as themselves:* Johnny Depp, Treat Williams, Jim Jarmusch, Benicio Del Toro, John Malkovich, Lara Flynn Boyle, James Brolin, Robert Evans, Dennis Hopper, Julian Lennon, Chris Penn, *and others.*

Running Time: 88 minutes *MPAA Rating:* None.

1996

Dead Man (May 10, 1996) 12 Gauge, JVC Entertainment, Miramax

Director/Writer: Jim Jarmusch *Producers:* Demetra J. MacBride, Karen Koch *Photography:* Robby Müller *Editor:* Jay Rabinowitz *Production Design:* Robert Ziembicki *Music:* Neil Young.

CAST: Johnny Depp (William Blake), Gary Farmer (Nobody), Lance Henriksen (Cole Wilson), Michael Wincott (Conway Twill), Mili Avital (Thel Russell), Iggy Pop (Sal Jenko), Billy Bob Thornton (Big George), Jared Harris (Benmont Tench), Crispin Glover (Train Fireman), Eugene Byrd (Johnny "the Kid" Pickett), Michelle Thrush (Nobody's Girlfriend), Robert Mitchum (John Dickinson), Gabriel Byrne (Charlie Dickinson), John Hurt (John Scholfield), Alfred Molina (Trading Post Missionary), Steve Buscemi (Bartender, uncredited).

Running Time: 120 minutes *MPAA Rating:* R.

1997

Donnie Brasco (February 10, 1997) Tristar

Director: Mike Newell *Producers:* Mark Johnson, Barry Levinson, Louis DiGiaimo, Gail Mutrux *Executive Producers:* Patrick McCormick, Alan Greenspan *Writer:* Paul Attanasio, based upon the book by Joseph D. Pistone with Richard Wooley *Photography:* Peter Sova *Casting:* Louis DiGiaimo, Brett Goldstein *Music:* Patrick Doyle *Executive Music Producers:* Budd Carr, Allan Mason *Costume Design:* Aude Bronson-Howard, David Robinson *Film Editor:* John Gregor *Production Design:* Donald Graham Burt.

CAST: Al Pacino (Lefty), Johnny Depp (Donnie Brasco), Michael Madsen (Sonny), Bruno Kirby (Nick), James Russo (Paulie), Anne Heche (Maggie), Željko Ivanek (Tim Curley), Gerry Becker (Dean), Robert Mianno (Sonny Red), Brian Tarantina (Bruno), Rocco Sisto (Richie Gazzo), Zack Grenier (Dr. Berger), Walt MacPherson (Sheriff), Terry Serpico (Strip Club Owner), Gretchen Mol (Sonny's Girlfriend), Tony Lip (Philly Lucky), Ronnie Farer (Annette), George Angelica (Big Trin), Val Avery (Trafficante), Madison Arnold (Jilly), Delanie Fitzpatrick, Katie Sagona, Sara Gold (Daughters), Larry Romano (Tommy), Tim Blake Nelson, Paul Giamatti (FBI Technicians), James Michael McCauley (FBI Agent), Jim Bulleit (U.S. Attorney), Andrew Parks (Hollman).

Running Time: 128 minutes *MPAA Rating:* R.

The Brave (Released July 30, 1997, France) Acapella Pictures, Majestic

Director: Johnny Depp *Producer:* Charles Evans Jr., Carroll Kemp *Co-Producer:* Diane Batson-Smith *Writers:* Paul McCudden, Johnny Depp, D. P. Depp, from the novel *The Brave*, by Gregory McDonald *Associate Producer:* Buck Holland *Music:* Iggy Pop, Mark Governer, J.J. Holiday, Chuck E. Weiss *Production Design:* Miljen Kreka Kljakovic *Photography:* Vilko Filac *Art Direction:* Branimir Babic *Editors:* Pasquale Buba, Hervé Schneid.

CAST: Johnny Depp (Rafael), Marlon Brando (McCarthy), Marshall Bell (Larry), Elpidia Carrillo (Rita), Frederic Forrest (Lou, Sr.), Clarence Williams III (Father Stratton), Max Perlich (Lou, Jr.), Luis Guzman (Luis), Cody Lightning (Frankie), Nicole Mancera (Marta), Floyd "Red Crow" Westerman (Papa), Iggy Popp (Man Eating Bird Leg), Pepe Serna (Alessandro), Lupe Ontiveros (Maria), Alexis Cruz (Heyman), Chuck E. Weiss (Whizzy), Buck Holland (Scoutmaster), Tricia Vessey (Luis's Girl #1), Tricia Peters (Luis's Girl #2), Jack Polick (Bartholomew Ender), Sam Sarkar (Freedo), Peter Mountain (Queen Carl), Jeff Johnson (Clerk), Shawn Mancera (Maria's Kid #1), Joseph Murphy (Khaki Man), Sharon McCreedy (Lou's Village Dancer), Leonardo Sessa (Villager #5), Robert De Leon (Villager #2), also Badja Djola, Bruce Corkham, Gibby Haynes, Elena St. John.

Running Time: 123 minutes (UK) *MPAA Rating:* None.

1998

Fear and Loathing in Las Vegas (May 22, 1998) Rhino Films, Shark Prod., Universal

Director Terry Gilliam *Producers:* Laila Nabulsi, Patrick Cassavetti, Stephen Nemeth *Writers:* Terry Gilliam & Tony Grisoni, and Tod Davies & Alex Cox, based on the book by Hunter S. Thompson *Photography:* Nicola Pecorini *Editor:* Lesley Walker *Production Design:* Alex McDowell *Music:* Ray Cooper.

CAST: Johnny Depp (Raoul Duke), Benicio Del Toro (Dr. Gonzo), Christina Ricci (Lucy), Gary Busey (Highway Patrolman), Ellen Barkin (North Star Waitress), Harry Dean Stanton (Judge), Katherine Helmond (Reservation Clerk), Tobey Maguire (Hitchhiker), Cameron Diaz (Reporter on Elevator), Michael Jeter (L. Ron Bumquist), Jenette Goldstein (Maid), Michael Lee Gogin (Uniformed Dwarf), Lyle Lovett (Road Person), Craig Bierko (Lacerda), Larry Cedar (Car Rental Agent).

Running Time: 118 minutes *MPAA Rating:* R.

LA Without a Map (Apparently not released in theaters in U.S., general release around the world 1999) Dan Films, Euro American Films S.A.

Director: Mika Kaurismaki *Writers:* Kaurismaki & Richard Rayner, based on his novel *Executive Producer:* Deepak Nayar *Producers:* Pierre Assouline, Julie Baines, Sarah Daniel *Co-Producer:* Mika Kaurismaki *Line Producer:* Brent Morris *Original Music:* Sebastien Cortella *Photography:* Michel Amathieu *Editor:* Ewa J. Lind *Casting:* Steve Brooksbank, Randi Hiller *Production Design:* Caroline Hanania *Set Decoration* Marcia Calosio, Eliza Solesbury.

CAST: Johnny Depp (Himself/William Blake), David Tennant (Richard), Vincent Gallo (Moss), Tony Peers (Vicar), Steve Huison (Billy), Margo Stanley (Mrs. Blenkinsop), Vinessa Shaw (Barbara), Saskia Reeves (Joy), Malcolm Tierney (Joy's Dad), Margi Clarke (Bradford Woman), Monte Hellman (Himself), Jean-Pierre Kalfon (Jean-Mimi), Julie Delpy (Julie), Kevin West (Spielberg Man), Lisa Edelstein (Sandra), Michael Campbell (Young Porter), Joe Dallesandro (Michael), Cameron Bancroft (Patterson), Matthew Faber (Joel), Brent Morris (Aviator Shades Cop), Mista Taboo (Rapper), Dijon Talton (Kid), Joey Perillo (McCrea), Amanda Plummer (Red Pool Owner), Dominic Gould, Sakke Jarvenpaa, Veeti Kallio (Leningrad Cowboys), Jerzy Skolimonski (Minister), Don Ranvaud (Man with Script), Debra Carroll (Waitress), James LeGros (Takowsky), Tootie (Lippy Blonde), Christa Lang (Woman on Bus), Michael Franco (Barman), Nathalie Huot (Tall Woman), Joseph Arsenault (Jealous Man), Robert Davi (Himself), Kenneth Hughes (Smoking Guest), Andy Bradford (Corpse), Anouk Aimée (Herself).

Running Time: 107 minutes *MPAA Rating:* None.

1999

The Source (Filmed 1999, apparently never released theatrically) Beat Productions, Calliope

Director/Writer/Producer/Editor: Chuck Workman *Associate Producer:* Mark Apostolon *Music* David Amram, Philip Glass *Photography:* Andrew Dintenfass, Tom Hurwitz, Don Lenzer, José Louis Mignone, Nancy Schreiber *Production Design:* Marc Greville-Masson *Executive Producer:* Hiro Yamagata.

CAST: Johnny Depp (Jack Kerouac), Dennis Hopper (William S. Burroughs), John Turturro (Allen Ginsberg). *And in archival footage:* Allen Ginsberg, Philip Glass, Robert Creeley, Ann Charters, George Steade, David Amram, William S. Burroughs, Ed Sanders, Gregory Corso, Kyle Roderick, Lawrence Ferlinghetti, Ken Kesey, Gary Snyder, Jerry Garcia, Jack Micheline, Michael McClure, Stephen Ronin, Philip Whalen, Terry Southern, Timothy Leary, Paul Krassner, Diane DiPrima, Tom Hayden, David Dellinger, John Sampas, Steve Allen, Amiri Baraka, Paul Bowles, William F. Buckley, Lenny Bruce, Mortimer Burroughs, John Cage, Neal Cassady, Shirley Clarke, Walter Cronkite, Richard J. Daly, Bob Dylan, Dizzy Gillespie, Brion Gysin, Abbie Hoffman, Billie Holiday, J. Edgar Hoover, Lyndon Johnson, Bob Hope, Robert F. Kennedy, Jack Kerouac, Jan Kerouac, Martin Luther King, John Luguizamo, Norman Mailer, Steve Martin, Groucho Marx, Gilbert Millstein, Robert Motherwell, Deborah Norville, Peter Orlovsky, Stuart Perkoff, Marlon Riggs, Henry Rollins.

Running Time: 88 minutes *MPAA Rating:* None.

The Astronaut's Wife (Released August 27, 1999) Mad Chance, New Line

Director/Screenplay: Rand Ravich *Producer:* Andrew Lazar *Executive Producers:* Mark Johnson, Brian Witten, Donna Langley *Photography:* Allan Daviau *Original Music* George S. Clinton *Editors:* Tim Alverson, Steve Mirkovich *Production Design:* Jay Roelfs.

CAST: Charlize Theron (Jillian Armacost), Johnny Depp (Spencer Armacost), Clea DuVall (Nan), Samantha Eggar (Doctor), Donna Murphy (Natalie Streck), Nick Cassavetes (Captain Alex Streck), Gary Grubbs (NASA Director), Blair Brown (Shelly McLaren), Tom Noonan (Jackson McLaren), Tom O'Brien (Allen Dodge), Lucy Lin (Shelly Carter), Michael Crider (Pat Elliott), Jacob Stein (Calvin, 2nd Grade Student), Timothy Wicker (Wide Eyed Kid #1), Sarah Dampf (Paula, 2nd Grade Student), Charles Lanyer (Spencer's Doctor), Conrad Bachmann (Reporter), Rondi Reed (Dr. Conlin).

Running Time: 109 minutes *MPAA Rating:* R. Note: The movie scene shown on the television set in the film is from *Penny Serenade* (1941).

Sleepy Hollow (November 19, 1999) American Zoetrope, Mandalay, Paramount

Director: Tim Burton *Writer:* Andrew Kevin Walker, based on the story "The Legend of Sleepy Hollow," by Washington Irving *Screenstory* Kevin Yagher and Andrew Kevin Walker *Producers:* Scott Rudin, Adam Schroeder *Co-Producers:* Kevin Yagher, Andrew Kevin Walker *Executive Producers:* Francis Ford Coppola, Larry Franco *Associate Producer:* Mark Roybal *Music* Danny Elfman *Photography:* Emmanuel Lubezki *Production Design:* Rick Heinrichs *Art Direction:* Ken Court, John Dexter, Andrew Nicholson *Editors:* Chris Lebenzon, Joel Negron *Sound Recording:* Harry Higgins, Bob Olari *Sound Mixer:* Tony Dawe *Production Manager:* Dusty Symonds *First Assistant Director:* Chris Newman *Costumes:* Colleen Atwood *Special Effects:* Carmila Gittens, Joss Williams *Stunt Coordinator:* Nick Gillard.

CAST: Johnny Depp (Ichabod Crane), Christina Ricci (Katrina Van Tassel), Miranda Richardson (Lady Van Tassel, Western Woods Crone), Michael Gambon (Baltus Van Tassel), Casper Van Dien (Brom Van Brunt), Jeffrey Jones (Reverend Steenwyck), Christopher Lee (Burgomaster), Richard Griffiths (Magistrate Samuel Philipse), Ian McDiarmid (Dr. Thomas Lancaster), Michael Gough (Notary James Hardenbrook), Marc Pikering (Young Masbath), Lisa Marie (Ichabod's Mother), Steven Waddington (Mr. Killian), Christopher Walken (Hessian Horseman), Claire Skinner (Midwife Elizabeth Killian), Alun Armstrong (High Constable), Mark Spalding (Jonathan Masbath), Jessica Oyelowo (Sara), Tony Maudsley (Van Ripper), Gabrielle Lloyd (Dr. Lancaster's Wife), Richard Sella (Dirk Van Garrett), Michael Feast (Spotty Man), Jamie Foreman (Thuggish Constable), Philip Martin Brown (Constable), Sam Fior (Young Ichabod Crane), Tessa Allen-Ridge (Young Lady Van Tassel), Cassandra Farndale (Young Crone), Martin Landau (Peter Van Garrett).

Running Time: 105 minutes *MPAA Rating:* R.

2000

The Ninth Gate (March 10, 2000) Araba Films, Kino Vision, Le Studio Canal+

Director/Producer: Roman Polanski *Writers:* John Brownjohn, Enrique Urbizu and Roman Polanski, based on the novel *El club Dumas*, by Arturo Pérez-Reverte *Executive Producers:* Wolfgang Glattes, Michel Cheyko *Director of Photography:* Darius Khondji *Editor:* Hervé de Luze *Music* Wojciech Kilar *Music Editor:* Suzana Peric *Sound:* Jean-Marie Blondel and (music) John Timperley *Sound Editor:* Laurent Quaglio *Casting:* Howard Feuer *Production Design:* Dean Tavoularis *Art Direction:* Gérard Viard *Set Decoration* Philippe Turlure *Special Effects:* Gilbert Pieri *Costumes:* Anthony Powell *Make-up:* Paul Le Marinel and Liliane Rametta *Stunt Coordinators:* Dominique Fouassier and Jean-Claude Lagniez.

CAST: Johnny Depp (Dean Corso), Lena Olin (Liana Telfer), Frank Langella (Boris Balkan), James Russo (Bernie), Jack Taylor (Victor Fargas), José López Rodero (identical twins Pablo and Pedro Ceniza/1st and 2nd Workmen), Allen Garfield (Witkin), Barbara Jefford (Baroness Frieda Kessler), Emmanuelle Seigner (the Girl), Tony Amoni (Liana's Bodyguard), Willy Holt (Andrew Telfer), Jacques Dacqmine (Old Man), Joe Sheridan (Old Man's Son), Rebecca Pauly (Daughter-in-Law), Catherine Benguigui (Concierge), Maria Ducceshi (Secretary), Jacques Collard (Gruber), Dominique Pozzetta (Desk Clerk), Emmanuel Booz (Baker), Lino Ribeiro de Sousa (Hotel Porter), Asil Rais (Cabby), Bernard Richier and Marinette Richier (Café Owners).

Running Time: 133 minutes *MPAA Rating:* R.

2001

Chocolat (Released January 5, 2001) David Brown Prod., Fat Free, Miramax

Director: Lasse Hallström *Producers:* David Brown, Kit Golden, Leslie Holleran *Writer:* Robert Nelson Jacobs, *based on the novel by* Joanne Harris *Music* Rachel Portman *Executive Producers:* Alan C. Blomquist, Meryl Poster *Photography:* Roger Pratt *Film Editor:* Andrew Mondshein *Production Design:* David Gropman *Art Direction:* Lucy Richardson.

CAST: Juliette Binoche (Vianne Rocher), Judi Dench (Armande Voizin), Johnny Depp (Roux), Alfred Molina (Comte Paul de Reynaud), Carrie-Anne Moss (Caroline Clairmont), Aurelien Parent Koenig (Luc Clairmont), Antonio Gil-Martinez (Jean-Marc Drou), Hélène Cardona (Francoise Drou), Harrison Pratt (Dedou Drou), Gaelan Connell (Didi Drou), Elisabeth Commelin (Yvette Marceau), Guillaume Tardieu (Baptiste Marceau), Hugh O'Conor (Père Henri), John Wood (Guillaume Blerot), Lena Olin (Josephine Muscat), Peter Stormare (Serge Muscat), Leslie Caron (Madame Audel).

Running Time: 121 minutes *MPAA Rating:* PG13.

Before Night Falls (January 26, 2001) El Mar Pictures, Grandview Pictures, Fine Line

Director: Julian Schnabel *Producer:* Jon Killik *Writers:* Cunningham O'Keefe, Lázaro Gómez Carriles and Julian Schnabel, from the book *Before Night Falls*, by Reinaldo Arenas *Producer:* Jon Kilik *Associate Producer:* Matthias Ehrenberg *Music* Carter Burwell *Photography:* Xavier Pérez Grobet, Guillermo Rosas *Production Design:* Salvador Parra *Art Direction:* Antonio Muño-Hierro *Editor:* Michael Berenbaum *Sound:* Christian Wangler.

CAST: Javier Bardem (Reinaldo Arenas), Olatz Lopez Garmendia (Reinaldo's Mother), Giovanni Florido (Young Reinaldo), Lolo Navarro (Reinaldo's Grandmother), Sebastian Silva (Reinaldo's Father), Johnny Depp (Bon Bon/Lt. Victor), Carmen Beato (Teacher), Cy Schnabel, Olmo Schnabel (School Children), Vito Maria Schnabel (Teenage Reinaldo), Pedro Armendariz, Jr. (Reinaldo's Grandfather), Diego Luna (Carlos), Lia Chapman (Lolin), Sean Penn (Cuco Sanchez).

Running Time: 133 minutes *MPAA Rating:* R.

Blow (April 6, 2001) Apostle Pictures, Avery Pix, New Line

Director/Producer: Ted Demme *Writers:* David McKenna & Nick Cassavetes, *based on the book by* Bruce Porter *Producers:* Denis Leary, Joel Stillerman *Photography:* Ellen Kuras *Production Design:* Michael Z. Hanan *Editor:* Kevin Tent *Music* Graeme Revell.

CAST: Johnny Depp (George Jung), Penelope Cruz (Mirtha Jung), Franka Potente (Barbara Buckley), Rachel Griffiths (Ermine Jung), Paul Reubens (Derek Foreal), Ray Liotta (Fred Jung), Jordi Mollà (Diego Delgado), Miguel Sandoval (Augusto Oliveras), Ethan Suplee (Tuna), Kevin Gage (Leon Minghella), Max Perlich (Kevin Dulli), Jesse James (Young George), Dan Ferro (Cesar Toban).

Running Time: 124 minutes *MPAA Rating:* R.

The Man Who Cried (May 21, 2001) Adventure Pictures, Studio Canal+

Director/Writer: Sally Potter *Co-Producer:* Simona Benzakein *Producers:* Tim Bevan, Erik Fellner, Christopher Sheppard *Photography:* Sacha Vierny *Editor:* Herve Schneid *Casting:* Irene Lamb *U.S. Casting:* Mary Colquhoun *Original Music* Osvaldo Colijov *Costume Designer:* Lindy Hemming.

CAST: Christina Ricci (Suzie), Cate Blanchett (Lola), John Turturro (Dante Dominio), Johnny Depp (Cesar), Oleg Yankovsky (Father), Claudia Lander-Duke (Young Suzie), Danny Scheinman (Man in Suit), Anna Tzelniker (Mother of Man in Suit), Barry Davis (Man in Village), Thom Osborn, Frank Chersky, Daniel Hart, Peter Majer (Men in Village), Hana Maria Pravda (Grandmother), Ayala Meir, Abraham Hassan, Lloyd Martin, Uri Meir (Children), Harry Flinder (Boy in Cart), Danny Richman (Man in Cart), Victor Sobchak (Man at Port), Sue Cleaver (Red Cross Woman), Clifford Berry, Paul Clayton (English Port Officials), Diana Hoddinott, Richard Albrecht (Foster Parents), Ornella Bryant, Sam Friend, Isabella Melling (Playground Bullies), Alan David (Welsh Teacher), Imogen Claire (Audition Mistress), Miriam Karlin (Madame Goldstein), Harry Dean Stanton (Felix Perlman), Katia Labèque, Marielle Labèque (Pianists), George Yiasoumi (Reporter).

Running Time: 100 minutes *MPAA Rating:* R.

From Hell (October 19, 2001) 20th Century–Fox, Underworld

Directors: Albert and Allen Hughes *Writers:* Terry Hayes & Rafael Yglesias, *based on the graphic novel by* Alan Moore and Eddie Campbell *Producers:* Jane Hamsher, Don Murphy *Executive Producers:* Thomas Hammel, Amy Robinson, Allen Hughes, Albert Hughes *Music* Trevor Jones *Photography:* Peter Deming *Editors:* George Bowers, Dan Lebental.

CAST: Johnny Depp (Inspector Frederick Abberline), Heather Graham (Mary Kelly), Ian Holm (Sir William Gull), Robbie Coltrane (Sergeant Peter Godley), Ian Richardson (Sir Charles Warren), Jason Flemyng (Netley, the Coachman), Terence Harvey (Benjamin "Ben" Kidney), Katrin Cartlidge (Dark Annie), Susan Lynch (Liz Stride), Paul Rhys (Dr. Ferral), Lesley Sharp (Kate Eddowes), Estelle Skornik (Ada), Nicholas McGaughey (Officer Bolt), Annabelle Apsion (Polly Nichols), Joanna Page (Ann Crook), Mark Dexter (Albert Sickert/Prince Edward), Danny Midwinter (Constable Withers), Samantha Spiro (Martha Tabram).

Running Time: 122 minutes *MPAA Rating:* R.

2002

Inside the Actors Studio: Johnny Depp One of a series of interviews, *Inside the Actors Studio,*

done for Bravo cable network. The program was Season 5, Episode 19, and aired on September 8, 2002. *Director:* Jeff Wurtz. Available on DVD.

2003

Pirates of the Caribbean: The Curse of the Black Pearl (July 9, 2003) Jerry Bruckheimer Films, Disney

Director: Gore Verbinski *Writers:* Ted Elliott & Terry Rossio *Story:* Ted Elliott & Terry Rossio and Stuart Beattie and Jay Wolpert *Producer:* Jerry Bruckheimer *Associate Producer:* Pat Sandston *Music* Klaus Badelt, Hans Zimmer *Photography:* Dariusz Wolski *Production Design:* Brian Morris *Art Direction:* Derek R. Hill, James E. Tocci, Donald B. Woodruff *Editors:* Stephen Rivkin, Arthur Schmidt, Craig Wood *Sound* Lee Orloff.

CAST: Johnny Depp (Captain Jack Sparrow), Geoffrey Rush (Barbossa), Orlando Bloom (Will Turner), Keira Knightley (Elizabeth Swann), Jack Davenport (Norrington), Jonathan Pryce (Governor Weatherby Swann), Lee Arenberg (Pintel), Mackenzie Crook (Ragetti), Damian O'Hare (Lt. Gillette), Giles New (Murtogg), Angus Barnett (Mullroy), David Bailie (Cotton), Michael Berry, Jr. (Twigg), Isaac C. Singleton, Jr. (Bo'sun), Kevin McNally (Joshamee Gibbs), David Schofield (Mercer), Treva Etienne (Koehler), Zoe Saldana (Anamaria), Nej Adamson (Short Sailor), Guy Siner (Harbormaster), Ralph P. Martin (Mr. Brown), Paula J. Newman (Estrella), Paul Keith (Butler), Dylan Smith (Young Will), Lucinda Dryzek (Young Elizabeth), Luke de Woolfson (Frightened Sailor), Michael Sean Tighe (Seedy Looking Prisoner), Greg Ellis (Officer), Dustin Seavey (Sentry), Georges Trillat (Skinny Man), Israel Aduramo (Crippled Man), Christian Martin (Steersman), Trevor Goddard (Grapple), Vince Lozano (Jacoby), Ben Wilson (Seedy Prisoner #2), Robbie Gee (Shrimper), Antonio Valentino (Seedy Prisoner #3), Lauren Maher (Scarlett), Matthew Bowyer (Sailor), Brye Cooper (Mallot), Mike Babcock (Seedy Prisoner #4), Owen Finnegan (Town Clerk), John Boswell (Wyvern), Ian McIntyre (Sailor), Vanessa Branch (Giselle), Christopher Adamson (Jimmy Legs / Dutchman), Sam Roberts (Crying Boy), Ben Roberts (Crying Boy), Martin Klebba (Marty), Felix Castro (Moises: Jack's Crew), Mike Haberecht (Kursar: Jack's Crew), Rudolph McCollum (Matelot: Jack's Crew), Gerard J. Reyes (Tearlach: Jack's Crew), M. Scott Shields (Duncan: Jack's Crew), Christopher Sullivan (Ladbroc: Jack's Crew), David Keyes (Scuttled Ship Helmsman), Craig Thomson (Crimp: Jack's Crew), Fred Toft (Quartetto: Jack's Crew), D. P. FitzGerald (Weatherby: Barbossa's Crew), Jerry

Gauny (Ketchum: Barbossa's Crew), Maxie J. Santillan, Jr. (Maximo: Barbossa's Crew), Michael Earl Lane (Monk: Barbossa's Crew), John Mackey (Turkish Prisoner #1), Spider Madison (Turkish Prisoner #2), Tobias McKinney (Dog Ear: Barbossa's Crew), Bud Mathis (Turkish Prisoner #3).

Running Time: 143 minutes *MPAA Rating:* PG13.

Once Upon a Time in Mexico (September 12, 2003) Columbia, Dimension *Writer/Photography/Editor/Original Music:* Robert Rodriguez *Producers:* Elizabeth Avellan, Carlos Gallardo, Robert Rodriguez *Co-Producers:* Sue Jett, Tony Mark, Luz Maria Rojas.

CAST: Antonio Banderas (El Mariachi), Salma Hayek (Carolina), Johnny Depp (Sheldon Jeffrey Sands), Mickey Rourke (Billy Chambers), Eva Mendes (Ajedrez), Danny Trejo (Cucuy), Enrique Iglesias (Lorenzo), Marco Leonardi (Fideo), Cheech Marin (Belini), Rubén Blades (FBI Agent Jorge Ramirez), Willem Dafoe (Armando Barillo), Gerardo Vigil (General Marquez), Pedro Armendáriz Jr. (El Presidente), Julio Oscar Mechoso (Advisor Nicholas), Tito Larriva (Cab Driver), Miguel Couturier (Dr. Guevera), José Luis Avendaño (Alvaro), Rudolfo De Alexandre (Omar).

Running Time: 102 minutes *MPAA Rating:* R.

Lost in La Mancha (January 21, 2003) Eastcroft Productions, Low Key

Director/Writers: Keith Fulton & Louis Pepe *Producers:* Lucy Darwin, Andrew J. Curtis, Rosa Bosch *Music* Miriam Cutler.

CAST: (as themselves) Toni Grisoni (Co-Writer), Terry Gilliam (Director, storyboard illustrator), Philip A. Patterson (First Assistant Director), René Cleitman (Producer), Nicola Pecorini (Director of Photography), José Luis Escolar (Line Producer), Barbara Perez-Solero (Assistant Set Decorator), Benjamin Fernandez (Production Designer), Andrea Calderwood (Former Production Head, Pathé), Ray Cooper (Gilliam colleague), Gabriella Pescucci (Costume Designer), Carlo Poggioli (Co-Costume Designer), Bernard Bouix (Executive Producer), Jean Rochefort (Actor as Don Quixote), Johnny Depp (Actor), Vanessa Paradis (Actor), Fred Millstein (Completion Guarantor), Jeff Bridges (Narrator).

Running Time: 93 minutes *MPAA Rating:* R.

2004

King of the Hill (Animated Television Series) "Hank's Back" (Season 8, Episode 20) Broadcast May 9, 2004. Johnny Depp (Yogi Victor, Voice).

Finding Neverland (November 24, 2004) Film Colony

Director: Marc Forster *Writer:* David Magee, from the play *The Man Who Was Peter Pan,* by Allan Knee *Producers:* Nellie Bellflower, Richard N. Gladstein *Associate Producer:* Tracey Becker *Executive Producers:* Gary Binkow, Neal Israel, Michelle Sy, Bob Weinstein, Harvey Weinstein *Music* Jan A.P. Kaezmarek *Photography:* Roberto Schaefer *Editor:* Matt Chesse *Production Design:* Gemma Jackson *Art Direction:* Peter Russell.

CAST: Johnny Depp (Sir James M. Barrie), Kate Winslet (Sylvia Llewelyn Davies), Julie Christie (Mrs. Emma du Maurier), Radha Mitchell (Mary Barrie), Dustin Hoffman (Charles Frohman), Freddie Highmore (Peter Llewelyn Davies), Joe Prospero (Jack Llewelyn Davies), Nick Roud (George Llewelyn Davies), Luke Spill (Michael Llewelyn Davies), Ian Hart (Sir Arthur Conan Doyle), Kelly Macdonald (Peter Pan), Mackenzie Crook (Mr. Jaspers), Jimmy Gardner (Mr. Snow), Oliver Fox (Gilbert Cannan).

Running Time: 106 minutes *MPAA Rating:* PG.

Happily Ever After (*Ils se marièrent et eurent beaucoup d'enfants*) (in France, August 25, 2004) Pathé Renn, Hirsch, Kino on Video

Writer/Director: Yvan Attal *Producer:* Claude Berri *Photography:* Remy Chevrin *Editor:* Jennifer Augé *Set Design:* Katia Wyszop *Executive Producer:* Pierre Grunstein.

CAST: Charlotte Gainsbourg (Gabrielle), Yvan Attal (Vincent), Alain Chabat (Georges), Alain Cohen (Fred), Emmanuelle Seigner (Nathalie), Angie David (La Maîtresse), Anouk Aimée, Claude Berri, Jérôme Bertin, Johnny Depp (Given special credit at closing of film).

Running Time: 105 minutes, Kino on Video (USA) *MPAA Rating:* None, but merits an R.

Secret Window (March 12, 2004) Grand Slam Prod., Columbia

Director: David Koepp *Writer:* David Koepp, from the story "Secret Window, Secret Garden" in *Four Past Midnight,* by Stephen King *Producer:* Gavin Polone *Executive Producer:* Ezra Swerdlow *Photography:* Fred Murphy *Editor:* Jill Savitt *Art Direction:* Gilles Aird *Set Decoration* Francine Danis *Costumes:* Odette Gadoury, *Music* Philip Glass *Production Design:* Howard Cummings.

CAST: Johnny Depp (Mort Rainey), John Turturro (John Shooter), Maria Bello (Any Rainey), Timothy Hutton (Ted Milner), Charles S. Dutton (Ken Karsch), Len Cariou (Sheriff Dave Newsome),

Joan Heney (Mrs. Garvey), John Dunn Hill (Tom Greenleaf), Vlasta Vrana (Fire Chief Wickersham), Matt Holland (Detective Bradley), Gillian Ferrabee (Fran Evans), Bronwen Mantel (Greta Bowie), Elizabeth Marleau (Juliet), Kyle Allatt (Busboy), Richard Jutras (Motel Manager), Sarah Allen (Sheriff's Niece), Chico (the Dog, Himself).

Running Time: 96 minutes *MPAA Rating:* PG13.

2005

The Libertine (March 10, 2005) Mr. Mudd Productions

Director: Laurence Dunmore *Writer:* Stephen Jeffreys, based upon his play *Producers:* Lianne Halfon, John Malkovich, Russell Smith *Executive Producers:* Chase Bailey, Louise Goodsill, Ralph Kamp *Music* Michael Nyman *Production Design:* Ben van Os *Photography:* Alexander Melman *Art Directors:* Patrick Rolfe, Fleur Whitlock *Editor:* Jill Bilcock *Sound:* John Hayes *Production Manager:* Marshall Leviten, *Special Effects:* Rob Tucker *Stunts:* Peter Pedrero.

CAST: Johnny Depp (Rochester), John Malkovich (Charles II), Samantha Morton (Elizabeth Barry), Clare Higgins (Molly Luscombe), T. P. McKenna (Black Rod), Freddie Jones (Betterton), Robert Wilfort (Huysmans), Rosamund Pike (Elizabeth Malet), Tom Hollander (Etherege), Rupert Friend (Downs), Paul Ritter (Chiffinch), Stanley Townsend (Keown), Francesca Annis (Countess), Johnny Vegas (Sackville), Richard Coyle (Alcock), Tom Burke (Vaughan), Hugh Sachs (Ratcliffe), Kelly Reilly (Jane), Jack Davenport (Harris), Trudi Jackson (Rose).

Running Time: 130 minutes *MPAA Rating:* R.

Charlie and the Chocolate Factory (July 15, 2005) Warner

Director: Tim Burton *Writer:* John August, *based on the book by* Roald Dahl *Producers:* Brad Gray, Richard Zanuck *Executive Producers:* Patrick McCormick, Felicity Dahl, Michael Siegel, Graham Burke, Bruce Berman *Co-Producer:* Katterli Frauenfelder *Casting:* Susie Figgis *Visual Effects: Supervisor* Nick Davis *Music* Danny Elfman *Costume Design:* Gabriella Pescucci *Editor:* Chris Lebenzon *Production Design:* Alex McDowell *Director of Photography:* Philippe Rousselot.

CAST: Johnny Depp (Willy Wonka), Freddie Highmore (Charlie Bucket), Helena Bonham Carter (Mrs. Bucket), Noah Taylor (Mr. Bucket), David Kelly (Grandpa Joe), Missi Pyle (Mrs. Beauregarde), James Fox (Mr. Salt), Deep Roy (The Oompa Loompas), Christopher Lee (Dr. Wonka), Adam Godley

(Mr. Teavee), Franziska Troegner (Mrs. Gloop), Annasophia Robb (Violet Beauregarde), Julia Winter (Veruca Salt), Jordan Fry (Mike Teavee), Philip Wiegratz (Augustus Gloop), Blair Dunlop (Little Willy Wonka), Liz Smith (Grandma Georgina), Eileen Essell (Grandma Josephine), David Morris (Grandpa George).

Running Time: 115 minutes *MPAA Rating:* PG.

Tim Burton's Corpse Bride (Corpse Bride) (September 23, 2005) Warner

Directors: Mike Johnson, Tim Burton *Producers:* Tim Burton, Allison Abbate *Writers:* John August and Caroline Thompson and Pamela Pettler *Songs and Score* Danny Elfman *Editors:* Jonathan Lucas, Chris Lebenzon *Photography:* Pete Kozachik *Production Design:* Alex McDowell *Executive Producers:* Jeffrey Auerbach, Joe Ramft.

CAST: (Voices) Johnny Depp (Victor Van Dort), Helena Bonham Carter (Corpse Bride), Emily Watson (Victoria Everglot), Albert Finney (Finis Everglot), Joanna Lumley (Maudeline Everglot), Tracey Ullman (Nell Van Dort/Hildegarde), Paul Whitehouse (William Van Dort/Paul/Mayhew), Richard E. Grant (Barkis Bittern), Christopher Lee (Pastor Galswells), Michael Gough (Elder Gutknecht), Jane Horrocks (Black Widow Spider/Mrs. Plum), Enn Reitel (Maggot/Town Crier), Deep Roy (General Bonesapart), Danny Elfman (Bonejangles), Stephen Ballantyne (Emil), Lisa Kay (Solemn Village Boy).

Running Time: 76 minutes *MPAA Rating:* PG.

2006

Pirates of the Caribbean: Dead Man's Chest (July 7, 2006) Jerry Bruckheimer Films, Disney

Director: Gore Verbinski *Writers:* Ted Elliott & Terry Rossio *Story:* Ted Elliott & Terry Rossio and Stuart Beattie and Jay Wolpert *Producer:* Jerry Bruckheimer *Associate Producer:* Pat Sandston *Music* Hans Zimmer *Photography:* Dariusz Wolski *Production Design:* Rick Heinrichs *Supervising Art Direction:* John Dexter *Editors:* Stephen Rivkin, Arthur Schmidt, Craig Wood.

CAST: Johnny Depp (Captain Jack Sparrow), Orlando Bloom (Will Turner), Keira Knightley (Elizabeth Swann), Jack Davenport (Norrington), Bill Nighy (Davy Jones), Jonathan Pryce (Governor Weatherby Swann), Lee Arenberg (Pintel), Mackenzie Crook (Ragetti), Damien O'Hare (Lt. Gillette), Kevin McNally (Gibbs), David Bailie (Cotton), Stellan Skarsgård (Bootstrap Bill), Tom Hollander (Cutler Beckett), Naomie Harris (Tia Dalma), Martin

Klebba (Marty), David Schofield (Mercer), Alex Norton (Captain Bellamy), Lauren Maher (Scarlett), Nej Adamson (Short Sailor), Jimmy Roussounis (Large Sailor).

Running Time: 143 minutes *MPAA Rating:* PG13.

Pirates of the Caribbean: At World's End (May 25, 2007) Jerry Bruckheimer Films, Disney

Director: Gore Verbinski *Writers:* Ted Elliott & Terry Rossio *Story:* Ted Elliott & Terry Rossio and Stuart Beattie and Jay Wolpert *Producer:* Jerry Bruckheimer *Associate Producer:* Pat Sandston *Music* Hans Zimmer *Photography:* Dariusz Wolski *Production Design:* Rick Heinrichs *Art Direction:* John Dexter *Editors:* Stephen Rivkin, Craig Wood.

CAST: Johnny Depp (Captain Jack Sparrow), Orlando Bloom (Will Turner), Keira Knightley (Elizabeth Swann), Jack Davenport (Norrington), Bill Nighy (Davy Jones), Jonathan Pryce (Governor Weatherby Swann), Lee Arenberg (Pintel), Mackenzie Crook (Ragetti), Yun-Fat Chow (Captain Sao Feng), Keith Richards (Captain Teague), Kevin McNally (Gibbs), David Bailie (Cotton), Stellan Skarsgård (Bootstrap Bill), Tom Hollander (Cutler Beckett), Naomie Harris (Tia Dalma), Martin Klebba (Marty), David Schofield (Mercer).

Running Time: 168 minutes *MPAA Rating:* PG13.

Sweeney Todd: The Demon Barber of Fleet Street (December 21, 2007) Dreamworks, Warner

Director: Tim Burton *Writer:* John Logan, based upon the musical by Stephen Sondheim and Hugh Wheeler, and the play by Christopher Bond *Producers:* John Logan, Laurie MacDonald, Richard D. Zanuck, Walter Parkes *Photography:* Dariusz Wolski *Editor:* Chris Lebenzon, *Production Design:* Dante Ferretti *Set Decoration* Francesca Lo Schiavo *Costume Design:* Colleen Atwood.

CAST: Johnny Depp (Sweeney Todd), Helena Bonham Carter (Mrs. Lovett), Alan Rickman (Judge Turpin), Timothy Spall (Beadle Banford), Sacha Baron Cohen (Adolfo Pirelli), Jamie Campbell Bower (Anthony Hope), Laura Michelle Kelly (Beggar Woman), Jayne Wisener (Johanna), Edward Sanders (Toby).

Running Time: 120 minutes *MPAA Rating:* R.

2008

This American Life (May 4, 2008) Depp narrates the Season Two premiere of the documentary series focusing on interesting Americans, in this case a disabled young man who can barely move or speak, yet communicates through a computer. Like the man depicted in Julian Schnabel's *The Diving Bell and the Butterfly* (2007), the episode shows man's triumph, however tenuous, over adversity.

2009

Gonzo: The Life and Work of Dr. Hunter S. Thompson (2009) Director Alex Gibney *Writers:* Alex Gibney and Hunter S. Thompson.

Cast Johnny Depp (as narrator), and a large cast in new and archival footage of people who knew Thompson.

Running Time: 120 minutes *MPAA Rating:* R.

The Imaginarium of Doctor Parnassus (2009) Davis Films

Director: Terry Gilliam *Writers:* Terry Gilliam and Charles McKeown *Producers:* Amy Gilliam, Samuel Hadida, William Vince *Photography:* Nicola Pecorini *Editor:* Mick Audsley *Original Music:* Jeff Danna, Mychael Danna.

CAST: Heath Ledger, Johnny Depp, Jude Law, Colin Farrell (Tony), Christopher Plummer (Dr. Parnassus), Tom Waits (Mr. Nick), Verne Troyer (Percy), Andrew Garfield (Anton), Lily Cole (Valentina), Michael Eklund (Tony's Aide), Quinn Lord (Young Son), Paloma Faith (Sally), Johnny Harris (Policeman), Mark Benton (Dad), Fraser Aitcheson (Dancing Policeman), Richard Riddell (Martin), Simon Day (Inspector), Peter New (Paramedic #1), Michael Jonsson (Paramedic #2), Emma Karwandy (Valentina's Daughter), Mackenzie Gray (Substitute Monk), Ryan Grantham (Little Anton), Ian A. Wallace (Fourth Monk), Brad Dryborough (Repulsed Diner), Joseph Cintron (Monk).

Public Enemies (2009) Forward Pass, Misher Films, Tribeca

Director: Michael Mann *Writers:* Michael Mann, Ronan Bennett, Ann Biderman, based on a book by Bryan Burrough *Producers:* Michael Mann, Kevin Misher *Co-Producers:* Bryan H. Carroll, Gusmano Cessaretti, Kevin De La Noy *Photography:* Dante Spinotti *Editors:* Jeffrey Ford, Paul Rubell *Original Music:* Elliot Goldenthal *Production Design:* Nathan Crowley *Art Direction:* Patrick Lumb, William Ladd Skinner *Costume Design:* Coleen Atwood.

CAST: Christian Bale (Melvin Purvis), Johnny

Depp (John Dillinger), Channing Tatum (Pretty Boy Floyd), Billy Crudup (J. Edgar Hoover), Stephen Dorff (Homer Van Meter), Leelee Sobieski (Polly Hamilton), Emilie de Ravin (Anna Patzke), Giovanni Robisi (Alvin Karpis), Marion Cotillard (Billie Frechette), Rory Cochrane (Carter Baum), David Wenham (Pete Pierpont), Lili Taylor (Sheriff Lillian Holley).

Running Time: 140 minutes *MPAA Rating:* R.

Bibliography

Film Reviews

Arizona Dream

<http://cinema-scope.com/cs26/col_rosenbaum_dvd.htm>, accessed July 20, 2008.

The Astronaut's Wife

Harti, John, *Courier Mail* (Queensland, Australia), 1 Nov., 1999, *News*: 10.

Leydon, Joe, *Daily Variety*, 30 Sept., 1999: 4.

Maslin, Janet, *New York Times*, 28 Aug., 1999: B14.

Schembri, Jim, *The Age* (Melbourne, Australia), 5 Oct., 1999: E9.

Before Night Falls

Arnold, Gary, *Washington Times*, 3 Feb., 2001: D3.

Clark, Jay, *Boston Globe*, 2 Feb., 2001: D1.

Fink, Mitchell, with Lauren Ruben, *Daily News*, 20 Nov., 2000: G18.

Harrison, Hugh, "Letter," *Newsweek* (International Edition), 17 July, 2006.

Stuart, Jan, *Advocate*, 19 Dec., 2000: 57.

Turan, Kenneth, *Los Angeles Times*, 22 Dec., 2000.

Benny & Joon

Ansen, David, *Newsweek*, 26 April, 1993: 64.

Dargis, Manohla, *Village Voice*, 13 April, 1993: 58.

Levy, Emmanuel, *Variety*, 29 March, 1993.

Medved, Michael, *New York Post*, 17 April, 1993: 15.

Monk, Claire, *Sight and Sound*, July 1993: 37.

Rainer, Peter, *Los Angeles Times*, 16 April, 1993: C 4.

Blow

Corliss, Richard, *Time* (Europe), 30 April, 2001: 63.

Denby, David, *New Yorker*, 9 April, 2001: 138.

Lumenick, Lou, *New York Post*, 16 April, 2001: 43.

Mathews, Jack, *Daily News* (New York), 18 April, 2001: N55.

Morgenstern, Joe, *Wall Street Journal*, 6 April, 2001: W1.

Raven, Charlotte, *New Statesman*, 6 April, 2001: 48.

Rea, Stephen, *The Philadelphia Inquirer*, 6 April, 2001: W3.

Sterritt, David, *Christian Science Monitor*, 16 April, 2001: 15.

Travers, Peter, *Rolling Stone*, 12 April, 2001, website, posted 15 Mar., 2001.

The Brave

Cheshire, Godfrey, *Variety*, 19 May, 1997: 56.

Giammarco, David G., *The Globe and Mail* (Canadian), 7 Mar., 1999: D3.

Kalhatsu, Jane B., *Daily Yomiuri*, 22 April, 1998.

Pickerill, Martha, *Time*, 26 May, 1997: 124.

Schwarzbaum, Lisa, *Entertainment Weekly*, 30 May, 1997: 30.

Charlie and the Chocolate Factory

Gilbey, Ryan, *Sight and Sound*, Sept. 2005: 58–59.

Lane, Anthony, *The New Yorker*, 25 July, 2005: 100.

Scott, A. O., *New York Times*, 15 July, 2005: E1.

Thomson, David, *Independent on Sunday* (London), 24 July, 2005: F9.

Travers, Peter, *Rolling Stone*, website, posted 14 July, 2005.

Chocolat

Anderson, John, *Newsday*, 15 Dec., 2000: 86.

Ansen, David, *Newsweek*, 15 Dec., 2000: 77.

Lumenick Lou, *New York Post*, 15 Dec., 2000: 86.

Mount, John, *Sight and Sound*, March 2001: 42.

Schickel, Richard, *Time*, 25 Dec., 2000: 148.

Thomas, Kevin, *Los Angeles Times*, 15 Dec., 2000: C 2.

Cry-Baby

Billson, Anne, *Monthly Film Bulletin*, August 1990: 222.

Corliss, Richard, *Time*, 23 April, 1990: 90.

Denby, David, *New York*, 9 April, 1990: 88.

Edelstein, David, *New York Post*, 6 April, 1990: 25.
Giddins, Gary, *Village Voice*, 10 April, 1990: 66.
Grant, Edmond, *Films in Review*, 7 June, 1990: 359.
Kelleher, Terry, *Newsday*, 16 April, 1990: 80.
Kempley, Rita, *Washington Post*, 7 April, 1990: C1.
Kroll, Jack, *Newsweek*, 16 April, 1990: 86.
Maslin, Janet, *New York Times*, 16 April, 1990: 10.
Moore, Suzanne, *New Statesman and Society*, 27 July, 1990: 38.
Rafferty, Terrence, *The New Yorker*, 19 April, 1990: 88.
Rainer, Peter, *Los Angeles Times*, 6 April, 1990: C6.
Variety, 6 April, 1990: 24.

Dead Man

Adams, Thelma, *New York Post*, 10 May, 1996: 53.
Ebert, Roger, 28 June, 1996 (rogerebert.com).
Denby, David, *New York*, 13 May, 1996: 59.
Hoberman, J., *Village Voice*, 14 May, 1996: 65.
Jones, Kent, *Cineaste*, 22: 2 (1996): 45.
Mathews, Jack, *Los Angeles Times*, 10 May, 1996: C1.
Sterritt, David, *Christian Science Monitor*, 8 June, 1996: 12.
Thompson, Ben, *Sight and Sound*, July 1996: 41–42.

Don Juan DeMarco

Adams, Thelma, *New York Post*, 7 April, 1995: 7.
Francke, Lizzie, *New Statesman and Society*, 19 May, 1995: 33.
Giles, Jeff, *Newsweek*, 25 April, 1995: 64.
Greenman, Ben, *Village Voice*, 18 April, 1995: 60.
Hinson, Hal, *Washington Post*, 7 April, 1995: D1.
Kemp, Philip, *Sight and Sound*, June 1995: 41.
Lane, Anthony, *New Yorker*, 10 April, 1995: 103. Reprinted in *Nobody's Perfect*, NY: Knopf, 2002, pp. 114–117.
Levy, Emanuel, *Variety*, 27 March, 1995: 75.
Mathews, Jack, *Newsday*, 7 April, 1995: B5.
Rainer, Peter, *Los Angeles Times*,7 April, 1995: C1.

Donnie Brasco

Adams, Thelma, *New York Post*, 28 Feb., 1997: 35.
Anderson, John, *Newsday*, 28 Feb., 1997: B3.
Ansen, David, *Newsweek*, 3 March, 1997: 69.
Denby, David, *New York*, 11 March, 1997: 55.
Doherty, Thomas, *Cineaste*, 23:1 (1997): 42.
Hoberman, J., *Village Voice*, 4 March, 1997: 65.
Kauffmann, Stanley, *New Republic*, 31 March, 1997: 26.
Kempley, Rita, *Washington Post*, 28 Feb., 1997: C1.
Klawans, Stuart, *Nation*, 31 March, 1997: 35.
Lane, Anthony, *New Yorker*, 17 March, 1997: 121.
Maslin, Janet, *New York Times*, 28 Feb., 1997: C4.
McCarthy, Todd, *Variety*, 24 Feb., 1997: 75.
Sterritt, David, *Christian Science Monitor*, 28 Feb., 1997: 12.

Turan, Kenneth, *Los Angeles Times*, 28 Feb., 1997: C2.
Wrathall, John, *Sight and Sound*, May 1997: 40–41.

Ed Wood

Ansen, David, *Newsweek*, 10 Oct., 1994: 71.
Chuma, Peter N. II, *Films in Review*, 9–10 (1995): 55.
Corliss, Richard, *Time*, 10 Oct., 1994: 82.
Denby, David, *New York*, 17 Oct., 1994: 71.
Hoberman, J., *Village Voice*, 4 Oct., 1994: 51.
Lewis, Kevin, *Films in Review*, 1–2 (1995): 80.
Mathews, Jack, *Newsday*, 28 Sept., 1994: B2.
Maslin, Janet, *New York Times*, 23 Sept., 1994: C4.
McCarthy, Todd, *Variety*, 12–18 Sept., 1994.
Medved, Michael, *New York Post*, 23 Sept., 1994: 53.
Newman, Kim, *Sight and Sound*, May 1995: 44.
Turan, Kenneth, *Los Angeles Times*, 28 Sept., 1994: C1.

Edward Scissorhands

Ansen, David, *Newsweek*, 10 Dec., 1990: 87.
Bernard, Jami, *New York Post*, 17 Dec., 1990: 65.
Billson, Anne, *New Statesman & Society*, 21 July, 1991: 32.
Corliss, Richard, *Time*, 10 Dec., 1990: 87.
Denby, David, *New York*, 10 Dec., 1990: 101.
Hoberman, J., *Village Voice*, 11 Dec., 1990: 69.
Howe, Desson, *Washington Post*, 14 Dec., 1990, weekend: 65.
Kael, Pauline, *New Yorker*, 7 Dec., 1990: 116.
Kempley, Rita, *Washington Post*, 14 Dec., 1990: B2.
Klawans, Stuart, *Nation*, 7–14 Jan., 1991: 22.
Leland, John, *Newsday*, 7 Dec., 1990: B94.
Maslin, Janet, *New York Times*, 7 Dec., 1990: C1.
Sterritt, David, *Christian Science Monitor*, 16 Jan., 1991: 110.
Strick, Philip, *Sight and Sound*, July 1991: 42.
Variety, 10 Dec., 1990: 84.
Welsh, James M., *Films in Review*, 3–4 (1991): 110.
Wilmington, Michael, *Los Angeles Times*, 17 Dec., 1990: C1.

Fear and Loathing in Las Vegas

Anderson, John, *Newsday*, 22 May, 1998: 83.
Dreher, Rod, *New York Post*, 22 May, 1998: 49.
Hoberman, J., *Village Voice*, 26 May, 1998: 132.
Kronke, David, *Los Angeles Times*, 22 May, 1998: C14.
Williams, Linda Ruth, *Sight and Sound*, Nov. 1998: 48.

Finding Neverland

Ansen, David, *Newsweek*, 18 Nov., 2004: 52.
Burr, Ty, *Entertainment Weekly*, 25 March, 2005: 59.

Dalton, Stephen, *BBC Two/Times* (London), 1 Nov., 2008: F19.

Erickson, Martin, *Journal of Feminist Family Therapy*, Spring 1995: 77–81.

Geer, Jennifer, "J. M. Barrie Gets the Miramax Treatment," *Children's Literature Association Quarterly*, 32:3 (2007): 193–212.

Kauffmann, Stanley, *New Republic*, 13 Dec., 2004: 30–31.

Lane, Anthony, *New Yorker*, 22 Nov., 2004: 103.

Tibbets, John C., *American Historical Review*, 4 (2005): 553–554.

From Hell

Bromley, Carl, *Cineaste*, 12:22 (2001): 36–37.

Giles, Jeff, *Newsweek*, 29 Oct., 2001: 12.

Kerr, Phillip, *New Statesman*, 4 Feb., 2002: 44.

Lumenick, Lou, *New York Post*, 19 Oct., 2001: 51.

Mitchell, Elvis, *New York Times*, 19 Oct., 2001: 16.

Overpeck, Deron, *Film Quarterly*, 2 (2002): 41.

Rainer, Pete, *New York*, 22 Oct., 2001: 92.

Richards, Andy, *Sight and Sound*, March 2002: 45.

Lady Blue, "Birds of Prey," TV episode

<http://www.youtube.com/watch?v=amklJRdZzWA&feature=related>, accessed May 20, 2008.

The Libertine

<http://www.nytimes.com/books/00/2002/20/specials/greene-monkey.html>.

Dargis, Manohla, *New York Times*, 25 Nov., 2005: 28.

Gleiberman, Owen, *Entertainment Weekly*, 2 Dec., 2005: 60–61.

Lane, Anthony, *New Yorker*, 28 Nov., 2005: 186–189.

Lowing, Rob, *The Sun Herald* (Sydney), 30 July, 2006, Insert: 18.

Maher, Kevin, *Sight and Sound*, Dec. 2005: 63–64.

Puig, Claudia, *USA Today*, 25 Nov., 2005: D3.

Stratton, David, *Weekend Australian*, 29 Sept., 2006, Insert: 22.

Travers, Peter, *Rolling Stone*, 1 Dec., 2005: 136.

Lost in La Mancha

Ansen, David, *Newsweek*, 10 Feb., 2003: 66.

Slotek, Jim, *Toronto Sun*, 11 Mar., 2003: E5.

The Man Who Cried

Foreman, Jonathan, *New York Post*, 25 May, 2001: 49.

Hoberman, J., *Village Voice*, 29 May, 2001: 119.

Mitchell, Elvis, *New York Times*, 25 May, 2001: E14.

Rainer, Peter, *New York*, 22 Oct., 2001: 92.

Stuart, Jan, *Los Angeles Times*, 25 May, 2001: C10.

Vincendeau, Ginette, *Sight and Sound*, Jan. 2001: 53.

Young, Deborah, *Variety*, 18–24 Sept., 2000: 37.

Nick of Time

Anderson, John, *Newsday*, 22 Nov., 1995: B19.

Maslin, Janet, *New York Times*, 22 Nov., 1995: C14.

Medved, Michael, *New York Post*, 22 Nov., 1995: 41.

Newman, Kim, *Sight and Sound*, May 1996: 57.

Thomas, Kevin, *Los Angeles Times*, 22 Nov., 1995: 12.

A Nightmare on Elm Street

Frumkes, Roy, *Films in Review*, 2 (1985): 109.

Sterritt, David, *Christian Science Monitor*, 18 Nov., 1984: 109.

Thomas, Kevin, *Los Angeles Times*, 19 Nov., 1984: C4.

Variety, 7 Nov., 1984: 19.

The Ninth Gate

Foreman, Jonathan, *New York Post*, 10 March, 2000: 57.

Hoberman, J., *Village Voice*, 21March, 2000: 135.

Kauffmann, Stanley, *New Republic*, 31 April, 2000: 25.

Lane, Anthony, *The New Yorker*, 20 March, 2000: 144.

Rainer, Peter, *New York*, 20 March, 2000: 21.

Romney, Jonathan, *New Statesman*, 5 June, 2000: 48.

Sterritt, David, *Christian Science Monitor*, 10 March, 2000: 15.

Strick, Philip, *Sight and Sound*, Sept. 2000: 45.

Stuart, Jan, *Newsday*, 10 March, 2000, Part II: B3.

Turan, Kenneth, *Los Angeles Times*, 10 March, 2000: C27.

Once Upon a Time in Mexico

Conlogue, Ray, *The Globe and Mail* (Canada), 13 Sept., 2003: R22.

Pryke, Chris, *Birmington Post*, 15 March, 2004: F13.

Puig, Claudia, *USA Today*, 12 Sept., 2003: E9.

Walls, Brendan, *Brisbane News* (Australia), 25 Oct., 2004: 38.

Pirates of the Caribbean: The Curse of the Black Pearl

Ansen, David, *Newsweek*, 14 July, 2003: 56.

Corliss, Richard, *Time*, 14 July, 2003: 61.

Denby, D., *New Yorker*, 28 July, 2003: 61.

Etherington, Dan, *Sight and Sound*, Sept. 2003: 59–60.

Travers, P., *Rolling Stone*, 7 August, 2003: 78–79.

Pirates of the Caribbean: Dead Man's Chest

Binelli, Mark, *Rolling Stone* website, posted 29 June, 2006.

Edelstein, D., *New York*, 17 July, 2006: 61–62.

Felperin, L., *Sight and Sound*, August 2006: 65–66.

Kirkland, Bruce, *Toronto Sun*, 12 July, 2006 (LexisNexisAcademic).

Klawans, Stuart, *The Nation*, 13 July, 2006: 22–24.

Lane, Anthony, *New Yorker*, 24 July, 2006: 82–83.
Roddick, N., *Sight and Sound*, Nov. 2006: 10.
Schickel, Richard, *Time*, 17 July, 2006: 72.
Scott, A. O., *NewYork Times*, 17 July, 2006: E1.
Smith, Sean, *Newsweek*, 26 June, 2006: 42–48.
Travers, Peter, *Rolling Stone* website, posted 28 June, 2006.

Pirates of the Caribbean: At World's End

Ansen, David, *Newsweek*, 4 June, 2007: 88–90.
Catsoulis, Jeannette, *New York Times*, 14 May, 2007.
Charity, C., *Sight and Sound*, August 2007: 73.
Clark, Mike, *USA Today*, 7 Dec., 2007: E9.
Gleiberman, Owen, *Entertainment Weekly*, 1 June, 2007: 48–49.
Lane, Anthony, *New Yorker*, 4 June, 2007: 88–90.
Toto, Christian, *Washington Times* (Lexis-Nexis Academic).

Platoon

Kramer, Sydelle, *Cineaste*, Fall 1987: 49–50.

Private Resort

Variety, 25 Dec., 1985.

Public Enemies

Droganes, Constance, CTT.ca, website, posted 1 July 2009.
Moore, Roger, *Orlando Sentinel* website, posted 1 July 2009.
Reed, Rex, *New York Observer* website, posted 23 June 2009.
Travers, Peter, *Rolling Stone*, Video Review, posted 30 June 2009.

Secret Window

Felperin, Leslie, *Sight and Sound*, May 2004: 70–72.
Griffin, John, *The Gazette* (Montreal), 12 March, 2004: D1.
Horowitz, Jane, *Washington Post*, 12 March, 2004: T39.
Howell, Peter, *Toronto Star* (Canada), 12 March, 2004: F1.
Kendall, Nigel, *Times* (United Kingdom), 1 May, 2004: 5.
Morgenstern, Joe, *Wall Street Journal*, 12 March, 2004: W1–W7.
Puig, Claudia, *USA Today*, 8 March, 2004: D1.
Rea, Stephen, *Philadelphia*, 12 March, 2004: W4.
Reyes, Damaso, *New York Amsterdam News*, 11 March, 2004: 20.
Tyrangiel, Josh, *Time*, 15 March, 2004: 76–78.

Sleepy Hollow

Clark, Mike, *USA Today*, 19 Nov., 1999: E7.
Foreman, Jonathan, *New York Post*, 19 Nov., 1999.
Giles, Jeff, *Newsweek*, 22 Nov., 1999.

Hoberman, J., *Village Voice*, 30 Nov., 1999: 133.
Howe, Desson, *Washington Post*, 19 Nov., 1999: N51.
Lowing, Rob, *Sun Herald* (Sydney Australia), 20 Jan., 2000, "Time Out": 11.
Maslin, Janet, *New York Times*, 19 Jan., 1999: E1.
Mathews, Jack, *Daily News* (New York), 19 Nov., 1999.
Rainer, Jonathan, *New York*, 29 Nov., 1999.
Ross, Jonathan, *The Mirror*, 7 Jan., 2000, Features: 6.
Schoemer, Karen, *Newsweek*, 19 April, 1999: 66.

Sweeney Todd

Ansen, David, *Newsweek*, 17 Dec., 2007: 70.
Dart, Gregory, *Times Literary Supplement*, 2 Feb. 2008: 18.
Ebert, Roger, *Chicago Sun-Times*, 21 Dec., 2007 (rogerebert.com).
Hischak, Thomas S., *USA Today*, 20 March, 2008: D3.
Lane Anthony, *New Yorker*, 24 Dec., 2007: 150–152.
Marks, Peter, *Washington Post*, 21 Dec., 2007 (washingtonpost.com).
Puig, Claudia, *USA Today*, 21 Dec., 2007: E6–E7.
Pwyser, Marc, *Newsweek*, 17 Dec., 2007: 70.
Scott, Mike, *Times-Picayune* (New Orleans), 21 Nov., 2007: E4, 10.
Scott, Walter, *Parade*, 27 Jan., 2008: 2.
Shay, Estelle, "Chas Jarrett on *Sweeney Todd*," *Cine-Fex*, April 2008: 25–32.

Tim Burton's Corpse Bride

Christopher, James, *The Times* (London), 22 Nov., 2005.
D'Angelo, Mike, *Esquire*, Oct. 2005: 72–74.
Diones, Bruce, *New Yorker*, 17 Oct., 2005: 45.
Gleiberman, Owen, *Entertainment Weekly*, 23 Sept., 2005.
Hynes, Eric, *Interview*, Sept. 2005: 156.
Klawans, Stuart, *Nation*, 10 Oct., 2005: 34–36.
Mathews, Jack, *Daily News* (New York), 16 Sept., 2005.
Terrell, M. K., *Christian Science Monitor*, 23 Sept., 2005.

What's Eating Gilbert Grape

Anderson, John, *Newsday*, 12 Dec., 1993, Part II: 48.
Medved, Michael, *New York Post*, 17 Dec., 1993: 44.
Powers, John, *New York*, 17 Jan., 1994: 55.
Rainer, Peter, *Los Angeles Times*, 14 Dec., 1993: C1.

General Bibliography

Allen, Richard, and Murray Smith, eds. *Film Theory and Philosophy*. Oxford: Oxford University Press, 1997.
Allon, Yoram, Del Cullen, and Hannah Patterson.

Contemporary North American Film Directors. London: Wallflower Press, 2001.

Arenas, Reinaldo. *Before Night Falls.* Trans. Dolores M. Koch. New York: Viking, 1993.

Barrie, J. M. *Peter Pan.* Ed. Jack Zipes. New York: Penguin Books, 2004.

Bell, Jeff. "The Director Function: Auteur Theory and Poststructuralism," *Fotogenia: storia e teorie del cinema* 3 (1996): 187–194.

Benfey, Christopher. "The Barber and the Meaning of Life," *New Republic,* 27 Feb., 2008: 27–28.

Binelli, Mark. "The Last Buccaneer." *Rolling Stone* website, posted 29 June, 2006.

Birkin, Andrew. *J. M. Barrie and the Lost Boys.* New York: Clarkson N. Potter, 1999.

Blitz, Michael, and Louise Krasniewicz. *Johnny Depp: A Biography.* Westport, CT: Greenwood Press, 2008.

Bosworth, Patricia. *Marlon Brando.* New York: Viking, 2001.

Brewer, John. *The Pleasures of the Imagination: English Culture in the Eighteenth Century.* Chicago: University of Chicago Press, 1997.

Brinkley, Douglas. "Johnny Depp's Great Escape." *Vanity Fair,* July, 2009: 56–65, 124–26.

Carlaw, Darren Richard. "In from the Cold: The Forgotten Life and Novels of H. L. Humes," *Times Literary Supplement,* 12 Sept., 2008: 14–15.

Cartwright, Derrick R. "Schnabel, Julian." *The Dictionary of Art.* New York: Grove, 1986.

Cawthorne, Nigel. *A History of Pirates.* New York: Chartwell Books, 2004.

Chilton, Bruce. "Abraham's Curse," *Chronicle of Higher Education,* 15 Feb., 2008: B11.

_____. *Abraham's Curse.* New York: Doubleday, 2008.

Christie, Ian, ed. *Gilliam on Gilliam.* London: Faber, 1999.

Clemons, Walter. "A Martyr to Sin," *New York Times,* 15 Sept., 1974: <http://www.nytimes.com/books/00/02/20/specials/greene-monkey.html>, accessed 30 April, 2008.

Cole, Toby, and Helen Krich Chinoy, eds. *Actors on Acting,* 3rd Edition. New York: Crown, 1957.

Cuddon, J. A. *The Penguin Dictionary of Literary Terms and Literary Theory, Fourth Edition.* Revised by C. E. Preston. London: Penguin Books, 1999.

Dionne, E. J. Jr. "Commentary," *The Advocate* (Baton Rouge), 20 April, 2008: 7B.

Donahue, Joseph. "Actors and Acting," in *The Cambridge Companion to Victorian and Edwardian Theatre.* Ed. Kerry Powell. Cambridge: Cambridge University Press, 2004, 17–35.

Dudgeon, Piers. *Captivated: J. M. Barrie, the Du Mauriers and the Dark Side of Neverland.* London: Chatto and Windus, 2008.

Edelstein, David. "Savage Grace," *New York,* 3 Dec., 2007: 84–85 (on *The Diving Bell and the Butterfly*).

Erickson, Hal. *Syndicated Television: The First Forty Years, 1947–1987.* Jefferson, NC: McFarland, 1989.

Girard, René. *The Girard Reader.* Ed. James G. Williams. New York: Crossroad, 1996.

_____. *The Scapegoat.* Trans. Yvonne Freccero. Baltimore: Johns Hopkins University Press, 1989.

_____. *Violence and the Sacred.* Trans. Patrick Gregory. Baltimore: Johns Hopkins University Press, 1989.

Goodall, Nigel. *The Secret World of Johnny Depp.* London: Blake Publishing, 2007. (This book, with a different title and cover, is merely an expanded edition of Goodall's earlier work *What's Eating Johnny Depp?*)

_____. *What's Eating Johnny Depp?* London: Blake Publishing, 2004.

Greene, Graham. *Lord Rochester's Monkey: Being the Life of John Wilmot, Second Earl of Rochester.* New York: Viking Press, 1974.

Hanson, Bruce K. *The Peter Pan Chronicles.* New York: Birch Lane Press, 1993.

Harris, Mark. "Dillinger Captured by Dogged Filmmaker!" *New York Times,* 28 June, 2009, Arts, 1, 10.

Hirsch, Foster. *Acting, Hollywood Style.* New York: Abrams, 1991.

_____. *Otto Preminger: The Man Who Would Be King.* New York: Knopf, 2007.

Hughes, Derek. *Culture and Sacrifice: Ritual Death in Literature and Opera.* London: Cambridge University Press, 2007.

James, Olive. "Michael Mann," in *Cultural Amnesia.* New York: W.W. Norton, 2007.

Johnson, James William. *A Profane Wit: The Life of John Wilmot, Earl of Rochester.* Rochester, NY: University of Rochester Press, 2004.

Johnstone, Nick. *Johnny Depp: The Illustrated Biography.* London: Carlton Books, 2006.

Kanfer, Stefan. *Somebody: The Reckless Life and Remarkable Career of Marlon Brando.* New York: Alfred A. Knopf, 2008.

Katz, Ephraim. *The Film Encyclopedia, 4th Edition.* Revised by Fred Klein and Ronald Dean Nolen. New York: Harper-Collins, 2001.

Keats, John. *The Letters of John Keats, 1814–1821,* 2 Volumes. Ed. Hyder Edward Rollins. Cambridge: Harvard University Press, 1958.

Kermode, Frank. "Offered to the Gods," *London Review of Books,* 5 June, 2008: 10–11. (A review of *Culture and Sacrifice,* by Derek Hughes.)

Kerouac, Jack. *The Subterraneans.* New York: Grove/Atlantic, 1996.

Kristeva, Julia. *Black Sun: Depression and Melancholia.* Trans. Leon S. Roudiez. New York: Columbia University Press, 1989.

Lee, Lance. *The Death and Life of Drama*. Austin: University of Texas Press, 2005.

Levy, Ariel. "Still Waters," *New York*, 31 March, 2008: 18–23, 90.

Louvish, Simon. *Cecil B. DeMille: A Life in Art*. New York: St. Martin's Press, 2007.

Lurie, Allison. *The Subversive Power of Children's Literature*. Boston: Little, Brown, 1990.

Mack, Robert L. *Wonderful and Surprising History of Sweeney Todd*. London: Continuum Books, 2007.

McCabe, Bob. *Dark Knights & Holy Fools: The Art and Films of Terry Gilliam*. London: Orion, 1999.

McKeen, William. *Outlaw Journalist: The Life and Times of Hunter S. Thompson*. New York: W. W. Norton, 2008.

McNeil, Alex. *Total Television*. New York: Penguin, 1996.

Meikle, Denis. *Johnny Depp: A Kind of Illusion*, 2nd Edition. London: Reynolds and Hearn, 2005.

Moore, Alan (text), and Eddie Campbell (graphics). *From Hell*. Marietta, GA: Top Shelf Productions, 2006.

Nichols, Bill. *Movies and Method: An Anthology, Vol. 1*. Berkeley: University of California Press, 1976.

Nieland, Justus. "Graphic Violence: Native Americans and the Western Archive in Dead Man," *The New Centennial Review*, Fall 2001: 171–200.

Ocasio, Rafael. *Cuba's Political and Sexual Outlaw, Reinaldo Arenas*. Gainesville: University Press of Florida, 2003.

Pérez-Reverte, Arturo. *The Club Dumas*. Trans. Sonia Soto. New York: Harcourt, 1996.

Pierpont, Claudia Roth. "Method Man," *The New Yorker*, 27 Oct., 2008: 66–73.

Poe, Edgar Allan. *Collected Works of Edgar Allan Poe, Vol. 1, Tales and Sketches: 1831–1842*. Cambridge, MA: Harvard University Press, 1978.

Pomerance, Murray. *Johnny Depp Starts Here*. New Brunswick, NJ: Rutgers University Press, 2005.

Robb, Brian J. *Johnny Depp: A Modern Rebel*, 2nd Edition. London: Plexus, 2004.

Rosenbaum, Jonathan. *Dead Man*. London: British Film Institute, 2000.

Russo. G. "The Chocolate and the Factory: A Depp Fairy Tale," *Cineforum*, Nov. 2005: 2–6.

Salisbury, Mark, ed. *Burton on Burton*, 3rd Edition. Foreword by Johnny Depp. London: Faber, 2006.

_____. *Sweeney Todd: The Demon Barber of Fleet Street*. Foreword Tim Burton. London: Titan Books, 2007.

Sandford, Christopher. *Polanski: A Biography*. New York: Palgrave Macmillan, 2008.

Seabrook, John, "Suffering Souls," *The New Yorker*, 10 Nov., 2008: 64–73.

Segal, Erich. *The Death of Comedy*. Cambridge, MA: Harvard University Press, 2001.

Shaw, Deborah. "*Blow*: How a Film Created a Hero from a Top-Level Drug Trafficker and Blamed the 'Colombians' for His Downfall," *Quarterly Review of Film and Video*, 24.1 (2007): 31–40.

Singer, Michael. *"Bring Me That Horizon": The Making of Pirates of the Caribbean*. New York: Disney Editions, 2007.

Sterritt, David, and Lucille Rhodes, eds. *Terry Gilliam: Interviews*. Jackson: University of Mississippi Press, 2004.

Suárez, Juan A. *Jim Jarmusch*. Urbana: University of Illinois Press, 2007.

Surrell, Jason. *Pirates of the Caribbean: From the Magic Kingdom to the Movies*. New York: Disney Press, 2006, 432–440.

Thompson, Hunter S. *Fear and Loathing in Las Vegas and Other American Stories*. New York: Modern Library, 1996.

_____. *Hell's Angels on Wheels: A Strange and Terrible Saga*. Introd. Douglas Brinkley. New York: Modern Library, 1999.

Thomson, David. *Have You Seen...?* New York: Knopf, 2008.

_____. *The New Biographical Dictionary of Film*. New York: Knopf, 2002.

Tóibín, Colm. "I Could Sleep with All of Them," *London Review of Books*, 11 June, 2008: 3–10.

Torrey, Beef, and Kevin Simonson, eds. *Conversations with Hunter S. Thompson*. Oxford: University Press of Mississippi, 2008.

Walker, Andrew Kevin. *The Art of Sleepy Hollow*. Introd. Tim Burton. New York: Pocket Books, 1999. (Contains Walker's screenplay for the Burton film and a wonderful selection of the artwork.)

Warshow, Robert. *The Immediate Experience*. Enlarged edition. Cambridge: Harvard University Press, 2001. (Includes "Robert Warshow: Life and Works," by David Denby; and "Epilogue: After Half a Century," by Stanley Cavell.)

Wenner, Jann S., and Corey Seymour, eds. *Gonzo: The Life of Hunter S. Thompson*. Introd. Johnny Depp. New York: Little Brown, 2007. (Not a traditional biography, but a collection of statements from people who knew Thompson.)

William, James G. *The Bible, Violence, and the Sacred: Liberation from the Myth of Sanctioned Violence*. San Francisco: Harper, 1991.

Wloszcyna, Susan. "The Artistic Mayhem of Depp and Burton," *USA Today*, 14 Dec., 2007: E12.

_____. "More Smoke and Mirrors," *USA Today*, 3 Dec., 1997: 4D. (On Julian Schnabel.)

Woods, Paul A., ed. *Tim Burton: A Child's Garden of Nightmares*. London: Plexus, 2002.

Index

Numbers in **bold italics** indicate main entries in the text.